OXFORD STUDIES IN AFRICAN AFFAIRS

General Editors
JOHN D. HARGREAVES *and* GEORGE SHEPPERSON

TRADE WITHOUT RULERS

TRADE WITHOUT RULERS

Pre-Colonial Economic Development in South-Eastern Nigeria

By

DAVID NORTHRUP

CLARENDON PRESS · OXFORD
1978

Oxford University Press, Walton Street, Oxford OX2 6DP

OXFORD LONDON GLASGOW
NEW YORK TORONTO MELBOURNE WELLINGTON
IBADAN NAIROBI DAR ES SALAAM LUSAKA CAPE TOWN
KUALA LUMPUR SINGAPORE JAKARTA HONG KONG TOKYO
DELHI BOMBAY CALCUTTA MADRAS KARACHI

© *Oxford University Press 1978*

British Library Cataloguing in Publication Data

Northrup, David
  Trade without rulers,—(Oxford studies in
  African affairs)
  1. Slave trade—Nigeria—History
  2. Produce trade—Nigeria—History
  I. Title   II. Series
  382′.44′096694   HT1394.N5   78-40069
  ISBN 0-19-822712-4

*Printed in Great Britain by
Butler & Tanner Ltd, Frome and London*

Acknowledgements

M Y fascination with the history of south-eastern Nigeria began in 1965–6 while teaching at Central Anang Secondary School, Ikot Ekpene, and I gratefully acknowledge the importance of my students and their families in prodding me to undertake this project. A return visit to that area in 1972–3 was made possible by a generous grant from the Fulbright-Hays Commission of the United States Office of Education, during the course of which I received extraordinary and immediate co-operation from a multitude of Nigerian officials, university personnel, chance acquaintances, and individuals well-informed in local history. It is especially for these village elders named at the end of this book, many of whom I fear have by now passed on to the status of ancestors, that my deepest expression of gratitude must be reserved.

In addition, special thanks are due to Professor G. I. Jones, whose work on this area has been a constant help and inspiration and who very kindly made extensive and helpful suggestions for improving an earlier version of this study, and to the members of my doctoral dissertation committee at the University of California, Los Angeles: Professors E. A. Alpers, T. O. Ranger, Arnold Rubin, and Hilda Kuper. I am also very thankful to Dr. R. C. C. Law and to my colleague Professor Felicia Ekejiuba for many helpful comments. Finally, I owe very special gratitude for patient advice, criticism, and encouragement on hundreds of occasions to my wife and fellow historian of Africa, Dr. Nancy Rutledge Northrup.

This study has been gratefully facilitated by the kindness of the following institutions in making their holdings available, the consulting of some of which was made possible by grants from the Fulbright-Hays Commission and the Patent Fund of the University of California: Graduate Research Library, University of California, Los Angeles; Hoover Institution for War and Peace Library, Stanford University; Butler Library, Columbia University; Missionary Research Library, Union Theological Seminary; New York Public Library; University of Ibadan Library; National Archive, Ibadan; National Archive, Enugu; Public Record Office, London; British Museum; Museum of Mankind, London; National Maritime

Museum, London; National Library of Scotland, Edinburgh; Edinburgh University Library; New College Library, Edinburgh; Biblioteca da Sociedade de Geografia de Lisboa; Mugar Memorial Library, Boston University.

Portions of Chapter I originally appeared under the title, 'The Growth of Trade among the Igbo before 1800', *Journal of African History*, XIII (1972), 217–36, and are repeated here with the kind permission of the publisher, Cambridge University Press.

Preparation of the final manuscript was assisted by a grant from Boston College.

Contents

		page
LIST OF MAPS, FIGURES, TABLES		ix
ABBREVIATIONS		x
INTRODUCTION		1
1. Themes and sources		1
2. Land and people		10
I.	THE DEVELOPMENT OF TRADE BEFORE 1500	16
	1. The economy of Igbo-Ukwu	17
	2. Long-distance trade	22
II.	PEOPLES AND POLITIES OF THE SIXTEENTH AND SEVENTEENTH CENTURIES	30
	1. Patterns of settlement: the Ngwa and their neighbours	33
	2. Cross River peoples: the Aro and Efik	34
	3. Communities of the Niger Valley and Delta	43
III.	THE SLAVE TRADE	50
	1. The slave trade before 1700	50
	2. Slave-trade statistics, 1700–1840	54
	3. Ethnic origins of those enslaved	58
	4. Means of enslavement	65
	5. The slave trade and depopulation	80
IV.	THE ORGANIZATION OF THE SLAVE TRADE	85
	1. Coastal trading states	86
	2. Hinterland trading organization	89

	3. Hinterland trading communities	100
	4. Religion and the rise of capital	107
V.	THE GOD-MEN OF THE SLAVE TRADE	114
	1. Theories of Aro success	114
	2. Areas of Aro activity	119
	3. Conclusions	137
VI.	THE SLAVE TRADE AND ECONOMIC DEVELOPMENT	146
	1. The marketing infrastructure	149
	2. Trading currencies	157
	3. The impact of the imports	164
	4. Internal trade	171
VII.	THE GROWTH OF AGRICULTURAL EXPORTS	177
	1. The provisioning trade	177
	2. Palm-oil production	182
	3. Palm-oil middlemen	188
VIII.	AGRICULTURAL EXPORTS AND ECONOMIC DEVELOPMENT	197
	1. Hinterland palm-oil traders	199
	2. Nineteenth-century imports	208
	3. The new hinterland economy	214
	CONCLUSION	224
	APPENDICES	231
	SOURCES	240
	INDEX	259

List of Maps

1. South-eastern Nigeria and the Bight of Biafra 2
2. Peoples and Places in South-eastern Nigeria 32
3. Towns Attending the Onitsha Market in 1854 96
4. Major Trade Routes in the Era of the Slave Trade 120
5. Aro Trade with the Ibibio 123
6. Aro Ndizuogu and its Neighbours 132
7. Palm-Oil Trade 193

List of Figures

1. Slaves Shipped from the Bight of Biafra, 1700–1850 55
2. Slaves Shipped from Bonny in 1821 61
3. Slaves Shipped from Old Calabar in 1821–2 61
4. Slaves Shipped from Bonny and Old Calabar, 1821–2 61
5. Sierra Leone Census, 1848: Bight of Biafra 61
6. Hinterland Currencies 161

List of Tables

1. Age and Sex of Slaves from the Bight of Biafra, 1659–1702, Based on the Records of Five Ships 78
2. Age and Sex of Slaves from the Bight of Biafra Emancipated in Sierra Leone, 1821–39, Based on the Records of 109 Ships 78
3. Manner of Enslavement of Koelle's Informants by Percentage of Known Instances 80
4. Palm-Oil Trade (in tons), 1815–64 183
5. 'An Abstract of a Cargo Suitable to Purchase 100 tons of Palm Oil at [Old] Calabar, at £14 per ton' 209
6. Cargoes Suitable for the Purchase of Palm-Oil at Old Calabar 210
7. Trade Items for Old Calabar as Percentages of Total Cargo 210

Abbreviations

CALPROF	Calabar Provincial Office Papers
C.O.	Colonial Office, Great Britain
CSE	Colonial Secretary, Enugu
CSO	Colonial Secretary's Office, Lagos
F.O.	Foreign Office, Great Britain
JAH	*Journal of African History*
JHSN	*Journal of the Historical Society of Nigeria*
JRGS	*Journal of the Royal Geographical Society* (London)
NAE	National Archive, Enugu
NAI	National Archive, Ibadan
NLS	National Library of Scotland
Parl. Papers	*Parliamentary Papers*, Great Britain

Introduction

1. THEMES AND SOURCES

THE West African peoples bordering the Gulf of Guinea differ in many aspects of their cultural and political history, but their commercial history has followed generally similar lines. Their earliest trade was centred round local markets with many areas enjoying regular commerce with more distant parts of West Africa. Beginning with the arrival of the Portuguese in the late fifteenth century, a pattern of trade developed which lasted until the advent of the colonial era in the second half of the nineteenth century. European ships of many nations called at trading ports situated on the coast or a few miles up navigable rivers. At these ports African goods from inland communities were exchanged for the goods brought by the Europeans, which the coastal Africans in turn traded with hinterland peoples. It was the western end of the Gulf which first achieved prominence: in the sixteenth century its exports of gold earned it the name Gold Coast. During the era of the slave trade, from the mid-seventeenth to the mid-nineteenth century, the entire Guinea coast participated in a vigorous commerce in slaves through these ports. Eventually, toward the beginning of the nineteenth century, English demand for soap and lubricants called into being a trade in palm-oil, though in this case it was the eastern end of the Gulf—called the Oil Rivers—which started earliest and achieved the greatest success in this new trade.

The growth and organization of these enduring commercial ties have been examined from both the European and the African sides.[1] Yet a strange imbalance exists in the literature covering the commercial organization of this trade within West Africa. Along the western portion of the Gulf, known as the Bight of Benin, researchers have examined the activities both of the hinterland peoples who originated the export trade—the Ashanti of modern Ghana, the Fon of Dahomey, the Yoruba of south-western Nigeria—and, to a lesser degree, the entrepreneurial coastal ports which were the middlemen

---

[1] The best synthesis is A. G. Hopkins, *An Economic History of West Africa* (New York: Columbia Univ. Press, 1973), pp. 87–135.

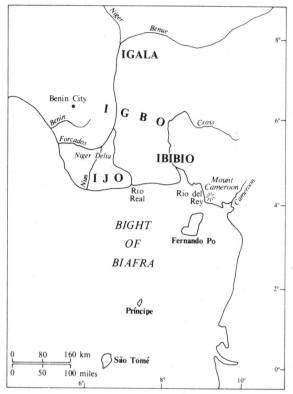

MAP 1. South-eastern Nigeria and the Bight of Biafra.

in the trade.[2] The commercial history of the peoples east of the Niger River, along the Bight of Biafra, has received a very different

[2]The classic treatment of a hinterland kingdom and its coastal outlet is by Margaret Arnold, 'A Port of Trade: Whydah on the Guinea Coast' in *Trade and Markets in the Early Empires*, ed. K. Polanyi, *et al.* (Glencoe: Free-Press, 1957) and Karl Polanyi, *Dahomey and the Slave Trade* (Seattle: Univ. of Washington Press, 1966). Corrections of some of Polanyi's excesses may be found in I. A. Akinjogbin, *Dahomey and its Neighbours, 1708–1818* (Cambridge: At the Univ. Press, 1966). Descriptions of the Oyo Kingdom by Peter Morton-Williams and of the Ashanti Confederation by Ivor Wilks are in Daryll Forde and P. M. Kaberry, eds., *West African Kingdoms in the Nineteenth Century* (London: Oxford Univ. Press, 1967). See also Ivor Wilks, *Asante in the Nineteenth Century* (Cambridge Univ. Press, 1975); K. Y. Daaku, *Trade and Politics on the Gold Coast, 1600–1720* (Oxford: Clarendon Press, 1970); and Peter Morton-Williams, 'The Oyo Yoruba and the Atlantic Trade', *JHSN* III (1964), 25–45. Studies with an economic focus are Edward Reynolds, *Trade and Economic Change on the Gold Coast, 1807–1874* (London: Longmans, 1974) and the following studies in *The Development of Indigenous Trade and Markets in West Africa*, ed.

treatment. The Igbo,[3] Ibibio, and other peoples of the hinterland have been almost totally neglected, while the middlemen of the coastal city-states have been the subject of several studies.[4] Even the more general surveys of African history have retained this bias. For example, a recent history of West Africa devotes thirty-one pages of text to this part of the continent: twenty-nine of them to the coastal communities, only two pages to the hinterland peoples.[5]

In large part this skewed treatment has been due to the obvious differences in political structure between the peoples of south-eastern Nigeria and those of the south-west. While the Ashanti, Fon, and Yoruba all ordered their political lives and oversaw their commercial activities through centralized kingdoms or federations, the peoples east of the Niger created no political structures above the local level.

The preoccupation of historians with African state systems is understandable in terms of the available sources (earlier visitors to the Guinea coast also having been drawn to write about the kingdoms and empires) and the thematic unity they give to historical narratives, but it has introduced some serious distortions into African history. Historians of Africa have tended either to ignore 'stateless' societies completely or to write of them in timeless anthropological terms or to force them into the more familiar moulds of

---

Claude Meillassoux (London: Oxford Univ. Press, 1971): Kwame Y. Daaku, 'Trade and Trading Patterns of the Akan in the Seventeenth and Eighteenth Centuries'; Catherine Coquery-Vidrovitch, 'De la traite des esclaves à l'exportation de l'huile de palme et des palmistes au Dahomey: xixᵉ siècle'; and Colin W. Newbury, 'Prices and Profitability in Early Nineteenth Century West African Trade.' For the situation at Benin see A. F. C. Ryder, *Benin and the Europeans, 1485–1897* (London: Longmans, 1969).

[3] The name of this people and their language is often spelled *Ibo*, but *Igbo* is to be preferred on linguistic grounds.

[4] K. Onwuka Dike, *Trade and Politics in the Niger Delta, 1830–1885* (Oxford: Clarendon Press, 1956); D. Forde, ed., *Efik Traders of Old Calabar* (London: Oxford Univ. Press, 1956); G. I. Jones, *The Trading States of the Oil Rivers* (London: Oxford Univ. Press, 1963); E. J. Alagoa, *The Small Brave City-State: a History of Nembe-Brass in the Niger Delta* (Ibadan: Ibadan Univ. Press, 1964), 'Long-distance Trade and States in the Niger Delta', *JAH* XI (1970), 405–19, and *A History of the Niger Delta* (Ibadan: Ibadan Univ. Press, 1972); K. K. Nair, *Politics and Society in South Eastern Nigeria: a Study of Power, Diplomacy and Commerce in Old Calabar* (London: Frank Cass, 1972); A. J. H. Latham, *Old Calabar 1600–1891* (Oxford: Clarendon Press, 1973) and 'Currency, Credit and Capitalism on the Cross River in the Pre-Colonial Era', *JAH*, XII (1971), 249–60.

[5] E. J. Alagoa, 'The Niger Delta States and their Neighbours, 1600–1800', in J. F. A. Ajayi and Michael Crowder, eds., *History of West Africa* (London: Longmans, 1971, 1974), I, 269–303.

political centralization by speaking of trading 'empires' or 'incipient state formation'. In south-eastern Nigeria all three approaches have been tried. The conceptual limitations of one respected historian are revealed in these remarks on the area: 'During the nineteenth century there is not much to tell about the Ibo and Ibibio. They were not integrated into kingdoms seeking conquest. They produced no hierarchy of rulers whose lives and careers could provide for dramatic stories.'[6] This author then gives an ahistorical description of the political organization of the region and examines the activities of one of the most important trading peoples, the Aro, who from their home at Arochukwu spread out to found settlements and colonies in many parts of the hinterland. Other, less cautious, writers have exhibited a sort of 'Aromania' in their eagerness to attribute exclusive economic and even political control to the Aro. But even serious scholars have gone overboard in their attempt to find in the Aro or in the small city-states of the coast and Niger valley the Holy Grail of state-building.[7]

Anthropologists have done much better in understanding small-scale African societies. Instead of viewing them as a primitive form of society which under favourable circumstances will bloom into large-scale states, they have accepted them on their own terms as mature and complex forms of social and political organization, quite capable of participating in cultural and economic systems much larger than their political units.[8] This ability of small-scale societies

[6] J. C. Anene, 'Benin, Niger Delta, Ibo and Ibibio Peoples in the Nineteenth Century', in J. F. A. Ajayi and Ian Espie, eds., *A Thousand Years of West African History* (Ibadan: Ibadan Univ. Press, 1965), p. 304.

[7] The growth of this theory is described in §1 of Chapter IV and criticized in §3 of that chapter.

[8] The first major analysis of small-scale African societies was by Meyer Fortes and E. E. Evans-Pritchard, eds., *African Political Systems* (London: Oxford Univ. Press, 1940). Elaborations of their category of 'stateless' were made by John Middleton and David Tait, eds., *Tribes without Rulers* (London: Routledge and Kegan Paul, 1958), who delineated three types of segmentary lineage systems. A still more complete typology has been proposed by S. N. Eisenstadt, 'Primitive Political Systems: a Preliminary Comparative Analysis', *American Anthropologist*, LXI (1959), 200–20. Important contributions to the study of small scale political organization in south-eastern Nigeria have been made by: C. K. Meek, *Report on the Social and Political Organization in Owerri Division* (Lagos: Government Printer, 1934); G. I. Jones, *Report on the Position, Status and Influence of Chiefs and Natural Rulers in the Eastern Region of Nigeria* (hereinafter, *The Jones Report*) (Enugu: Government Printer, 1958); Daryll Forde, *Yakö Studies* (London: Oxford Univ. Press, 1964); Malcolm Ruel, *Leopards and Leaders: Constitutional Politics among a Cross River People* (London: Tavistock Publications, 1969); Laura Bohannan, 'Political Aspects of Tiv Social Organization', in Middleton and Tait, *Tribes*; Simon Ottenberg, *Double Descent in an African Society*:

to participate in large and complex networks of trade has also been recognized, though somewhat grudgingly, in recent historical studies of African trade.[9] If there is then no necessary correlation between large-scale trade and large-scale political institutions, one has an additional reason for examining the commercial life of south-eastern Nigeria where the volume of trade was among the highest in Africa for many centuries. For it is very likely that the institutions which functioned there were also in use in the West African states, but have not been appreciated because of the emphasis on political matters.

The chapters which follow are concerned not with the internal political organization of south-eastern Nigeria, but with the institutions and personnel of its commercial organization: markets and market networks, regional and long-distance trade, commodities and currencies, trade routes and professional traders, for it is in this economic approach that both the thematic unity and the main thrust of the history of this region are most clearly revealed.

While south-eastern Nigeria is composed of several ecological zones and inhabited by a number of ethnolinguistic groups, in terms of its economic history it may be considered as a single region.[10]

the Afikpo Village Group (Seattle: Univ. of Washington Press, 1968) and Leadership and Authority in an African Society: the Afikpo Village Group (Seattle: Univ. of Washington Press, 1971); and Richard Neal Henderson, The King in Every Man: Evolutionary Trends in Onitsha Ibo Society and Culture (New Haven: Yale Univ. Press, 1972).

It is not surprising that the best effort so far at approaching the history of stateless societies is by an anthropologist: Robin Horton, 'Stateless Societies in the History of West Africa', in Ajayi and Crowder, History, I, 78–119. Horton's stimulating essay nevertheless reaches the depressing conclusion that 'the difficulties of writing a "history" [of stateless societies of the same type as that of] the great pre-colonial states are virtually insuperable'. A notable exception to this stricture is the outstanding history by another anthropologist, Jones, Trading States, for an area with relatively abundant written historical records.

[9] Richard Gray and David Birmingham, eds., Pre-Colonial African Trade: Essays on Trade in Central and Eastern Africa before 1900 (London: Oxford Univ. Press, 1970), p. 3, conclude: 'In Eastern and Central Africa ... close links between states and organized trade have not, on the whole, been established.' The members of a recent seminar on West African trade likewise 'did not consider it established in any clear way that trade was everywhere encouraged by the existence of state systems'; see Meillassoux, Development of Indigenous Trade, p. 74.

[10] The Bight of Biafra and the Cameroon Mountains provide clear frontiers of the region on the south and east. The Niger River is a convenient frontier on the west, but of course it was a commercial artery not a barrier. The northern frontier is also imprecisely defined, although population densities grow thinner north of the Igbo to the Benue valley before increasing again. The exact nature of the western and northern frontiers bears further investigation.

As subsequent chapters will indicate, the hinterland became increasingly cross-cut by networks of markets and trade routes, while its external ties remained channelled through narrow outlets. To the north the region was connected to the central Sudan by the Niger–Benue river system, although this contact may have declined in importance as the trade to the coast grew. At the coast trade with Europeans was confined to a few coastal towns whose numbers actually decreased as the overseas trade became concentrated at a few favoured ports. In the days of the slave trade most of the slaves shipped from these coastal ports originated within the hinterland. Moreover, the end of the slave trade did not end the close integration of the region even though the remaining export of palm-oil came only from the southern portion of the hinterland since internal trade between the northern and southern portions remained high.

Because the coastal zone formed an integral part of this economic region it is included within this study, though these ports will occupy a much smaller place in this work than they have in earlier studies. The reason for this change of emphasis is not to challenge their very considerable importance in the commerce of the eastern Guinea coast but rather to place it in a larger historical and geographical context.

To gain a proper perspective on the economic history of this region it is important to broaden one's focus in time as well as in space. Too many writers have paid scant attention to topics and relationships which had no direct bearing on trade with Europeans, yet this trade, though very significant, needs to be viewed in the general context of trading relations of the region. For that reason this study begins by examining the state of economic life during the centuries before the arrival of the Portuguese. Though less is known of this early period than one would like, it is clear that the first trade with Europeans began in a context defined by pre-existing African institutions.

The slave trade also appears in a new perspective when examined in terms of African rather than European trade. Far too often the slave trade has been evaluated as a moral principle rather than as a part of history. Having condemned the immorality of the trade, historians felt constrained to affirm its uniformly destructive impact on Africa, selecting only that evidence which supported their preconceived ideas.[11] The more serious study of the slave trade has been

[11] The most recent evaluations of the impact of the slave trade on south-eastern

aided greatly by the statistical work of Curtin, and the revisions of traditional judgements suggested by Fage and Hopkins.[12] The present study also weighs the impact of the slave trade, both on the society of south-eastern Nigeria and on its commercial institutions, in the hopes of adding a useful case study to the process of reinterpretation.

Only by re-examining the slave trade in the context of hinterland trading institutions is it possible to understand how the trade was about to grow so rapidly and how south-eastern Nigeria, alone of West African regions, was able to develop a gigantic trade in palm-oil during, as well as after, the overseas slave trade. Therefore, in addition to studying the role of this region in the slave and palm-oil trades, the role of these trades in the commercial life of the hinterland must be examined, for the institutions which accommodated the overseas trade antedated it and persisted during it. At the same time, these institutions were also altered, producing a larger, more complex and integrated internal economy in the process.

The materials upon which this re-examination rests are varied. Except along the Niger and Cross rivers, European explorers and missionaries did not visit the interior until much later than the period being considered, but there does exist a substantial body of information on the coastal area. In many cases observers recorded information about the hinterland which they learned from Africans at the coast.[13] Additional information about parts of the interior is also

Nigeria are no exceptions to this pattern. R. Olufemi Ekundare, *An Economic History of Nigeria, 1860–1960* (London: Methuen, 1973), pp. 35–6, can see only negative effects, though he makes no effort to harmonize this opinion with the facts of pre-colonial economic history. Elizabeth Isichei, *The Ibo People and the Europeans* (London: Faber and Faber, 1973), p. 43, prefaces her highly selective analysis of the trade with this profession of faith: 'It is the belief of the present writer that the effects of the slave trade, both in Iboland and elsewhere, were overwhelmingly destructive, and retarded and distorted the historical development of African societies.'

[12] Philip D. Curtin, *The Atlantic Slave Trade: a Census* (Madison: Univ. of Wisconsin Press, 1969); John D. Fage, 'Slavery and the Slave Trade in the Context of West African History', *JAH* X (1969), 393–404 and chapter 6, 'The Slave Trade and Economic Change', of his *A History of West Africa* (Cambridge: At the Univ. Press, 1969); Hopkins, *Economic History*, pp. 101–12; Roger Anstey, *The Atlantic Slave Trade and British Abolition, 1760–1810* (London: Macmillan, 1975), pp. 58–88. An important case study by Walter Rodney of an area which seems to have been exceptional in the West African context should also be consulted: 'African Slavery and Other Forms of Social Oppression on the Upper Guinea Coast in the Context of the Atlantic Slave Trade', *JAH* VII (1966), 431–43.

[13] The most useful sources for the period before 1700 are Duarte Pacheco Pereira, *Esmeraldo de Situ Orbis*, ed. Raymond Mauny (Bissau: Centro de Estudos da Guiné

available from Africans who lived in or visited interior parts. Two eighteenth-century Africans wrote their own accounts and others, who were enslaved and shipped away from home, described their homelands to missionaries in other parts of Africa and in the New World.[14] A major difficulty with this body of contemporary evi-

---

Portuguesa, 1956) for the beginning of the sixteenth century; Olfert Dapper, *Description de l'Afrique*, tr. from the Dutch edition of 1668 (Amsterdam: Waesberge, Boom and van Someren, 1686); John Barbot, 'A Description of the Coasts of North and South Guinea', including his brother James's 'Abstract of a Voyage to *New Calabar* River, or *Rio Real*, in the Year 1699', both in Awnsham and John Churchill, comps., *Collection of Voyages and Travels*, vol. V (London: H. Lintot and John Osborn, 1746); William F. Hutchinson, 'A Seventeenth Century Slaver's Diary', *Elder Dempster Magazine*, IV (1925), 60–2, 141–3; V (1926), 32–4; and Alexander Falconbridge, *An Account of the Slave Trade on the Coast of Africa* (London: J. Phillips, 1788).

For the late eighteenth century and the first half of the nineteenth the most useful accounts of the coast are Capt. John Adams, *Remarks on the Country Extending from Cape Palmas to the River Congo* (London: G. & W. B. Whittaker, 1823); Capt. Hugh Crow, *Memoirs of the Late Capt. Hugh Crow of Liverpool* (London: Longmans, 1830); and R. M. Jackson, *Journal of a Voyage to the Bonny River* (Letchworth: Garden City Press, 1934).

Accounts of early expeditions up the Niger are Richard and John Lander, *Journal of an Expedition to Explore the Course and Termination of the Niger* (London: J. Murray, 1832), reissued as *The Niger Journal*, ed. Robin Hallett (New York: Praeger Publishers, 1965); Macgregor Laird and R. A. K. Oldfield, *Narrative of an Expedition into the Interior of Africa ... in 1832, 1833, and 1834*, 2 vols. (London: Richard Bentley, 1837); 'Substance of a Letter Received from J. Becroft [*sic*], Esq., Relative to his Recent Ascent of the Quorra, dated Fernando Po, 28th February, 1836', *JRGS* VI (1836), 424–6, and John Beecroft, 'On Benin and the Upper Course of the River Quorra or the Niger', *JRGS* XI (1841), 184–90; William Allen and T. R. H. Thomson, *A Narrative of the Expedition ... to the River Niger in 1841*, 2 vols. (London: Richard Bentley, 1848); James Frederick Schon and Samuel Crowther, *Journals of the ....
Expedition up the Niger in 1841* (London: Church Missionary Society, 1842); William Balfour Baikie, *Narrative of an Exploring Voyage up the Rivers Kwora and Binue in 1854* (London: John Murray, 1856); The Revd. Samuel Adjai Crowther, *Journal of an Expedition up the Niger and Tshadda Rivers ... in 1854* (London: Church Mission House, 1855); Thomas Joseph Hutchinson, *Narrative of the Niger, Tshadda and Binue Exploration* (London: Longmans, 1855).

Early explorations of the Cross River were fewer: R. A. K. Oldfield, 'A Brief Account of an Ascent of the Old Calabar River in 1836', *JRGS* VII (1837), 195–198; J. B. King, 'Details of Explorations of the Old Calabar River, in 1841 and 1842 by Captain Becroft [*sic*] ... and Mr. J. B. King', *JRGS* XIV (1844), 260–83.

The best accounts of early missions are Samuel Adjai Crowther and John Christopher Taylor, *The Gospel on the Banks of the Niger* (London: Dawsons, 1859); Hope Masterton Waddell, *Twenty-Nine Years in the West Indies and Central Africa* (London: Thomas Nelson, 1863) and the extant volumes of Waddell's 'Journal of the Old Calabar Mission' (1846–58), United Presbyterian Church papers, NLS, MSS. 7739–7743 and 8953.

[14] The autobiography of an enslaved Igbo and the diary of an Old Calabar trader have appeared in modern editions: *Equiano's Travels. His Autobiography. The Interesting Narrative of the Life of Olaudah Equiano or Gustavus Vassa the African*, abr.

dence, even excusing its fragmentary nature, is determining the specific places referred to by each informant. Most employed ethnographic and place-names which are no longer in use. Much time has been spent by the present writer, often aided by the suggestions of other scholars, in establishing the meaning of these terms, and the effort has produced a very useful body of data for periods of time usually thought to be irretrievable by the historian. Especially when used in combination with each other and with other sources, these bits and pieces of information enable one to trace patterns of hinterland trade which other researchers have not perceived.

In supplementing these sources extensive use has also been made of non-contemporary material, primarily in the form of oral testimony. Some of this was collected and published earlier in this century by British missionaries and colonial officials.[15] A great amount of additional oral testimony was incorporated into the unpublished Intelligence and Assessment Reports of district officers and their subordinates written in the 1920s and 1930s and now stored in Nigerian archives. While few of these officials were trained researchers, many were highly skilled and conscientious amateurs, whose work has the distinct advantage of covering all portions of the region and of having been completed before the period of greatest

---

and ed. by Paul Edwards (New York: Frederick A. Praeger, 1967); a portion has appeared as 'Early Travels of Olaudah Equiano', edited, with an introduction entitled 'Olaudah Equiano of the Niger Ibo', by G. I. Jones, in *Africa Remembered: Narratives by West Africans from the Era of the Slave Trade*, ed. Philip D. Curtin (Madison: Univ. of Wisconsin Press, 1967); and 'The Diary of Antera Duke', ed. Donald C. Simmons, in Forde, *Efik Traders*. Seventeenth-century slaves from south-eastern Nigeria were interviewed in Latin America by Alonso de Sandoval, *Naturaleza ... de Totos Etiopes* (Sevilla: Francisco de Lira, 1627), reissued as *De Instauranda Aethiopum Salute* (Bogota: Empressa Nacional de Publicaciones, 1956). Eighteenth-century slaves from this region were interviewed in the West Indies and in North America by C. G. A. Oldendorps, *Geschichte der Mission der Evangelischen Brüder auf den Caribischen Inseln*, 2 vols. (Barby: Christian Fredrich Laux, 1777). Nineteenth-century liberated Africans from this region were interviewed in Sierra Leone by S. W. Koelle, *Polyglotta Africana* (London: Church Missionary House, 1854). See also S. J. S. Cookey, 'An Igbo Slave Story of the Late Nineteenth Century and its Implications', *Ikenga*, I.2 (July 1972), 1–9.

[15] The work of P. Amaury Talbot is of special importance: *In the Shadow of the Bush* (London: William Heinemann, 1912), *Life in Southern Nigeria* (London: Macmillan, 1923), and the *Peoples of Southern Nigeria* (London: Oxford Univ. Press, 1926). See also N. W. Thomas, *Anthropological Report on the Ibo-Speaking Peoples of Nigeria*, 4 vols. (London: Harrison, 1913–14) and the Revd. G. T. Basden, *Among the Ibos of Nigeria* (Philadelphia: J. B. Lippincott, 1921) and *Niger Ibos* (London: Seeley Service, 1938).

social change. More recently systematic collection of oral testimony has been undertaken by historians and social scientists doing case studies within this region.[16] Finally the present writer conducted extensive personal interviews in 1972–3, concerning those subjects most pertinent to this present study. Many of these interviews (see §I of Sources) were conducted among the Ibibio because their homeland had been given less attention by other researchers, because it could test a number of hypotheses concerning the region as a whole, and because it was best known to the author from a previous residence in that area. Interviews were also conducted at Arochukwu, among the Ngwa and Ndoki Igbo, and in the Onitsha area of the Niger valley. In many cases it was possible to interview elders of communities which had been mentioned in the older written sources, thus enabling written sources and oral recollections to act as checks upon each other and to give a more detailed history of key places.

2. LAND AND PEOPLE

The economic history of south-eastern Nigeria has been strongly influenced by its geography, so this study must start with a survey of the region's main variations of vegetation and topography as well as ethnography. Lying between four and eight degrees north of the equator, the region has a hot, humid climate. In prehistoric times rainfall patterns produced two east–west vegetation zones: a tropical rain forest extending inland for approximately 100 miles in the zone of heaviest rainfall (80–140+ inches per year), above which the forest thinned out to a more open savanna. In the course of centuries of relatively dense human settlement these zones have been greatly modified. Much of the woodland of the northern savanna zone was cleared for cultivation and firewood producing a more open countryside than in prehistoric times. In the south much of the three-tiered canopy of the rain forest was reduced by cultivation practices to 'secondary scrub' containing high concentrations of oil-palms. These oil-palms are now the most characteristic vegetation of this area reaching *average* densities of 100–150 adult trees per acre in places. Favoured by humans for their edible oil though not actually cultivated until the twentieth century, these trees multiplied along with the human population, especially on abandoned homesteads. These modifications of the original vegetation zones took place over many centuries, and, it would appear, largely before the period under

[16]See note 8, above.

study. Only east of the Cross River, where population densities were not so high, did the original rain forest remain largely intact.

The rivers draining this region have also limited the distribution of the pure rain forest. In the south-west the Niger River created a vast delta of meandering creeks, swamps, and low-lying islands. This broken coastline was re-created on a smaller scale by other rivers all along the seaboard to the east. In the saline parts of the delta mangrove forest predominated and in the salt-free parts of the delta there was freshwater swamp forest. Early European mariners failed to recognize the broken coast as the delta of the Niger River—this discovery coming only in the nineteenth century—naming each outlet as a separate river. Many of these 'rivers' and others along this coast still retain their Portuguese names. Of the many 'rivers' of the delta the most important for this study is the Rio Real, the outlet of both the New Calabar and Bonny rivers, which were named after the two leading trading communities of the eastern delta. At the eastern end of the coast, in contrast with the many outlets of the single river Niger, is a large estuary which serves as an outlet for several rivers draining the Cameroon highlands. The largest and most important of these is the Cross River (Rio da Cruz) which also gives its name to the estuary; other confluents are the Old Calabar (or Calabar) River, the Kwa (Qua) River and the Akpa Yafe River. Just beyond the Cross River Estuary is a false estuary called the Rio del Rey, which is fed by some small streams. The south-central portion of the hinterland is drained by two rivers, the larger and more important Imo River, which drains the central and southern Igbo area, and the Kwa Ibo River, which drains the southern and western Ibibio area. Although all of these rivers have sand-bars at their mouths which were a hazard to European ships, the main rivers of the Bight of Biafra are unusual for African rivers in being largely free of obstacles to navigation along their inland courses. The Niger and Cross are both navigable for their entire lengths within Nigeria, and the Imo, and Kwa Ibo are readily usable by canoes. All the rivers east of the Cross, however, are blocked by waterfalls a few miles from their mouths.[17]

Geographical variations within south-eastern Nigeria produced two main occupational specializations: fishing at the coast and along the rivers, and, for many more people, farming in the inland areas.

[17] Reuben K. Udo, *Geographical Regions of Nigeria* (Berkeley: Univ. of California Press, 1970), pp. 1–9, 46–98.

These were not mutually exclusive categories for, where possible, the wives of fishermen raised garden crops, and farmers near rivers and ponds also did some fishing.

The fishing communities along the major rivers and at the coast came to play quite special roles in the history of this region. Unable to raise sufficient crops on their limited arable land, they were forced to trade with their hinterland neighbours for vegetable foods, supplying dried fish and salt in return. Because of the skills they developed in constructing and operating large canoes and the mobility which fishing required, they also possessed skills which were readily transferable to full-time trading. It was the fishermen who first came into contact with European traders, and they were able to retain a monopoly on direct contact throughout the period of the overseas trade. Thus in many coastal communities trading came to overshadow fishing as the main economic activity.

Throughout both the northern and southern portions of the hinterland farming practices and crops are largely similar. Nearly all farmers practice 'rotational fallow' whereby land once cultivated is allowed to lie fallow for several years before being cleared and replanted. Fields tend to be small and care is taken not to disturb useful trees, especially palms, during the clearing process. Cultivation is continuous on the garden plots around homesteads, usually called 'compounds'. On the farmland the most ancient food plants are the raphia and oil-palm, the common yam (*dioscorea rotundata*) and the kolanut, which are all indigenous to the area. These have remained basic to the agricultural economy, although the addition of crops of the Malaysian complex (cocoyam, plantain, water yam, *et al.*) at some distant time and of West Indian crops introduced by the Portuguese within the last 500 years (rice, oranges, coconuts, some types of onions, and cassava) has added considerable variety to the diet and stability to the food supply. Only in the twentieth century have yams been replaced by cassava as the staple food in much of the hinterland because of cassava's greater yield per acre.[18]

[18] Udo, *Geographical Regions*, pp. 1–9, 46–98. For linguistic evidence of plant cultivation see Kay Williamson, 'Some Plant Names in the Niger Delta', *International Journal of American Linguistics*, XXXVI 1970), 159–63. For other descriptions and analyses of human interaction with the vegetation of this region see: D. G. Coursey, *Yams* (London: Longmans, Green, 1967), pp. 18–20; William Orville Jones, *Manioc in Africa* (Stanford: Stanford Univ. Press, 1959), pp. 73–9; C. W. S. Hartley, *The Oil Palm* (London: Longmans, 1967); Anne Martin, *The Oil Palm Economy of the Ibibio Farmer* (Ibadan: Ibadan Univ. Press, 1956); W. B. Morgan, 'The Forest and Agriculture in West Africa', *JAH* III (1962), 238–9.

Despite the losses during the overseas slave trade, the population of south-eastern Nigeria has attained densities among the highest in rural Africa, in some cases in excess of 800 persons per square mile. Since there have been no major migrations into the area within recent centuries,[19] this density must have occurred through natural reproduction, indicating a relatively dense population for several centuries before the present era. The reasons for this density cannot be fully explained in the absence of adequate sources, but a large part of the explanation must rest on skilful exploitation of the environment and the complex marketing system which expanded along with the population.[20]

Despite this density, the people of south-eastern Nigeria have generally lived in dispersed compounds among their fields.[21] Here, in sharp contrast to the urbanized Yoruba to the west of the Niger, compact settlements were a distinct rarity in the pre-colonial era. Even 'villages' were customarily only political and social units, not actual clusters of dwellings, and the family compounds of a village were normally scattered throughout its territory. Only the coastal ports, fishing villages cramped for dry land, and places fortified against attack were compact settlements.[22]

Political units, like residential settlements, tended to be limited in size and cohesiveness. The basic political unit was the localized patrilineage, generally the subdivision of a village, which managed its own internal affairs. Matters between lineages were regulated at the village level and the largest unit of regular political action was a group of villages claiming ancestral ties. Only in rare cases (especially among the Ibibio) were members of the same clan capable of

[19] The idea of 'distinct waves of migration' into the hinterland in historic times as suggested by Dike, *Trade and Politics*, pp. 21–30, can not be sustained by any reasonable reading of the evidence.

[20] See below, Chapters IV and VII.

[21] According to a mid-nineteenth-century account of the Ibibio: 'There are no towns in the country, the people living scattered in family settlements on their farms ...'; see Hugh Goldie, *Dictionary of the Efik Language* (Glasgow: Dunn and Wright, 1962), p. 358.

[22] Fortified villages were most common in the vicinity of Arochukwu and may have been in defence against the Abam warriors (see below, Chapter V, §2). The eastern Igbo generally have compact walled settlements according to Daryll Forde and G. I. Jones, *The Ibo and Ibibio-Speaking Peoples of South-Eastern Nigeria* (London: International African Institute, 1950), p. 52. The existence of fortified settlements among the nearby Ibibio was confirmed in interviews with Chief Akpan Udo Essien, the Obong Ikpa Isong of Ikpe Clan at Ebam Ukot on 20 Dec. 1972, and with Chief Ekpenyong Akpan at Ekoi Atan Ubom, Ikpe, on the same date.

collective action in war, in some religious festivals, and in making judicial decisions.[23]

The inhabitants of south-eastern Nigeria belonged to several ethnolinguistic groups of considerable antiquity. The largest of these were the Igbo and the Ibibio, most of whom lived north of the delta between the Niger and Cross rivers. The eastern delta was inhabited by the Ijo (Ijaw), though during the period under study many Igbo also came to live there, primarily as domestic slaves. East of the Cross River lived the Efik branch of the Ibibio and a number of smaller groups which may usefully be encompassed by the term Cross River peoples.[24] South of the Benue River lay several groups of which the largest were the Igala, who alone of the inhabitants of this region had a monarchy, and the Tiv.

Although the Igbo and Ibibio have much in common culturally and have deceptively similar names, they lie on opposite sides of one of the major dividing-lines of the Niger–Congo language family. Igbo is the easternmost extension of the Kwa sub-family of Niger–Congo languages, while Ibibio is one of the westernmost extensions of the Benue–Congo sub-family. The languages most closely related to Igbo, though they are very distant by the standards of Bantu Africa, are spoken by its western neighbours the Ijo, Yoruba, Edo, Igala, as well as by the geographically more distant Ewe and Akan of Ghana and the Kru of Liberia. Ibibio's nearest linguistic relatives are the languages of the Cross River peoples, though Benue–Congo includes a large number of languages spoken along the Benue and upper Cross rivers, as well as the entire Bantu group of languages which dominate in Africa south of the equator.[25] The degree of differentiation among the many languages of each sub-family in this region is such as to imply several millennia of separate development, and that between sub-families must be much greater. At the same time the relative geographical distribution of the languages and language groups implies that the speakers of these languages have

[23]The political organization of the region is considered at greater length in Chapter II, §4.

[24]The Cross River peoples are sometimes called Ekoi after one of the larger dialect clusters in that area, but this is not very useful, or accurate. Where possible in this study individual Cross River peoples will be identified by their proper names.

[25]Joseph H. Greenberg, *The Languages of Africa*, 2nd edn. (London: Frank Cass, 1966), p. 8, and C. F. and F. M. Voegelin, 'Languages of the World: African Fascicle One', *Anthropological Linguistics*, VI. 6 (May 1964), 14–16.

resided in their present locales for most, if not all, of the period of linguistic differentiation.

Despite the importance of ethnolinguistic frontiers no worse error could be made than to exaggerate the significance of these divisions in the economic history of the region. Divided into small political units and spread across different ecological zones, the larger peoples of the hinterland were also divided into distinct cultural and dialectical sub-groups. The largest Igbo subdivisions are customarily named after the points of the compass: Northern, Western, Southern, Eastern, and North-Eastern. A portion of the Southern Igbo are often designated as Central or Owerri Igbo. The Ibibio are composed of three large groups, the Anang, Ibibio Proper, and Efik, and the smaller Enyong, Eket, and Delta (Andoni-Ibeno) divisions.[26] In pre-colonial times the largest unit of identity for most inhabitants does not appear to have been the primary ethnic unit such as Igbo or Ibibio, but rather the smaller dialect or cultural group. For example, Igbo-speakers enslaved in the 1820s and liberated in Sierra Leone claimed never to have heard the name Igbo in their homelands and could identify themselves only by names designating very much smaller units.[27] Because of this the main linguistic boundaries proved no real barrier to trade, and trade routes cut across them. Members of one ethnic group might attend the markets of another and vice versa. This is not to say that ethnicity counted for naught, but economic transactions between cultural sub-groups took place as readily across linguistic frontiers as within them. Thus little if anything is to be gained by writing the history of each ethnic group separately as has been the unfortunate practice of some historians, while much understanding of the economic interdependence of the region will be lost by such an approach. The chapters that follow will pay far more attention to economic relations than to ethnic ones, not out of any personal predilection of the author, but because the citizens of south-eastern Nigeria during the centuries under study were also much more concerned with trade than with tribe.

[26]These are the divisions and names used by Forde and Jones, *Ibo and Ibibio.*

[27]Koelle, *Polyglotta,* pp. 7–8. To this day no one name is universally accepted by speakers of the Ibibio language. Ibibio is the name of the largest dialect, but is not accepted by most Anang and Efik as a proper name for themselves. With apologies to those who call themselves by other names the name Ibibio will be applied to the entire language and its speakers.

CHAPTER I

The Development of Trade Before 1500

PROFESSOR Dike opened his now classic study of the Niger Delta with the remarkable pronouncement: 'The history of modern West Africa is largely the history of five centuries of trade with European nations ...'[1] Certainly for the coastal entrepôts of south-eastern Nigeria which are the focus of Dike's study this would be hard to dispute.[2] Their development from fishing villages[3] to city states and their considerable wealth and power were largely dependent upon their monopoly of trade with Europeans. The growing volume of trade passing through these ports likewise had its impact on the Delta hinterland, forging into a continuous network the local markets of the disparate political communities, promoting the wealth and interests of several merchant peoples, and creating a demand for European minerals and manufacturers which had an important influence on local life.

Yet, important though this European trading presence was, it did not dominate modern West African history to the extent Dike claimed. Even in the area of trade it is clear that the European trade was but one facet of a system of exchange which, before the coming of the first European traders, linked the peoples of West Africa to

[1] Dike, *Trade and Politics*, p. 1.

[2] Nevertheless, a stimulating and vigorous attack has been mounted against Dike's thesis and a similar point of view by Latham, *Old Calabar* (whose conclusion, p. 146, begins, 'From 1600 to 1891 the economic demands of the expanding international economy were the main force acting for change in Efik society ... the changes which took place in Efik society were side-effects of this commerce.') by A. E. Afigbo, 'Mono-causality and the African Historiography: the Case of Efik Society and International Commerce', *Transactions of the Historical Society of Ghana* XVI.1 (1973), 11–27. Afigbo justifiably draws attention to the capacity for change inherent in coastal societies and the stimuli for change which also came from neighbours further inland, but he somewhat exaggerates the element of 'mono-causality' in his opponents' arguments since both do make efforts to avoid that error (Dike's 'largely', Latham's 'main force').

[3] Or an even earlier farming community: see E. J. Alagoa, 'The Development of Institutions in the States of the Eastern Niger Delta', *JAH* XII (1971), 269–78. See also Robin Horton, 'From Fishing Village to City-state: a Social History of New Calabar' in *Man in Africa*, ed. Mary Douglas and Phyllis M. Kaberry (London: Tavistock Publications, 1969), pp. 37–58.

each other and with the world beyond. Although south-eastern Nigeria was not the centre of this early trade, neither was it a backwater. Before the arrival of the Portuguese it had developed an economy which was able to support a growing population and whose artisans had attained a high degree of skill. Exchange was facilitated through local and regional markets, the more important of which were connected by regular overland and water routes.

1. THE ECONOMY OF IGBO-UKWU

The earliest information about the economic life of south-eastern Nigeria derives from the excavations of an elaborate burial and two related sites in the village of Igbo-Ukwu, about twenty-five miles south-east of Onitsha. Four of the five carbon samples from these sites yielded radio-carbon dates in the eighth to eleventh century (A.D.) range, a dating which their excavator, Thurstan Shaw, does not feel is contradicted by any of the other archaeological evidence.[4] Owing to an unfortunate laboratory malfunction, no radio-carbon dates were obtained for the richest site, a repository or treasury of ritual or ceremonial objects. Since the style and workmanship of the objects found there suggest to Shaw that it is the youngest of the three sites and because of other circumstantial problems with dating the finds, the terminal date of the Igbo-Ukwu finds could extend to about 1500 but not beyond, since no evidence of European contact from the coast was discovered.[5]

The material remains of the Igbo-Ukwu sites are rich and varied, representing a culture whose craftsmen possessed considerable technical virtuosity and artistic imagination. Because of the quality of its metal-working, weaving, and pottery-making, and the type of

[4] A fifth sample produced a much later date, presumably as the result of contamination. For a full report of the findings and a discussion of the comment and criticism which they generated see Thurstan Shaw, *Igbo-Ukwu* (London: Faber and Faber, 1970), and Thurstan Shaw, 'Those Igbo-Ukwu Radiocarbon Dates: Facts, Fictions and Probabilities', *JAH* XVI (1975), 503–17.

[5] Shaw believes that the greater use of the *cire perdue* technique and the greater quantity of metalwork at the repository site suggest that it is more recent than the other two sites (*Igbo-Ukwu*, I, 257–8). He also argues that the bead evidence 'does not favour a date after the sixteenth century but that it does not preclude a considerably earlier date' (Ibid., 260). In his article, 'Those Igbo-Ukwu Dates', pp. 511, 515, he has defended this interpretation of the bead evidence against his critics, and has allowed (p. 515) that a twelfth- to fifteenth-century date would best fit what is known of African trading patterns. I am grateful to Dr. Shaw for pointing out inaccuracies in my earlier attempts to summarize his findings and conclusions. I hope those errors have been corrected here.

society these would presuppose, Igbo-Ukwu is the most impressive archaeological complex yet exhumed in this part of Africa. This fact, along with the unexpectedly early dating, has made Igbo-Ukwu a matter of some controversy. Yet the evidence as presented by Shaw is not only internally consistent but fits in very well with what is known of the economic life of this area from other sources.

The most impressive finds are those made of metal. The three sites yielded 110 major and 575 minor copper and copper alloy objects with a combined weight of over 74 kg. Because these objects are of very high quality and of a very distinctive design with no clear stylistic affinities with any other West African bronze-making area, Shaw concludes that they probably were cast within the general region of their discovery.[6] Although iron objects can survive a long burial less easily, several were found at Igbo-Ukwu along with pieces of slag, which would suggest the existence of a local smelting and smithing industry.[7] One does not have to look far for a source of such iron. Slag-heaps, indicating a long period of iron-mining, can be found in numerous places to the north-east of Igbo-Ukwu in the hills from Oji River to Enugu. The blacksmiths of nearby Awka received supplies from this area until imported iron stole the market.[8]

Since little additional archaeological work has been done in this area, it is difficult to elaborate on the development of iron-working. The proximity of Awka to the Igbo-Ukwu sites and the general similarity of many of the items would suggest that Awka smiths were the fabricators of the metal objects. However, the time-span involved is very long, and the Awka smiths have not, at least in recent times, exhibited certain of the artistic and technical traits which were typical of the Igbo-Ukwu work. Another archaeological dig in the Awka area has yielded fifteen iron gongs and an iron sword similar to those still made by the Awka smiths, as well as a large number of cast bronze bells. These objects have been radio-carbon dated to A.D. 1495 ± 95.[9]

Textiles of two types were preserved at Igbo-Ukwu. One type was

[6] Shaw, *Igbo-Ukwu*, I, 106–7, 271.

[7] Ibid., 64, 67, 261.

[8] [J. S. Boston], 'Ethnographic Field Work', *Annual Report of the Antiquities Service for the Year 1956–57* (Lagos: Federal Government Printer, 1961), p. 5.

[9] Donald Hartle, 'Bronze Objects from the Ifeka Garden Site, Ezira', *West African Archaeological Newsletter*, No. 4 (Mar. 1966), 26 and 'Radio-carbon Dates', *West African Archaeological Newsletter*, No. 9 (May 1968), 73. Iron knives were made in Benin perhaps as early as the thirteenth century according to Graham Connah, *The Archaeology of Benin* (Oxford: Clarendon Press, 1975), p. 251.

'composed of flat ribbon-like fibres resembling grass or leaf fibres, ... a cross between a textile and a fabric made on the bark-cloth or papyrus principle, whereby different layers of fibres running at right-angles are made to adhere by soaking or beating'.[10] The other textile was woven of a cotton-like fibre, the yarns of which suggest 'that the craftsmen possessed a high degree of technical skill, as does the quality of the woven materials'.[11] A critic of Shaw's has argued that these cloth fragments could not possibly have been preserved for so long a period as the radio-carbon dates would indicate and that for this and other reasons, the dates of Igbo-Ukwu must be moved several centuries forward.[12] But recent excavations have uncovered similar textiles in Benin City which have been dated to the thirteenth century. The Benin cloths were described as 'fragments of possibly raphia and of probably cotton-textiles, the latter of a complex weave'.[13] It is possible that the Igbo-Ukwu textiles were imports from Benin, whose cloths they so closely resemble, yet there is no reason to think that Benin made all of its own cloth or had a monopoly on the trade.

A great wealth of glass and stone beads, numbering 165,000 in all, were unearthed at Igbo-Ukwu, some of which were of local or West African origin.[14] It is tempting to try to identify some of these with the bead or beads called *acori* which were so important an item of early trade in the Gulf of Guinea and which came from several points not far from Igbo-Ukwu. However, any such identification breaks down as no positively identified *acori* beads have survived.[15] Still, it is hard to imagine that Igbo-Ukwu was without some of these

[10] Shaw, *Igbo-Ukwu*, I, 242–3.

[11] Ibid., 242.

[12] Babatunde Lawal, 'Dating Problems at Igbo-Ukwu', *JAH* XIV (1973), 2–3.

[13] Graham Connah, 'Archaeology in Benin', *JAH* XIII (1972), 31. For more detail see M. Greeves, 'Identification of Fibres and Weaves in Cloth Fragments from Feature 21 in Cutting II on the Clerks' Quarters Site' in Connah, *Archaeology of Benin*, pp. 236–7. This description in turn bears an astonishing resemblance to the first recorded description of Benin cloths, by an Englishman in 1588, who also observed two types: one 'made of the barke of palme trees', the other 'made of Cotton wool very curiously woven'. See 'A Voyage to Benin beyond the Country of Guinea made by Master James Welsh (1588)' in Hakluyt's *Voyages*, VI, 457. The Portuguese had purchased cloths (type unknown) on the Forcados River south of Benin at the start of the sixteenth century; see Pereira, *Esmeraldo*, p. 138.

[14] Shaw, *Igbo-Ukwu*, I, 225–39.

[15] J. D. Fage, 'Some Remarks on Beads and Trade in Lower Guinea in the 16th and 17th Centuries', *JAH* III (1962), 343–7. Cf. Raymond Mauny, 'Que faut-il appeler "pierre" d'agris?' *Notes Africains*, IV.42 (1949), 33–6, and 'Akori Beads', *JHSN* I (1958), 210–14.

highly-prized beads which could once command their weight in gold on the Gold Coast.

The 20,000 fragments of pottery recovered from Igbo-Ukwu are hardly less interesting than the beads or metal objects. They fall into two basic types: one of a plain utilitarian design, the other highly ornate. According to Shaw 'The characteristic Igbo-Ukwu ware ... has a marvellous wealth of form and decoration, executed with great verve and boldness. It gives the impression of the same delight in exploiting to the full the possibilities of the *cire perdue* process.'[16]

Taken as a whole, the material remains of Igbo-Ukwu are evidence of a craft industry highly developed in skill and artistry. While both earlier and richer than other evidence, the Igbo-Ukwu finds do not diverge from the general trends of cultural development in southern Nigeria. Yet these craft industries were but the summit of an economy about whose base Igbo-Ukwu gives very little information. Despite this lack of direct evidence, it is clear that such specialists and their customers could only have existed in a society producing an agricultural surplus capable of supporting them. The economy of that era, while lacking many of the West Indian plants introduced in the course of the Atlantic trade, would still have had yams and palm-oil as staple foods. Several varieties of yams are indigenous to West Africa, dating from pre-iron age times, and have been a staple crop in this zone for many centuries.[17] The oil-palm is also thought to be West African in origin, and is found in its greatest profusion in south-eastern Nigeria. The spread of oil-palms follows the clearing of the primeval forest and they are thus closely associated with continuous agricultural activity.[18] While sleeping sickness prevented the maintenance of large animals, goats, sheep, fowls, and a resistant breed of dwarf cattle have long been raised in the area. The cows and sheep are mentioned in the earliest Portuguese account.[19]

Hunting is another activity certain to have been practised in this area for food as well as for other animal products. Shaw has suggested, that because of the prominence of elephant motifs in the bronzes of Igbo-Ukwu and the presence of a tusk in the burial site, elephant hunting must have been an important occupation and that

---

[16]Shaw, *Igbo-Ukwu*, I, 209.
[17]Coursey, *Yams*, pp. 8, 10.
[18]Hartley, *Oil Palm*, pp. 1–9.
[19]Pereira, *Esmeraldo*, p. 146.

ivory was the most likely item of exchange for the expensive metal and bead imports.[20] Hunting was decidedly an important activity by the early fifteenth century, for Pereira mentions trade in both ivory and leopard skins. The ivory trade was especially active in the Benin River area, among the Opuu (Igbo), and in the vicinity of Mount Cameroon, while the eastern delta furnished some ivory as well.[21]

Fishing would also have been important during this early period in the many rivers of the hinterland and especially in the Niger Delta, where it would have been the major source of livelihood along with salt-making. At the time of Pereira's description the salt-water marshes and islands of the delta were generally well-populated and he mentions one very large village of 2,000 souls at the mouth of the Rio Real which specialized in making salt.[22] References to other 'salt towns' in later accounts make it clear that this was not the only such place.[23] According to G. I. Jones, 'Andoni and Bonny legends suggest a salt boiling industry in the Bonny area before the arrival of the European traders ...'[24]

The fishermen of the coast and the farmers of the hinterland did not live in isolation from each other. Rather from an early date there had developed a regional pattern of exchange between the two both in food and in the products of their other special industries. In part this trade was based on a nutritional necessity: large portions of the delta are too swampy and saline to support much agriculture or live-stock, while most of the hinterland lacks natural salt deposits. In the resulting exchanges yams, palm-oil, and livestock from the hinterland were traded in return for salt and dried fish from the delta. But the trade was not a simple subsistence exchange between comple-mentary ecological zones. A number of craft items had entered the trade as well. Pereira records a trade in cotton cloth on the Forcados River, and on the Rio Real, where the inhabitants wore no clothing, the men normally carried double-edged swords, evidently a product

[20]Shaw, *Igbo-Ukwu*, I, 284–5.

[21]Pereira, *Esmeraldo*, pp. 134, 136, 140, 148.

[22]Ibid., 140, 146.

[23]A salt town at the mouth of the Cross River is mentioned by Barbot, 'Descrip-tion', p. 382. Willem Bosman, *A New and Accurate Description of the Coast of Guinea* (London: J. Knapton, 1721), pp. 288–9, says Africans all along the coast made salt by drying brine or boiling sea water.

[24]Jones, *Trading States*, p. 35. Cf. M. D. W. Jeffreys, 'Report on the Andoni Clan', 1930, quoted by C. T. C. Ennals, 'Intelligence Report on the Ndoki Clan', 1933, p. 12, NAI, CSO 26/3/29281.

of the hinterland smithies. In the early sixteenth century the inter-
zonal trade was of such a volume that it was being carried on the
largest canoes known in West Africa, holding up to eighty men
each.[25]

2. LONG-DISTANCE TRADE

Had the development of commerce proceeded no further than the
regional exchanges just outlined, the peoples of south-eastern
Nigeria would have been adequately prepared to adapt themselves
to the challenges of overseas trade. In fact by the arrival of the Portuguese the region was already a veteran of longer-distance trade both
up the Niger and westward to the Gold Coast, and in the case of
the inter-coastal trade it was the Europeans who had to make the
adaptation to existing African patterns. The proof of the existence
of such an inter-coastal trade is admittedly not conclusive, but it
is suggestive enough to have won the support of two specialists in
Gold Coast history.[26] The evidence for this early trade is of two
types: first the behaviour of the Portuguese mariners; second, the
preferences of the Gold Coast Africans.

The Portuguese were in many ways ill-equipped to open up the
intercontinental sea routes in the fifteenth century. While sufficiently
daring and ruthless, and possessing adequate ships, they were
desperately lacking in products to trade with the distant peoples they
reached. The scorn with which their humble gifts to the Sultan of
Madras were met is a well-known illustration of this Portuguese
dilemma. To earn sufficient capital to buy the Asian and African
products they desired, the Portuguese were forced to enter into the
carrying trade, plying ancient routes between traditional customers.
Through a combination of force and technological skill they gained
for themselves a sufficient share of the profits of the China–Japan
and Indian Ocean trades eventually to bring home the cargoes they
sought. In West Africa the situation was much the same. To obtain
the gold and ivory (as well as pepper) they needed for the home market, the Portuguese had to expend a good deal of energy as middlemen, carrying goods along the western coast. Pereira makes this
pattern quite explicit in his description of the Portuguese trade in

---

[25] Pereira, *Esmeraldo*, pp. 138, 140. For additional details of early delta trade see
Alagoa, 'Long-distance Trade', pp. 319–29.

[26] Ivor Wilks, 'A Medieval Trade-Route from the Niger to the Gulf of Guinea',
JAH III (1962), 339 and Fage, 'Beads and Trade', pp. 343–4.

the Niger Delta at the beginning of the sixteenth century. The Portuguese buy slaves, he relates, on the Benin River 'and from here they
are traded to the fortress of Sam Jorze da Mina where they are sold
for gold'. On the Forcados River they buy slaves, cotton cloth,
leopard skins, palm-oil, and beads—'all this has value at the castle
of Sam Jorze da Mina, [where] our prince's factor sells this for gold
to the black merchants'. Pereira does not state that the trade on the
Rio Real was similarly conducted, but there is no reason to think
that the pattern did not apply there as well.[27]

Whether the Portuguese were intruding on an already established
trade is harder to demonstrate. Certainly their actions elsewhere
suggest this as a likely possibility. Indirect confirmation may be seen
in the fact that the same key items that Pereira reported were so
marketable at the Gold Coast in the sixteenth century continued to
find a market there during the next century. At the beginning of the
seventeenth century a Swiss surgeon on a Dutch ship reported that
certain beads from near Mount Cameroon of the same type purchased earlier by the Portuguese for Elmina were worth their weight
in gold at the Gold Coast.[28] At the end of the seventeenth century
John Barbot reported that a type of well-made assagai from the Rio
del Rey, similar to the type Pereira reported at the Rio Real, was
proper for the Gold Coast trade.[29] Of course, proof that a trade
in certain goods from the Bight of Biafra to the Gold Coast existed
later than the Portuguese period does not prove that it had preceded
the Portuguese as well, but it does not seem likely Gold Coast Africans would have accepted new African products from the Portuguese
and later would have resisted so strongly competition from European goods of a similar type. The logic of the situation favours root-
ing the pattern of trade in the pre-Portuguese period.

While the evidence for the inter-coastal route remains tantaliz-
ingly scanty, that for an ancient route from south-eastern Nigeria
to the north can be supported from a variety of sources. The finds
at Igbo-Ukwu indicate that it was in existence several centuries
before the arrival of the Portuguese. According to Shaw the copper
in the Igbo-Ukwu bronzes was necessarily of Saharan or trans-

[27] Pereira, *Esmeraldo*, pp. 134, 138, 146.
[28] Samuel Brun, *Schiffarten* (1624) quoted by Edwin Ardener, 'Documentary and
Linguistic Evidence for the Rise of the Trading Polities between Rio del Rey and
Cameroons, 1500–1650', in *History and Social Anthropology*, ed. I. M. Lewis (London: Tavistock Publications, 1968), pp. 103–4.
[29] Barbot, 'Description', p. 384.

Saharan origin, while a considerable quantity of the beads were of Indian manufacture with some evidently coming from Venice.[30] This trade, though perhaps small in over-all quantity at that date, shows clearly that this area was linked, through numerous inter-mediaries, to the trading states of the Sudan and beyond.

The long-distance trade reaching Igbo-Ukwu from the north prob-ably completed the final stages of its journey on the Niger River. The volume of trade at that time may have been small, but by the time of the first European visitors to the delta, trade on the Niger was of some importance. As three and a half centuries would elapse between the arrival of the Portuguese and the discovery of the exist-ence of the lower Niger, early accounts of the delta region make no effort to describe trading patterns on the Niger. They do, however, mention some details of trade in the interior which, when put in the context of trading patterns on the lower Niger described by nine-teenth-century explorers, begin to make much more sense. It is thus necessary to approach this subject by first describing the patterns of the second quarter of the nineteenth century and then examining the evidence from around 1500.

In the first half of the nineteenth century trade below the Niger-Benue confluence was in the hands of three major groups: the states of the delta, the Igbo of Aboh at the head of the delta, and the Igala kingdom further north. From the delta goods went up the Niger in large canoes passing through a succession of middlemen. The cities of Aboh and the Igala capital of Idah were the hubs of the inland trade routes, storage depots, and the home ports of the major traders, but a major amount of the riverain trade took place at special markets at the fringes of these kingdoms, where traders from a number of lesser riverain states also assembled.

The pattern for the merchants of Aboh, who were called 'the most enterprising and industrious traders on the Niger',[31] is evident from this 1841 description:

They go to the Eggarah market [at Igala Bank near Asaba] directly after the new moon; the journey there and back takes about five days; after resting a day, they go to the station below. At the upper one they receive the produce of the interior brought there by the Eggarah people ...; this produce they exchange at the lower market with the traders from Brass and Bonny.

---

[30] Shaw, *Igbo-Ukwu*, I, 225–39.
[31] Laird and Oldfield, *Narrative*, I, 102.

This is the general method of intercourse with the merchants who never traverse a foreign state to visit a distant market.[32]

The pattern just described was more the ideal than the reality in the first half of the nineteenth century, since traders from Brass regularly came up as far as Aboh rather than stopping at the lower frontier market, Bonny traders could be found as far north as Idah, and Aboh traders ventured as far as the Igbira town of Panda north of the confluence.[33] But this ideal pattern perhaps represented an earlier historical reality.

The market at the northern limits of Aboh's power was held on a sand-bar, or in canoes when the water was high. This Igala Bank market was near the town of Asaba (opposite Onitsha) and was the centre of a complex of riverain and overland trade routes. To Asaba came traders from as far west as Benin; the Igbo on the east bank sent their products through Aboh, Onitsha, and other towns. From the south, delta products and European goods came upstream in the hands of Aboh traders, and the Igala traders of Idah and Adamugu, who gave their name to the market, brought downstream the produce and horses of the Igala hinterland. All met at the Igala Bank market, where the Asaba people also sold a planned agricultural surplus.[34] Even for the mid-nineteenth century it is impossible to make a reliable estimate of the trade of this market, but it appears to have been considerable. In the early 1830s some 300 canoes were seen going up to the market.[35]

Another important market was held 30 miles north of Idah, also on a sand-bar. This 'Ikiri' market met every ten days for up to three days at a time, drawing traders from as far south as Aboh (and even a few from Bonny) and as far north as the kingdom of Nupe on the Niger and the Igbira metropolis of Panda, a weaving and smithing centre of 30,000 inhabitants near the Benue. The volume of the trade here appears to have exceeded that of Igala Bank, drawing as it did upon the commerce of the two great rivers as well as of overland routes. In 1832 the Muslim traders there were observed selling Nupe mats, straw hats, ivory, long robes, Indian corn, rice, flour, small horses, slaves, locally made blue beads and cloth,

[32] Allen and Thomson, *Narrative*, I, 237.
[33] Ibid., 237–8; Laird and Oldfield, *Narrative*, I, 102, 124, 166.
[34] Allen and Thomson, *Narrative*, I, 270. Elizabeth Isichei, 'Historical Change in an Ibo Polity: Asaba to 1885', *JAH* X (1969), 424–5.
[35] Laird and Oldfield, *Narrative*, II, 178.

'country beer', coconuts, sheep, goats, and dogs. All market exchanges were computed in cowries, which impressed early European visitors, as did the size of the market. One witness estimated the market crowd at 6,000 and another estimated the number of slaves sold there annually at 11,000; a third commented that 'there appeared to be twice as much traffic going forward here as in the upper parts of the Rhine'.[36]

While the volume of the Niger trade is impressive, it is the antiquity of that trade which would tell most about the economic history of this region. Since seventeenth-century sources suggest that the Niger Delta trade passed through a series of middlemen as it moved inland,[37] the pattern of trade observed in the nineteenth century may have existed, at least in the broad outlines, at that time. There is other more specific evidence which indicates that this pattern was still older. Pereira reports that one of the items the Portuguese purchased on the Forcados River in the early fifteenth century was a blue bead called *cori*.[38] One of the places where Benin traded for these beads in the seventeenth century was 'Gaboe', which was eight days from Benin City by canoe. Both the name and the distance support the identification of Gaboe with Aboh, the Igbo town at the head of the delta whose traders so impressed the Niger explorers.[39] The most direct water route from Benin to Aboh is via the Forcados River. It is thus very likely that Aboh had a role in the bead trade in 1500 as well.

Additional information about Niger trading patterns at the beginning of the sixteenth century can be gleaned from Pereira's comments on a mysterious hinterland people: 'A hundred leagues [*c.* 400 miles] up the main branch of the Rio Formoso [the Benin River] one encounters a land of Negroes called Opuu, where there

[36] This market was also called *Bocqua* and *Okiri* by the explorers; it was described by Laird and Oldfield, *Narrative*, I, 124–33, 165–7, 409 and II, 254, 305, 318–22. Political turmoil in Igala brought the market to an end in mid-century according to Crowther, *Journal*, pp. 171–3. See J. S. Boston, *The Igala Kingdom* (Ibadan: Oxford Univ. Press, 1968), pp. 110–11.

[37] Dapper, *Description*, pp. 315–16; Barbot, 'Description', p. 381.

[38] Pereira, *Esmeraldo*, p. 138. Basden, *Niger Ibos*, p. 198, locates the source of a similarly named bead, which he says was highly prized by the Igbo, in the area north of Benin.

[39] The reference to Gaboe is from Dapper, *Description*, p. 312. The identification of Gaboe with Aboh was first suggested by Talbot, *Peoples*, III, 922. That Gaboe and Jaboe, another state mentioned by Dapper, are both to be identified with Ijebu, a Yoruba town west of Benin, has been suggested by A. F. C. Ryder, 'Dutch Trade on the Nigerian Coast during the Seventeenth Century', *JHSN* III.2 (1965), 197–8.

is much pepper, ivory, and some slaves'.[40] Mauny has suggested, perhaps because of the distance and the name, that Opuu was Nupe.[41] However, one can hardly trust Pereira's round number, for in the words of Shakespeare's *Henry V*, 'Who hath measured the ground?' Samuel Crowther on the 1854 Niger Expedition also heard of a people whom the Igala called Opù. By questioning knowledgeable informants, Crowther learned that the Opù were the Igbo.[42] More extensive research in central Nigeria by the explorer Baikie showed that the Igbira and Nupe also used the name Opù for the Igbo people.[43]

It is curious, however, that Pereira used what—by the nineteenth century at least—was an Igala term for the Igbo, since he must have obtained his information in the Benin Kingdom which he says he had visited four times. The trading patterns of the nineteenth century may offer a clue to the explanation. The nearest point to Benin City on the Niger is Asaba, less than 100 miles away. If Benin traders had attended the Asaba sand-bar market in 1500 as they did in the nineteenth century, the presence of so many Igala traders could explain the borrowing of the Igala name for the Igbo.

Further evidence of early Niger trading patterns can be derived from Pereira's description of another commercial relation in the delta:

At the mouth of the Rio Real ... is a very large village in which dwell 2,000 souls; much salt is made there, and in this land there are canoes made from a single trunk, which are the largest known in all of Guinea; some of them are large enough to hold 80 men. These come down this river for a hundred leagues and more and convey many yams ..., and many slaves, cows and sheep ..., all of which is sold to the Negroes of the aforesaid village.[44]

Again, little weight should be attached to the distance mentioned. If the nineteenth-century trading patterns were in existence in Pereira's time, one would expect the up-river market to be at or just

[40] Pereira, *Esmeraldo*, p. 136.
[41] Mauny in ibid. note 284, p. 191. P. E. H. Hair, 'Ethnolinguistic Continuity of the Guinea Coast', *JAH* VIII (1967), 262, rejects Mauny's suggestion, arguing that the Opuu must have been the Ijo, '*opu*- forming part of many Ijaw toponyms, e.g. Opobo....'
[42] Crowther, *Journal*, 167, 174. Ryder, *Benin*, p. 36, also suggests that the Opuu be identified with the Igbo, but he does not explain how he reached that conclusion.
[43] William B. Baikie, 'Synonyms of the Principal Countries and Towns of Sudan', enclosure in Baikie to Russell, 17 Jan. 1862, *Parl. Papers* 1863 lxxi (3160), 72–3. See his earlier identification of Opuu as an Igala word for Aboh in *Narrative*, p. 437.
[44] Pereira, *Esmeraldo*, p. 146.

below Aboh. In fact the trade Pereira records was duplicated almost exactly at Aboh in the mid-nineteenth century. The Lander brothers in 1830 noticed that salt was made near Brass: 'It is an item of trade, and appears to be taken in large quantities to the Eboe [Aboh] market where it is exchanged for yams.'[45] A couple of years later it was noted that at Aboh 'Yams, plantain, bananas, Indian corn, and peppers are grown in abundance ... The Eboe people also rear bullocks of a small breed, goats, and fowls, which are bartered in exchange for powder and cottons, with the natives of Bonny, Brass, and, I believe, [New] Calabar.'[46] Thus one finds confirmation in the middle of the nineteenth century of trade in the same items that Pereira noted at the beginning of the sixteenth: food crops (especially yams) and livestock in exchange for salt. Of course, new items had entered the trade during these 350 years (especially slaves, trade in whom had waxed and waned in the meantime), but the kind of trade which had been basic in 1500 was still basic in the 1830s.

Three hypotheses have been advanced in this chapter about trade in the lower Niger about 1500: (1) that Gaboe is to be identified with Aboh as a source of beads in Benin, (2) that the Pereira's Opuu were Igbo, and (3) that Aboh or a market near it was the market whose traders came to trade for salt at the mouth of the Rio Real. If these hypotheses are accepted, then it seems likely that many of the general patterns of trade between the lower Niger and the coast noted in the early nineteenth century can be traced back several centuries. There are no comparable records to document earlier patterns of trade from the lower Niger to the north, but here too antiquity and durability could be expected. While it is impossible to push the evidence to a point much earlier than 1500, it is not unlikely that some such trading patterns had delivered the copper and the beads to ancient Igbo-Ukwu. Thus it is apparent that before the arrival of the first European traders major segments of south-eastern Nigeria had already attained a significant level of economic and commercial development. Important craft industries specialized in the production of metal products, cloth, beads, and pottery, often exhibiting very great skill of design and execution. The economy in many places had developed beyond subsistence production to production for exchange, and the products of hinterland farmers, fishermen, and hunters, as well as craftsmen, supported a vigorous commercial life.

[45] Lander and Lander, *Niger Journal*, p. 286.
[46] Laird and Oldfield, *Narrative*, I, 379–80.

While most communities were no doubt still relatively untouched by these developments, others had already begun to trade over long distances. The arrival of the Portuguese thus necessitated no abrupt changes in the trading life of this region; they were instead accommodated within well-established patterns of commercial organization.

CHAPTER II

Peoples and Polities of the Sixteenth and Seventeenth Centuries

THE present inhabitants of south-eastern Nigeria must have occupied this region for many centuries, probably for several millennia, for their traditions retain no memory of a previous homeland or of any prior residents of the region.[1] Instead, the languages of the Ijo, Igbo, and Ibibio appear to have developed and separated into their component dialects during a very long period of residence in their present locale.[2] Linguistics aside, no specific information has survived about their internal organization or the degree of cultural differentiation of one group from another during the period before 1500, but the earliest European guides to this coast record the existence of all three peoples and several of their subdivisions. The Ijo and Igbo are mentioned at the beginning of the sixteenth century, while several Ijo groups, two Ibibio groups, and the Igbo are named in an account from a century later.[3]

[1] Forde and Jones, *Ibo and Ibibio*, pp. 11, 68; E. J. Alagoa, 'Oral Tradition among the Ijo of the Niger Delta', *JAH* VII (1966), 413.

   The temptation to invent prestigious ancestral homelands has given rise to some elaborate embellishments of the remote past. The similarities between some of their customs and those of the Biblical Hebrews have led many Ibibio and Igbo Christians to posit a Palestinian or an Egyptian homeland, while similarities of personal names have led some Efik to propose an Akan ancestry. See A. Kalada Hart, *Report on the Enquiry into the Dispute over the Obongship of Calabar* (Enugu: Government Printer, 1964), pp. 24–38 (hereafter cited as the *Hart Report*). The Revd. A. Okokon of Ikot Offiong has spent half a century writing a lengthy history of the Ibibio on the premise that they are the direct descendants of Abraham and the Hebrews and kindly allowed me to examine his manuscript. The Hebrew origins of the Igbo were first proposed by James Africanus Horton over a century ago in his *West African Countries and Peoples* (Edinburgh: At the Univ. Press, 1969), pp. 164–71, and his opinion has been seconded privately and in print since then by an array of scholars too numerous to list here. The fashion among Nigerian peoples of claiming such prestigious origins led a Chief of the Anang to propose that his branch of the Ibibio must have been the only people on hand to serve as a welcoming committee.

[2] Cf. Greenberg, *Languages of Africa*, p. 8.

[3] Pereira, *Esmeraldo*, pp. 136, 140, where the 'Ijo' and the 'Opuu' (Igbo) are named. Sandoval, *De Instauranda*, pp. 17, 94, where the 'Done': (Andoni Ibibio) and 'Moco' (Anang Ibibio) are named. For the identification of Sandoval's peoples see below, Chapter III, §1.

This stable continuity for the region as a whole should not obscure the existence of smaller population movements at the local level, movements which were very important in the formation of local ethnic identities and communities. A variety of circumstances—population pressure, internal disputes, economic changes—appear to have made it common for bands of settlers to leave their parent communities. Farmers sought more abundant or more fertile farmland. Fishermen migrated along the broken coastline and up the major rivers in search of more abundant catches. As trade expanded, especially after European ships began regular visits to this coast, other settlers were drawn to the more advantageous trading positions. It was characteristic of the region that such migrations occurred gradually, in small groups, and without undue conflict.

These shifts of population are traceable only through oral traditions which, although they tend to compress and standardize the actual historical complexities, remain worth examining for several reasons. First, such legends are the only historical sources for most of the hinterland in this early period. Second, they record the origins and development of the major trading communities and thus provide clues to their structure and success. Finally, these traditions provide an insight into the workings of an unusual system which dealt with growing population and economic development by a proliferation of small autonomous communities rather than the aggregation of the population into a smaller number of larger units.

To examine every tradition of migration would be neither possible nor profitable. The most important are those which describe the emergence of the leading trading communities along the Niger and Cross rivers and in the Niger Delta. It is useful, however, to begin with the settlement of a zone of contact between the Igbo and Ibibio since it illustrates a number of general principles about such movements. The meeting of the Igbo and Ibibio took place along a large arc sweeping from the Cross River along the Imo River to the eastern Niger Delta. It is impossible to assign certain dates to the events described in these traditions, but they probably went through their main phases in the sixteenth and seventeenth centuries with additional periods of consolidation in the eighteenth and nineteenth centuries.

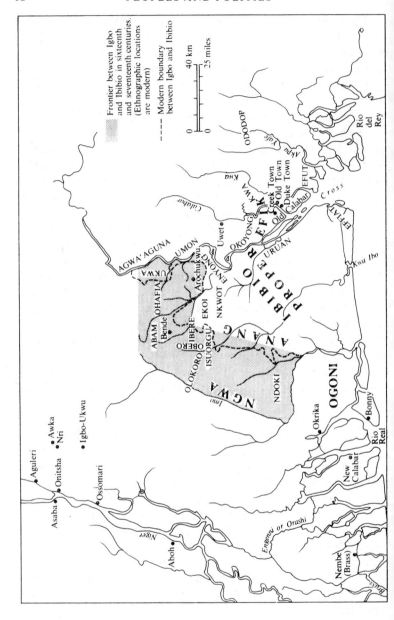

1. PATTERNS OF SETTLEMENT: THE NGWA AND THEIR NEIGHBOURS

One of the largest areas of settlement in this zone involved the Ngwa Igbo, whose traditions were collected forty years ago by J. G. C. Allen. In his account the evolution of the Ngwa went through three phases. During the first phase, the territory east of the Imo River was inhabited, though sparsely, by the Ibeme, a people who were predominantly Ibibio in language and culture with some admixture if Igbo elements. While the Ibeme were spread thinly across this large forested area, the Igbo west of the Imo were beginning to experience the pressures of an expanding population and small groups began to cross the river. Tradition says that the first group of settlers was led by Ngwa Uku and that he and his followers were given land for their use by the hospitable Ibeme.

The arrival of Ngwa Uku's group began the second phase, during which there was a great expansion of the Ngwa, as all of the new settlers came to call themselves. Allen writes, 'This pioneer band of settlers proved to be the thin edge of the wedge, and very soon the Ibeme were fleeing before the advancing tide of Ngwas.'[4] Against this tide the small Ibeme communities eventually united and brought an end to the conquest tactics of the Ngwa. But the Ibeme were either unable or unwilling to halt the influx of Ngwa settlers; the peace settlement provided only that the Ngwa should recognize the Ibeme (whom the Ngwa call Mboko) as the rightful first owners of the land and accord them the honours and ritual prerogatives due to senior lineage members.

During the next phase Ngwa settlement continued at a rapid pace, but on a more peaceful basis. Where the Ibeme (Mboko) were strongest the agreement to recognize their seniority was kept, and to this day the names and customs of many Ngwa village groups include a respectful reference to the Ibibio forefathers. Where the Ibeme were fewer, new villages were formed. Over-all, the culture and language of the area became predominantly Igbo, although with a strong persistence of Ibibio social structures.[5]

The Ngwa case may be taken as an example of the general manner

---

[4] J. G. C. Allen, 'Supplemental Intelligence Report No. 3 on the Ngwa Clan, Aba Division', 1934, p. 6, NAE, CSE 1/85/3710.

[5] J. G. C. Allen, 'Supplementary Intelligence Report No. 1 on the Ngwa Clan, Aba Division', 1933, NAE, CSE 1/85/3708 and Allen, 'Intelligence Report No. 3, Ngwa', pp. 6–18. See also Forde and Jones, *Ibo and Ibibio*, pp. 42–4.

of population shift in this region. Settlers came in small autonomous bands under a leader. Land was not so scarce that such settlers were seen as enemies; provided they were willing to respect local traditions, they were made welcome and given land. It is important to notice that it was local tradition which was paramount in this region of small communities; the fact that the Ngwa belonged to a different ethnolinguistic group did not appear to trouble the Ibeme so long as the Ngwa settlers were willing to respect their prior rights. Some conflict was inevitable as the newcomers were joined by ever increasing numbers from across the river, but it ended in a *modus vivendi* that governed relations for a long period. In the end the cultural identity of the area changed, but it did so through the gradual multiplication of autonomous communities which reflected the political traditions of the newcomers and the original inhabitants.

Further north the territory now inhabited by the Igbo-speaking Ibere, Obero, Olokoro, Isuorgu, and Bende appears to have been settled at about the same time and under circumstances similar to those in the Ngwa area. Although Igbo language and culture predominates in the area, some groups preserve only the legends of origin of the original Ibibio inhabitants and several senior villages retain their original Ibibio names.[6]

2. CROSS RIVER PEOPLES: THE ARO AND EFIK

To the north-east of the Ngwa there was another meeting of the Ibibio and Igbo between the Enyong Creek and the Cross River in an area which became the home of the famous Aro traders of Arochukwu and which also figures in the traditions of the important Efik traders of Old Calabar. Both the Aro and the Efik have relatively coherent traditions of their origins, although in both cases some manipulation of them to serve twentieth-century political ends has occurred. These manipulations, the complexities of the events themselves, and efforts by some writers to make the traditions fit certain theories of African migrations have produced considerable variations in the interpretation and dating of these events.

The traditions concerned with the foundations of Arochukwu were first recorded during the colonial era as a result of a series of court cases and have subsequently been collected by various

---

[6] Forde and Jones, *Ibo and Ibibio*, pp. 42–4; L. T. Chubb, 'Intelligence Report on the Ibere Clan, Bende Division', 1933, pp. 3–5, NAI, CSO 26/3/28869.

researchers.[7] Although variations exist, the basic story told by the Aro, as well as by their Igbo neighbours, relates that the land they now occupy was first inhabited by Ibibio. Igbo settlers in the area (by some accounts slaves) were unable to take effective control from the Ibibio until they formed an alliance with a group from east of the Cross River called the Akpa. The identity of the Akpa is not entirely clear, but it would appear that they were part of a general population movement into this area from east of the river and are possibly to be identified with an offshoot of the Agwa'aguna.[8] The resulting community of Arochukwu was composed of villages of Igbo, Akpa, and Ibibio origin. Associated with the rise of Arochukwu was the Long Juju, the oracular shrine of the High God Chukwu, also known as Ibritam and Ibiniukpabi, which may have been acquired at this time from the Ibibio.[9]

Assuming that these traditions preserve a memory of the actual events involved in the founding of Arochukwu, one has a situation parallel to the Ngwa case examined earlier, but more complex and dramatic in its outline. The events described need not have involved particularly large numbers of people, and appear from the traditions themselves to have taken place over several generations. Because of the nature of the sources, determining when these events occurred

[7] A very helpful introduction to the circumstances under which the earliest compilations of Aro traditions were made and to the early historiography on this subject is A. E. Afigbo, 'The Aro of Southern Nigeria: a Socio-Historical Analysis of Legends of Their Origin', *African Notes*, VI (1971), 31–46 and VII (1972), 91–106. Afigbo's analysis and conclusions are stimulating but are unlikely to end the debate on this subject. Other accounts based on archival and oral research are: Talbot, *Peoples*, I, 182; T. M. Shankland, 'Intelligence Report on the Aro Clan', 1933, pp. 8–13, NAI, CSO 26/3/29017; G. I. Jones, 'Who are the Aro?' *Nigerian Field*, II (1939), 100–103; Forde and Jones, *Ibo and Ibibio*, pp. 51–6; E. Ilugu, 'Inside Arochukwu', *Nigeria*, no. 53 (1957), 100–18; F. Ifeoma Ekejiuba, 'The Aro Trade System in the Nineteenth Century', *Ikenga*, I (1972), 13–14.

[8] Forde and Jones, *Ibo and Ibibio*, p. 56. The Akpa raiders also occur in the traditions of neighbours of the Aro along the Enyong Creek as does the movement of peoples from east of the Cross River; see J. V. Dewhurst, 'Intelligence Report on the Ututu Clan, Arochukwu District', 1932, pp. 5–6, NAI, CSO 26/3/28779; and Forde and Jones, *Ibo and Ibibio*, pp. 53–4, 85. This circumstance makes more difficult Afigbo's argument ('The Aro', pp. 45–6) that the presence of the Akpa in Aro traditions of origin is not due to a real historical event, but results from intimate co-operation between the Aro and Akpa over a long time after the foundation of Arochukwu. The weakening of his Akpa explanation in turn weakens his argument that Arochukwu did not result from a merging of ethnically heterogeneous peoples but from 'solid Ibo stock'.

[9] Oral accounts claiming variously that the shrine was originated by the Aro or that it had been taken over from the Ibibio are quoted by Afigbo, 'The Aro', pp. 31–46.

is difficult. Estimates have ranged from the early fourteenth century to as late as the mid-eighteenth century, the former date being a guess while the latter is based on the statement in some accounts that the Akpa used fire-arms during the conquest.[10] Dating the events from the presence of fire-arms, while tempting, is risky. In the first place fire-arms were not mentioned in the earliest accounts collected and could easily be a later intrusion. Secondly, given the absence of any systematic documentation of the trade along this coast, it is impossible to be sure when fire-arms were first imported in any quantities. Instead, one probably can do no better than to infer from the time needed for the Aro to have put together their elaborate trading network and the numerous colonies that served it (see Chapter V), that Arochukwu must have been founded at least as early as the seventeenth century.[11]

The origin of the Efik towns of Old Calabar is known only from oral sources. The traditional accounts were first written down by Scottish missionaries in the mid-nineteenth century and have been recorded in more detail in the twentieth century by colonial and Nigerian officials. The missionary versions say only that the Efik, having settled for a time with the Ibibio Proper, lost out in a civil dispute with their hosts and emigrated to the other side of the river,

[10] Talbot, *Peoples*, I, 182, gives the earlier date. The later date, based on the 'crucial' evidence of the guns and on surviving accounts of trade on this coast, is in Latham, *Old Calabar*, p. 27. Afigbo, 'The Aro', p. 100, reports no mention of the fire-arms in oral accounts until 1927. Other scholars, citing more general trading patterns to Africa have used fire-arms to arrive at dates for the founding of Arochukwu in the seventeenth century (Ekejiuba, 'Aro Trade System', p. 13) and the sixteenth century (Forde and Jones, *Ibo and Ibibio*, p. 85).

[11] On the basis of his own studies, Simon Ottenberg concludes 'that the Aro may have existed as controllers of an organized oracular and trading system from 1700' in 'Centralized and Non-centralized Politics: Was there an Ibo State?' paper presented to the U.C.L.A. African Studies Center Symposium on States and Kingdoms in West Africa in the Nineteenth Century, 1969, p. 16. Ekejiuba, 'Aro Trade System', p. 13, supports a mid-seventeenth-century date based in part on the genealogies of the oldest Aro families. The earliest recorded mention of the Aro would appear to be from an Igbo enslaved near the middle of the eighteenth century who ended up in Pennsylvania. In giving an account of his region of Africa to a missionary there the man named neighbouring peoples including the 'Bibi' (Ibibio), who he said were far from his home, and the 'Alo', who were not far away. For reasons not explained, the missionary identified 'Alo' with Egypt, but it is more likely that the Aro were what was meant. The r/l sound shift is common in this area. For the account see Oldendorps, *Geschichte der Mission*, p. 286. If this can be taken as evidence that the Aro were well known by the mid-eighteenth century then dating the foundation or at least the expansion of Arochukwu to the seventeenth century or earlier seems not unreasonable.

founding Mbiabo and Old Calabar. The twentieth-century versions are more elaborate, often beginning with fanciful migrations from Palestine, North Africa, or ancient Ghana. After these modern embellishments, they tell of a period of residence among the Ibibio that had at least two phases: earlier settlements in the shifting frontier zone along the Enyong Creek (including connections with the village of Ibom now in Arochukwu), and then a movement to the Uruan clan of the Ibibio Proper near the Cross River for a lengthy residence before their dispersal. One must be extremely careful in drawing historical events out of these traditions since they have a stong tendency to compress and synthesize remote periods, but it does seem that the first phase of Efik origins may have been associated with the same area and complex of events that gave rise to Arochukwu.[12]

The first Efik settlement on the Calabar River was at Ikot Itunko, called Creek Town by the English traders. Before long, however, disputes among the residents of Creek Town had led to one party moving across the Calabar River to found Old Town on land they had procured from the Kwa. Because of its more accessible location Old Town was able to take the lion's share of the slave trade which led to 'a continual state of warfare between the two towns, until a number of families of Creek Town procured land from the Qua people further down the river than Old Town; and ... built Duke Town ...'[13]

As in the case of Arochukwu, widely varying dates have been proposed for the foundation of the Efik towns of Old Calabar. Nineteenth-century missionaries thought the Efik had moved to Old Calabar only during the previous century,[14] but European sources

[12] The missionary accounts are to be found in Waddell, *Twenty-Nine Years*, pp. 309–10 and Goldie, *Dictionary*, p. 356. Goldie's is the purer version, Waddell's being mixed with his speculations about the causes and dates of the key events. Colonial Intelligence Reports add details which are summarized and discussed in Forde and Jones, *Ibo and Ibibio*, pp. 89–90. The most detailed published versions are in the *Hart Report*, pp. 24–38. For further discussion see Kannan K. Nair, *The Origins and Development of Efik Settlements in Southeastern Nigeria* (Ohio Univ.: Center for International Studies, 1975); Latham, *Old Calabar*, pp. 3, 8–13; and A. E. Afigbo's stimulating but tendentious 'Efik Origins and Migrations Reconsidered', *Nigeria*, no. 87 (1965), 267–80, with rejoinders by M. D. W. Jeffreys, 'Efik Origins', *Nigeria*, no. 91 (1966), 297–9, and by Edet A. Udo, 'The Ibo Origin of Efik by A. E. Afigbo: A Review', *Calabar Historical Journal*, I.1 (1976), 154–72. All of the *Hart Report* informants name Ibom as an early stage in the migrations. The first earliest account to include Ibom was recorded from the 'head chief' of Mbiabo on 22 June 1932 by H. J. M. Harding, 'Mbiabo Clan Intelligence Report,' 1932, pp. 5–7, NAI, CSO 26/3/28862.

[13] Goldie, *Dictionary*, p. 356.

[14] Waddell, *Twenty-nine Years*, p. 309; Goldie, *Dictionary*, p. 356.

first mention trading there in the second half of the seventeenth century.[15] Indeed, as G. I. Jones has perceptively pointed out, the Efik had already settled all three of the towns of Old Calabar (Creek Town, Old Town, Duke Town) by 1698, for a list of the principal Cross River traders composed in that year named the heads of each of these towns.[16] Allowing for these towns to have been founded in the sequence given in the traditions, the foundation of the original settlement at Creek Town must have taken place no later than the first half of the seventeenth century, a date which is also supported by genealogical calculations.[17] As their stay in Uruan had lasted for several generations, the Efik's initial movements must have occurred in the mid-sixteenth century or earlier. Finally, if the conclusion reached by one scholar that the departure of the Efik from the Enyong area was occasioned by the events associated with the Akpa capture of the Long Juju is true,[18] then the foundation of Arochukwu may also be dated to this period.

Whether or not the early histories of Arochukwu and Old Calabar were linked to each other, there is a strong possibility that their early histories were connected with the beginnings of European trade. In order to demonstrate this connection it is necessary to examine the larger ethnographic and commercial history of this area at the time of the earliest European contacts.

In the mountainous country east of the Cross River and among the creeks, swamps, and islands along the coast to the south-east lived ethnic groups very much smaller in size and fewer in number than the peoples west of the river. In the mountains were several dispersed communities whom the Efik have given the name Ekoi. Along the middle section of the river lived a people called the Akunakuna or, more properly, the Agwa'aguna, and another called Umon,

[15] Nair, *Politics and Society*, p. 4. Nair is relying on Count C. N. de Cardi's 'Short Description of the Natives of the Niger Coast Protectorate', in Mary Kingsley, *West African Studies* (London: Macmillan, 1899), p. 566, which is based on the fictionalized account of Old Calabar in 1668 by John Watts, *A true Relation of the inhuman and unparallel'd Actions, and barbarous Murders of Negroes or Moors committed on three Englishmen in Old Calabar in Guinny* (London: Thomas Passinger, 1672). De Cardi correctly reasons that the people described in the account cannot have been the Efik, but fails to perceive that they were figments of Watts's imagination.

[16] G. I. Jones, 'Introduction to the Second Edition' of Waddell, *Twenty-Nine Years* (London: Frank Cass, 1970), pp. xviii–xix, who is inferring from Barbot, 'Description', p. 465.

[17] Latham, *Old Calabar*, pp. 11–12.

[18] M. D. W. Jeffreys, 'Notes on the Ibibio', 1930, cited by Forde and Jones, *Ibo and Ibibio*, p. 90.

both of whom were important in the early trade and politics of this region. Preceding the Efik at Old Calabar were the Kwa, a small group who were partially absorbed by the newcomers and after whom the Kwa (or Great Kwa) and Little Kwa rivers are named. Small communities of Bantu-speaking peoples from the east were also migrating into the area north, east, and south-east of Old Calabar. One of these, the Efut, were living south-east of the Kwa at the time the Efik arrived. Another Bantu-speaking group, the Ododop, may also have been in the vicinity of Old Calabar at the time the Efik settled there; by the nineteenth century they had split into two groups, the Ododop branch living east of the Kwa River and a branch called Okoyong living above Old Calabar on the Calabar River.[19]

Early European sources tell less about the coast from the Cross River to Mount Cameroon than one would like, but enough, as was suggested in the previous chapter, to imply that there was a fifteenth-century trade from this area to the Gold Coast. Pereira's description of the coast and its trade about 1500 jumps abruptly from the Andoni, Imo, and two unnamed smaller rivers (none of which had any trade at that time) to the Island of Fernando Po and then to the coast near Mount Cameroon without even a mention of the Cross River or of the broken coast between it and the mountain. Navigational difficulties, which apparently were not solved until the seventeenth century, kept sailing ships from visiting much of the coast of the Bight of Biafra, except for those parts which could be reached by oarred vessels from Fernando Po, evidently the reason for the course of Pereira's narrative.[20] The Cross River (*Rio da Cruz*) was sighted and named about this time for it appears on Portuguese maps from 1502, but it evidently was not explored until later for an otherwise reliable Dutch description from the mid-seventeenth century makes the erroneous statement that the mouth of the river was blocked by a great reef.[21] The broken coast to the west of the

[19] Talbot, *In the Shadow*, p. 163; Forde and Jones, *Ibo and Ibibio*, p. 90; L. Sealy-King, 'Intelligence Report on the Okoyong Clan of the Calabar Division', 1932, pp. 7–8, NAI, CSO 26/3/27674.

[20] Ardener, 'Documentary and Linguistic', pp. 105–6.

[21] A. Teixeira da Mota, *Topónimos de Origem Portuguesa na Costa Ocidental de Africa* (Bissau: Centro de Estudos da Guiné Portuguesa, 1950), p. 302. The Cross River does not appear on Dutch maps until much later. It is absent from the 1606 map of Guinea by Jodocus Hondius, but was added to the 1631 edition by Heinricus Hondius. See Egon Klemp, ed., *Africa on Maps* (Leipzig: Edition Leipzig, 1968), maps 15, 16, 17, 56. The Cross River reef is mentioned in an anonymous

Cross appears on maps of the early sixteenth century as the *Golpho* (later *Rio*) *del Rey*.[22]

The earliest European trade along this part of the coast took place at the shores of Mount Cameroon, where Pereira recorded a trade in beads, large tusks of ivory, and slaves,[23] and in the Rio del Rey. In the early sixteenth century there was also a trade in *acori* beads from this region[24] and by Dapper's day the centre of this trade was firmly positioned on the Rio del Rey: 'The main trade of this river is in slaves, which are exchanged for little bars of copper ... The Blacks here sell *acori*, assagais, knives and ivory, three [tusks] of which ordinarily equal a hundredweight. In some years 400 hundred-weights of elephant teeth and 500 slaves have been carried away.'[25] On the basis of a mid-seventeenth-century word list for this area, it has been established that the traders at the Rio del Rey spoke Ibi-bio and thus were probably the ancestors of the fishermen who still live in that area.[26]

None of the sources indicate where the goods purchased from the Africans at the Rio del Rey had come from, but it is profitable in light of the later movement of the trade to the Cross River to suggest the most likely possibilities. It is not hard to imagine the proven-ance of the tusks since even in the nineteenth century the country north and north-east of the Rio del Rey had a large elephant popu-lation.[27] This ivory had long been traded by the Ekoi and Ododop inhabitants there.

The assagais and knives suggest that there was another trade route to the north-west from the Rio del Rey which could have involved

---

description on the coast of Africa appended to an edition of Leo Africanus published in Rotterdam in 1665 by Arnout Leers, whose significance is explained by Ardener, 'Documentary and Linguistic', pp. 100–1, 106. The text refers to the Cross as the 'Olde Calborch' river, which may be the first reference to Old Calabar.

[22] Mota, *Topónimos*, p. 305.

[23] Pereira, *Esmeraldo*, pp. 146, 148.

[24] Samuel Brun's *Schiffarten* quoted by Ardener, 'Documentary and Linguistic', p. 103.

[25] Dapper, *Description*, p. 316. This information is probably from the first half of the seventeenty century.

[26] Leers's source, quoted by Ardener, 'Documentary and Linguistic', pp. 101–3. Ardener gives the original word list with a translation and notes on pages 119–22. By Dapper's time the small trade of these Ibibio had been disrupted by Bantu-speak-ing traders to the east. See Ardener, pp. 102–7, for the complexities.

[27] H. H. Johnston to Earl of Iddesleigh, 17 June 1886, enclosure No. 13: 'Sketch Map of the Cameroons Region', F.O. 403/73. H. H. Johnston, 'Map of the Rio del Rey', F.O. 84/1882/92.

the Efut, Kwa, Okoyong, and Agwa'aguna. John Barbot says that
the assagais and knives of the Rio del Rey were made 'to perfection'
and were 'proper for the trade of the Gold Coast'; if the knife he
illustrates came from this region, the work was very excellent indeed.[28] Where the knives came from is puzzling since there is no
tradition of metal working in the immediate vicinity of the Rio del
Rey and even in the nineteenth century Old Calabar relied on Igbo
blacksmiths for work of high quality.[29] The closest source of the
implements would have been the Abiriba smiths, who at present live
north of Arochukwu and are Igbo-speaking, but whose traditions
describe a migration from the Agwa'aguna peoples.[30] Before European iron captured the market the Abiriba smiths had access to iron
deposits in the Kwa Mountains east of the Cross River and in the
Okigwi-Arochukwu ridge to the west.[31]

If the metal implements did come from the Abiriba, there is an
indication that the mysterious *acori* beads may have passed along
the same route. In 1850 the Revd. Hope Waddell visited the town
of Uwet north of Old Calabar which had once been on an important
trade route from Old Calabar to Arochukwu and could have been
on an earlier route to the Rio del Rey. He found the Uwet Chief
wearing ancient blue beads which accord perfectly with early descriptions of *acori*:

... his only ornaments [were] a peculiar blue bead in strings round his neck,
wrists and ankles. This kind of bead, somewhat long and coarse looking, is
not now an article of trade, nor can be easily if at all made exactly the right
old kind now. They are rare and very precious and obtained chiefly from the
leeward coast of Guinea where it is said they are found in the ground. The
possession of them indicates rank and wealth almost beyond anything else.
The origin of them is not well ascertained. Their value consists not so much
in their beauty as in their rarity.[32]

This reconstruction of the inland sources of the goods traded at
the Rio del Rey is of course highly speculative, but a number of circumstances support the hypothesis that the goods, which included
ivory, beads, fine metalwork, and a relatively large number of slaves,

[28] Barbot, 'Description', p. 384 and plate 26.
[29] Waddell, *Twenty-Nine Years*, p. 326.
[30] Forde and Jones, *Ibo and Ibibio*, pp. 54–5.
[31] Waddell, *Twenty-Nine Years*, p. 326. S. N. Nwabara, 'Ibo Land: a Study in
British Penetration and the Problem of Administration, 1860–1930', Ph.D. dissertation, Northwestern University, 1965, p. 48n.
[32] Waddell, 'Journal', VIII, f. 43.

came from the peoples to the north and north-west. The emergence of the Efik towns and the shift of the trade to the Cross River, as well as the development of the trading system of Arochukwu must be considered in the context of the Rio del Rey trade and its inland connections. Although Aro traditions do not mention trade as a reason for taking control of Arochukwu, that location would have provided important commercial advantages by intercepting the route that ran from the Abiriba smiths via the Agwa'aguna to the Rio del Rey. Since it is clear that trade did develop between the Aro and both of these groups such a rationale may have been a factor in some phase of the events. Similarly, the Efik migrations to Old Calabar may have been based on commercial considerations. It is quite likely that Efik fishermen had already explored the Cross River, its tributaries, and the waterways of the Rio del Rey in search of fish before their first settlement at Old Calabar, and thus were aware of the possibilities of the overseas trade. Oral traditions do not state a reason for the choice of Creek Town as a refuge from Uruan, but do specifically relate Old Town's rise to the slave trade, and also tie Duke Town's foundation to commercial considerations. In any event, whether by initial design or not, the Efik were successful in diverting the European traders from the Rio del Rey to Old Calabar by the late seventeenth century.

In suggesting such a link between overseas commerce and the Aro and Efik migrations one must be careful of reducing complex events to simple economic reflexes. Even omitting consideration of social and political considerations, the economy of this area was too complex and the volume of foreign trade too small to govern African actions in so deterministic a fashion. As was shown earlier, the trade along the Bight of Biafra and in its hinterland antedated the arrival of European traders and the ports the Europeans frequented were those which had already achieved some commercial importance. It was thus the increased flow of goods through these ports, not its commencement, that encouraged the development of new trading settlements. It is no more reasonable to view the settlement of the Efik and the Aro as simple responses to European initiatives than to view the arrival of the Dutch and English traders in the same area at about the same time as European responses to African initiatives. Both sides were interacting in a much broader and more complex set of economic and historical circumstances.

3. COMMUNITIES OF THE NIGER VALLEY AND DELTA

At the same time as these events were taking place in the eastern part of this region, a similar nexus of culture, population, and commerce was developing to the west on the lower Niger and to the south in the Niger Delta. Here the population movements and cultural exchanges were well underway before 1500 but as was the case along the Cross River the growth of overseas trade produced great changes in history of these areas. The upper edge of the delta had been a zone of contact between the delta Ijo and the hinterland Igbo and others for several centuries. The details of these contacts are necessarily vague, but the communities which developed along this frontier often grew into bilingual and bicultural societies or into new ethnolinguistic communities divergent from both.[33]

The traditions of the two leading trading states of the eastern delta, Elem Kalabari (New Calabar) and Ibani (Bonny), tell of gradual migrations out of their original homes in the central delta, east to the northern margin of the eastern delta where they were in contact with Igbo people, and then south to their present homes. The migrants who settled Elem Kalabari mixed with the autochthonous residents (apparently also of Ijo stock) and incorporated other later immigrants, some said to be from Efik and others from Igbo, as is evidenced by Igbo names in the genealogies of important families in the seventeenth century. The founders of Bonny migrated as far east as the Ndoki on the Imo River before turning south; they retained strong ties through trade and intermarriage with the Ndoki afterwards. Possibly as a result of these early contacts and surely in the course of later slave trading both Ijo and Igbo came to be spoken in Bonny, a fact which led to many conflicting reports about its ethnic identity. Both communities had a king named Kamalu, a name common to the Arochukwu area, and suggestive of ties in that direction as well.[34] There is no accurate way to date the foundation of either settlement, but both are thought to have been in place

[33] Several of the former are explained below. The linguistic status of three of the latter, the Ekpeye, Ogba, and Ikwerre, is discussed by David J. Clark, 'Three "Kwa" Languages of Eastern Nigeria', *Journal of West African Languages*, VIII (1971), pp. 27–36. It is notable that all three chose to be a part of the Rivers State rather than the East Central State in 1971 when Nigeria's political subdivisions were redesigned.

[34] Alagoa, *History*, pp. 89–160; Jones, *Trading States*, pp. 24–32, 105, 133–4; J. G. Mackenzie, 'Intelligence Report on the Emohua Clan, Ahoada Division', 1933, p. 3, NAI, CSO 26/3/28871; Ennals, 'Intelligence Report, Ndoki', pp. 8–11.

by about 1500. If this is so, the large salt-making village the early Portuguese found at the mouth of the Rio Real may well have been Bonny.[35]

The founders of Okrika and Ndoki (or a portion of them) can also be traced to the same general and no doubt prolonged dispersal as the Ibani and Elem Kalabari from the central delta, but did not follow them south. The Okrika at the northern edge of the eastern delta remained predominantly Ijo in culture but later additions of Igbo settlers (as traders and as a buffer against the neighbouring Ogoni) and the growth of trade from Bonny to the hinterland led to bilingualism and a division of the town into two traditional factions, the 'fisherfolk' and the 'traders'. The Ndoki, further inland on the Imo River, gradually lost the use of the Ijo language and became predominantly Igbo-speaking with a considerable admixture of Ibibio as well. Both the Okrika and the Ndoki were important intermediaries between the coastal communities and the more densely populated areas further inland.[36]

Along the Niger River above the delta was another area of interaction among the Ijo, Edo, Igala, and Igbo peoples. The roots of this contact must go back for a considerable time before 1500 since among the Igbo west of the river those elements of Edo culture which antedate the rise of the Benin Empire (*c.* 1300) are more widespread than those which can be associated with Benin. The influence of early Edo culture is detectable east of the Niger as well.[37] Likewise, as will be shown below, the cultural influence of early Igala migrants can be detected all along the Lower Niger valley. So complex is the ethnographic history of his area that there is a danger of anachronism in speaking of the Edo, Igala, and Igbo with reference to the centuries before 1500, since, while these three were no doubt differentiated from each other in language and customs by that date, there is no way of knowing the degree of this differentiation or the degree of homogeneity within each of the three.[38]

[35] Pereira, *Esmeraldo*, p. 146. This identification is supported by Alagoa, *History*, p. 154, who dates the settlement of Bonny to the fifteenth century (p. 158). See also Jones, *Trading States*, pp. 29–30, who does not disagree with this dating.

[36] Alagoa, *History*, pp. 144–50; J. C. Porter, 'Intelligence Report on the Okrika Clan, Degema Division', 1933, pp. 8–11, NAI, CSO 26/3/29004; Ennals, 'Intelligence Report, Ndoki', pp. 8–11; Forde and Jones, *Ibo and Ibibio*, p. 43.

[37] Forde and Jones, *Ibo and Ibibio*, p. 46.

[38] This is not to suggest that the Igbo-Ukwu culture may not be called Igbo, but that the 'Igbo' of that day must have borne much the same relation to modern Igbo as ancient Franks and Allemagni did to modern French and Germans.

An important example of this early complexity can be seen in the culture of Igbo-Ukwu. Thurston Shaw has suggested that the sites he excavated there were probably connected with the *Eze Nri*, the Priest-King of the town of Nri or Aguka which is only a few miles away. Today the priests of Nri are highly respected representatives of an ancient religious tradition among the Igbo. For many centuries they have occupied a unique position as divine intermediaries, especially among the Igbo east of the Niger. The origins of the Nri are a matter of debate. The official version says the apical founder, Eri, and his wife fell from the sky. One of Eri's sons founded Nri while another founded the Igala capital of Idah.[39] A more prosaic account is recorded by another branch of the Children of Eri (*Umueri*), the Aguleri, who live to the north of Nri. They say Eri was the leader of an Igala military expedition whose descendants 'founded' several towns in the area, including Aguleri and Nri.[40] Whatever the origins of Nri, it may be that the Nri priests once had political influence equal to their religious powers, like the priest-kings of the Igala, for in later times they were a source of royal legitimization of the lower Niger, rivalling the king-making powers of the Benin and Igala monarchs.[41]

In the sixteenth and seventeenth centuries the increasing importance of the European connection in the Niger trade gradually restructured the trading priorities on the Lower Niger, greatly increasing the importance of those communities close to the Atlantic at the expense of the more northern ones that previously had prospered because of their Hausa and Saharan connections. During this era new dynasties were established at several places along the Niger as a result of expanding Benin and Igala influence. In many cases both Benin and Igala origins are blended in the new dynasties in a way that underlines the cultural complexity of this Lower Niger area.

A case in point is Aboh, on the west bank of the Niger just at

[39] Shaw, *Igbo-Ukwu*, I, 164. The most detailed study of Nri traditions is by M. D. W. Jeffreys, 'Umundri Traditions of Origin', *African Studies*, XV (1956), 119–31. A similar tradition and a list of 19 Eze Nri was compiled by Thomas, *Anthropological Report*, I, 49–50.

[40] Aguleri traditions can be found in B. G. Stone, 'Intelligence Report on the Umueri Villages of Awka and Onitsha Divisions', 1932, pp. 1–6, NAI, CSO 26/3/28323 and Onuora Nzekwu, 'Gloria Ibo', *Nigeria*, No. 64 (1960), p. 75.

[41] R. L. Bowen, 'Nri Tradition', *Nigeria*, No. 54 (1957), 280; Jeffreys, 'Umundri Traditions', p. 124; Isichei, 'Historical Change', p. 428.

the neck of the delta. The legend now told at Aboh traces its origin to the losing contender for the throne of Benin, who, on the eve of Portuguese arrival, had to flee eastward with his supporters and, after founding a series of other communities, eventually occupied the site of Aboh.[42] His reasons for this choice are not given but it is hard to imagine trade was not a major one as Aboh commands three major channels of the Niger which meet nearby: the Nun branch to the south, the Forcados west to Warri and Benin, and the Engenni east to New Calabar and Bonny. A rival tradition of Aboh's foundation is told in Igala: '.. Aboh was founded in a migration of families from Idah, the Igala capital. It is also claimed that the chief of Aboh were formerly subject to the Ata 'Gala, and that each new chief of Aboh had to spend three months at Idah before investiture, performing rituals, and receiving instructions from the king's eunuchs.'[43]

In the sixteenth century, and the first half of the seventeenth, three other Niger towns in the crucial middle area between Aboh and Idah received new dynasties: Ossomari and Onitsha on the east bank serving the densely populated Igbo hinterland and Asaba on the west bank with connections to Benin. Of these three, Ossomari has a clear tradition of connections to the Igala from the sixteenth to the nineteenth century.[44] Onitsha and Asaba, which face each other across the river, have a curious blend of traditions. Onitsha on the east bank traces its origin to Benin to the west, while Asaba on the west bank claims foundation from an Umueri town to the east. In any event Asaba was soon sending its kings to Benin for coronation with the requisite symbols of office, while Onitsha was drawn increasingly into the cultural focus of Nri.[45]

Despite the complexity of these traditions along the lower Niger some over-all conclusions can be drawn. The immigrant bands which established these dynasties were not mass movements of population

[42] Ikenna Nzimiro, *Studies in Ibo Political Systems* (London: Frank Cass, 1972), pp. 11–12. For Igala and Benin ties with Lower Niger towns not treated here, see Stone, 'Intelligence Report, Umueri', pp. 6–7.

[43] J. S. Boston, 'Notes on Contact between the Igala and the Ibo,' *JHSN* II (1960), 53–4.

[44] F. Ekejiuba, 'Omu Okwei, the Merchant Queen of Ossomari', *JHSN* III (1961), 635; Esama Kaine, *Ossomari, A Historical Sketch* (Onitsha: the author, 1963), pp. 1–4.

[45] Henderson, *King in Every Man*, pp. 76–82; Julius Spencer, 'The History of Asaba and its Kings', *Niger and Yoruba Notes*, VIII, No. 87 (Sept. 1901), 20–1; Isichei, 'Historical Change', pp. 427–33.

such as Dike imagined,[46] nor were they the first to occupy their respective sites. A careful reading of the traditions themselves in several cases reveals that they were small but tightly organized groups that succeeded in establishing themselves as the rulers of their respective towns. The indigenous peoples either accepted them as such, or, being unable to expel them, moved on to other places. The site of Bonny was previously occupied by Abalama and Iyankpo communities which were either driven out or incorporated; the Igbo-speaking Akri were at Aboh when the Benin group arrived; and only the ruling house and two other sections of Ossomari trace their origins from Igala.[47] Both Onitsha and Asaba, because of the key sites they occupy on high ground at the edge of the river, must have been important trading centres long before their modern traditions of origin would indicate.[48]

These immigrant bands on the Niger were part of a long-standing involvement of Igala and Benin in the Niger trade, but they do not appear to represent a conscious effort of these monarchies to gain control of the growing trade in these centuries. The Igala groups seem to have been free agents rather than royal emissaries. While Benin kings had made vigorous efforts to expand to the Niger in the fifteenth century, these efforts were not continued. It is instructive that the new settlers at two prime locations on the river, Aboh and Onitsha, were losers in power struggles in Benin. Perhaps it would not be too far-fetched to suggest that they represented a party advocating a more expansionist policy.[49]

The evidence presented in this chapter on the movements and interactions of the peoples of south-eastern Nigeria points up the danger of describing the history of this area in terms of distinct and mutually hostile ethnic groups. During the centuries considerable interaction, not always peaceful but by no means generally acrimonious, took place between the different ethnolinguistic communities of this region. Continuous contact between contiguous groups produced broad zones of culturally and sometimes linguistically mixed communities rather than sharply delimited frontiers. Along the Cross River and the Niger River these processes were most complex, but

---

[46] Dike, *Trade and Politics*, pp. 25–7.

[47] Jones, *Trading States*, p. 105; Henderson, *King in Every Man*, p. 47; Baikie, *Narrative*, p. 298; Ekejiuba, 'Omu Okwei', p. 635.

[48] Henderson, *King in Every Man*, pp. 35–7.

[49] Boston, 'Notes on Contact', pp. 52–8, and Boston, *The Igala Kingdom*, p. 16, Ryder, *Benin*, p. 15.

similar if simpler processes were also taking place in the regions of
contact between the Ibibio and the Igbo, between the Igbo and the
Ijo, and between the Igala and the Igbo.

In some cases the growth of trade was an important element in
promoting the influx of diverse peoples into an area, as in the case
of at least some of the Efik towns, of Arochukwu, and of the
numerous Aro colonies in the central portion of the hinterland. As
time went on most of the major trading communities incorporated
many immigrants from elsewhere in the region and the acculturation
of these newcomers became a major concern.[50] Even where ethnic
diversity was not initially due to trade, it could facilitate trade
between the component parts of a community. This was the case
in the Okrika and Ndoki communities which geographically and
ethnically straddled the line between the delta and its hinterland,
trading with both sides. Another example is the Aro, who were able
to trade so freely among the Igbo, the Ibibio, and the peoples east
of the Cross River in part because the original Arochukwu community had been formed by representatives of all these groups. This
close connection between trade and ethnic diversity in south-eastern
Nigeria was paralleled in contemporary Europe, where, Professor
Trevor-Roper has argued, immigrants, especially those from late
medieval centres of commerce, were to be found at the heart of the
developing commercial capitalism in north-eastern Europe.[51]

Another way in which the population movements of these centuries influenced trade was in partitioning the region into distinct
spheres of influence whose interstices were generally dominated by
communities of mixed origins. No single trading community,
whether coastal or inland, ever gained control of the trade from start
to finish. Instead, trade passed through several different trading communities on its way to or from the coast. The Aro, who traded so
widely in the hinterland, did not deal directly with the European
merchants or even with the coastal African traders. From their own
spheres of trade hinterland traders transferred their goods to intermediate communities mostly along the rivers leading to the coastal
ports. Thus along the Cross River the Enyong and Uwet were inter-

---

[50] For acculturation efforts at New Calabar see Horton, 'From Fishing Village',
pp. 37–58. For the role of the Ekpe Society in Old Calabar see below, Chapter IV,
§4. For Aro efforts to sustain a distinct cultural identity see below, Chapter V, §3.

[51] H. R. Trevor-Roper, *The European Witch-Craze of the Sixteenth and Seventeenth
Centuries and Other Essays* (New York: Harper and Row, 1969), pp. 19–21.

mediaries between the hinterland and Old Calabar, on the Imo River the Ndoki stood between the hinterland and Bonny, and on the Niger riverain communities handled the trade between inland traders of the western portion of the hinterland and the delta.

CHAPTER III

The Slave Trade

THROUGHOUT the peak years of the slave trade a large proportion of the slaves reaching the Americas came from ports in the Bight of Biafra. This chapter examines several aspects of this important subject. The most basic task is to trace the growth of the overseas slave trade in this region and determine its volume during the peak years of the trade. Next, the origins of the slaves within the hinterland and the means by which they were enslaved are considered. Finally, an attempt is made to gauge the demographic impact of the slave trade. Later chapters will examine the economic impact of this trade, particularly the profound alterations in the commercial structure of the region which accompanied the overseas slave trade.

1. THE SLAVE TRADE BEFORE 1700

While the trade in slaves achieved a dominant position in the commerce of the Bight of Biafra only in the mid-eighteenth century, it began almost with the appearance of the first European sailing ships. To encourage Portuguese settlement on the island of São Tomé the privilege of trading in slaves and other goods with coastal Africans from the Rio Real to the Kingdom of the Congo was granted to the islanders in March 1500. Pereira's account of these early years confirms the purchase of slaves on the Rio Real and the Cameroon River, but not on the Cross River, where trade did not become important for another century and a half. Within a few years São Tomé had become the Portuguese base of operations for the Gulf of Guinea and the Congo and a major exporter of sugar and slaves.[1]

The next description of the slave trade in the Bights was written in 1617–19 by a Jesuit missionary in Peru. Working from mariners' accounts and from interviews with African slaves in Lima, Alonso de Sandoval was able to compile an account of the trade which is astonishingly detailed for the Bight of Biafra.[2] In his day São Tomé

---

[1] John William Blake, ed. *Europeans in West Africa, 1450–1560* (London: Hakluyt Society, 1942), I, 57–63 and document 13. Pereira, *Esmeraldo*, pp. 146ff.

[2] Sandoval, *De Instauranda*, pp. 17, 94.

was still the base of operations for the Portuguese, whose kingdom had been attached to Spain, and to the island Spanish ships brought small cargoes of slaves from the entire Gulf of Guinea. The São Tomé blacks, as all these slaves were called, were not so highly prized as those from the upper Guinea Coast, but they were considered superior to slaves from the Congo and Angola. The gradually accumulating cargoes of slaves on São Tomé must have been transported to the Americas only at infrequent intervals, as Sandoval reports that the blacks there learned to speak a corrupt form of Portuguese which was used as a *lingua franca*. In the Bight of Biafra the main trade was with the 'Caravalies', who can be identified as the Kalabari Ijo. There were some forty or fifty villages of different clans and nations who traded with these 'pure or natural Caravalies' and all of them were called Caravalies as well. According to Sandoval none of these had any kings, which is the earliest indication of the manner of political organization in this area. The Caravalies are said to have been addicted to war among themselves, at least partly for the purpose of capturing slaves, and many were also known to sell their wives and children.

Sandoval lists the names of eighteen of these generic Caravalies. Of those which can be identified, most are Ijo, but the Igbo ('Ibo') and Ibibio ('Done' and 'Moco') are also mentioned.[3]

The name 'Caravalies' has passed into the nomenclature of this area in two places: later traders called the main Kalabari trading settlement New Calabar and the cluster of Efik towns were termed Old Calabar. Why the Kalabari, who were so clearly the earliest of the coastal peoples to engage in regular trade with the Europeans, should have been termed 'New' while the Efik, who appear in the records only in the seventeenth century were called 'Old' is unclear.[4] Bonny, the major port on this coast in the eighteenth and nineteenth centuries, does not appear on the list of Caravalies, although one of the communities it displaced, Abalama ('Abalomo'), does. Since Bonny traditions hold that their first king, Ashimini, learned the secrets of the trade from Owerri Daba of Kalabari, whom Jones

[3] For the identification of the names of many of the Caravalies see Hair, 'Ethnolinguistic Continuity,' pp. 262–3. The 'Done' were most likely the Andoni branch of the Ibibio, who occupy the islands and marshes west of Bonny. The Moco are to be identified with the Western Ibibio (Anang); see David Northrup, 'New Light from Old Sources: Pre-Colonial References to the Anang Ibibio', *Ikenga*, II.1 (Jan. 1973), 1–5.

[4] Jones, *Trading States*, p. 21.

calculates to have ruled about 1600, these two circumstances suggest that the rise of Bonny to commercial importance dates from the early seventeenth century.[5]

The establishment of sugar plantations in the West Indies in the mid-seventeenth century greatly added to the volume of the slave trade and occasioned the entry of the Dutch, English, and French into the Bight of Biafra on a regular basis. Dapper, whose survey was first published in 1668, but which reflects the life of earlier decades, indicates that there was a considerable trade in slaves at Bonny and New Calabar, particularly by the Dutch, and that in some years 500 slaves could be purchased on the Rio del Rey.[6]

In the latter half of the seventeenth century competition between Bonny and New Calabar increased along with the volume of the trade. New Calabar, which was closer to the interior markets and could provide better food supplies, held on to its premier position for most of the century. The Royal African Company was trading there regularly for slaves by 1672 and a rare R.A.C. diary records the purchase of nearly 350 slaves at New Calabar in 1678.[7] But Bonny, nearer the coast, had been strengthening its ties with the Ndoki Igbo, who were at a main terminus of the hinterland trade routes. Bonny was clearly an important port by mid-century, for the Dutch ship *St. Jan* was able to collect a cargo of 219 slaves there in a relatively short time in the spring of 1659.[8] By the end of the century Bonny was the dominant port. John Barbot, who had visited the Rio Real in 1678 and 1682 and had consulted later accounts, reported, 'Very few ships go as high as *New Calabar* town', preferring instead to anchour inside the mouth of the estuary at a place where they were less molested by mosquitoes and could draw upon slaves and supplies from New Calabar, Bonny, and lesser towns.[9] There was also considerable rivalry among the European nations trading in the Rio Real at that time; Barbot estimated that 'the *Dutch* have the greatest share in the trade; the *English* next, and after them the *Portugueses*, from *Brasil*, *St. Thome*, and *Prince's islands*; and altogether export thence a great number of slaves yearly to America,

[5] Jones, *Trading States*, 26, 105.

[6] Dapper, *Description*, pp. 315–16.

[7] Barbot, 'Description', p. 461; Hutchinson, 'Slaver's Diary', p. 143; Donnan, *Documents*, I, 226–34.

[8] Donnan, *Documents*, I, 141–2; Jones, *Trading States*, pp. 28, 105.

[9] Barbot, 'Description', p. 379.

besides a considerable quantity of good elephants teeth and abundance of provisions.'[10]

Old Calabar was less favoured as a port. Located 40 miles up the Cross River estuary it lacked the ocean breezes which most contemporary Europeans associated with a healthy African climate. Because it drew upon a less densely populated hinterland and had weaker ties to inland traders, assembling a cargo of slaves at Old Calabar took longer than at Bonny. Finally, the currents at the mouth of the estuary forced ships leaving Calabar to sail south-east along the coast for a considerable distance before they could turn westward. The Dutch avoided Old Calabar almost completely; yet the English traders of the Royal African Company in 1672 found that, as in New Calabar, slaves and ivory were available there 'in great Plenty'.[11] John Barbot, while noting Old Calabar's disadvantages, reported its estuary easy to navigate even for large ships (unlike the Rio Real, which had a treacherous bar at its mouth), provisions readily available, and the inhabitants 'good civiliz'd people'.[12] One English ship is known to have purchased 300 slaves from there in 1678; another, the *Dragon*, took on 212 in 1698; the *Eagle Galley* of London obtained a cargo of 400 in 1704.[13]

Clear evidence of the great activity of the slave trade in these ports at the end of the seventeenth century may be seen in the instructions of a London shipowner to his captain in 1700. He advised the captain that New Calabar was the most likely place to obtain a cargo of slaves without excessive delay, since 'there are more Shipps go to Bandy [Bonny] than new Callebar especially Dutch and Portugueese' and 'there is soe many Ships gone to Old Callebarr that you cann have no trade there'. Yet as it turned out there were five English ships ahead of him when the captain got to New Calabar.[14] If New

---

[10] Ibid., 381.

[11] Donnan, *Documents*, I, 193.

[12] Barbot, 'Description', p. 383.

[13] Ibid., 379; Barbot, 'Abstract of a Voyage', p. 465; William Snelgrave, *A New Account of Some Parts of Guinea and the Slave-Trade* (London: James, John, and Paul Knapton, 1734), p. 165. Additional slaving voyages to Old Calabar in the seventeenth century are cited in Latham, *Old Calabar*, pp. 17–18.

[14] Letters of Thomas Starke to James Westmore, Oct.–Nov. 1700, in Donnan, *Documents*, IV, 74, 82. The trade of the Gulf of Guinea was important enough to warrant Royal Navy patrols in the 1670s and 1680s to guard the R.A.C. monopoly. The number of private English traders licensed by the Company to operate east of the Volta River increased after 1689 and especially after 1695; see K. G. Davies, *The Royal African Company* (New York: Atheneum, 1970), pp. 115, 119, 126.

Calabar were the least favoured of the three ports, there would have
been some twenty slave-ships working that coast, which with cargoes
of only 200–250 each would have carried away 4,000–5,000 persons.
Such an estimate of the annual slave trade of the Bight of Biafra
at the end of the seventeenth century seems reasonable, but cannot
be documented further.

2. SLAVE-TRADE STATISTICS, 1700–1840

The slave trade of the eighteenth century is better known thanks to
Philip Curtin's excellent studies, which project the slave exports of
the various coasts of Africa by decade from 1711 to 1810.[15] His
figures for the Bight of Biafra appear to be entirely reasonable from
1731, but their accuracy for the earlier two decades is open to serious
question since he records no trade at all from the Bight of Biafra
in 1711–20 and a *total* of only 4,500 slaves for the entire decade 1721–
30. Unless one is to hypothesize that there was a dramatic fall from
the totals of the turn of the century, these figures must be amended.
Incomplete records show that Virginia alone imported an average
of 800 slaves a year from the Bight of Biafra late in the second decade
of the eighteenth century and at least twice that number by the
middle of the third decade.[16] Curtin's figures for the 1730s indicate
that some 4,500 slaves a year were being shipped from the Bight of
Biafra. Since this also accords with the estimate made above for the
beginning of the century, one should not go too far wrong in using
that number for the first three decades as well. In view of the numbers known to be entering Virginia from the Bight of Biafra, it may
be considered a conservative estimate.

After the 1730s the volume of the trade increased sharply as hinterland traders responded to the increasing demand by European
slavers at the coast. An average of 7,100 slaves per annum were
shipped during 1741–50 and about 12,500 per annum in the 1760s
and 1770s. The trade from this coast reached its peak in the 1790s
when it averaged 17,400 slaves a year, but it fell to 9,200 a year
in the first decade of the nineteenth century, largely as a result of
the reduced French and British shipping during the Napoleonic
wars and blockade. Over-all from 1761 to 1810 the Bight of

[15] Curtin, *Slave Trade*, table 66, and (for revised estimates of the Bight of Biafra
in 1761–1810) Philip D. Curtin, 'Measuring the Atlantic Slave Trade', table 3, in *Race
and Slavery in the Western Hemisphere: Quantitative Studies*, ed. Stanley L. Engerman
and Eugene D. Genovese (Princeton: Princeton Univ. Press, 1975).

[16] Donnan, *Documents*, IV, 183–5, 187.

Biafra supplied better than one slave in every six in the Atlantic trade.[17]

Figures for the last decades of the overseas trade are as difficult to compute as those for the early decades. With the departure of the British from the trade in slaves after 1807, the subsequent banning of slave imports into a number of American territories, and the establishment of Joint Commissions in Sierra Leone to enforce the treaties against slave trading in West Africa, the trade took on a

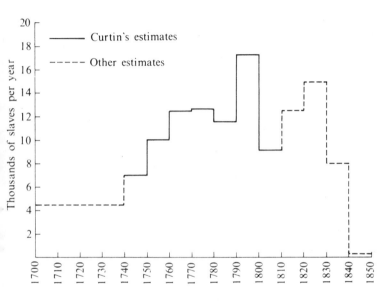

FIG. 1. Slaves Shipped from the Bight of Biafra, 1700–1850.

clandestine character which discouraged the keeping of precise records. However, Curtin's figures show that despite the patrols and other measures there was no abrupt drop in the over-all volume of the Atlantic slave trade until after 1850.[18] In the Bight of Biafra French traders were rejoined by Spanish, Portuguese, Brazilian, and Dutch, who frequented this coast in large numbers with São Tomé again becoming a collection point.

[17] The Bight of Biafra's share of the total trade is computed by comparing these export figures with Curtin, *Slave Trade*, table 65 ('Estimated Slave Imports into American Territories, 1701–1810'), adjusted for a 15 per cent mortality in transit.
[18] Curtin, *Slave Trade*, pp. 267, 269.

No longer able to document the distribution of the trade by decade and coast of origin after 1810, Curtin does provide several calculations intended to give a general indication of the nineteenth-century trade.[19] He points out that most of these may not give an entirely reliable picture of the trade in the Bight of Biafra. The one calculation which Curtin does consider (with qualifications) 'reasonably accurate' for the West African trade of 1817–43 is based upon the Sierra Leone census of recaptives in 1848. Curtin's redistribution of this by coast of origin indicates that 20·2 per cent of these recaptives had come from the Bight of Biafra, which (by further calculations involving the Cuban slave trade) would assign this coast between 9·9 and 13·6 per cent of the over-all Atlantic slave trade in those years.[20] As Curtin considers the lower percentage likely to be more reliable, this would indicate that the Bight of Biafra's share of the slave trade had fallen from one-sixth in the decades before 1810 to one-tenth in those after 1816.

There are, however, several reasons to doubt that these calculations from the Sierra Leone census actually present a true picture of the historical reality. The first set of reasons concerns the figures themselves. It is difficult to assign the recaptives to their actual coast of origin with perfect accuracy. Curtin arbitrarily assigns all Hausa recaptives to the Bight of Biafra, although he is aware that by no means all were actually shipped from that coast. Moreover, the number of recaptives landed in Sierra Leone from the Bight of Biafra was inversely proportional to its share in the slave trade, being lowest in the decades when the trade was at its peak and highest in the middle thirties when the trade was in decline. Finally, the census was only a sampling, counting fewer than 10 per cent of the slaves from the Bight of Biafra actually registered in Sierra Leone in those years.

Two other attempts have been made to estimate the slave trade from the Bight of Biafra during its last decades. The first, based primarily on the sightings, seizures, and estimates of the British West African patrol, concludes that from Curtin's calculation of 9,200 a year in 1801–10 the trade rose to some 15,500 in 1820, averaging perhaps 12,500 for the decade. After 1820 the export of slaves continued to rise, possibly reaching a peak of 20,000 or more in 1826, but averaging closer to 15,000 for the decade. Not until the mid-

[19] Curtin, *Slave Trade*, tables 69, 71, 72, 74, 76.
[20] Ibid., 244–7, 258 and tables 71–2.

1830s did the trade in slaves from the Bight of Biafra begin to fall precipitously, but then the end came quickly with only a trickle of a few hundred slaves a year continuing into the 1840s.[21] The second attempt, part of a much larger study of the volume of the entire Atlantic slave trade in the years 1821–43, is largely based on the records of slave imports to the Americas and on calculations of their probable losses en route. It concludes that the slave trade from the Bight of Biafra averaged about 12,500 a year in 1821–30 with a peak of about 17,000 in 1825. The trade fell to an annual average of a little over 10,000 in the first four years of the next decade, but reached a level of about 18,500 in 1835, the highest single year total in the period under study. Then the trade declined rapidly to only a few hundred a year in 1841–2. Over-all, this study concludes, some 227,000 slaves were shipped from this region, representing 15·3 per cent of the total Atlantic slave trade in that period.[22] While these two approaches do not accord perfectly, their conclusions are re-markably close and both suggest that the Bight of Biafra retained its earlier share of the overseas slave trade through the 1830s.

By 1840 the overseas slave trade had run its course in the Bight of Biafra except for occasional clandestine voyages. Old Calabar and Bonny were too easily observed by the British patrols and con-centrated on the expanding palm-oil trade. New Calabar and Brass were less open to inspection and continued trading for some time after 1840, drawing to them some of the trade that had once gone to Bonny.[23] Other slaves were shipped from the hinterland via inter-coastal waterways to Lagos or beyond where the trade also con-tinued for a time.[24] Portuguese ships from São Tomé also continued

[21] David Northrup, 'The Compatibility of the Slave and Palm Oil Trades in the Bight of Biafra', *JAH* XVII (1976), 355. The figures originally given for 1811–20 have been revised downward here in light of Curtin's downward revision of the totals for 1801–10, upon which those of the next decade are dependent. See note 17 above.

[22] David Eltis, 'The Export of Slaves from Africa 1821–1843', *Journal of Economic History*, XXXVII (1977), 429 and fig. 3.

[23] Slave schooners from New Calabar were observed by the newly appointed Con-sul for the Bights of Benin and Biafra, John Beecroft, in 1850 and 1851. See F.O. 84/816, Africa (West Coast) Consular No. 1: Beecroft to Palmerston, 4 May 1850, and F.O. 84/858 Africa (West Coast) Consular No. 40: Beecroft to Palmerston, 3 June 1851. Cf. Dike, *Trade and Politics*, pp. 52–3.

[24] Schön and Crowther, *Journals*, p. 43, report that 'much traffic went from the lower Niger to Lagos and Whydah in 1841'. This was evidently true earlier in the century as a Portuguese schooner seized by the British Navy at Lagos in 1822 carried a cargo of whom nine-tenths were 'Ibo' and 'Calabar'. See the case of the *Esperança Felis*. F.O. 84/15, British Commissioners, Sierra Leone (General): Woods to Bandinel, 5 Jan. 1823.

to trade in the unpatrolled lesser rivers of the Bight such as the Kwa Ibo, picking up small cargoes of slaves which were taken to that island in much the same manner as in the sixteenth century until there were enough to send across the ocean.[25]

Yet even when these last gasps of the overseas trade had died out, the internal trade in domestic slaves continued along the old routes and in the old markets. This internal slave trade would not come to an end until well into the twentieth century.

3. ETHNIC ORIGINS OF THOSE ENSLAVED

The raw statistics of the annual exports of slaves from the Bight of Biafra indicate the tremendous volume of the trade, yet they tell nothing of its impact on the hinterland. Before this subject can be approached detailed information is needed on where these slaves came from, how they became enslaved, and how such large numbers were assembled in the ports for sale to the European slavers.

The sources for these details are few. Since, except on the Niger, Europeans did not penetrate beyond the coast until long after the overseas trade had ended, there are no direct observations by explorers or missionaries. Even those Europeans who were frequent visitors to the ports have left few reports on these matters. The major contemporary sources on the internal organization of the trade come from Africans who either were literate observers themselves or who were interviewed after leaving this area. Two sources of the former type have survived from the eighteenth century. One is the autobiography of an Igbo, Olaudah Equiano or Ekwuno, who tells of being kidnapped as a child about 1750 and sold into the overseas trade.[26] The other source is the pidgin English diary of the years 1785–8 by Antera Duke, an Efik slave trader of Duke Town, Old Calabar.[27] A European contemporary described Duke as 'having a bold and daring countenance, with some appearance of malignity about it: he possesses great activity of mind'.[28]

Interviews with Africans living abroad have come mainly from

[25] Talbot, *Life*, p. 335.

[26] Edwards, *Equiano's Travels*.

[27] The surviving portions of the original diary, with notes and a modern translation, are in Forde, *Efik Traders*.

[28] Letter from Henry Nicholls to the African Association, 15 Feb. 1805, in Robin Hallett, ed., *Records of the African Association 1788–1831* (London: Thomas Nelson, 1964), p. 199.

missionaries, both among the slaves in the new world and among
the emancipated recaptives in Sierra Leone. The earliest such source
is Sandoval's at the beginning of the sixteenth century, which draws
on interviews with slaves in Peru. A second account, contemporary
to Equiano's and Duke's, by C. G. A. Oldendorps is based on interviews in the West Indies and Pennsylvania.[29] Nineteenth-century
sources are more detailed. The Sierra Leone commissions have provided some general information on the origin, age, and sex of those
it emancipated. The most useful source, however, is S. W. Koelle's
Polyglotta Africana, which contains brief biographies of each of the
informants Koelle used in compiling his vocabularies of the African
languages spoken by freed Sierra Leoneans.[30] The biographies of
informants from the hinterland of the Bight of Biafra are particularly
rich since Koelle frequently records the circumstances of their enslavement and journey to the coast.

The problem of tracing slaves back from the port of embarkation
to their actual homeland is a complex one. Although the New World
slave buyers developed preferences for slaves from certain parts of
Africa, these tell very little about the actual origins of the slaves since
such preferences were most often expressed in terms of a coast or
port of origin, such as Sandoval's 'São Tomé blacks', rather than
a specific group. Tracing slaves shipped from the Bight of
Biafra is made easier by evidence that most slaves were obtained
from quite close to the ports in the sixteenth century, evidently
through already existing trade connections, and even as the trade
developed, most still came from among the Igbo and Ibibio. Pereira's
belief that in the sixteenth century slaves were brought to the coast
from a distance of 'a hundred leagues and more', is not born out
by Sandoval, whose 'Calavaries' were mostly coastal Ijo along with
a few Igbo and Ibibio. Two centuries later Oldendorps similarly identifies slaves from this coast as 'Kalabari' Ijo, Igbo, and Ibibio, but
he devotes more attention to the latter two groups which by then
had become the main source of the overseas trade from this coast.
More precise information comes from Equiano's mid-eighteenth-
century account which indicates that slave routes may have extended
among the Northern Ika Igbo 100–125 miles from the coast and
beyond, for Igbo traders regularly brought slaves through his village

[29] Oldendorps, *Geschichte der Mission.*
[30] Koelle, *Polyglotta.*

on their way to the coast. After their capture he and his sister were transported along the same route.[31]

The first indications of the relative distribution of the slave trade among hinterland peoples comes only after the establishment of the Slave Trade Commissions in Sierra Leone in 1819. For a short time at the beginning of their effort the Commissioners recorded the 'tribe' of origin, along with the port of embarkation, of all of the recaptives they emancipated. As these records, whose results are shown in Figures 2–4, include only seven cargoes of slaves shipped from the Bight of Biafra in 1821–2 (four from Bonny and three from Old Calabar), they may not be fully representative. However, they can be taken as a rough indication of the ethnic groups drawn on by these two ports. As might be expected from Bonny's location adjacent to the Igbo hinterland, three-quarters of its slaves were Igbo, a figure which corresponds closely with contemporary estimates.[32] Old Calabar's high proportion of Igbo slaves (56 per cent) is testimony to the importance of its trading connections with Arochukwu, which are discussed in Chapter V.

The composite Bonny–Old Calabar ratios shown in Figure 4 cannot be used to represent the total slave trade of the Bight of Biafra without two reservations. First, there were probably larger numbers of persons not of Igbo or Ibibio origin than shown there. A greater number of Hausa and other peoples to the north would have passed down the Niger and through the delta ports of Brass and New Calabar than were shipped from Bonny and Old Calabar. In addition, ports just east of Old Calabar would have shipped a higher proportion of North-west Bantu peoples. Second, the ratio of Ibibio to Igbo (about 2 : 5 in Figure 4) seems too high, as the Ibibio population was likely, then as now, to have been only a quarter that of the Igbo. The Ibibio may have furnished slaves beyond their relative numbers, but there is also a distortion caused by the absence of statistics from New Calabar, Brass, and other ports to the west which shipped many Igbo but few Ibibio slaves.

These two faults are corrected (and indeed over-corrected) in Figure 5, which is based upon Curtin's presentation of the 1848 Sierra Leone census. For the reasons cited earlier, this distribution

[31] Equiano, 'Early Travels', pp. 75, 85–92; Jones, 'Olaudah Equiano', p. 61.

[32] Adams, *Remarks*, pp. 116, 129. Evidently referring to the late eighteenth century, Adams stated that the Igbo constituted 80 per cent of the slaves exported from Bonny, with no slaves coming from any people north of the Igbo.

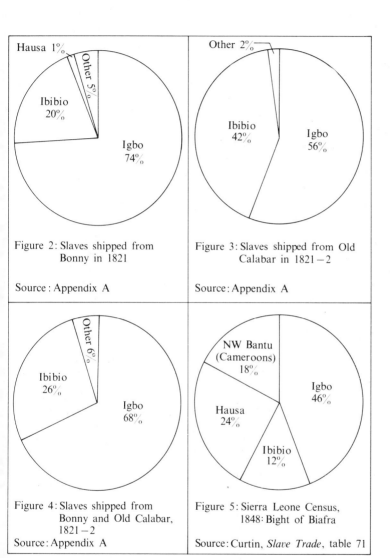

Figure 2: Slaves shipped from
Bonny in 1821

Source: Appendix A

Figure 3: Slaves shipped from Old
Calabar in 1821–2

Source: Appendix A

Figure 4: Slaves shipped from
Bonny and Old Calabar,
1821–2
Source: Appendix A

Figure 5: Sierra Leone Census,
1848: Bight of Biafra

Source: Curtin, *Slave Trade*, table 71

includes too many Hausa and also seems to include too low a proportion of Igbo. Possibly many Igbo, who have shown an exceptional willingness in the twentieth century to settle far from their homeland, formed a disproportionate share of those who left Sierra Leone in the 1840s to accept work elsewhere in West Africa and in the West Indies. If forced to hazard a guess on the proportions of slaves in this period, I would say that the Ibibio and North-west Bantu must each have provided a sixth, the Igbo 60 per cent, with the Hausa and others accounting for the remainder.

Besides the probable proportions of the slave trade supplied by different hinterland ethnic groups, it would be helpful to determine, in the cases of the larger groups (the Igbo and Ibibio), the sub-units from which the slaves were chiefly drawn. In part this will be indicated when treating the organization of the trade, but as those sections have been pieced together from a great variety of sources and rely heavily on information derived from later traditions, it is not possible to be very precise about the *relative* intensity of the trade in any one place or at any single time. However, much can be learned about the areas from which most Igbo and Ibibio slaves came by examining the general descriptions Koelle gives of each of these peoples. It must be remembered that Koelle's preoccupation is primarily with linguistic differences, but with care his information can be put to other uses.[33]

Because of the dialectical variations in the Igbo language, and also, one suspects, because of the large number of Igbo in Sierra Leone, Koelle decided to treat Igbo as five related dialect groups. His informants for two of the dialects, 'Isoama' and 'Abadsha', reported that there were large numbers of their particular groups in Sierra Leone, indicating a heavy slave trade. The 'Isoama' can be identified with the Isuama Igbo (see Appendix B), who inhabit Orlu and neighbouring divisions south-east of Onitsha in the new Imo State of Nigeria. As will be shown later, the Isuama were a source of slaves both to the Aro of Ndizuogu to their north-east and to the riverain Ossomari to the west. The 'Abadsha' are the Agbaja of modern Udi Division, north-east of Onitsha, a source of slaves to their eastern neighbours, the Nike, who were agents of the Aro. The informants of both places were captured about 1820 and could well have been on the ships which furnished the records for Figure 4.

The other three dialect groups had produced relatively few slaves.

[33] Koelle, *Polyglotta*, p. 8 (for the Igbo) and p. 18 (for the Ibibio).

The Aro dialect in fact was represented only by an Isuama man who had been kidnapped from his home about 1810 and raised in Arochukwu. There were six slaves from Ohafia to the north of Arochukwu and four from Ishielu to the east of Nike and Agbaja.

Koelle lists eleven other Igbo 'countries', though he does not explain on what basis he compiled this list. It is most likely that they represent those Igbo groups which were most numerous in Sierra Leone since they correspond so well with the known Aro trading areas. Some, like the Ngwa and Elugu were major Igbo sub-units; others, like Ozuzu, were village-groups whose names were applied to a larger territory.[34]

Koelle's information on the Ibibio is perhaps even more enlightening about the slave trade. Although modern linguists have called this language either Efik, after the first dialect to be written, or Ibibio, after the largest dialect, Koelle names the language Anang. This evidently indicates that the Anang Ibibio were the most numerous Ibibio group in Sierra Leone, even though they were, then as now, probably no more than a third of the total Ibibio population. Koelle divided the 'Anang' into six 'districts'. Three of these, 'Anang', 'Bie or Bibie' (Ibibio), and 'Efik' are readily identifiable with the three largest divisions of the Ibibio-speaking people. The other three are obscure: ŋkuo, Okua, and Ekoe. Yet if Koelle were basing his districts on the number of representatives he found among the Ibibio recaptives in Sierra Leone, it would be reasonable to seek these districts in areas which may have produced disproportionate numbers of slaves in that era. Quite small groups might have appeared as major divisions. On that assumption the following identifications are proposed:[35] ŋkuo = Nkwot, a large group of villages in Ikono Clan, Itu Division; Okua = Ukwa, a large group of villages inhabiting the right bank of the Cross River north-east of Arochukwu;[36] Ekoe = Ekoi, a group of villages in the Ikpe Clan, Itu Division. The three are all within twenty miles of Arochukwu. While the elders of the one Ukwa village it was possible to visit had no traditions of many slaves coming from their area, interviews in Nkwot and Ekoi confirmed that there had been an extensive trade in slaves with the Aro and in those places. The Ekoi lay fortified against attacks

[34] For Umudioka/Umudi Awka see Forde and Jones, *Ibo and Ibibio*, pp. 31–2.
[35] See map 2.
[36] The Ukwa are the northern most offshoot of the Ibibio and the subject of a proverb which also names their neighbour, Ito: *Asanga osim Ito ye Ukwa*: He/it has reached Ito and Ukwa, i.e. the furthest parts. Quoted by Goldie, *Dictionary*, p. 361.

by the slave-raiding and head-hunting Abam Igbo, the 'friends in arms' of the Aro.[37]

While most slaves shipped from ports in the Bight of Biafra came from the Igbo and Ibibio hinterland, a small number came from much further inland. Among Koelle's informants were an 'Mbarike' who had come from somewhere beyond Bauchi (a town itself some 350 miles from the Niger-Benue confluence), an Igbira of Panda near the confluence, several Igala, as well as some Igbo who had passed through Igala hands.[38] Slaves of Nupe, Kakanda, and Hausa origins to the north and north-west also passed into the Niger trade.[39] From the Igala riverain markets, which were visited by traders from as far away as Aboh and Bonny, slaves were taken south to the Igala Bank and Aboh markets. The latter place in 1830 was said to be the principal slave market on the lower Niger, from which in turn slaves were taken to Brass, New Calabar, Bonny, and other ports to the west.[40]

Another long-distance route led from Old Calabar through the sparsely settled Cameroon foothills to the Bamenda Grasslands in modern Cameroon. The number of informants from this area in Koelle makes it clear that raids by the Fulani and others in the 1820s and 1830s were producing a large number of slaves which supplied the internal demands of the Fulani emirates to the north and the overseas markets to the south at Old Calabar and the Cameroon River.[41]

[37] Interviews with Ekpenyong Akpan, Ekoi Atan Ubom, Ikpe, 20 Dec. 1972; Akpan Udo Essien, Ebam Ukot, Ikpe, 20 Dec. 1972; Ekara Udo Ebiong, Odoro Ikpe, 26 Jan. 1973; Odiong Udowong, Ukwa Eburutu, 14 Feb. 1973. F. D. D. Winston, 'Nigerian Cross River Languages in the Polyglotta Africana', *Sierra Leone Language Review*, III (1964) and IV (1965) was the first to suggest (IV, 123) that Koelle's 'Okua' may be the Ukwa; however, his suggestion (III, 82), that Koelle's 'Ekoe' may refer to the Ekoi peoples east of the Cross River fails to account for the important fact that these Ekoi speak languages entirely different from the Ibibio dialects.

[38] Koelle, *Polyglotta*, pp. 6, 8, 9, 20. The Mbarike are identified with the Zumper people of West Cameroon by Philip D. Curtin and Jan Vansina, 'Sources of the Nineteenth Century Atlantic Slave Trade', *JAH* V (1964), 207.

[39] According to Simon Jonas in Schön and Crowther, *Journals*, p. 233.

[40] The judgement on Aboh's importance is from the Landers' *Niger Journal*, p. 253. On the next Niger expedition (1832–4) Macgregor Laird met two men at Idah 'from King Peppel of Bonny, buying slaves for their master...' He also encountered traders from Aboh at the Igbira market town of Panda, some 50 miles beyond the Niger–Benue confluence, and was told that they regularly attended the 'Bocqua' or Ikiri market between Idah and the confluence. Laird and Oldfield, *Narrative*, I, 102, 124, 132 ff. See also Oldfield's observations, ibid., I, 409, and II, 254, 305, 318 ff.

[41] See below Chapter IV, §3.

Although these routes indicate the distances that slaves were brought from, the majority of those shipped from this coast came from the densely populated Igbo and Ibibio areas between the Niger and the Cross rivers. The organization of trade routes within this area will be described in Chapters IV and V.

4. MEANS OF ENSLAVEMENT

The manner in which slaves were procured within Africa for sale into the overseas trade has not always been treated objectively. Those wishing to bring out the cruelty of the system to those enslaved or the negative impact on Africa have concerned themselves with the more brutal techniques of the trade, such as wars and raids. Yet there is considerable evidence that various other techniques were in use in West Africa and that in many cases the raid or war played only a minor role in the procurement of slaves. In south-eastern Nigeria, for example, the most detailed study of the topic, done by J. S. Harris thirty-five years ago, lists seven modes of enslavement plus many subdivisions without finding it necessary to even mention raids.[42] Since Harris used only oral sources from the Bende area, his study has too narrow a base to generalize from, but his work is an indication of the kind of research that can be done on this topic.

This section will examine the modes of enslavement in the hinterland using a wide range of oral sources, contemporary written records, and statistical interpolations. Although the records are scantier than one would like, it is possible to group the reasons for enslavement under four general headings and to evaluate the relative importance of each technique. A concluding section relates the modes of enslavement to the demographic impact of the slave trade and to the trading techniques of the hinterland peoples.

Wars and raids

In the historiography of the slave trade the slave raid or war occupies a special place, for it brings to mind simultaneously the personal terror and suffering endured by captured slaves and the social destruction and chaos which the trade unleashed in Africa. There is certainly clear evidence that these techniques were used in south-eastern Nigeria. In the sixteenth and seventeenth centuries, when most slaves were obtained from relatively near the coast,

[42] J. S. Harris, 'Some Aspects of Slavery in Southeastern Nigeria', *Journal of Negro History*, XXVII (1942), 37–54.

prisoners of war may have been a major staple of the trade. Both
Sandoval and Dapper imply that trade and war were about equally
important in procuring slaves without indicating whether these wars
were fought primarily for the purpose of obtaining prisoners or for
other reasons.[43] Oral traditions from the delta communities give
little additional light on this period, beyond indicating that it was
a time of civil strife.[44] However, by the end of the seventeenth century prisoners, at least from the delta area, were no longer a source
of slaves.[45]

More specific information on the ways of obtaining slaves is available for the Cross River area in the eighteenth century. Thomas
Clarkson has left this description of the conjunction of trading and
raiding by Duke Town (New Town) residents in the 1770s:

I had two opportunities of seeing how slaves were procured in the Rivers of
Old Calabar. I resided with the king of New Town for four months, and he
allowed me to go up the river with him to trade for slaves. I went with him
twice within that time. In the first expedition, there was a fleet consisting of
from ten to twelve canoes, which were properly manned and armed. With
this fleet we set out to trade. In the day time we called at the villages as we
passed, and purchased our slaves fairly; but in the night we made several excur-
sions on the banks of the river. The canoes were usually left with an armed
force: the rest, when landed, broke into villages, and, rushing into the huts
of the inhabitants, seized men, women, and children promiscuously. We
obtained about fifty negroes in this manner, in our first expedition.[46]

The second expedition Clarkson went on was organized in a similar
manner and yielded a somewhat larger total of slaves.

Another account of the slave trade in Old Calabar, which substan-
tiates Clarkson's, is provided by an English seaman, Isaac Parker,
who spent five months in Duke Town in 1765. Parker accepted the
invitation of Dick Ebro, 'who was a king's son' and an important
trader, to raid upriver for slaves. On the two expeditions described
Parker and Ebro dispensed with trading entirely, confining their
activity to raids on the riverain villages. On each occasion their
expeditions of several canoes took about forty-five prisoners in the

[43] Sandoval, De Instauranda, p. 17; Dapper, Description, p. 315.
[44] Jones, Trading States, p. 134.
[45] Barbot, 'Abstract of a Voyage', p. 459, where he indicates that slaves were
obtained by purchase from inland markets.
[46] Thomas Clarkson, 'Essay on the Efficiency of Regulation or Abolition' (1789)
quoted in Donnan, Documents, II, 572.

space of eight or nine days.[47] Two years later in 1767 a civil war
in Old Calabar between Old Town and Duke Town ended quickly
with several Old Town notables being sold as slaves, and signalled
the supremacy of Duke Town in the slave trade on that river.[48]

Slave raids could not, however, long continue in the immediate
vicinity of a major slaving port without becoming counter-produc-
tive to the trade. Just as the eastern delta states had ceased to resort
to raids by the end of the seventeenth century, so did Old Calabar
come to obtain its slaves by purchase at the surrounding markets
some time late in the next century. Raiding for slaves was even prohibited at Calabar.[49] Although it is unlikely that this prohibition
could have been enforced perfectly, it is significant that when the
slave trader Antera Duke encountered a lone Ibibio fisherman on
the Cross River in 1785, he drew near only to offer the man a drink
of brandy in exchange for some fish.[50] This event, trivial in itself,
contrasts sharply with the raids of the previous decades and illustrates the completion of the process of evolution to orderly marketing practices. The difference in techniques between the Old Calabar
traders and their suppliers further inland is brought out clearly in
an interview between the Revd. Hope Waddell and King Eyo
Honesty II of Creek Town. The overseas slave trade ended, King
Eyo remained an active trader in domestic slaves, but objected
strongly to the missionary calling him a 'man-stealer':

He did not employ men to steal slaves for him; nor would he knowingly buy
those which were stolen. He bought them in the market, at the market price,
without being able to know how they were procured ... He admitted that
they were obtained in various objectionable ways... ; but said that they came
from different far countries of which he knew nothing, and in which they had
no other trade. Calabar people did not steal, but only bought, slaves.[51]

Outside the coastal area, however, it is much harder to determine
the frequency of raiding or slave inspired warfare. King Obi, one
of the most powerful rulers on the lower Niger, told explorers on

[47] Testimony of Isaac Parker, *Parl. Papers* 1790 lxxxvii (699), 124–34. Dick Ebro
referred to this campaign up the river as a 'war' (p. 124), although he admitted to
Parker that in fact there was no dispute with the people being raided.
[48] Thomas Clarkson, *The History of the Abolition of the African Slave Trade* (London: Longman, 1808), I, 305–15.
[49] D. Simmons, 'An Ethnographic Sketch of the Efik People', in Forde, *Efik
Traders*, p. 7.
[50] Duke, 'Diary', pp. 38–9.
[51] Waddell, *Twenty-Nine Years*, p. 429.

that river in 1841: 'When other chiefs quarrel with me and make war, I take all I can as slaves', enslavement in this case evidently being one of the punishments of rebellious chiefs.[52] A century earlier Equiano reported that his people sold prisoners of war to slave dealers, though he was uncertain if the wars had been fought with that end in mind or for other reasons.[53] Likewise in the case of the incursions in the Cameroon Grasslands and the upper Cross River area it is impossible to say if slaves were the prime object of the fighting or only a by-product. The same is true of the battles fought by the Ndizuogu and Nike against their neighbours; either land or slaves may have been the primary motive.[54] Oral traditions from several parts of the hinterland attest that raids for the purpose of capturing slaves did exist. On the Niger traditions from both aggressors and victims indicate that Aboh and Ossomari traders raided the poorly defended inhabitants along the Aguleri River for slaves.[55] East and west of the lower Kwa Ibo River there are also traditions of slave raids, though it is impossible to judge the scale of such actions.[56] Finally, although Harris somehow missed it, there is clear evidence of slave raids by the Abam in the Bende area.[57]

Yet when all the evidence for raids and war is considered, there is no indication that these produced more than a small percentage of the slaves exported from the Bight of Biafra in the eighteenth and nineteenth centuries. Slave raiding was important further north where slave raids accompanied the consolidation of the Sokoto Caliphate. Nearer the coast the small scale of warfare produced fewer captives to enslave. 'Except in the more open and densely populated regions,' Talbot notes, 'war consisted more of a series of skirmishes

---

[52] Allen and Thomson, *Narrative*, I, 218.

[53] Equiano, 'Early Travels', pp. 75–7.

[54] For the Grasslands see Koelle, *Polyglotta*, pp. 11–13. For Nike see W. R. G. Horton, 'The Ohu System of Slavery in a Northern Ibo Village-Group', *Africa*, XXIV (1954), 311–36. For Ndizuogu see below, Chapter V, §2, 'The western area'.

[55] Kaine, *Ossomari*, pp. 51, 60. B. G. Stone, 'Intelligence Report on the Anam Villages, Onitsha Division, Onitsha Province', 1934, p. 6, NAI, CSO 26/3/29576.

[56] Talbot, *Life*, p. 335. Talbot identifies the villages of Mkpok and Ikot Akpa Atek as the perpetrators of raids west of the river, while raids on the Eastern Nsit and Obium clans east of the river are mentioned by E. H. F. Gorges, 'Intelligence Report on the Ubium Clan, Eket Division, Calabar Province', 1935, NAI, CSO 26/3/31351, p. 5, and by J. M. Lieber, *Efik and Ibibio Villages* (Ibadan: Institute of Education, Univ. of Ibadan, 1971), p. 36. Lieber's source attributes the raids to the Aro, but since the Aro are not mentioned in earlier accounts this may well be an intrusive 'modernization' of the tradition.

[57] See below, Chapter V, §2, 'The eastern area'.

in the bush between two towns than of regular battles.'[58] In places the accepted rules of war prevented prisoners from being sold as slaves. Some hinterland peoples took the heads of defeated enemies as trophies and others were said to eat captured warriors in the belief that it would give them a 'strong heart'.[59] Perhaps the clearest indication of the small role of war and raids in producing slaves is the testimony of a ship's surgeon who had been to Bonny twice in the 1780s and was emphatic in his opinion that warfare produced few slaves in that area:

It may not be here unworthy of remark, in order to prove that the wars among the Africans do not furnish the number of slaves they are supposed to do, that I never saw any negroes with recent wounds; which must have been the consequence, at least with some of them, if they had been taken in battle. And it being the particular province of the surgeon to examine the slaves when they are purchased, such a circumstance could not have escaped my observation.[60]

Judicial and extra-judicial processes

If many foreign analysts of the slave trade have exaggerated the numbers taken in wars and raids, there is a strong belief among present-day residents of the hinterland that wrongdoers sold by rightful authorities were the mainstay of the trade. A typical statement of this belief was given by an Ibibio elder, 'When a brother poisons a brother, he must be sold. A woman who commits adultery would be sold by her husband and the husband kept the money. Rogues, i.e. thieves, were sold and the money went to the elders whose responsibility it was to make the decision, who would keep it and use it to buy gunpowder for when there was a war.'[61]

---

[58] Talbot, *Peoples*, III, 823. In a similar vein Equiano described the battles he witnessed as a child as 'irruptions of one little state or district on another'. See Equiano, 'Early Travels', p. 77. The 'Great War' between Nnewi and Abiriba mercenaries lasted only one day according to John O. Alutu, *A Groundwork of Nnewi History* (Enugu: the author, 1963), pp. 150–5. Of a major war between Old Calabar and the Okoyong in 1868 an amused missionary wrote: 'I believe it to be a fact that thousands have fallen before their victorious swords and cutlasses—I mean thousands of small bushes, with a sprinkling of big trees. In so far as I am able to learn, the expedition has been entirely bloodless except among fowls and goats.' From William Anderson's 'Journal' for 30 Dec. 1868, quoted in William Marwick, *William and Louisa Anderson* (Edinburgh: Andrew Elliot, 1897), p. 438.

[59] Talbot, *Peoples*, III, 836–45. Roger Casement, 'Report of an Attempted Journey from Itu ... to the Opobo River', 10 Apr. 1894, p. 13, F.O. 2/63/322ff.

[60] Falconbridge, *Account of the Slave Trade*, p. 16.

[61] Interview with Chief Udonyah, Ikono.

Considerable evidence that enslavement was a common punishment for crime may be found in the Intelligence Reports written on this region in the late 1920s and early 1930s, which was soon enough after the end of the internal slave trade to be a fairly reliable guide. Since judicial processes were a matter of particular interest to the colonial authorities, these matters were carefully noted. Although customs varied in detail from place to place, certain general norms can be laid down. For serious crimes death or compensation seem to have been the traditional penalties. However, with the growth of the slave trade sale into slavery became a distinct and profitable alternative. A person was especially liable to be sold when he was unable to pay the compensation or fine required, the proceeds of the sale being used as compensation. At other times the sale was mandatory or the person might even be given away. Sale was the normal punishment for repeated or serious theft, particularly theft of agricultural produce which was a crime against the Earth Deity (Igbo: *Ala, Ale, Ani:* Ibibio: *Ndem Isong*). Crimes of revenge, such as destroying crops or arson, as well as poisoning and witchcraft were often punished by sale into slavery. The elder quoted above said a woman might be sold for adultery, but this was not usually grounds for the enslavement of a man unless the adultery had been with the wife of an important man. Kidnapping for the purpose of selling into slavery was regarded as an especially serious crime and universally punished, in the best tradition of the *lex talonis*, by the kidnapper being sold to the slave dealers. Confirmation of the antiquity of some of these customs may be found in sources contemporaneous with the overseas slave trade. Equiano reported that (in addition to prisoners of war) his people sold to the slave dealers, 'such among us as had been convicted of kidnapping, or adultery, and some other serious crimes which we esteemed heinous'.[62] In 1821 an Efik man named Duke was sold at Calabar for 'ravishing his father's wives' in preference to his being executed, since a slave ship was handy.[63]

In addition to these offences, which nearly all societies would recognize as crimes, the Igbo and Ibibio had another category of transgressions which concerned their cosmological beliefs. Serious penalties could also be invoked on those who might, generally inadvertently, depart from what was considered 'normal' human beha-

[62] Equiano, 'Early Travels', p. 75.
[63] F.O. 84/10, Sierra Leone (Portugal) No. 13: Gregory and Fitzgerald to Marquis of Londonderry, 10 Nov. 1821.

viour. The Ibibio and most of the Igbo considered the birth of twins to be a particularly abhorrent event. Believing only single births to be normal for humans, one of the twins was considered the incarnation of an evil spirit which must not be allowed to remain in human society. Both twins were customarily killed and their mother, who, having once allowed such a fiend to enter her womb, might do so again, might be killed as well or banished or sold away.[64] The Igbo recognized a wider range of 'abominations' (*nso*), such as a child whose upper teeth appeared before its lower, who walked or talked sooner than was usual, who had supernumerary fingers or toes, or who had any other deformity, or a woman who menstruated before attaining the 'proper' age, gave birth to twins, or climbed trees.[65] Depending on the circumstances such a person might be killed outright, ritually cleansed, or sold into slavery. The most ancient specialists in removing such abominations were the priests of Nri, the most respected and powerful Igbo religious figures. The Aro likewise promoted themselves as special intermediaries with the spiritual world. As the Eze Aro put it: 'Since the Aro set up a shrine to Chukwu for other people and made laws [concerning spiritually prohibited practices] anyone violating the law would be sent back to Arochukwu for "training", i.e. be sold as a slave.'[66] Thus by spreading the belief in the dangers of abominations and taboo violations, the Aro effectively promoted the profitable slave trade. The Long Juju functioned as a supreme court of appeals for much of the southern part of this region and in the course of its functions produced, as fines or victims, a considerable number of slaves for the export market. This Aro Oracle was not unique as there were other oracles operating among the Igbo just east of the Niger.[67]

In all of these judicial processes there was room for considerable perversion of justice. In part this was so because much of the administration of justice in the hinterland was rather informal. Only important or complex cases might be brought before the village elders and

[64] The mother of Chief Udo Akpabio of a prominent Anang Ibibio family had been sold to the Igbo after giving birth to twins. See W. T. Groves, 'The Story of Udo Akpabio of the Anang Tribe, Southern Nigeria', in *Ten Africans* ed. Margery Perham (London: Faber and Faber, 1936), pp. 43–4.

[65] Harris, 'Some Aspects of Slavery', p. 42.

[66] Interview with His Highness Chief Kanu Oji, Paramount Chief of Arochukwu, 12 Dec. 1972.

[67] For example, the Igwe-ke-Ala oracle at Umunoha near Owerri, and the Agbala oracle near Awka. See C. K. Meek, *Law and Authority in a Nigerian Tribe* (London: Oxford Univ. Press, 1937), p. 18; and Basden, *Niger Ibos*, pp. 77–91.

enforcement of their decisions was often left to the aggrieved party with the support of public opinion. Many cases could be decided within the kindred or family and other cases were settled only in the tribunal of public opinion and could thus be unfair especially to the weak and friendless. In such circumstances enslavement could be made the penalty for quite minor offences. Goldie was of the opinion that the Ibibio Proper were especially prone to such mis-carriages of justice. They sell, he wrote, 'not only strangers, but each other, on the merest pretexts. When an individual succeeds to the leadership of the family or clan, he is said to sell all the children of his predecessor.'[68] The Efik, who bought these victims, were themselves prone to a similar fault. Great Duke Ephraim, Old Calabar's leading merchant in the early nineteenth century, when very hard pressed by impatient European slave captains, was said to require each of his great men to furnish him with a quota of slaves 'by sending him every individual from the neighbouring villages, who have committed any crime or misdemeanor; and should he still continue unable to make up the specified demand, they sell their own servants to him.'[69] The more perceptive elders in the hinterland are quite aware that not all those sold as evil-doers were guilty of any crime. As one venerable chief put it:

Any person could be accused of being a wicked person. If I were in need of money, and I had a child of a brother or somebody like that, I could just go and say this child of my brother is a wicked person. Then the whole village would say, "He is a wicked man; let him be sold!" So that the number would be increased according to the demand for money ... Any man was free to sell his wife if he had any dislike for the woman or if he needed some money to do some other thing.[70]

While there is not sufficient evidence to indicate the exact con-tribution of judicial decisions to the slave trade, both contemporary and more recent sources indicate that it was considerable. Studies of the judicial systems of the hinterland communities indicate that violators of criminal and cosmological norms were regularly sold as slaves, especially to the Aro. Enslavement for crimes here, as else-where in West Africa,[71] was a penalty which originated with the

[68] Goldie, *Dictionary*, p. 358.

[69] James Holman, *Holman's Voyage to Old Calabar*, ed. Donald Simmons (Calabar: Hope Waddell Press, 1959), p. 16. Holman was in Old Calabar in 1828.

[70] Interview with Chief the Honourable Ntuen Ibok, M.B.E., Essene, Ikpa Nung Asang, 20 Feb. 1973.

[71] Rodney, 'African Slavery', p. 441.

overseas slave trade and was open to considerable exploitation. Quite minor infractions or entirely trumped-up charges could be made grounds for enslavement of the weak and friendless. Even the rich and powerful were not safe, since disputes originating in jealousy might force them into appeals to the Long Juju which might end up in their being sold too.[72]

Economic decisions: greed, debt, and famine

The literature of most societies is rich in stories of the unfortunate bargains made between shrewd traders and gullible peasants. Such situations were common in south-eastern Nigeria as well, where the goods brought by visiting traders proved irresistible to many. Yet there was little that could be given in exchange for such goods: ivory, salt, fancy textiles, metalware, and, of course, slaves. Until the palm-oil trade expanded agricultural crops were of negligible value except near the coast, and even then only the southern part of the hinterland lay within the palm belt. For many people slaves were the only real possibility. The more venturesome or powerful might hope to take a prisoner in war, sell an adulterous wife, or kidnap someone from a neighbouring village. But these actions, too, would not have been within the range of possibilities open to the average person.

Some, it appears, were tempted into debt, which cannot have been a common state before the arrival of traders in rare and exotic goods. In areas where population densities were high land might be pledged to obtain the price. Elsewhere the head of a family might pledge or 'pawn' family members, who, like land, would remain redeemable for decades, even into new generations. This does not seem to have been a rare occurrence. As one early colonial source reported: 'In the old days if anybody got into trouble or debt in the upper parts of the Cross River and wanted ready money, he used generally to "pledge" one or more of his children, or some other member of his family or household to one of the Akunakuna traders who paid periodic visits to his village.'[73] In theory pawns or pledges were distinguished from bought slaves in that they could not be sold away outside the country, but the Igbo used the same word, *ohu*, for both a domestic slave and a pledge. In most cases the distinction remained academic since redemption reportedly was rare.[74]

[72] See below, Chapter V, §3.

[73] Charles Patridge, *Cross River Natives* (London: Hutchinson, 1905), p. 72.

[74] Meek, *Law and Authority*, p. 204; Basden, *Niger Ibos*, pp. 244, 254–5. For the Ibibio see Waddell, *Twenty-Nine Years*, p. 315.

Domestic slaves might also be sold to raise money, at least by those wealthy enough to have them. As was indicated above, Efik men sometimes sold their slaves to pay trading debts. Some 30 per cent of Koelle's informants from the hinterland had evidently spent some time as domestic slaves before being sold into the overseas trade since a year or more passed between their original enslavement and their final sale.[75] Equiano had also spent a time as a domestic slave after being kidnapped from his home.[76] It cannot be determined how many of these were sold for debt, but it is probable that some were since they appeared unaware of any other reason. Koelle records two clear cases of purely economic transactions: one middle Cross River man had been sold by his family for a gun and powder and an upper Cross River man was sold to pay his father's debts.[77] A local history of Aro Ndizuogu says that some Igbo sold their children to get a fancy cloth for certain masquerade dances and adds in what sounds like a paraphrase of the trader's sales pitch: 'The cloth was very attractive and each colour shone as the mirrow [sic] on the sun. Anyone who had seen [the masquerades] would say that the people were not so foolish ... to make such exchanges with their sons.'[78]

Besides those traders and their customers who got into financial binds because of commercial transactions there were also people who faced economic choices because of food shortages. By the nineteenth century those parts of the central Igbo and Ibibio area which have such high population densities today, must have been reaching the productive capacity of arable land. It is clear that some communities were able to escape the consequences of land pressure by turning from farming to trading, the profits of which could be used to purchase food supplies elsewhere. But this was not a practical solution for all. King Eyo Honesty II of Creek Town recalled 'that he had seen [a famine] one year in a neighbouring country, when people sold themselves and children for a few yams or few coppers'.[79] One writer has gone so far as to suggest that over-population was a key factor in the slave trade:

[75] Koelle, *Polyglotta*, pp. 9–21.
[76] Equiano, 'Early Travels', pp. 85–92.
[77] Koelle, *Polyglotta*, pp. 11, 19.
[78] R. Ohizo Igwegbe, *The Original History of Arondizuogu from 1635–1960* (Aba: International Press, 1962), p. 78.
[79] Waddell, *Twenty-Nine Years*, p. 382.

From a study of past trading arrangements in this area it seems probable that one of the major determinants of the enormous number of slaves in Iboland before the advent of British Administration was the close juxtaposition of areas of exhausted, barren land with areas of great agricultural fertility; in such cases an exchange of men for yams was the quickest method of securing a more equitable distribution of both population and food.[80]

Since, as Afigbo has pointed out,[81] there may not have been an actual trade in food in that area at that time, the transaction may not literally have been 'men for yams'. But it does appear that some effort at regulation of people/food ratios was made by selling off the younger and weaker members of society. Perhaps this is the reason why, despite its densities, reports of famine were rare in the hinterland. Additional examples of this type of population limitation are not difficult to find. In the Ndizuogu area the Aro bought children from their neighbours who lacked good water and adequate food supplies: 'These people had many children and thought it wise to sell some of their children to feed others.'[82] On the Cross River the Afikpo 'occasionally also sold to the Aro some of their own people, particularly younger sons and daughters',[83] perhaps in time of financial distress. Traditions at Arochukwu also maintain that the Aro purchased 'surplus children' since families that 'lacked enough to eat would sell their children to the Aro'.[84]

Kidnapping

If the fear in which kidnapping was held in south-eastern Nigeria is any indication, there must have been many people enslaved in that fashion. During the slave-trade era fear of enslavement caused most

[80] Horton, 'Ohu System', pp. 311–12.

[81] A. E. Afigbo, 'Trade and Trade Routes in Nineteenth Century Nsukka', *JHSN* VII.1 (Dec. 1973), 78.

[82] Igwegbe, *Original History*, p. 75.

[83] Simon and Phoebe Ottenberg, 'Afikpo Markets: 1900–1960', in *Markets in Africa*, ed. Paul J. Bohannan and George Dalton (Evanston, Ill: Northwestern Univ. Press, 1961), p. 123.

[84] Interview, Chief Oji, Arochukwu. Lest it appear from all these instances of children being sold that the hinterland peoples were somehow lacking in proper parental feelings, the following comments by an anthropologist who has worked extensively in the region may serve to redress the balance: 'When Onitsha people assess the career of a person, their primary criterion is the number of children he has raised to support and survive him. Children are extolled in proverbs above any other good, even above the accumulation of wealth (*aku*); "children first, wealth follows" is a proverb affirming the route to success... The value of children is often affirmed in the personal names given them, for example, "Child surpasses money" (Nwa-ka-ego), "Child is shelter" (Nwa-bu-ndo).' From Henderson, *King in Every Man*, p. 106.

people to stay at home or to travel only in large, armed groups, and the memory of this danger remained vivid well into the twentieth century.[85] In the dense undergrowth of most of the hinterland ambush was easy and the small size of political units made it easy for kidnappers to flee from pursuit. Children at play or left at home while parents farmed were particularly easy victims. Equiano reported that it was common practice in his day for children to be brought to a neighbour's for safe keeping when the adults had to be absent and the children often spent their days in trees watching for kidnappers. But one day when he and his sister had been left alone they were seized by two men and a woman who ran off with them into the forest.[86] Although the Aro, like the coastal traders, did not find it good business to engage in kidnapping themselves, they had no compunction about dealing with those who did. The present Paramount Chief of Arochukwu says that such transactions even ended with a feast: 'In some cases when women left their children at home while they went to the farms, kidnappers would take them and sell them to the Aro, who would kill a goat for them.'[87] Another source reports that many people used to sell kidnapped children to the Aro to realize enough money to purchase prestigious titles.[88]

It is significant that one of the crimes mentioned frequently in the Intelligence Reports as grounds for sale into slavery was kidnapping. Evidently many were tempted to try their hand at child stealing, whether for titles, goods, or other riches. Dr. Falconbridge was of the firm opinion that, rather than to war, it was 'to *kidnapping*, and to crimes, (and many of these fabricated as a pretext) the slave trade owes its chief support'.[89]

How many were enslaved by each of these methods?

These four categories are by no means discrete. Kidnapping was merely raiding on a small scale and raiding of the scale described on the Cross River was little more than organized kidnapping. Nor, ultimately, is there much difference between selling a kinsman or

---

[85] Basden, *Niger Ibos*, p. 245. Harris, 'Some Aspects of Slavery', p. 42. Igwegbe, *Original History*, p. 75. R. Kanu-Umoh, *Slave Markets in East Nigeria* (Umuahia-Ibeku: Language Academy, n.d.), pp. 11–12.

[86] Equiano, 'Early Travels', p. 85.

[87] Interview, Chief Oji, Arochukwu.

[88] Igwegbe, *Original History*, p. 55.

[89] Falconbridge, *Account of the Slave Trade*, p. 15.

kidnapping a stranger when the purpose of the action is to raise the money to buy a gun, pay a debt, or escape hunger. Perversions of justice likewise blend into economic choices or legalized kidnapping. Yet while the four categories blend into one another, they do represent bins into which the actual cases might be sorted.

The evidence presented so far has been of an impressionistic nature and, while it suggests that more were enslaved in south-eastern Nigeria by kidnapping than by war, it does not enable any further weighting of the categories. However, certain other types of evidence do suggest more clearly how the categories should be quantified. As some modes of enslavement applied more to children than adults or women more than men, indications of the age and sex of those enslaved would give some clues as to the manner of their enslavement. By chance these figures are available for five ship-loads of slaves from the Bight of Biafra (one from Bonny and two each from Old Calabar and New Calabar) during a half century to-ward the beginning of the trade. By design the sex and estimated age of each slave emancipated in Sierra Leone were recorded during the first half of the nineteenth century. Most of the persons registered in Sierra Leone were between seven and thirty years of age, with those sixteen and above being considered adults. The nineteenth-century figures are more reliable, representing over 30,000 slaves shipped from the Bight of Biafra. Both sets of statistics are presented in tables 1 and 2.

While the percentage of adult men in each case is nearly identical, adult women were nearly three times as likely to be enslaved in the seventeenth century as in the nineteenth, despite the fact that the Royal African Company had instructed its captains in the seven-teenth century that a ratio of two males per female would produce the most saleable cargo. Hingston in his diary of the *Arthur's* voyage to New Calabar in 1677 explained that he had gone against this recommendation, buying instead three women for every four men, because he found the women to be in much better health.[90] The nine-teenth-century figures conform to the recommended ratio perfectly which seems to have been the case at least from the 1780s since Dr. Falconbridge reports that slaves from the Bight of Biafra 'consist chiefly of men and boys, the women seldom exceeding a third of the whole number'.[91] The most dramatic difference is in the

[90] Hutchinson, 'Slaver's Diary', p. 143.
[91] Falconbridge, *Account of the Slave Trade*, p. 12.

percentage of the children, who made up only 15 per cent of the
earlier cargoes, but 39 per cent of the latter. The actual proportion
of children in the trade may have been even higher since by the nineteenth century there was also a large market for children as domestic
slaves because they were more readily assimilated than adults.

TABLE 1

*Age and sex of slaves from the Bight of Biafra, 1659–1702, based on
the records of five ships*

| | Number | | | Percentage | | |
	Male	Female	Total	Male	Female	Total
Adult	500	424	924	47	40	86
Child	97	49	146	9	5	14
Total	597	473	1,070	56	44	100

Percentages do not add up because of rounding.
Source: Appendix C.

TABLE 2

*Age and sex of slaves from the Bight of Biafra emancipated in Sierra
Leone, 1821–39, based on the records of 109 ships*

| | Number | | | Percentage | | |
	Male	Female	Total	Male	Female	Total
Adult	11,171	3,713	14,884	46	15	61
Child	5,024	4,594	9,618	20	19	39
Total	16,195	8,307	24,502	66	34	100

Source: Appendix D.

These figures are highly instructive in evaluating the ways in which
people were enslaved. Children cannot have been sold for crimes
or debts of their own, or as victims of oracular decisions, nor can
the number of abnormal children have increased by itself. Since slave
raids do not seem to have been frequent in this period, one can only
conclude that over two-fifths of the slaves sold in the nineteenth century must have been kidnapped or sold by their families for some
reason.[92]

[92] With typical perceptivity Waddell noted in his diary that the Calabar people:
'pretend that the slaves they purchase are sold in payment of the debts they have

There is another way to test the relative importance of the various modes of enslavement in this region. In compiling his monumental *Polyglotta Africana*, S. W. Koelle recorded the ways in which many of his informants had been enslaved. Since some forty of these informants had passed through ports in the Bight of Biafra, they provide an indication of the prevailing methods by which people were enslaved in the 1820s. There are several biases built into these figures. Koelle's informants were nearly all men who had been enslaved in their adult years, yet as has been shown adult males constituted fewer than half of the slaves taken from the hinterland in this period. More seriously, since there is generally only one biography per language, the figures do not reflect the number of slaves produced by each linguistic group. Thus over half of the informants from this area were North-west Bantu from Cameroon, although this group produced only about a sixth of the slaves. The Ibibio, who produced as many slaves, have only a single informant.

While the reasons for enslavement given by those shipped from this coast were similar in distribution to those given by Koelle's informants throughout the continent,[93] when broken down further the responses reveal important variations within this region. By dividing the informants into two groups, those from the northern part of the region under study (Benue Valley and Cameroon Grasslands) and those from the southern part (Igbo, Ibibio, Cross River and coastal Cameroon), the most significant variations are brought out, as can be seen in Table 3. While nearly two-fifths of the informants from the northern zone, which was heavily raided by the Fulani and others during this period, were enslaved as a result of wars, not a single southerner was enslaved for this reason. In return, kidnapping was twice as frequent in the southern region as in the north. This seems to have been particularly true in the Igbo–Ibibio area where four out of the six informants reported being kidnapped. Finally, in the southern zone sale by relatives was over four times as frequent as in Africa as a whole. Since the earlier discussion of modes of enslavement in the hinterland indicated that children were more likely to be kidnapped than adults and both women and children to be sold

contracted, or for crime or as prisoners of war ... At the same time they don't deny the fact that they buy very many children who cannot have been sold for such causes...' Waddell, 'Journal', IX (1852), f. 120.

[93] See the analysis by P. E. H. Hair, 'The Enslavement of Koelle's Informants', *JAH* VI (1965), 193–203.

TABLE 3

Manner of enslavement of Koelle's informants
by percentage of known instances

Manner of Enslavement	Bight of Biafra		Total	All of Africa
	Northern Zone	Southern Zone		
Taken in war	38(10)[a]	— —	24(10)	34
Kidnapped	15(4)	33(5)	22(9)	30
Sold by relatives or superiors	4(1)	33(5)	15(6)	7
Sold to pay debts	8(2)	13(2)	10(4)	7
Judicial process	12(3)	13(2)	12(5)	11
Other reasons	23(6)	7(1)	17(7)	11
Totals	100(26)	100(15)	100(41)	100(143)

[a] Numbers in parentheses indicate number of informants in sample. Percentages do not add up because of rounding.
Sources: Koelle, *Polyglotta Africana*. The figures for all of Africa are from P. E. H. Hair, 'The Enslavement of Koelle's Informants', *JAH* VI (1965), 193–203, and personal communication from Dr. Hair.

by their relatives than men, both of these modes of enslavement were surely higher than Koelle's adult male examples indicate.

5. THE SLAVE TRADE AND DEPOPULATION

How great an effect the overseas slave trade had on African population densities is an important but not easily answered question. Although on first consideration a drop in population might be expected to have occurred, a sufficiently dense and fertile population could have added as many or more souls through normal reproduction as it lost through that trade and thus would have suffered a decline only in its rate of growth but not in the over-all size of its population. Indeed, a rapidly multiplying population might have found release from pressures on its resources through the forced export of some of its members.

The key to deciding which of these circumstances actually prevailed is a knowledge of the population size and growth rate at the time of the slave trade, a subject for which there is only the most limited information. Despite the absence of census figures or other estimates contemporary with the slave trade, Professor J. D. Fage has made a valiant effort to chart population change in West

Africa over the past several centuries. With the aid of his colleague, Dr. P. K. Mitchell, Fage reached this conclusion about the demographic effect of the slave trade in West Africa:

... extrapolating backwards from twentieth century censuses and estimates and rates of increase suggests that the population of West Africa may have been at least 25 million at the beginning of the eighteenth century, with a rate of natural increase of about 15 per 1000 [per decade] at the beginning of the century and of about 19 per 1000 at the end. If these estimates are anything like right, then at first sight the effect of the export slave trade in the eighteenth century may have been more or less to check population growth, the rates of slave exports and natural increases being of the same order. For other centuries, the effect of the slave trade would have been slight ...[94]

While calculations arrived at in so indirect a manner are poor substitutes for contemporary records, Fage has been sufficiently cautious in his assumptions that his over-all assessment is very probably correct. Nevertheless, his conclusion that the Atlantic slave trade no more than temporarily checked population growth in West Africa as a whole may conceal the magnitude of the trade's demographic effects in particular regions of West Africa, such as south-eastern Nigeria, which supplied a large share of the total trade.

Now as it happens Roger Anstey has recently used Fage's methods to calculate the effects of the slave trade on this very region.[95] On the basis of his calculation of an average of 14,000 slaves per year having been shipped from the Bight of Biafra during the period 1761–1810, Dr. Anstey asks how large a population would have been needed to supply such numbers without demographic loss at the growth rate assumed by Fage for this period. He finds that the area of colonial Eastern Nigeria–West Cameroon would have needed a population twice what Fage's method would give it even by 1850 to have done this. At this point the train of Anstey's thought becomes difficult to follow. Surprisingly in light of these calculations he concludes that this region did not suffer depopulation, because, he suggests, an 'unknown' but 'significant' number of slaves came from areas further north, or perhaps, as he speculates in a footnote, because the natural growth rate of the population in this region was greater than the figure Fage employed for West Africa as a whole.

[94] Fage, 'Slavery', pp. 399–400. See also J. D. Fage, 'The Effect of the Export Slave Trade on African Populations', in *The Population Factor in African Studies*, ed. R. P. Moss and R. J. A. R. Rathbone (London: Univ. of London Press, 1975), pp. 15–23.
[95] Anstey, *Atlantic Slave Trade*, pp. 70–82.

It is the second factor which is the more likely, especially since evidence presented earlier in this chapter suggests that even at the height of the nineteenth-century disturbances in Northern Nigeria only a small number of captives from that area were sold from the Bight of Biafra. Indeed, the very high population densities recorded in south-eastern Nigeria in the twentieth century have suggested to many observers, including Fage, that the region must have enjoyed a natural rate of growth sufficient to have offset the population loss due to the slave trade. More direct evidence that the population of the region was growing rapidly at the time the slave trade began to increase were cited above in Chapter II, of which the Igbo expansion into the Ngwa, Bende, and Arochukwu areas is the most dramatic.

Support for the argument that the export slave trade had only a moderate impact on this region's population growth may also be drawn from three other circumstances. First, while some slaves surely lost their lives before leaving the coastal ports, the fact that warfare was not an important means of procuring slaves in the southern and most populous part of the hinterland means that there would have been little loss of life in the process of enslavement. Secondly, since females were only one-third of the slaves exported during the peak years, the rate of natural increase was slowed only by a corresponding ratio. In a polygamous society such as that of the hinterland where women rarely remain unmarried during their fertile years the ability of the population to reproduce is affected only by loss of females. Although actual population loss would have resulted from the export of both males and females, the rate of natural increase would have been reduced only by the loss of females. Finally, there is every indication that slaves were procured from the hinterland in direct proportion to the population of each part. The indications in the previous chapter of the numbers produced by each ethnic group are in essential proportion to their present numerical importance. Although some trading communities such as the Aro and the Agwa'aguna were represented in Koelle's lists only by their domestic slaves who had originally come from elsewhere, there is little indication that any hinterland group were made to produce slaves over a long period of time in numbers disproportionate to their population. Both the Agbaja Igbo and the Isuama Igbo, who were so numerous in Sierra Leone, were among the largest Igbo groups in the twentieth century when censuses were first taken.[96]

[96] While one could not expect perfect accord based upon the estimates of Koelle's

Because slaves were obtained in small numbers and transported to the coast through a system of roads and markets that reached into every corner of the region, the trade tended to be very evenly distributed.

This essay has focused on those aspects of the slave trade in southeastern Nigeria which lend themselves to an objective treatment: the statistics, routes, ethnic origins, modes of enslavement, and demographic effects of the trade. In so doing it has run the risk of neglecting those aspects of the trade which do not lend themselves to such an analysis—aspects which the older treatments of the trade, for all their lack of objectivity, never lost sight of: the tremendous fear and injustice which the trade produced. In closing this section, therefore, one can do no better than to quote from Hope Waddell, a man who has been called 'an accurate and remarkably sympathetic, impartial and objective observer, ... a historian in spirit',[97] a man who perhaps because of these qualities occasionally found himself under attack by his fellow missionaries for being too sympathetic to African customs. In detailing the ways in which hinterland peoples became enslaved Waddell mentioned famine, misfortune, debt, war, and crime, but added:

Less by these means, however, than by others under the cover of them, was the system of slavery perpetrated and the trade supplied. Throughout the vast interior the poor and the orphan were everywhere harassed with claims of debt they could not pay, and for which they and theirs were sold. Every infringement of custom became a great offence, and every offence a crime, involving death or slavery. Plundering expeditions were made for the express purpose of capturing slaves; and kidnapping though everywhere condemned, was everywhere practiced.[98]

In another place Waddell recorded a conversation with King Eyo Honesty, who, as a dealer in slaves, was in an even better position to judge the system; the slaves, he said,

come from different countries and were sold for different reasons—some as prisoners of war, some for debt, some for breaking their country's laws, and

---

informants, the number of slaves from each Igbo group in Sierra Leone corresponds in rough proportion to that group's population as recorded in the first census of the region in 1921. The Ishielu, who were 0.2 per cent of the Igbo population in 1921, had 4 members in Sierra Leone; the Ohafia, who were about 0.7 per cent of the Igbo, had 6 in Sierra Leone; the Agbaja, who were 16.3 per cent of the Igbo, had 40 in Sierra Leone. See Koelle, *Polyglotta*, p. 8, and Talbot, *Peoples*, IV, 57.

[97] Jones, 'Introduction', p. ix.
[98] Waddell, *Twenty-Nine Years*, pp. 315–16.

some by great men, who hated them. The king of a town sells whom he dislikes or fears; his wives and children are sold in turn by his successor. A man inveigles his brother's children to his house, and sells them. The brother says nothing, but watches his opportunity, and sells the children of the other.[99]

Both of these quotations convey qualities of the trade impossible to capture in figures or objective analysis: its capriciousness and disruptiveness. For however much enslavement was regulated by the law of man and of the market-place, it was also subject to extreme lawlessness and cruelty.

[99] Waddell, *Twenty-Nine Years*, p. 429.

CHAPTER IV

The Organization of the Slave Trade

As a result of the tremendous expansion of the Atlantic slave trade in the eighteenth century the Bight of Biafra became one of the most important trading areas in sub-Saharan Africa, supplying one person in every six for that vast involuntary migration in the half-century from 1761 to 1810. During the next quarter century this region not only increased the volume of its slave trade, but also developed one of the most important 'legitimate' trades in Africa in palm-oil. The rapidity with which this overseas trade developed and the high level at which it was sustained over so many decades have aroused much curiosity about the institutions and persons behind it. This curiosity has been further whetted by the fact that this trade was not associated with any large states as it was in important slaving areas elsewhere along the Gulf of Guinea.

The organization and effects of the slave trade are the subject of the next three chapters. This chapter examines the political and economic institutions of the hinterland and the difficult changes which the slave trade produced in them. Chapter V will look more closely at the structure of one of the most interesting and controversial of the trading communities of the hinterland, the Aro of Arochukwu. Finally, Chapter VI will seek to place the economic effects of the trade in slaves in the broader context of over-all trade and economic development.

Most of the evidence for reconstructing the commercial and political history of the hinterland during the peak years of the slave trade is, unfortunately, indirect. Some information can be derived from oral histories, but much of the information must be based on descriptions of the institutions of the hinterland as they were during and just before the early colonial period. Nevertheless, it is possible to reconstruct the main outlines of change in the slave-trade era by combining this information with what has already been discovered about their entire history, aided by fragmentary oral traditions and isolated contemporary accounts.

It must be emphasized at the outset that there was nothing

inevitable or coerced about the role of this region in the slave trade. While the over-all dimensions of the Atlantic slave trade were fixed by European and American demand, the magnitude of the response in each region of western Africa was largely a product of local conditions, preferences, and capacities. In the western Niger Delta, for example, the Benin Kingdom, despite considerable commerce in other goods, 'either could not or would not become a slave-trading state on a grand scale'.[1] In contrast the eastern delta could and did expand its trade in slaves sufficiently during the eighteenth century to capture a major share of the Atlantic trade. How this expansion was accomplished has generally not been well understood by historians. Curtin, for example, is not out of the mainstream in suggesting that the unusually high level of trade may be explained by the political development of the coastal states and of Arochukwu.[2] The intent of this chapter is to revise traditional explanations through two shifts in emphasis: (1) paying primary attention to the traders of the hinterland rather than to the coastal middlemen, who depended on the former for their supplies of slaves which they passed on to European slavers; and (2) focusing on changes in economic institutions which were far more crucial to the growth of overseas trade than were those in political institutions.

1. COASTAL TRADING STATES

While the main focus of this chapter is on the trading communities of the hinterland, it is useful to begin by examining the coastal traders, notably those of New Calabar, Bonny, and Old Calabar. As was shown in earlier chapters, commerce in the Bight of Biafra began much earlier than the slave trade of the eighteenth century. Because of their ability to cover long distances in their canoes, the coastal fishermen had become active in trading marine products and other valued goods both with their immediate inland neighbours and, it seems, with other coastal communities. After the arrival of the first Portuguese mariners, a small but important overseas trade was added. Recent studies have demonstrated that in the eighteenth century, as the trade in slaves expanded, the coastal communities underwent gradual but decisive territorial growth, political central-

[1] Ryder, *Benin*, p. 198.
[2] Curtin, *Slave Trade*, p. 228.

ization, and commercial specialization which gave them their special character as trading states.[3]

The first feature of this transformation was a reduction in the number of communities trading with the Europeans and a corresponding expansion in the size, wealth, and power of those communities which remained active in the trade. In part the reduction in the number of trading states was due to the natural desire of European captains to be able to gather an entire cargo from a single port rather than taking on partial cargoes at each of several smaller ports. In part also the ports which prospered were those which were favoured by nature with safe anchorages and other geographical advantages. However, in greater measure this process appears to have been due to the efforts and proclivities of the citizens of the successful communities themselves. Of all the Kalabari Ijo settlements which had traded with Europeans in the earlier centuries, it was not Ifoko, located nearest to the anchorage, which captured the slave trade, but Elem Kalabari (the New Calabar of the trading records) which had better connections with the hinterland and a more competitive tradition than its neighbours.[4] Similarly in the western delta it was the Itsekiri town of Warri which became more important in the slave trade than Benin, which had been the object of so much earlier European interest, again largely through local initiative.[5]

The movements to a more limited number of coastal entrepôts had begun in the seventeenth century, but the process was accelerated during the eighteenth. For example, when James Barbot traded on the Cross River in 1698, he dealt with representatives of a dozen communities on both sides of the river, of which the Efik towns of Old Calabar were the most important.[6] During the subsequent decades, as Latham has shown, the Efik expanded their dominance over the entire lower river and 'excluded all other peoples from direct access to the Europeans, establishing and maintaining a position as monopolistic middlemen'.[7] Similar processes of monopolization were at work in the eastern delta, notably along the Rio Real, partly through the use of force, but also as a result of smaller

[3] The description of the changes in the coastal states in this period is drawn from Jones, *Trading States*, Chapters IV, V, X, XI, XII; Latham, *Old Calabar*, Chapters 3 and 4; Alagoa, 'Niger Delta States', pp. 269–303.

[4] Alagoa, 'Niger Delta States', p. 284.

[5] Ryder, *Benin*, pp. 75, 197–8.

[6] Barbot, 'Abstract of a Voyage', p. 465.

[7] Latham, *Old Calabar*, p. 49.

communities seeking the protection of one trading state against another.

The expansion of these coastal communities was more for commercial monopolization than for political aggrandizement. In most internal matters the formerly independent communities remained autonomous, but in their participation in the overseas trade they were subordinate to the major trading states. Even in the commercial sphere, however, the process of amalgamation was limited. No one trading state was ever able to dominate the entire coast. For example, Bonny and New Calabar, though they shared a common estuary, remained rival states. Nor during the peak years of the slave trade did the coastal states extend their commercial empires very far inland. Instead they traded through intermediaries which themselves traded with others still further inland. Bonny, for example, traded with Okrika, which controlled the trade to Ikwerre and Ogoni, and with Ndoki, via the Imo River, which had links with the Aro.

A second aspect of coastal life transformed during the eighteenth century was the government of these coastal communities. In New Calabar the largely ritual and ceremonial office of king developed into a far more powerful and authoritarian office under King Amakiri, the royal house effectively absorbing all other political structures into it. The situation in Bonny under King Pepple was similar though centralization was not carried quite so far. Among the Efik of Old Calabar the process differed significantly in detail but was analagous in over-all effect. By the second decade of the nineteenth century Duke Ephraim of Duke Town held both the office of King (Obong) and the highest title of the Ekpe Society (Eyamba) which dominated trading relations. In addition his ward had a virtual monopoly on the export trade. In part this process of political centralization in the coastal states can be traced to the desire of the European traders to negotiate the terms of trade and to collect debts through a single quasi-absolute ruler, but in this case as well the desire and skill of such rulers to use the wealth, power, and patronage which thus accrued to them to increase their political and economic power was the major factor for this transformation. Rulers like Amakiri, Pepple, and Duke Ephraim were men of tremendous imagination, energy, and determination who succeeded where lesser men would have failed.

The third major change in the coastal communities during the eighteenth century was a movement toward economic specialization that came close to eliminating all occupations unrelated to the overseas trade from the lives of their inhabitants. By the early nineteenth century the cultivation of crops was said to have ceased entirely at Bonny.[8] The results in the other coastal states were similar, though not necessarily so extreme. In the Ijo delta this economic specialization also manifested itself in the creation of canoe houses. The canoe house differed from the older lineage organization of these communities in several respects: (1) it commonly grew rapidly in size through the addition of large numbers of slaves from the hinterland, (2) it was led by men of talent promoted rigorously from among slave and free members alike who demonstrated the necessary abilities, and (3) it formed a single economic unit, a sort of trading company, owning giant trading canoes and jointly responsible for house profits and debts. In Old Calabar and in some waterside trading communities one stage removed from the coast, such as Okrika,[9] canoe houses did not develop a fully corporate economic structure, though lineage units tended to be directed much more toward commercial purposes than was formerly the case.

2. HINTERLAND TRADING ORGANIZATION

The trading states along the Bight of Biafra were not so different in size and organization from those elsewhere along the Guinea coast. The Akan states, Little Popo, Whydah, Porto Novo, and Lagos to the west were all small, specialized states built around ports visited by European ships. Where this region differed was in the organization of the hinterland which possessed no political units comparable to the Ashanti, Dahomean, or Yoruba kingdoms, despite the fact that by the eighteenth century many of the circumstances favouring state growth were present. The traditions of origin presented in Chapter II suggest that the population of the hinterland was increasing and expanding into once lightly settled areas. At the same time, along the Niger small bands of emigrants from the Igala and Benin monarchies were imparting the trappings and traditions of kingship to previously egalitarian communities. Finally, owing to this growing population, but more to the new contacts with Europeans, trade was expanding. In such circumstances the further growth of trade in the eighteenth century and, the continued population growth, might have been expected to promote the development

[8]Jackson, *Journal*, p. 148.
[9]Porter, 'Intelligence Report, Okrika', p. 18.

of larger, more centralized states. Yet this did not happen. Equiano, whose homeland was exposed to enough Benin influence for him to consider it an outlying province of the Benin Kingdom, could only describe its prevailing form of warfare as 'irruptions of one little state or district on the other'.[10] Nor did the passage of time do much to alter the scale of political sentiments in the hinterland. A century after Equiano, James Africanus Horton, whose father was an Igbo, wrote of the Igbo spirit: 'They would not, as a rule, allow anyone to act the superior over them; nor sway their conscience by coercion, to the performance of any act, whether good or bad, when they have not the inclination to do so; hence there is not that unity among them that is found among other tribes; in fact everyone likes to be his own master.'[11]

This spirit of individualism and the small scale of political organization which was intimately linked with it were not signs of excessive conservatism or an inability to organize effectively. The great volume of the trade which was built up and sustained in the eighteenth and nineteenth centuries clearly points up the ability of hinterland peoples to organize large-scale and complex activities. Yet, as this section will seek to demonstrate, the structures of the long-distance trade were closely linked to the traditions and customs of the small-scale and individualistic hinterland society. In order to study the commercial life of the hinterland, therefore, it is necessary to look first at the social and political institutions through which and round which the trading life was constructed.

Because there are few extant records, one cannot hope to describe the political organization of south-eastern Nigeria as it actually was in the early eighteenth century. Even for the early twentieth century evidence is scanty. Yet it is possible to sketch the structural principles which, though described only in recent decades, have long been the determinants of political life in this region. These determinants defined the normal operations of political life and suggest the manner in which the large volume of trade was organized.

The basic principle of social and political life south-eastern Nigeria was descent. People of common descent would normally reside together and order their common affairs. The basic unit of residence and of many economic activities consisted of a living patriarch and his sons with their wives, children, and other depen-

[10]Equiano, 'Early Travels', p. 77.
[11]Horton, *West African Countries*, p. 164.

dants. This 'extended family' was self-governing in all internal matters. Neighbouring extended families sharing descent from a deceased ancestor formed a larger descent group called *umunna* by the Igbo, *ekpuk* by the Ibibio, and referred to as a localized patrilineage or kindred in the anthropological literature.[12] The patrilineages were the basic political units of society and generally had the strongest allegiance of any unit. The ritual lineage head (Igbo: *Okpara*, Ibibio: *Ete Ekpuk*) had great moral authority as the guardian of the ancestral shrines and thus of the ultimate source of authority and lineage solidarity. Solidarity was also reinforced by the fact that the patrilineage was commonly the land holding group, all of whose members were entitled to an appropriate share.[13]

Neighbouring lineages formed a village, often named for an ancestor held common to all. Adjoining villages were frequently associated together in village-groups, also called 'towns', which commonly claimed descent from 'brothers' equal in number to the component villages. The village-group was usually the largest unit to function politically on any regular basis. Unity at the village and village-group level was strengthened by the possession of common guardian spirits (Igbo: *arosi*, Ibibio: *ndem*), common markets, and communal lands for hunting, meetings, shrines, etc.[14]

Above the village or village-group level there existed clans and dialect groups, which rarely had any political functions although their members often had a strong sense of solidarity. This was true of the Ngwa and Efik, for example. Clans and larger units, often claiming remote common ancestors and experiences, shared many customs and institutions, especially food taboos and shrines. The largest units differed from each other in dialect, social institutions and nomenclature, and a large variety of other customs. Much of this variation was due to the considerable borrowing and intermingling that had taken place across ethnolinguistic frontiers. For example, as was shown earlier, many Igbo along the Niger have

[12]Forde and Jones, *Ibo and Ibibio*, pp. 15–17, 71–2; C. K. Meek, *Report on the Social and Political Organization in Owerri Division* (Lagos: Government Printer, 1934), para. 11.

[13]L. T. Chubb, *Ibo Land Tenure*, 2nd edn. (Ibadan: Ibadan Univ. Press, 1961), pp. 17–18; S. N. C. Obi, *The Ibo Law of Property* (London: Butterworths, 1963), pp. 42–50; Martin, *Oil Palm*, p. 6; S. E. Johnson, 'Intelligence Report on the Ukanafun Clan, Abak District', 1933, p. 25, NAI, CSO 26/3/29627.

[14]In recent times such 'little states', as Equiano called them, have averaged only 2,000 to 10,000 citizens and may have been even smaller in his day; see Jones, 'Olaudah Equiano', p. 63.

adopted political structures and titles, art styles and techniques, and other customs from Benin, while other Igbo groups exhibit noticeable Igala, Ijo, Ekoi, and Ibibio influences.

Not only did a striking uniformity exist in the size of the political units in this region, but there was also a great similarity in their basic institutions of government. According to an official comparative study of the region by G. I. Jones, 'whether in the Ogoja, Rivers, Ibo or Ibibio provinces, [the traditional form of] the government of every local community consisted of a federation of equivalent segments whose leading men met together in a council which was said to consist of the senior age-grade in the community and was referred to collectively as the elders.'[15]

The organization of political life was essentially segmentary. Each descent group had total authority over its own internal affairs and combined with other units to regulate matters of mutual concern. Disputes between patrilineages, for example, were brought up at village council meetings; those between villages at village-group meetings. The lineage head and other leading members of the lineage represented their unit on the village council and the village head and its leading members sat on the village-group council. In theory such a system might have operated at higher levels as well, but the requirement of unanimity made that impractical.

The segmentary nature of this system was also evident in political fission. Despite the ties that bound them, land pressures and internal disputes might lead units to split, with small groups moving off to combine with other units or to found new communities. Although the insistence on descent might seem to make such reorganization impossible, in practice it was often easier to translate political realities into kinship idioms than vice versa. There seemed to be an optimum size for this type of organization and large village-groups might divide even when occupying contiguous farmland. More often distance forced the split as migrations to new lands, as in the case of the Ngwa crossing the Imo River, made attendance at common meetings and shrines impossible.

Such a political system lacked *rulers*, relying instead on a variety of official and unofficial *leaders*. Some of these held offices which were ascriptively filled, e.g. lineage and village heads were generally the oldest men in their respective units. As living symbols of their segment's unity, they were generally respected as prime inter-

---

[15] *Jones Report*, p. 6.

mediaries with the ancestral spirits and thus possessed enormous influence. But as political officers their authority was limited to presiding at council meetings. They could make no important decision outside of a council meeting, issue no orders, but only argue their point of view along with the rest. Decisions were made by the representatives of the component units of each council and no decision was binding on a unit not represented or not in agreement with the others. At a village council meeting each patrilineage was represented by its leading men. These were generally its senior office holder and other elders. Anyone, however, might attend and voice an opinion; the elders were only expected to represent lineage opinion, not make it.

In most aspects of life in south-eastern Nigeria leadership was achieved by personal talent and determination. The natural leaders of the community rose to the fore through their skill in oratory, valour in battle, success in farming, hunting, or trading, strength in wrestling, general intelligence, and good judgement. Those possessing these and other talents could command public respect. Such leaders and opinion-makers were a force in any community. For example, a quick-witted young man who was skilful with words might be invited to attend the village council meeting along with the elders and even act as their spokesman. Age alone was no sufficient qualification for leadership. As the Igbo proverb puts it, 'A child who washes his hands can eat with his elders.'[16]

By stressing the possibilities of personal achievement open to every citizen, this social system promoted individual initiative, the effort to bring out that potentiality which a recent author has termed 'the king in every man'.[17] At the same time society stressed a fundamental egalitarianism not only among the segments of a community united in balanced opposition, but at the individual level as well. An excess of individualism was held in check by the loyalty and obligations each citizen owed the members of his family, lineage, village, and town. No matter how tall it might be, the Ibibio proverb says, 'one tree doesn't make a forest'. The result of these social values and institutions was to encourage initiative in the new trade, but to discourage the development of autocratic government.

In large measure the slave trade in the hinterland was not

[16]Elechukwu N. Njaka, 'Igbo Political Institutions and Transition', Ph.D. dissertation, University of California, Los Angeles, 1971, p. 614.
[17]Henderson, *King in Every Man*.

conducted through institutions as centralized as those at the coast. This fact may be seen in Equiano's remembrances of traders in his home area near the middle of the eighteenth century:

We have also markets, at which I have been frequently with my mother. These are sometimes visited by stout mahogany-coloured men from the south-west of us: we call them Oye-Eboe, which term signifies red men living at a distance. They generally bring us firearms, gunpowder, hats, beads and dried fish. The last we esteemed a great rarity, as our waters were only brooks and springs. These articles they barter with us for odoriferous woods and earth, and our salt of wood-ashes.[18]

These traders also dealt in slaves and were occasionally sold slaves acquired in war by Equiano's people, though in this case the transactions took place though the village chief, not in the market-place. This account from a time when the overseas slave trade was expanding rapidly reveals several important aspects of commercial life in the hinterland. The trade in slaves appears not to have been a new creation, but was added to an older regional trade in which beads and fish were exchanged for forest products. The trade in slaves was conducted by itinerant professional traders whose homeland was afar off. Finally, there is no hint that these traders had or sought any influence over local politics. The description thus suggests that the new trade did not produce such radical internal changes in the hinterland as it had at the coast. Moreover, the absence both of direct European influence and of indigenous state systems in the hinterland precluded any totally new institutions being introduced or imposed from outside. It would appear, therefore, that the expansion of slave trading in the hinterland was accommodated by a proliferation of existing trading techniques in the hands of existing trading communities with some modifications to handle the size of the new trade.

One of the ways the eighteenth-century trade must have been organized was through a great expansion and extension of traditional forms of inter-personal and inter-group relations. In the small-scale communities of the hinterland a man's social ties were defined by descent, residence, and marriage. Through his father a man

[18] Equiano, 'Early Travels', p. 75. Ekejiuba strongly implies that these 'red' traders were Aro in her 'Aro Trade System', p. 14, while Alagoa has used the same source to argue against there having been any Aro influence in Equiano's time since no mention was made of oracles ('Niger Delta States', p. 299). Both conclusions are unwarranted if one accepts the convincing arguments of G. I. Jones that Equiano was from the Northern Ika Igbo west of the Niger, an area which was never within the Aro sphere of operations; see Jones, 'Olaudah Equiano', p. 61.

became a member of a particular extended family which was part of a land-holding, residentially localized patrilineage. Through his mother he also came to be a recognized affiliate of her lineage group and was entitled to certain forms of hospitality from them. Since a man's lineage was a part of a village and a village-group and/or clan, he also partook of the rights and duties of these residential groups and participated in their organizational structures. For example, many Igbo communities were divided into two halves or moieties for a variety of organizational purposes.[19] When a man married he acquired a new set of relations, his in-laws or affines. Since the localized patrilineages and sometimes larger units as well, such as villages and moieties, were exogamous, his marriage brought ties to a group of people from distance parts of his village-group or clan or from unrelated villages. Thus a man's social relations comprised maternal and paternal kinsmen, neighbours (generally sharing some distant ancestor), and one or more sets of in-laws.

Since movement from one part of the region was not defended by any organized police force nor rights of entry by any passport system, traders' rights and security could diminish sharply as they moved away from home. Before a strong climate of fear was engendered by the growth of slave trading it may well have been possible for traders bringing highly desired items to small rural communities not to have had to trouble themselves too much about their safety. By opening their packs they established their welcome. Anyone tempted to slay the goose that laid the golden eggs would be restrained by his neighbours. However, the dangers inherent in slave trading, the longer distances to be covered, and the absence of any large political units to offer protection meant that even for short distances it became necessary to travel armed and in groups. An Anang trader recalled that in the nineteenth century 'Ten miles' travel was a long journey. Before a man could go on such a task he had to be well armed with knives and a gun.'[20] Such a condition was also noted by an explorer among the neighbouring Ngwa, where 'not a man apparently moved a step without carrying a naked sword in one hand and a rifle at full cock in the other'.[21] To preserve their safety, traders attending the larger markets, such as Onitsha, which

[19]Forde and Jones, *Ibo and Ibibio*, p. 16.
[20]Chief Udo Akpabio quoted by Groves, 'Story of Udo Akpabio', p. 46.
[21] A. G. Leonard, 'Notes of a Journey to Bende', *Journal of the Manchester Geographical Society*, XIV (1898), 191.

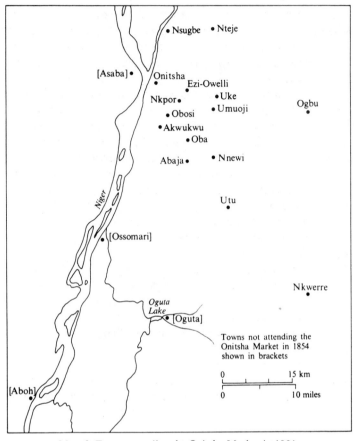

MAP 3. Towns attending the Onitsha Market in 1854.
Source: Crowther, *Journal*, p. 179

in 1854 drew people from 15 to 20 miles away to every session (see map), went in large groups of kinsmen and neighbours accompanied by armed defenders.[22]

Traders might add to their safety by travelling in armed groups and by attending only well-regulated markets, but on a journey of any length it was necessary to establish places where one could stop safely to rest, eat, and sleep. For this reason traders would also culti-

[22] Interview with Messrs. Anyeabosim Mefo and Maurice Ibe of Okozu, Oba, Idemile, 30 Dec. 1972; Oba men and some women travelled to the Onitsha market in armed groups and had regular hosts along the way.

vate the friendship of certain important men along their routes who would serve as their hosts. These friendships were cultivated through the custom of gift-exchange. The trader would present his host with some item of value and would be given something of value in return, including food, drink, and accommodation. Such bonds of hospitality could be brief or of lengthy duration and were renewed by additional gifts on suitable occasions. Termed a 'dash' by European traders, gift-exchanges were an essential preliminary to the opening of trade at the coast, and in one way or another the gifts were reciprocated by the African traders. European traders, missionaries, and early explorers understood gifts to be an essential social courtesy. African traders had long employed this custom as a means of expanding the limits of kinship relations. Traders had regular stopping places along their routes. According to an Ngwa Igbo informant: '... the heads of the families with which the traders lodged along the routes had to be given presents. The families would protect them and see them safely to the next resting place along the route. For example, I am from Mboko Ofokobe, about nine miles north of Aba; traders used to lodge with us and then we would hand them over to Ihie, some ten miles away.'[23]

In addition to gift-exchanges contacts between hosts and traders were often formalized by solemn oaths of alliance. Should either party violate the terms of the agreement, great harm would come to him through the agency of the 'medicine' or spirits sworn by. A more specialized agreement was the blood pact by which individuals and groups could create strong and enduring bonds between themselves. The rite involved each party swallowing some blood of the other and pledging to observe specified reciprocal obligations. A violation of such a pact was sure to be strongly condemned by public opinion since it was believed that the mystical sanctions it entailed would affect not only the parties who entered into it but their kindred and households as well. Because of their endurance, which often was renewed by the descendants of the original parties, and because they could be sworn between any two parties no matter how closely related or unrelated, these blood pacts were widely used to forge commercial agreements between traders and the leaders of communities they regularly visited. According to one detailed study, the Aro made such blood pacts by the thousand, which were 'the means through which Aro trade, and indeed Igbo trade up to the end of

[23] Interview with Mr. Wamua, Ngwa.

the nineteenth century, was carried on with a maximum assurance of protection and security to the traders'.[24]

Another type of protector a trader could depend on was an in-law, so it was not unusual for trading contacts to lead to marriage between the trader and a woman of his host's family. Such an alliance set up a complex set of reciprocal obligations between the two families. Some of the trading advantages may be seen in this description of an affinal relationship among the Anang Ibibio which was common throughout the region:

There is a very useful inter town relationship known as *eyeyen*. A woman from town B marries a man from town C. Her child is an eyeyen of her town. That is to say he has the freedom of both towns. He belongs to his father's town has the right of entry into his mother's town even though both towns are at active war. Such a system laid the way open for 'pour parlers' when hostilities existed and tended for peace and goodwill.[25]

With the expansion of trade and the need for more freedom of movement, great use was made of these social customs to enhance one's mobility. The more a trader prospered in the trade, moreover, the more he was able to marry additional wives and thus gain still greater mobility. The more wealthy, powerful, and numerous his in-laws, the more securely he could travel beyond his home community.

By the time of the first detailed accounts in the nineteenth century this system of trading alliances had been established on a grand scale. The most powerful trader on the lower Niger was King Obi of Aboh who controlled the slave and oil trade from Onitsha to the delta. While few details are known of his marriages, it is reported that he had 110 wives in 1841 who had been carefully chosen to keep his economic and political power intact. King Obi married one of his daughters to King Boy Amai-kunno of Brass Town in the Delta and by this marriage (plus the payment of a fee) King Boy was able to trade directly at Aboh Town instead of at an intermediate market.[26] Patterns of marriages between the important trading town of Oguta and trading communities on the Niger were well established, as well as between Oguta men and the women of other inland communities.

---

[24] Felicia Ekejiuba, 'Igba Ndu: an Igbo Mechanism of Social Control and Ajustment', *African Notes*, VII.2 (1972), 9–24; the phrase quoted is on p. 19.

[25] M. D. W. Jeffreys, 'Assessment Report on the Ikot Ekpene District, Calabar Province', 1927, p. 23, NAI, CSO 26/3/20678. *Eyeyen = eyeneyen*, literally, the child of a child.

[26] Allen and Thomson, *Narrative*, I, 237–9, 247.

There were also frequent marriages between the Igala and Igbo riverain communities.[27]

The trading network on the Cross River was similarly buttressed by an intricate web of marriage alliances. King Eyo Honesty II of Creek Town, the leading merchant of Old Calabar, scandalized the Scottish missionary Hope Waddell by the number of them he managed to centre on himself; Waddell wrote in his journal in 1851: 'I am distressed to look at his new women's yards—one for his wives, a large square containing thirty-eight domiciles of two or three rooms each with a small yard and apartments behind, for each woman and her maids; and another of less pretensions for the inferior class of "intimates," as Erasmus gently called them.'[28] King Eyo owed his political leadership of Creek Town to his connections to the town's leading families and he had made a number of strategic marriages with trading families in the hinterland of which the following are known: one wife was the daughter of the wealthiest man of Umon and another the daughter of a chief of Ikot Offiong, both important upriver trading centres.[29]

The marriage alliances were by no means confined to the riverain areas. Oral traditions collected by Ofonagoro uncovered patterns of such alliances in the Owerri–Oguta area,[30] and the present writer has found them common east of the Imo River. Throughout the region the Aro traders and settlers allied themselves with prominent local men by marrying their daughters, thus assuring themselves of a proper host in every area they visited. But they retained their separate identity and built up their numbers by refusing to allow Aro women to marry non-Aro since the children of such marriages would belong to the father's patrilineage. This practice was so strictly adhered to that the Aro departed from the ordinary Igbo rules of exogamy, marrying in the third generation even within an extended family.[31]

The techniques of eighteenth-century trade in the hinterland of

---

[27] V. H. Moult, 'Intelligence Report on the Oguta Native Court Area, Owerri Division, Owerri Province', 1934, p. 13, NAI, CSO 26/3/29835; J. O. Nzekwu, 'Onitsha', *Nigeria*, No. 50 (1956), 200.

[28] Waddell, 'Journal', VIII, 70.

[29] Ibid., 45, 75; Waddell, *Twenty-Nine Years*, p. 603; Hart Report, p. 48.

[30] Walter Ibekwe Ofonagoro, 'The Opening Up of Southern Nigeria to British Trade, and its Consequences', Ph.D. dissertation, Columbia University, 1972, pp. 87–90.

[31] Moult, 'Intelligence Report, Oguta', p. 16.

south-eastern Nigeria were not radically different from those used at the coast, where armed escorts, marriage patterns, and the kinship idiom were essential underpinnings of the canoe houses, but the hinterland's new trade, being less concentrated in locale, did produce less structural change. Thus any understanding of the commercial organization of this era must still begin with the network of individual and family alliances and ties, not at corporate units. This is true even when considering the larger communities of professional traders in the hinterland, which are the subject of the next section.

3. HINTERLAND TRADING COMMUNITIES

The possession of a network of friends, relatives, and in-laws to serve as hosts and escorts was necessary for anyone who wished to be a trader in the eighteenth century, but it was a technique used more successfully and on a larger scale by members of established trading communities than by newcomers. It would appear that a great many newcomers must have become involved as traders in slaves and its allied goods, as kidnappers and as hosts, but most of these seem to have operated only on a local level or as agents of the larger trading communities. Those communities which were already steeped in a trading tradition and which thus had established networks of customers, suppliers, and hosts, as well as organized means of protection, were better prepared to expand and adapt their operations to the new demands at the coast.

Prior experience gave the established communities an advantage in exploiting the slave trade, but there appear to have been considerable differences in the way they managed that trade. The longest, but not the busiest, trade routes ran along either edge of south-eastern Nigeria: along the Niger and its tributaries in the west, and both overland and along the Cross River to Old Calabar in the east.

The oldest and longest of the trade routes ran between the Niger Delta and the markets on the middle Niger and Benue to the north. Along its course to the delta ports this route was also punctuated by riverain markets which drew additional slaves into the trade. Just below the confluence of the Niger and Benue, near the Igala capital of Idah, was an important island market through which many slaves passed in this era. When first described by Niger explorers in the early 1830s this market, which met every ten days, was attended by

more than 6,000 persons, who came from considerable distances up
the Niger and Benue and from as far south as Aboh, at the head
of the delta. The slaves sold there, estimated at 11,000 annually or
about 300 per session, were said to come mostly from Nupe and
Kakanda, which were on the Niger above the confluence.[32] In addition to the Nupe and Kakanda it is clear from Koelle's interviews
among recaptives in Sierra Leone, that many other slaves were
bought from peoples along the river including many Igala and some
Igbo who had passed through Igala hands.[33] To the stream of slaves
descending the river from the north were added Igbo slaves from
both sides of the river. Aboh, identified as the principal slave market
on the lower Niger, supplied slaves to Brass, New Calabar and
Bonny.[34]

East of the Cross River peoples such as the Ekoi, Agwa'aguna,
and Umon who had a prior history of trading and others in that
area who did not, soon became active in the expanding slave-trade.
The Umon, who occupied the bank of the river north of the Efik
and a strategic island in the river near Arochukwu, traded with both
and were said in 1805 to have 'the richest and most powerful King
in the neighbourhood of [Old] Calabar'.[35] At least from the late
eighteenth century trade in the middle Cross River area north of
the Umon began to expand rapidly. Local peoples moved in to stake
out river-front property for trading purposes and the larger trading
peoples began to 'open up' this area to trade with the coast. Aro
traders moved into the area as did Agwa'aguna traders from just
north of Umon, while the Efik opened up an overland route to near
Ikom, on the upper river.[36] A number of Nde Ekoi (Atam) slaves
from this area who were liberated in Sierra Leone had been brought
to Old Calabar, perhaps along this route or via the Umon, and others
had gone via the Igbo territory to Bonny. A Sierra Leonean recaptive

[32] Laird and Oldfield, *Narrative*, I, 132 ff., 409; II, 254.

[33] Koelle, *Polyglotta*, pp. 6, 8–9, 20.

[34] Lander and Lander, *Niger Journal*, p. 253.

[35] By Otto Ephraim, a Liverpool-educated Efik, to Henry Nicholls, the European
Agent of the African Association in Old Calabar, in Hallett, *Records*, p. 203. Ephraim
called the king 'Eerick Boatswain'; Efik trader Antera Duke mentions Boostam as
a source of slaves for Old Calabar in his 'Diary' for 1785–7. Donald C. Simmons,
who annotated Duke's diary, suggested that Duke meant Mbiabo, a place which Duke
normally called 'Curcock'; see Forde, *Efik Traders*, pp. 30–41, 69. Umon was commonly called 'Bosun' by other in the nineteenth century and this is the more likely
meaning of both Ephraim's 'Boatswain' and Duke's 'Boostam'.

[36] Rosemary Harris, 'The History of Trade at Ikom, Eastern Nigeria', *Africa*, XLII
(1972), 122–39.

from the Boki, west of Ikom, reported having been sold at Old Calabar, while another Boki had gone to Bonny.[37]

The longest and evidently the busiest of the slave routes east of the Cross River ran overland from the Cameroon Grasslands and upper Cross River area through the sparsely populated Cameroon foothills to the Ododop people north-east of Old Calabar and then on to the Efik port. Goldie's 1865 Efik dictionary called this 'a principal slave route in former times' which still retained a small trade in his day. He named the principal stopping places along the route to a point near the modern Cameroon town of Mamfe, eight and a half days journey from Old Calabar.[38] From there the route connected with the Anyang three days further north, who in turn had connections with the Cameroon Grasslands around Bamanda.[39] Although raids by the Fulani and others in the Grasslands increased the number of slaves descending this route in the 1820s and 1830s, raids probably were not so important earlier.[40]

Despite the length of the routes on the Niger and east of the Cross River, the figures compiled in Chapter III suggest that persons from outside the Igbo–Ibibio area constituted only a relatively small portion of the slaves from the Bight of Biafra, probably not more than a quarter of the nineteenth-century total, less in the eighteenth century. Thus these long routes were less significant than the shorter trade routes in the densely populated areas between the rivers. As was shown in Chapter II the western section of the hinterland, along the Niger, was densely settled and had a tradition of trade which can be traced back to the days of Igbo-Ukwu. The course of the trading history of this section is little known, but by the early eighteenth century the people of Awka and Nkwerre, who were itinerant blacksmiths and craftsmen, must have been well established as

---

[37] Koelle, *Polyglotta*, pp. 10–11, 19. For the identification of these peoples I am indebted to Winston, 'Cross River Languages', pp. 78, 126.

[38] Goldie, *Dictionary*, p. 353, entry under 'Adadop'.

[39] The Anyang are a branch of the Bantoid cluster north of Mamfe, concerning whom see Murdock, *Africa*, 31:1. Goldie says the route extends to 'Mbudukom' which the list of place names which he gives under 'Mbudikom' makes clear is the Cameroon Grasslands area (*Dictionary*, p. 359).

[40] Koelle, *Polyglotta*, pp. 11–13, 20, records the capture of a number of these poor souls by the 'Tibara'; for identification of Koelle's languages see Winston, 'Cross River Languages', 78–80 and David Dalby, 'Provisional Identification of Languages in the *Polyglotta Africana*', *Sierra Leone Language Review*, III (1964), p. 87. For identification of the Tibara see Merran McCulloch, *et al.*, *Peoples of Central Cameroons* (London: Oxford Univ. Press, 1954), pp. 53, 93, *passim*.

traders as well.[41] In the central hinterland, in contrast, the population was less dense and many communities were of more recent foundation. As has been argued above, the community of Arochukwu may have been founded only a century or so before the great expansion of the overseas slave trade, though they were descended in part from earlier trading peoples from east of the Cross River. Despite being relative neophytes in a less thickly settled area of the hinterland, it was the Aro whose growth was the more dramatic and because of this can be more closely attributed to the slave trade than is the case among the older trading communities to the west.

There were many similarities in the basic manner of trading throughout the hinterland. Commercial units were generally based upon socio-political divisions of the parent community, and these larger units were organized into trading troupes, such as the one which periodically visited Equiano's village. Oral traditions recall that the traders and smiths of Awka, for example, were divided into two sections which went on the road in alternate years for nine-month tours, travelling in troupes of ten or twenty adults.[42] This form of organization had probably been fixed before the expansion of the overseas slave trade, but the addition of large numbers of slaves to the trade must have led to increases in the territory covered, the size of the troupes, and the frequency of tours to outlying areas. From the limited evidence available, however, there is no indication of any dramatic alteration in the trading techniques on the western hinterland, except along the Niger itself where the trading states such as Ossomari and Aboh developed and armed their trading canoes fore and aft with cannon and their men with fire-arms as well.[43] To a large measure the high density of this region did not necessitate any dramatic changes in techniques or spheres of operations.

[41] Afigbo, 'Trade and Trade Routes', p. 3.

[42] Ukwu I. Ukwu, 'The Development of Trade and Marketing in Iboland', *JHSN* III (1967), 651. The Abiriba likewise had two main groups, the Abiriba Bende and the Abiriba Amon (Umon) whose names and perhaps whose organization reflect the trading regions of the late eighteenth century; see Ogbonna O. Ekeghe, *A Short History of Abiriba* (Aba: International Press, 1956), pp. 52–3.

[43] For a recent sketch of these towns' trading history see Henderson, *King in Every Man*, p. 69. Ossomari was little mentioned by the nineteenth-century Niger explorers, but Allen and Thomson, *Narrative*, termed Aboh's king Obi Osai, 'the most powerful ruler' on the lower Niger (I, 239), whose 'sovereignty is acknowledged for about 55 miles along both sides of the river' (I, 233). Yet they cautioned against considering this sphere of influence a state: 'Notwithstanding all his proud declaration of absolute power, it is doubtful whether it can be considered as really more than a preponderating influence, of variable nature.' (Ibid.)

To the east, however, the Aro had lighter densities and a less well-established trading network to deal with, yet by the early nineteenth century, as the evidence from Koelle's informants in Sierra Leone illustrates, they had expanded up against the Awka–Isu areas and were trading in slaves from the densely-populated Isuama and Agbaja districts right out from under the noses of the older trading communities.[44] Because of this striking expansion of trading areas and the controversy which has surrounded their role in the slave trade, Aro operations are examined in detail in the next chapter, but for purposes of comparison it is useful to mention some of their main features here. Like other traders of the hinterland the Aro developed regular routes of trade covered by organized troupes, said to contain thirty or forty traders plus retainers and porters.[45] The leaders of these troupes established elaborate networks of trading friends, allies, and kinsmen. Unlike other trading peoples of the hinterland, however, the Aro established a network of permanent settlements and colonies throughout the central portion of the hinterland from which they conducted their trade. They also differed from others in the great awe in which they were held because of their reputed connections with the spiritual world.

All of the trading communities of the hinterland had some agreements or alliances with neighbouring communities to facilitate the movement of slaves and other goods into and out of their own trading area. The Aro appear to have a much greater number of such ties than any other group. To ensure themselves steady supplies of European goods they had trade agreements with the intermediary groups that traded with Old Calabar and with Bonny: with the Uwet on the Calabar River, with the Enyong on the Cross River, and with the Ndoki on the Imo River. To the north the Aro had other connections which supplied them with the horses and cows needed for sacrifices in title-taking ceremonies. There were also agreements with Abiriba and Nkwerre blacksmiths to supply them with iron, and agreements with others in all corners of the region to supply them with textiles. Finally, the Aro had trading agreements with the title-holders of Awka, perhaps even agreeing to split the Igbo territory into separate spheres of influence. These agreements were one of the important means by which the Aro or more accurately segments of

[44] Koelle, *Polyglotta*, p. 8. See above, Chapter II, §3, and below, Chapter V, §2, 'Western Area'.
[45] Ekejiuba, 'Aro Trade System', p. 17.

the Aro, were able to expand their trade over so wide an area of the hinterland.[46]

In addition to these alliances and trading agreements there was another element of commercial organization which came into existence with the burgeoning of the overseas slave trade: the great fairs of Bende and Uburu.[47] Although many analyses of how slaves were obtained, as well as Equiano's more direct testimony, stress that individuals did not pass into slavery via the local market-place, as slaves were assembled into larger groups for shipment to the coast they very often did pass through one of these great fairs and the larger markets, such as Old Umuahia,[48] which fed them. These major trading centres had special sections for slave-selling, but were also depots for all sorts of other goods, both locally made and imported, whose importance will be examined in Chapter VI.

The fair at Uburu in the northern part of the hinterland had developed out of a regional trading centre for the northern Igbo and southern Igala, specializing in salt from the nearby salt lake.[49] This northern fair met in fixed sequence to the southern one at Bende, so that goods moved freely from one to the other. Unlike smaller markets whose sessions lasted no more than a day, the fairs at their peak met for four-day sessions followed by a minor session of equal length. As a consequence the fairs did not meet so often as smaller markets; at their peak they are said to have met every twenty-four days.[50]

[46] For Aro agreements with smiths see Ukwu, 'Development of Trade', p. 651; A. J. Fox, *Uzuakoli: A Short History* (London: Oxford Univ. Press, 1964), p. 2; Ottenberg and Ottenberg, 'Afikpo Markets', p. 123. For the Aro as textile traders see below, Chapter VI, §4. See also Victor C. Uchendu, *The Igbo of Southeastern Nigeria* (New York: Holt, Rinehart, 1965), p. 35, and Ekejiuba, 'Igba Ndu', pp. 17–20.

[47] Strictly speaking, Bende and Uburu were only the usual sites of the fairs. On occasion the fairs were moved to alternate sites a few miles away: from Bende to Uzuakoli and from Uburu to Okposi. One source claims that the fairs alternated sites every eight years. See E. R. Chadwick, 'Intelligence Report on Olokoro Clan, Bende Division, Owerri Province', 1935, pp. 20–2, NAI, CSO 26/4/30829. This seems less likely than Ukwu's explanation that 'The Aro wanted to retain effective control of the fairs and competition between rival sites for their very profitable patronage ensured that they obtained the most favourable conditions.' See Ukwu, 'Development of Trade', pp. 653–4. In only one historical case are the reasons for changing sites known: the southern fair was moved from Bende to Uzuakoli after Leonard's expedition visited the former site in 1896. See Fox Uzuakoli, p. 2.

[48] Chadwick, 'Intelligence Report, Olokoro', p. 21.

[49] Onuora Nzekwu, 'Uburu and the Salt Lake', *Nigeria*, No. 56 (1958), 91. Cf. Uchendu, *Igbo*, p. 35.

[50] Ekejiuba, 'Aro Trade System', p. 21. Ukwu charts a more complex cycle of sessions in 'Development of Trade', p. 654.

While it has generally been assumed that these fairs came into existence as a result of the expansion of the slave trade in the eighteenth century and under the guidance of the Aro, proof of these hypotheses has been lacking. However, the observations of Europeans at the coast make it possible to date the formation of the fairs to the period of greatest growth in the slave trade. The fairs clearly were not meeting in 1699 when James Barbot reported that New Calabar traders bought their slaves and provisions at upriver markets meeting twice a week, i.e. at the main market of a traditional four-day market ring.[51] Eighteenth-century sources indicate that the coastal Africans went upriver less often for slaves and in very much larger groups. The most comprehensive description of these marketing arrangements was by a ship's doctor familiar with Bonny in the 1780s. Slaves, he reported,

are bought by the black traders at fairs, which are held for that purpose, at the distance of upwards of two hundred miles from the sea coast; and these fairs are said to be supplied from an interior part of the country ... At the fairs, which are held at uncertain periods, but generally every six weeks, several thousands are frequently exposed to sale, who had been collected from all parts of the country for a very considerable distance round. While I was upon the coast, during one of the voyages I made, the black traders brought down, in different canoes, from twelve to fifteen hundred negroes, which had been purchased at one fair ...

The preparations made at Bonny by the black traders, upon setting out for the fairs which are held up the country, are very considerable. From twenty to thirty canoes, capable of containing thirty or forty negroes each, are assembled for this purpose; and such goods are put on board them as they expect will be wanted for the purchase of the number of slaves they intend to buy. When their loading is completed, they commence their voyage, with colours flying and musick playing; in about ten or eleven days, they generally return to Bonny with full cargoes.[52]

Although the interval between the fairs was less in later times, this description fits in very well with what is known of the fairs from oral sources. One exception to the doctor's account is that Bonny traders would not have attended the fair itself, visiting instead one of the major markets along the Imo river which were supplied from Bende and thus operated in its cycle. No doubt the Rio Real traders

[51] Barbot, 'Abstract of a Voyage', p. 461.
[52] Falconbridge, *Account of the Slave Trade*, pp. 12, 16. Another writer, who visited the coast ten times between 1786–1800, gives an essentially similar description of Bonny's trade; see Adams, *Remarks*, pp. 129–30.

continued to attend the four-day markets for provisions, especially for palm wine which spoils quickly, and perhaps for some local slaves, but it is clear that most slaves were obtained through the integrated marketing network which had been put together in the mid-eighteenth century, most likely during the period when the slave trade from the Bight of Biafra jumped from 4,500 a year in the 1730s to 12,500 a year in the 1760s, in order to handle that volume. As the account indicates, the Bende fair could handle 600 to 1,200 slaves at a session.

The role of the Aro in the establishment of these fairs is more difficult to assess. No evidence now available describes how the fairs came into existence, but the date of their creation, coinciding with the period of greatest Aro expansion, the proximity of Bende to Aro-chukwu, and the usefulness of the fairs to the Aro all suggest that the Aro would have played a major role in their creation. In any event by the end of the nineteenth century the Aro are known to have had great influence over the fairs though they did not actually control them.[53]

4. RELIGION AND THE RISE OF CAPITAL

The rapid growth of the slave trade in south-eastern Nigeria has been shown in this chapter to have depended upon the existence of established trading communities and mechanisms for extending trading contacts. Despite the dramatic expansion of the Aro and the creation of a network of fairs, the dominant theme of the period is one of greater continuity and more gradual change than was the case at the coast. However, even when it occurs within a framework of familiar institutions economic growth can gradually alter a society by eroding, if not overturning, the values at its heart. The need of the hinterland traders, for example, to reach rapid decisions was at odds with the slow deliberative process of village councils; the wealth brought by successful trading challenged the respect customarily accorded to other accomplishments, to age, and to traditional wisdom; the demands of trading upon the time and attention of men of mature years drew them away from their customary concerns with maintaining harmonious relations in the community and the contemplation of traditional beliefs and values. How were these competing demands reconciled? While the evidence is far from conclusive, it favours the conclusion that in this arena, too, change was more

[53] See note 47.

gradual than might have been expected and that traditional values and concerns (even in trading communities) showed a surprising vitality. Though the region was on its way to becoming one of the most commercially oriented in sub-Saharan Africa, it managed during the period under study to do so without sacrificing the greater part of its traditional values and way of life.

This was accomplished in large degree through the growth in importance and in distribution of voluntary associations of prominent men especially among the trading communities. These associations were of several types. In one type, called secret societies because their rites and lore were carefully concealed from non-members, membership was open to all adult men (or, less commonly, adult women) and generally acted to support established authority by restraining the fissiparous tendencies of lineage organization. In some places these societies replaced village councils of elders as the primary structure of internal governance. Another type of association had a more limited membership, being open only to people who felt or exhibited in some way a special call to a quasi-religious position of influence and power. Men whose lives demonstrated unusual achievement (of which economic success was one type) could obtain special titles recognizing their achievement and granting them powerful roles as political leaders, judges, and peacemakers. It is a matter of regret that these title societies have been so little studied that their development and origins remain obscure. Whatever their earlier functions it is clear that the structures based upon association, like those based on descent, were very important in explaining the changes in political organization which occurred as a result of the expansion of trade in the eighteenth century.

One of the best illustrations of this process may be seen in Old Calabar, which differed from the Ijo coastal states in that the political power of its two leading kings and most important citizens was exercised through a remarkable secret society, Ekpe, known to contemporary Europeans as 'Egbo'. The various grades of Ekpe were open to men who could pay the increasingly heavy fees each grade required. The origins of Ekpe and aspects of its development are not clear, although it appears to have developed from a men's secret society named for the leopard (*ekpe* in Efik) which was common in the upper Cross River area. In a recent study of this type of society among the Banyang of that area, Malcolm Ruel stressed that leopard associations functioned as a way of reconciling the conflicting principles of individual interest with the need for united collective action. The purchase of the graded titles in the association provided advancement in status and power to the wealthy and ambitious, yet subjected them to the discipline of the association's rules, which reflected the norms of society at large.[54] Similarly an Efik historian has argued that in Old Calabar Ekpe:

helped the Efik society by curbing some of the blind desires of the wealthy and restraining their oppression of the weak and the poor, because the poor had every right to take his case to the Ekpe council in order to exact the justice due to him.... It kept each member of the fraternity striving to ascend the Ekpe ladder in order to obtain the privileges due to the next grade so that he could better his social and political status and gain recognition in the community; in this way he had to be as civil and law-abiding as the Fraternity's regulations prescribed.[55]

Since even slaves were eligible for membership in the lower grades of Ekpe at Old Calabar, the lowest elements in society were united in a common purpose with the highest. Because the top grades of Ekpe were very costly there was in effect a 'means test for those seeking social advancement'. The rich were encouraged 'to expend their wealth in a manner which was socially beneficial' rather than disintegrative since the power of Ekpe membership gave them 'an overriding common interest in preserving the stability of society and the social order ...'[56] The highest grade of Ekpe, Nyamkpe, acted as a governing council for all Old Calabar towns, each of which also had its own subordinate branch. Since one of the most important Ekpe functions came to be the collection of trading debts by imposing sanctions, European traders also found compelling reasons to purchase membership. For example, in his diary an English captain trading for palm-oil in 1841 recorded the purchase of two 'Egbo' grades, which facilitated the collection of outstanding debts before he set sail.[57]

From Old Calabar the Ekpe Society spread to many lower Cross

---

[54] Malcolm Ruel, *Leopards and Leaders: Constitutional Politics among a Cross River People* (London: Tavistock, 1969), pp. 241–6.

[55] Efiong U. Aye, *Old Calabar through the Centuries* (Calabar: Hope Waddell Press, 1967), p. 75.

[56] G. I. Jones 'Political Organization of Old Calabar', in Forde, *Efik Traders*, p. 138.

[57] Capt. Turner (presumed author), 'Voyage. Ship Magistrate towards old Calabar commencing Tuesday 15th Dec. 1840', National Maritime Museum, London, MS. LOG/M/23.

River communities which traded with the Efik. Although each community had its own totally independent branch (unlike the case of the Old Calabar towns), membership in a common society appears to have greatly facilitated trade between Old Calabar and these other communities.[58] Arochukwu acquired all seven grades of Ekpe from the Efik and the society spread to Aro settlements throughout the hinterland and to neighbouring Igbo and Ibibio communities.[59] During the nineteenth century Ekpe was very popular among the Ibibio and a similar society called Okonko spread in the Bende–Ngwa–Ndoki area. Although these secret societies were by no means exclusively concerned with economic matters, the fact that their highest grades could be afforded by those who had profited from commercial activities, made it natural for the societies to play an important role in the collection of debts.[60] Nevertheless, though the highest grade of Ekpe in Old Calabar came to function as a governing body, in the hinterland the secret societies appear to have acted less toward creating new political institutions and more toward directing the new wealth and its attendant power toward traditional social ends. This function is best illustrated by another type of association called title societies, which were based on achievement and special calling. There were several types of these in the hinterland but the most important and best-known flourished among the Igbo traders in the western part of the hinterland.

Probably the largest group of title-holders were the *Ndi Nze* or Ozo title-holders in the area east of the Niger. This system of graded

---

[58] Interview with Chief Philip Bassey Ikpe, Ikpa Uruan, Uyo Division, 5 Dec. 1972, and interview with Mr. Odiong Udowong, Ukwa Eburutu, Calabar Divison, 14 Feb. 1973.

[59] Waddell, *Twenty-Nine Years*, p. 315; Talbot, *Peoples*, III, 779–82; Igwegbe, *Original History*, pp. 54–5; R. Kanu Umo, *History of Aro Settlements* (Lagos: Mbonu Ojike, n.d.), *passim*.

[60] *Jones Report*, p. 22. H. J. M. Harding, 'Intelligence Report on the Ibiono Clan (Idioros and Strangers upon Ibiono Clan), Itu District, Enyong Division, Calabar Province', 1933, p. 28, NAI, CSO 26/3/28881; H. H. Marshall, 'A Report on the Umuma Area, Aba Division, Owerri Province', n.d., p. 22, NAE, CSE 1/85/5426A; E. G. Hawkesworth, 'A Report on the Okon and Afaha Clans of the Ikot Ekpene Division, Calabar Province', 1931, p. 14, NAI, CSO 26/3/26506; R. K. Floyer, 'Intelligence Report on the Uwet Sub-Tribe', 1931, p. 1, NAE, CALPROF 53/1/547. For Okonko see Allen, 'Intelligence Report No. 1, Ngwa', pp. 76–7; Ennals, 'Intelligence Report, Ndoki', pp. 34–5, 46–7; E. N. Dickenson, 'Intelligence Report on Ezennihitte Clan in Owerri Province', 1932, NAE, CSE 1/85/4817, pp. 9, 18; C. J. Pleass, 'Intelligence Report on the Ubakala Clan, Bende Division, Owerri Province', 1934, p. 6, NAI, CSO 26/3/29828. In 1896 Major Leonard observed Okonko Society houses along the road in Ngwa; see his 'Journey to Bende', 198 ff.

titles evidently originated among the Nri priests in that area. A title was taken in an elaborate ceremony which symbolized the title-holder's transition from ordinary human status to a higher, more spiritual status, which, while giving him many privileges such as great freedom of movement, exemption from assault and bodily labour, and judicial powers, also hemmed him in with strict moral obliga-tions enforced by spiritual sanctions and public opinion. A man could not, for example, hold a title and continue to be a trader. Title-holders were distinguished by special dress and regalia including an ivory 'trumpet'. Little is known of the early development of this society and of others like it, but by the nineteenth century titles and trading wealth were clearly linked.[61] Wealthy men sought to convert their new money into traditional offices of high social standing, while society sought to regulate and divert 'the intoxication of wealth and power' to sober social ends: 'When a person makes money and attains a powerful position in Igbo society, he is repudiated, ignored and taunted until he takes a title. . . . Having achieved all they need on earth their only obligation now is to do good and be good.'[62] Since each title was obtained through the payment of fees which were divided among those already holding titles the system, like Ekpe, had aspects of a financial investment and the number of title-holders increased sharply in the nineteenth century. In the 1850s title-holders in Onitsha numbered about 200 in the junior grade, who had paid fees of 100,000 cowries (perhaps £5 in contemporary money) and a large number of animals and yams, and about six senior title-holders, who had paid 'enormous sums'.[63]

Despite the financial aspects of the title societies, membership acted more to draw men away from the pursuit of material gain and toward the contemplation of traditional spiritual values and the

[61] *Jones Report*, pp. 18–21; C. K. Meek, 'Social Organization in Owerri Division: Interim Report on the Isu Group', 1932, p. 9, NAI, CSO 26/3/28057; G. I. Jones, 'Intelligence Report on the Isu Clan, Okigwi Division, Owerri Province', 1935, pp. 15–19, NAI, CSO 26/4/31354. For another title society, the *Eze*, common among the Northern Igbo, see Jones, *Oil Rivers*, p. 178.

[62] Njaka, 'Igbo Political Institutions', pp. 262, 264.

[63] Crowther and Taylor, *Gospel on the Banks*, pp. 443–4. In the 1920s the cost of a senior Ozo title was put at £200 by Talbot, *Peoples*, III, 774. There was a similar growth in the number of title-holders across the Niger at Asaba in the nineteenth century; see Isichei, 'Historical Change', pp. 423, 430. In the latter part of that century and in the twentieth century there appears to have been an increasing commercializa-tion of titles and a subsequent loss of respect for title-holders; see Basden, *Niger Ibos*, pp. 133–4, 145; and J. B. Webster and A. A. Boahen, *History of West Africa* (New York: Praeger, 1970), pp. 172–3.

maintenance of peaceful and harmonious relations among neighbouring social units. According to a 1935 report on the Isu Igbo:

One of the most important functions of all these societies and associations, was that they in some measure brought together a number of people from the village area whose collective interests would not necessarily coincide with the collective interests of the other groupings. They thus tended to keep the village area united together and prevent undue separatism on the part of kindreds and quarters ... There is no doubt that in the past it was the Ndi-Nze who controlled the affairs of the village area and of its kindreds, and who settled disputes, tried cases and convened meetings, and because of their wealth and following had the most say in public matters generally.[64]

One might see in the political role of the title-holders a trend toward political centralization analagous to that in the coastal states, but the differences are more striking. Instead of building up a base of autocratic power, the *Ndi Nze* acted to preserve the political structures of the area during a difficult period of economic change.

Earlier studies of the slave trade era along the Bight of Biafra have concentrated on the commercial organization of the coastal middlemen and the dramatic changes which European contact and the pressures of the trade produced in their coastal states. In seeking to understand the over-all organization and effects of the slave trade from this coast it is necessary to consider the region from which most of the slaves were drawn. By doing so one sees very different effects. In the hinterland, as at the coast, the trade in slaves was taken up by communities which had developed an affinity for commerce much earlier. Yet their growth did not (except along the Niger) produce political units anywhere near as large or as centralized as those at the coast. Despite the pressures of population and of the wealth brought by the new trade, the loosely structured and egalitarian societies of the hinterland strove to retain their earlier form. Indeed one of the most significant developments of this era was the spread of various men's associations among the communities enriched by the trade which directed the energies of the traders toward the promotion of traditional values and social harmony.

It was more through economic rather than political changes that the new trade was handled, though in this case too previous experience and techniques shaped the eighteenth-century trends. The older market structure added a new upper layer of monthly fairs. The established regional traders expanded their routes and volumes, but

[64] Jones, 'Intelligence Report, Isu', pp. 16–17.

retained much of their former structure and techniques. The major trading divisions of the hinterland were based on social divisions in the parent communities. The Aro carried this concept furthest by founding resident communities outside of Arochukwu but still attached to the parent community's kindreds. Yet as the next chapter will show this extended the lineage system beyond its capacities. The outlying settlements, especially the larger colonies such as Ndizuogu, often came to be tied more closely to localized interests than to Arochukwu. There was no single Aro system, nor indeed was there any institution in the hinterland with the corporate economic responsibility of the eastern delta canoe house. Even the Aro troupe did not function as an economic unit. Individual members, who did not have to be Aro, were free to make whatever deals they could in the markets and rest stops along the way. It was one of the essential features of the commercial life in this region that trading was basically an individual enterprise. In this regard the economic system of the hinterland reflected the structures and values of the political system. An excellent recent study of Ontisha has brought out this point concerning their structures: '... in Onitsha as elsewhere [on the Niger] trade relations were segmented in that each Onitsha village has its own distinctive favored external ties; they were non-collective in that within each village persons had diversifying external ties to different sets of maternally linked kinsmen.'[65]

[65] Henderson, *King in Every Man*, pp. 495–6.

CHAPTER V

The God-Men of the Slave Trade

IT has long been argued that the Aro were the most important of the trading peoples of south-eastern Nigeria. Moving out from their hometown of Arochukwu near the Cross River, they traded and settled, in large groups and small, throughout the region, buying and selling slaves and a host of other valuable items and serving as agents for their oracle and for the hiring of mercenary soldiers. At a time when most inhabitants of the hinterland considered travelling beyond the confines of their native villages a foolhardy and possibly fatal venture, the Aro moved in relative freedom across the myriad political units and through the no-man's-lands between them. Their *forte* was the slave trade, much of which passed through their hands before reaching the coast. Yet at the same time as they were notorious a slave dealers, they were also known as 'the children of God'.

1. THEORIES OF ARO SUCCESS

The explanation of this dramatic and improbable success has intrigued all those who have studied them and has led to the formulation of a variety of theories, stressing religious, military, economic, and political factors as the key to their success. Few analysts have felt the evidence sure enough or the situation simple enough to adhere to a single factor, but nearly all have had a favourite. Before examining the Aro system in detail, therefore, it is worth while reviewing the main theories of Aro success.

The oldest explanation is also the most dramatic: that the Aro were cynical hucksters playing on the religious credulity of the masses. By an incredible promotional campaign they transformed a local shrine into an oracle of Delphic dimensions, capable of solving (for a stiff fee) all problems personal or political. Like a race of Elmer Gantrys, the Aro, according to this theory, promoted themselves as the sole interpreters of the Divine Will. By escorting petitioners to the shrine they were able to extract a series of lucrative fees for food, lodging, sacrifices, and other expenses. An added bonus accrued to the Aro in the form of the slaves which the oracle demanded as sacrifices, but which were actually sold into the overseas trade. Finally, the Aro exploited their position as divine intermediaries to obtain immunity from assault, enabling them to trade peacefully throughout the region.

The earliest version of this theory, by the nineteenth-century explorer William Baikie, is worth quoting at length for it has inspired all more recent versions and is the only version based on interviews with people who had first-hand knowledge of the shrine's workings in its heyday:

When a man goes to Áro to consult *Tshúku*, he is received by some of the priests outside of the town, near a small stream. Here he makes an offering, after which a fowl is killed, and, if it appears unpropitious, a quantity of red dye, probably camwood, is spilt into the water, which the priests tell the people is blood, and on this the votary is hurried off by the priests and is seen no more, it being given out that *Tshúku* has been displeased, and has taken him. The result of this preliminary ceremony is determined in general by the amount of the present given to the priests, and those who are reported to have been carried off by *Tshúku* are usually sold as slaves. Formerly they were commonly sent by a canoe, by a little creek, to Old Kalabár, and disposed of there. One of my informants had met upwards of twenty such unfortunates in Cuba, and another had also fallen in with several at Sierra Leone. If, however, the omen be pronounced to be favourable, the pilgrim is permitted to draw near to the shrine, and after various rites have been gone through, the question, whatever it may be, is propounded, of course, through the priests, and by them also the reply is given. A yellow powder is given to the devotee, who rubs it round his eyes, which powder is called in Ígbo, *Édo*. Little wooden images are also issued, as tokens of a person having actually consulted the sacred oracle, and these are known as *Ófo-Tshúku*, and are afterwards kept as djú-dju. A person who has been at Áro, after returning to his home, is reckened djú-dju or sacred for seven days, during which period he must stay in his house, and people dread to approach him. The shrine of *Tshúku* is said to be situated nearly in the centre of the town, and the inhabitants of Aro are often styled *Ómo-Tshúku*, or God's children.[1]

Even as more became known of other aspects of Aro organization, the oracle of Chukwu continued to be seen as the touchstone of Aro success. In his monumental work on Southern Nigeria, Talbot listed the 'Aro Chuku juju' as the prime factor in Aro power.[2] Likewise the pioneering history of Professor Dike, though cautioning against attributing Aro success *exclusively* to the oracle, still considered it

---

[1] Baikie, *Narrative*, pp. 313–14.
[2] Talbot, *Peoples*, III, 821.

the most important factor, 'the *medium* through which the slaves exported from Delta ports were largely recruited', and estimated that half or more of the slaves from this region had passed through its mysterious portals.[3]

Another popular theory stresses the military dominance of the Aro. Right from the foundation of Arochukwu, it is argued, the Aro have enjoyed a near monopoly on fire-arms in most of the hinterland because of their control of European goods from the coast. Able to turn these weapons against any place that resisted them, the Aro were free to expand and settle at will. The guns were also used to guard bands of traders on their way to market and to supply their allies with weaponry to use in raiding for slaves. Moreover, when the Aro met strong resistance, according to this theory, they called upon their allies and neighbours the Abam, Ohaffia, Abiriba, and Ada, who, under the name 'Abam', had the reputation as the warriors *par excellence* among the Igbo. Specializing in warfare the way other groups specialized in trading, farming, or fishing, the Abam trained their youth early in the use of weapons and armour. No one among them could be recognized as a man until he had brought home a human head in battle.[4] Some maintain that the Abam were entirely under Aro control, to be used for Aro ends or hired out to allies.

The military theory became popular at the beginning of the twentieth century, partly as a result of a British penchant for attributing every act of opposition to Aro plotting. Talbot mentions this use of the Abam, though he does not consider it a main reason for Aro success.[5] Dike argues that the Abam, armed by the Aro with firearms, were the second prop of Aro power essential to enforce 'universal belief in the Oracle as the supreme deity'.[6] Most recently the theory has been endorsed by Udo, who maintains that 'Aro domination of vast areas of the Eastern States was made possible by their Abam mercenaries . . .'[7]

The tendency of the most recent scholarship has been to emphasize

[3] Dike, *Trade and Politics*, pp. 39–41. The most recent champion of this theory is Austin Metumara Ahanotu, 'Economics and Politics of Religion', Ph.D. dissertation, Univ. of California, Los Angeles, 1971.

[4] Only two brief studies of the Abam have appeared: M. D. W. Jeffreys, 'Ibo Warfare', *Man*, LVI (1956), 77–9, and N. Uka, 'A Note on the "Abam" Warriors of Igbo Land', *Ikenga*, I.2 (1972), 76–82.

[5] Talbot, *Peoples*, I, 184 and III, 821.

[6] Dike, *Trade and Politics*, p. 39.

[7] Udo, *Geographical Regions*, p. 91.

a third factor for Aro success, their commercial organization and skill. Based upon a reconstruction of pre-colonial commercial life, this theory stresses that the Aro were not primarily priests or conquerors, but traders; their success as traders depended upon their ability to meet the demands of the market-place. The Aro had to construct and maintain excellent relations with thousands of suppliers and customers over a vast area. This was done through a network of mutually beneficial agreements negotiated between individual Aro in scores of settlements throughout the hinterland and important local leaders. In addition the Aro promoted and maintained a series of important markets, including two regional fairs at Bende and Uburu, which were connected by a series of trails, bridges, and rest stops, and linked to coastal entrepôts. Along these routes moved regular trading troupes supplying the interior with a variety of foreign and domestic goods in return for slaves and other other items.

Although much of this theory is based upon recent field-work, Talbot was fully aware of the importance of Aro commercial organization in their success, though he did rank it second to the Oracle.[8] The work of reconstructing the Aro trade routes and marketing techniques owes much to the research of Ottenberg, Ukwu, Fox, Umo, and Igwegbe, and particularly to Ekejiuba's detailed descriptions of the inner workings of the trading system.[9]

A fourth theory attributes the success of the Aro to their creation of a trading *state*. Through their control of the economy, the main routes, the military forces of the Abam, the highest court of appeal (the Oracle), and an incipient state organization, the Aro are said to become the virtual rulers of the hinterland. Although this theory has received an elaborate presentation in a recent work,[10] it is in fact part of an older theory of Aro success. The political theory is currently popular among many Aro and among many peoples with whom they have long traded. One does not spend long in this part of Nigeria before being told by village spokesmen that 'the Aro were

[8] Talbot, *Peoples*, III, 821.

[9] Simon Ottenberg, 'Ibo Oracles and Intergroup Relations', *Southwestern Journal of Anthropology*, XIV (1958), 63–85; Ukwu, 'Development of Trade', pp. 647–62; Fox, *Uzuakoli*; Umo, *Aro Settlements*; Igwegbe, *Original History*; Ekejiuba, 'Aro Trade System', pp. 11–26; F. I. Ekejiuba, 'The Aro System of Trade in the Nineteenth Century', *Ikenga*, I.2 (1972), 10–21.

[10] R. F. Stevenson, *Population and Political Systems in Tropical Africa* (New York: Columbia Univ. Press, 1968).

the Government in those days'. This interpretation developed into an obsession among British officials in the period immediately preceding the Aro Expedition of 1902 and for some twenty years afterwards, as investigations by Anene and Afigbo have shown.[11] The Aro were believed to have control over the activities of everyone in the hinterland and to be using this control to organize opposition against the Colonial Government.

The first scholarly presentation of this political explanation of Aro success was by Dike, who argued that, through their position as 'spokesmen of the Almighty', the Aro established 'what amounted to a theocratic state over eastern Nigeria'.[12] More recently the theory has been recast in more comprehensive terms by Stevenson. After reviewing the interaction of population density and state formation elsewhere in Africa, he takes up the apparently exceptional case of south-eastern Nigeria, which, despite some of the highest population densities in Africa, is generally held not to have had any comprehensive state structures until the colonial era. Stevenson argues that, on the contrary, the Aro, while falling short of a 'full blown state', did produce 'a certain type of state' by dominating regional trade, the apex of judicial administration, and large-scale warfare, while relegating other political functions to local governing institutions. Caught up in the dynamic onslaught of his argument, Stevenson gradually escalates the Aro achievement from a cautiously ambiguous 'partial state formation' to 'a fairly well-defined state organization', and finally, an organization 'which in terms of the major functions it fulfilled must be considered a state'.[13]

At least in their cruder forms, all of these theories share a single underlying assumption: that there was an Aro system, that throughout much of the hinterland there was some sort of underlying uniformity of operations which can be understood in terms of a key factor or the interaction of several key factors, that the Aro operation was something more than the co-operation of a group of individuals who shared a common ethnic identity and a predilection for commerce. To test this assumption the description of Aro operations which follows will be approached regionally. Only at the conclusion to the chapter will the existence of an Aro 'system' be mooted and

[11] J. C. Anene, 'The Protectorate Government of Southern Nigeria and the Aros 1900–1902', *JHSN* I (1956), 20–6; A. E. Afigbo, 'The Eclipse of the Aro Slaving Oligarchy of South-Eastern Nigeria, 1901–27', *JHSN* VI (1971), 3–24.

[12] Dike, *Trade and Politics*, p. 38.

[13] Stevenson, *Population and Political Systems*, pp. 190, 204, 231.

its underlying structure examined in the terms of these four popular theories. The regions serving as the basis of this examination are not entirely discrete or homogeneous, but they are different enough from each other and correspond closely enough to ethnographic, historical, and economic subdivisions of the region to be used for this purpose.

2. AREAS OF ARO ACTIVITY

The eastern area

Shortly after the emergence of Arochukwu, the Aro established contact with neighbouring peoples to the north along the Cross River and west along the Enyong Creek. The peoples to the north were most closely related to the Aro and, like them, a mixture of Igbo groups moving in from the west and other peoples from east of the Cross River. The more southerly group, the Abam, and the northern group, the Ada, were aggressively warlike and had head-hunting societies. Their raids were greatly feared by neighbouring peoples, especially along the upper Enyong Creek which, as was indicated in Chapter II, had been inhabited by Ibibio but was being colonized by Igbo groups from both east and west. Since the Aro had established themselves on good terms with the Abam and Ada, communities in these turbulent zones reportedly invited the Aro to settle among them to protect them from these raids.[14]

The Abam continued to raid communities without Aro protection in this area, taking heads and selling captive women and children to the Aro. One group which the Abam continued to raid into the nineteenth century was the Ikpe clan of the Ibibio, just across the Enyong Creek from the Abam homeland. The Abam entered into an agreement with the elders of Odoro Ikpe, the clan centre, which permitted them to make joint raids on neighbouring territories, including parts of the same clan. The Ekoi whom Koelle found so numerous among the Ibibio recaptives in Sierra Leone were most likely the Ekoi village-group of this clan.[15]

One of the markets regularly visited in this area by both Aro and Abam traders was also in this clan at Ikpe Ikot Nkon which commanded the main trade route between Arochukwu and the Anang country and which was also connected to the fair at Bende. Although

---

[14] Umo, *Aro Settlements*, pp. 26–34.
[15] Interview with Chief Akpan, Ikpe; with the Revd. Inyang, Ikpe; and with Chief Ekara Udo Ebiong, Odoro Ikpe, Ikpe, 26 Jan. 1973. Koelle, *Polyglotta*, p. 18.

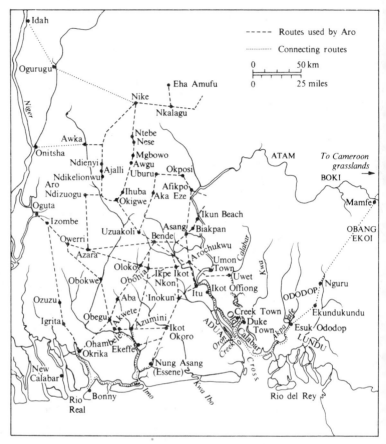

MAP 4. Major Trade Routes in the Era of the Slave Trade.
Based on maps in Ottenberg, 'Ibo Oracles', p. 300, Ukwu, 'Development of Trade',
p. 625, Cookey, 'Igbo Slave Story', p. 9, and Aro Expedition Sketch Map, 1901, in
Moore to C.O., 24 Nov. 1901, C.O. 520/10/381.

the Ikpe and Bende markets remained under the control of the local
inhabitants, the Aro could and did apply strong pressure to get their
way about market operation.

The largest Aro enclave in this eastern area was along the Cross
River at Afikpo in the Ada group, which has been extensively studied
by Ottenberg. Over several generations, while the Aro were founding
settlements south of Afikpo, Ada Igbo were moving into the Afikpo
and mixing with the original inhabitants. Because Afikpo was situated conveniently to the Uburu fair and the middle Cross River—
as well as to Arochukwu—the Aro moved to establish themselves

there in numbers, settling in nearly every Afikpo village and eventually forming some 20 per cent of the population. Through their trading wealth and the religious aura attached to them as representatives of the Oracle of Chukwu, the Aro were able to dominate the culturally fluid Afikpo society to a degree rare in the hinterland. They appear to have exercised some sort of veto power in village council meetings and were highly regarded (and paid) as negotiators in local disputes. The Aro 'held a special and powerful shrine, *otosi*, to which they sold rights of use to some other Afikpo', who then were entitled to share in most Aro privileges. Protective shrines and charms were also made available to local citizens, which further enhanced the Aro influence. While protecting Afikpo from outside attack, the Aro encouraged the Afikpo warriors to engage in raids and in kidnapping for slaves. Finally, the Aro escorted groups to Arochukwu to consult the Oracle, 'especially for land cases that the Afikpo elders had difficulty in settling and for "troubles" such as barrenness and illness, that local herbalists and diviners could not end'.[16]

The general pattern that emerges from an examination of the eastern Aro area shows Aro groups using their economic and religious superiority to promote their status and interests. While a political force in Afikpo, elsewhere the Aro were more economic imperialists than colonizers. Except where their interests were at stake they left local politics to follow its usual course. In most places the Aro settlers were only small groups and their influence was dependent on alliances with powerful local leaders and groups. The Aro were able to safeguard places from Abam attack, but they did not control Abam activities elsewhere. The Aro also had a close relationship with the Abiriba smiths (an Abam group) who supplied iron products to Aro traders and weapons to the whole area. At Bende and Afikpo the participation of the local traders and elders was a part of the system. Although these 'junior partners' might not be in a position to operate on their own, neither could the Aro have operated without a vast number of allies to act as their local agents. The Aro retained their high status as priests and traders by relying on others to do the dangerous work of capturing slaves. Local criminals, such as Okon, a native of Ohafia (Abam group) who was sold for adultery in about 1820, also fed the slave trade.[17]

---

[16] Simon Ottenberg, *Leadership and Authority in an African Society: The Afikpo Village-Group* (Seattle: Univ. of Washington Press, 1971), pp. 24–6.

[17] Koelle, *Polyglotta*, p. 8.

The south-eastern area

The organization of the Aro among the Ibibio has been one of the topics most neglected by students of the Aro who have paid more attention to ethnographic boundaries than the Aro themselves ever did. For this reason, and because this area illustrates several patterns of Aro organization and behaviour so well, it is worth considering in particular detail.

The association between the Aro and the Ibibio is at least as old as Arochukwu itself, since some of the founding villages of Arochukwu were Ibibio-speaking. During the era of the slave trade the association was expanded as a result of both economic and geographical circumstances. The Ibibio possessed a dense population, surrounded Arochukwu on three sides, controlled the major slave port of Old Calabar, and lay astride the most direct route from Arochukwu to the eastern delta ports. It was natural that those villages of Arochukwu which were Ibibio in origin and whose citizens continued to retain the Ibibio language and elements of its culture, should have become the trading partners with the Ibibio.

The ties between Old Calabar and Arochukwu were very important to both of these trading communities. Arochukwu was a major source of the slaves sold at Calabar, while Calabar was an important supplier of European goods to the Aro. Nevertheless, perhaps to reduce friction, direct contact between the two was limited; most trade took place through intermediaries. One route ran overland from Arochukwu through the Ito group of Northern Ibibio, across the Cross River, and on to Uwet on the Calabar River. From there the slaves passed on to Old Calabar, but out of Aro hands.[18] Another route (that mentioned by Baikie) ran down a connecting stream to the Enyong Creek to Enyong Ibibio markets at Asang and Itu, from where they were taken to Old Calabar.[19]

Like Aro trade elsewhere these routes were in the hands of specific subdivisions of the Arochukwu community. The village of Amasu maintained the route to Uwet; Ujari and Ibom villages traded with the Enyong; and Amanagwu dealt with Itu.[20] A fifth Arochukwu village, Obinkita, operated in the western part of the Ibibio area. Obinkita's role and method of operations differed from those on the routes to Old Calabar, which were primarily concerned with moving

[18] Ekejiuba, 'Aro Trade System', p. 15.
[19] Interview with Chief Ekpenyong Ibah, Ikot Nya Asaya, Enyong, 19 Dec. 1972.
[20] Shankland, 'Intelligence Report, Aro', Appendix IV.

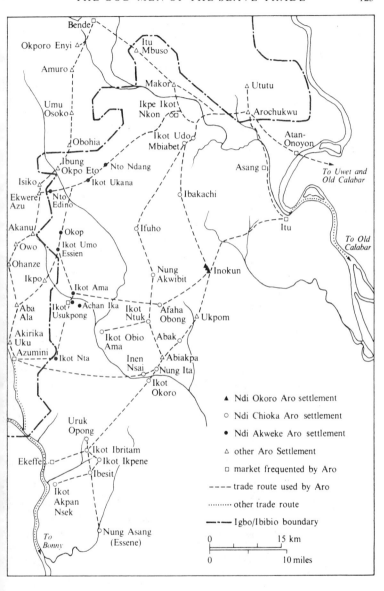

MAP 5. Aro Trade with the Ibibio.

relatively large volumes of slaves and trade goods. The Obinkita were specialists in the collecting end of the hinterland trade, selling goods and buying slaves in small units in local Ibibio markets and villages. While those trading to Old Calabar established only resting-places along their relatively short routes (under thirty miles to Uwet, under twenty to Itu), the Obinkita established dozens of permanent settlements among the western section of the Ibibio from which they conducted their trade. Both because Obinkita became one of the most powerful villages in Arochukwu, and because its pattern of organization is typical of Aro settlements elsewhere, it is worth ex-amining in some detail.

The Arochukwu village of Obinkita was divided into five patri-lineal kindreds (*umunna*); four of these operated among the Ibibio and one among the neighbouring Ngwa Igbo. Just as trade among the Ibibio was divided among several Aro villages, trade in the west-ern Ibibio area was divided among these four Obinkita lineages. The divisions corresponded roughly to ethnographic divisions among the western Ibibio. Thus, Ndi Akweke lineage operated among the northern Anang, Ndi Chioka among the southern Anang, Ndi Otu in the Opobo area, and Ndi Okoro in the Ibiono clan of the Ibibio Proper. Over time as the number of Aro settlements expanded there was a certain amount of overlapping in the border areas, though these basic divisions in trade and settlement remained up until the time of the Nigerian Civil War.[21]

While the other three Obinkita lineages each founded several small settlements in the western Ibibio area, the Ndi Okoro founded a single settlement which in time grew to a village of several com-

---

[21] Interview with Mr. Fidelis Emmanuel Sunday Okoro, Obinkita, Arochukwu, 13 Feb. 1973; interview with Mr. Kanu Merem and Mr. Kanu Nwankwo, Obinkita, Arochukwu, 13 Feb. 1973; interview with Chief Robert N. Asiegbu, Obinkita, Aro-chukwu, 13 Feb. 1973.

The importance of Obinkita as a trading town is well attested to in the older sources. Talbot, *Peoples*, I, 184, goes so far as to say that Bonny was under Obinkita control, which was hardly the case. In 1894 Casement was told by some Aro whose pride may have led them to exaggerate, that the Arochukwu villages of Obinkita, Ibom, and Atani were all larger and more important than the market town of Bende; see Roger Casement, 'Report of an attempted Journey from Itu on the Cross River to the Opobo River', 10 Apr. 1894, F.O. 2/63/322–36, p. 10. Obinkita was the only village of Arochukwu listed in the geographical section of Goldie's *Dictionary* (p. 358). The name Obinkita, which in Igbo means 'the heart of the dog', is puzzling. Goldie records the name as *Ibibinkita* and in one place (p. 7) Casement calls it *Ibibio Nkita*, which suggest that the original name may have been transmuted into something more Igbo sounding, just as Bende was originally the Ibibio village of *Mbente*. Could the original name have been *Ibibio Ŋkiwa* (Old Ibibio) since the area once belonged to the Ibibio?

ponent parts. The settlement originated in the no-man's-land between two Ibibio Proper clans, Itak and Ibiono, and adjacent to a third, Ediene. Locally the settlement was known as 'Inokun', the Ibibio name for the Aro, and stretched from Nung Okoro to Ekpemiong with compounds in many neighbouring villages. A 1931 Intelligence Report put the foundation 'at least four generations ago'.[22] According to Ibibio traditions as the settlement grew the Aro began to flex their economic and demographic muscles, demanding authority over the internal affairs of the Ibibio and more land. On one occasion (or perhaps several, the traditions are sketchy) fighting broke out, though the Aro were successful in defeating their more numerous, but divided, neighbours by calling in Abam mercenaries. In the course of the fighting the Aro took a number of Ibibio prisoners, whom they sold, and land, which they kept.[23]

When Roger Casement penetrated this far in March 1894, he concluded from the veritable wall of Aro settlements facing him that he had reached the boundary of Aro territory rather than a single settlement. He reported that there were several Aro 'towns' and that they were divided into two rival factions. Although these factions joined to assist Casement in his intention to continue on to Essene (near Opobo), they were refused passage by the 'king of Anang', no doubt a powerful chief in the vicinity of Abak, who acted after consulting another Obinkita group, most likely Ndi Chioka. Casement retraced his steps to Itu, which appears to have been the only route open to the Ndi Okoro as well, since the roads to Akwete, Bende, Opobo, and Arochukwu itself were all closed to them by feuds and wars.[24]

The three other Obinkita lineages operating in this area had generally more peaceful relations with their Ibibio neighbours and a more complex settlement pattern. Instead of a single large settlement, these three had many enclaves within the Ibibio villages.

It would be useful to know when the first Aro settlements were made and to trace the sequence of Aro expansion, but it does not seem possible to do so for lack of evidence. The Intelligence Report cited above put the foundation of 'Inokun' four generations (80–100 years?) or more prior to 1931. Another report of the same era

[22] R. J. N. Curwen, 'Intelligence Report on the Ediene and Itak Clans of the Ikot Ekpene Division, Calabar Province', 1931, p. 17, NAI, CSO 26/3/27615.
[23] Interviews with Chief James Russell of Ikot Akpan Odung, Itak, and Chief Thompson Ekpo of Ibiaku Ikot Udo, Ibiono, 28 Nov. 1972.
[24] Casement, 'Report from Itu', pp. 4–11 and map in F.O. 2/64/30A.

dates two other settlements to ninety years earlier, a figure probably
arrived at by counting generations.[25] This writer's interviews in this
area likewise produced genealogies three to five generations deep in
Aro settlements. Although it is possible that some Aro settlements
were founded at the time when the wealth of the new palm-oil trade
made this area more attractive to traders, it does not seem likely
that nearly all of them should date from the mid-nineteenth century.
The number of slaves taken from this area before that time, and the
weight of the cultural evidence, suggest that the Aro were no newcomers. The Aro alone are known to the Ibibio by a special name
(*Inokun*) that distinguishes them from other Igbo (*Uneghe*).[26] The
Aro and their Oracle are also the subject of popular sayings, such
as, 'A man can't go to Arochukwu with a light heart' and 'The Oracle
demands a person; you're a person, aren't you?'[27] Thus it is likely
that the generation counts represent only the length of remembered
ancestry rather than the actual length of settlement, three to five
generations being the maximum one is likely to record anywhere in
the western Ibibio area.[28]

If, however, it is impossible to devise an absolute chronology of
Aro settlement in the area, the oral sources do allow for the hypo-
thetical reconstruction of the general sequence of contact between the
Aro and the Ibibio. The Aro would first have appeared as itinerant
traders and religious specialists and built up a sequence of resting-
places along routes leading toward the Imo River where contact was
made with the Bonny traders. Each resting-place would be at the
compound of a prominent Ibibio who was compensated for his
troubles. The first settlement in the area, according to one source
was at Essene, at the very end of the route from Arochukwu.[29]
Gradually the more important resting-places became trading centres

[25] S. E. Johnson, 'Intelligence Report on the Afaha Obong Village Group of the
Afaha Clan of the Anang Sub Tribe', 1932, p. 3, NAI, CSO 26/3/28242.

[26] Both are in Goldie, *Dictionary*, pp. 359, 361.

[27] *Owo ikaha Inokun ke mfon ekere. Ibritam ete eno owo; afo udogho owo?*

[28] This is a common complaint among the writers of the intelligence reports in
the hinterland. One typical report says that among the Okon clan of the Anang,
'Generally tradition does not go back for more than two generations and all they
can tell of their past is a confused account of petty fights with their neighbours'
(Hawkesworth, 'Intelligence Report, Okun and Afaha', p. 7). Another writer
lamented, 'In every village visited by me the people professed complete ignorance of
their origin and early history' (W. E. Aston-Smith, 'Intelligence Report on Otoro or
Northern Anang Group, Ikot Ekpene Division, Calabar Province', 1933, p. 1, NAI,
CSO 26/3/28780).

[29] Interview with Chief Asiegbu, Arochukwu.

and finally Aro settlements. From these in turn new settlements were founded, owing either to Aro initiative or the invitation of a local citizen eager to attract some of the trading wealth to his village. According to one Ndi Chioka elder the mode of expansion went like this: 'Sometimes a man would come to an Aro settler and give him a goat and a cow and so many things to beg him to give them an Aro man to come and live in his place.... It was just like the Christian churches, which were first established in one town and the people came and took them down to their place and asked them to establish themselves there, too. We didn't go by force, but by invitation.'[30] On the whole Ibibio sources agree with this analysis.

Generally the decision to invite the Aro to settle permanently would have been made at a general village meeting, since it involved the alienation of village land. At this meeting the advantages of a permanent Aro settlement (wealth, disposal of criminals and other undesirables, exotic goods and 'medicines', access to the Oracle) would have been weighed against the disadvantages. (The words *isin-enyin* and *ŋkari-ŋkari*, meaning 'open-eyed', i.e. greedy, and 'tricky' occur with astonishing frequency in conversations about the Aro, even with Ibibio who are well-disposed toward them.) According to one Anang elder, his ancestors had allowed the Aro to settle in their village 'because they were clean people; they were honest; they were not thieves; and they would purge the village of evil doers. The chiefs had the leader [of the Aro] bring all his people to the village to swear that they would not do any evil. So the chiefs were not afraid of them and they gave them a place of settlement.'[31]

Once a settlement was formed, marriages were generally negotiated with local families. This was a form of alliance and also served to increase the size of Aro groups since, while freely marrying local women the Aro men never permitted their daughters to marry a non-Aro. The children of these marriages, raised by Ibibio mothers and living in an Ibibio community, naturally became increasingly acculturated into Ibibio society. Up to a point this was viewed as a good thing by the Aro for the less distinctive they were, the less likely they were to arouse hostile feelings. An Aro told with pride how his people were still greeted as *eyen ete*, i.e. brother (literally, son of one father) in the Ikot Ibritam area. At the same time it was essential

---

[30] Ibid.
[31] Interview with Chief Udo Udo Akpan Ntuk of Ikot Obio Ama, Abak, 14 Dec. 1972.

for the Aro to maintain their distinctive sense of identify as an élite community if they were to be more than just local traders. In part this was done through meetings held with other Aro in the area at the compound of the most prominent trader at which matters of policy and tactics could be agreed upon. In part, too, it appears to have been encouraged by a constant repetition of claims of Aro superiority. 'We ruled the Ibibio in those days', is a claim one hears constantly when discussing these Aro settlements. Although hardly true in any literal sense, the claim does reflect an attitude of superiority which the Aro encouraged to make themselves distinct from the Ibibio without remaining foreigners. In general the most successful Aro traders seem to have been able to operate comfortably in both cultures, an Aro among Aro, an *eyen ete* among the Ibibio.[32]

Although intended as a description of just one part of Anang, these comments from an old Intelligence Report apply quite well to the position of the Aro throughout that area: 'The Aros appear to have penetrated into the district in early days but seem to have been kept at arm's length by the people. They were allowed to trade in slaves and merchandise and settle in the country but it appears they were given little or no active share in the life of the country. Their Long Juju was however made known to and much feared by the people.'[33] Aro success among the Ibibio was due more to trade than to any other factor. They rarely resorted to force, being too few in number to hope for success except in a couple of their larger settlements, relying instead on the natural attractiveness of the goods they sold and their alliances with prominent Ibibio citizens. The Aro had one great advantage over other traders: the protection of their renowned Oracle. Even the notoriously pugnacious Anang feared to attack them lest they be punished by the god with whom the Aro claimed so close an association. But, as the Ibibio proverbs show, the Oracle was more feared than resorted to. Goldie says that in the mid-nineteenth century Calabar residents no longer sought its decisions.[34] Still less did the Aro exercise any significant political

[32] Interview with Chief Asiegbu, Arochukwu.

[33] H. P. James, 'Assessment Report on the Abak District, Ikot Ekpene Division, Calabar Province', 1927, p. 3, NAI, CSO 26/3/20678.

[34] Goldie, *Dictionary*, p. 359. Waddell tells of a man plagued by the misfortunes of Job and having exhausted the remedies of the local priests, who 'went to the Ibo country, and swore to some reputed god there'. See Waddell, *Twenty-Nine Years*, p. 451. This surely refers to the Oracle at Arochukwu, but it is indicative of the infrequency of such actions that the usually well-informed missionary was quite ignorant of the Oracle's existence.

influence in the area, outside their one large settlement, being unable at the end of the century to escort Casement across the few miles of territory without permission of the Ibibio chief. But within the sphere of trade their achievement was impressive; if the impressions of present-day residents are correct, few slaves from this area reached the coast without passing through Aro hands.

The south-western area

From the Bende fair the most direct route to the coast ran through the Ngwa people to the Ndoki on the Imo River and from there either across the river to the Okrika at the edge of the delta or down the river to Bonny. The Aro had evidently established trading connections through this territory to Bonny and New Calabar in the eastern Niger Delta by the seventeenth century, for king-lists from that period for both these towns include rulers named Kamalu, a name which Jones points out is typically Aro. The Kalabari Kamalu was an Igbo 'doctor', while the Bonny Kamalu was the child of a marriage between a Bonny king and the daughter of an Ndoki chief.[35] The Ndoki have strong connections with the Aro area since one of their principal trading towns, Ohambele, was founded by Abam mercenaries who chose not to return home.[36] As was indicated in Chapter II, the Ngwa were comparatively recent arrivals in their area and, like the Afikpo, thus offered the Aro an opportunity to profit from a fluid situation. A large number of small Aro settlements were made in Ngwa rather on the pattern of those among the neighbouring Anang. Here, too, these settlements served both as trading stations and as resting-places on the trade routes which ran to the Ndoki towns on the Imo River. The Ngwa–Ndoki area was a major nexus for trade since through it ran routes from Bende and points north, from Oguta and Owerri, and from the Anang country. In general the relations between the Aro and the local inhabitants appear to have been peaceful. The only record of fighting connected with the Aro was an attack on Obegu by the Abam in 1901 when the British were trying to break Aro power.[37]

[35] Jones, *Trading States*, pp. 28, 105, 133.
[36] Ennals, 'Intelligence Report, Ndoki', p. 21. This was confirmed in an interview with the Ohambele Elders, Ndoki.
[37] John Jackson, 'Assessment Report upon the Asa Native Court Area of the Aba Division', 1927, p. 13, NAI, CSO 26/3/20610. This was also the only example mentioned in an interview with Mr. Wamuo, Ngwa.

Further west there were several Aro settlements near Oguta,[38] a town with excellent connections by water to the lower Niger ports such as Aboh and via the Orashi–Engenni River with New Calabar. Between Oguta and the delta among the Ikwerre Igbo there were also several Aro settlements 'allied with the indigenous population by marriage and custom'.[39] Through these the Aro had additional contacts with the Kalabari and Okrika traders.

The influence of the Aro Oracle in the eastern delta seems to have been surprisingly strong and oral traditions date the introduction of it into New Calabar from 'the time of Owerri Daba' in the seventeenth century. During the nineteenth century frequent recourse was had to *suku obiama*, as the Oracle was known in that district, both to settle succession disputes and as a political weapon.[40] The Ikwerre and their neighbours also made use of the Oracle.[41] At least by the nineteenth century the people of Aboh, the important trading town on the Niger River, also held the Oracle in high regard and travelled to it via the delta and the Ndoki country. In 1841 the Oracle of Chukwu was said to decide all matters of importance, and pilgrims went there from Aboh even in the rainy season when the trip was said to take three months.[42] In 1854 Crowther met an Aro man and his son in a village south of Aboh, who were probably on oracular business though they may have been traders, too.[43]

The south-western area of the hinterland was vitally important to the Aro for it linked them to the eastern delta ports. Along the trade routes from Bende to Ndoki the Aro moved a large portion of the slaves reaching Bonny. Close relations were established with the Ngwa, through whose territory these routes passed, and further west with the Ikwerre and Oguta traders. As was the case on the Cross River, these links to the coastal ports were not direct but passed via intermediate trading peoples.

[38] Moult, 'Intelligence Report, Oguta', p. 11.

[39] R. T. Savory, 'Intelligence Report on the Ikwerri Clan, Ahoada Division, Owerri Province', 1939, p. 3, NAE, CALPROF 53/1/577.

[40] Jones, *Trading States*, pp. 70, 87, 134, 147.

[41] Jackson, 'Assessment Report, Asa', p. 12; W. F. H. Newington, 'Intelligence Report on the Ekpeya Clan, Ahoada Division, Owerri Province', 1931, pp. 8–9, NAI, CSO 26/3/28956; G. A. Williams, 'Intelligence Report on Okpu Mbu Tolu Clan, Ahoada Division, Owerri Province', 1932, pp. 6–7, NAI, CSO 26/3/28074.

[42] Schön and Crowther, *Journals*, pp. 51–2.

[43] Crowther, *Journal*, p. 193. Cf. Allen and Thomson, *Narrative*, I, 270, quoted in the next section of this chapter concerning the route followed from Aboh to the Oracle and the discussion there on whether it was the Oracle at Arochukwu or another at Aro Ndizuogu which was being consulted.

The western area

In the western part of the hinterland the Aro faced a very different set of circumstances from the eastern and southern areas. This was the Igbo heartland whose dense, well-established village groups could not be manipulated as the culturally fluid Afikpo area could. This was also the home of the ancient Nri priests, who commanded great authority and respect in all religious matters. Finally, this area, like the delta, already had a number of well-established trading communities: the riverain traders of Asaba, Ossomari, Oguta, and Aboh and the land-traders of Onitsha, Awka, and Isu (including the Nkwerre). Against these formidable obstacles one would not expect the Aro to have achieved much success and the map quite clearly shows their settlements halt at the edge of this area. Yet by adopting a different set of methods the Aro also became a major force in this area. In the hills on the upper Imo River on the eastern fringe the Aro founded a settlement which eventually became larger in population than Arochukwu itself. Moreover, by effectively promoting their oracle they were able to establish themselves in this area as experts in spiritual matters. Finally, the Aro made alliances with the established trading towns and made this area one of the hubs of their trading system. Each of these achievements will be examined below.

The origins of the first Aro settlement in this area, at a place called Ndizuogu, are obscure. While probably not founded so early as the 1635 date suggested by one source,[44] it was surely in place by the eighteenth century, founded, it is said, on land unoccupied at the time. If its origins were peaceful, the oral traditions of neighbouring peoples attest that conflict was the hallmark of its subsequent growth. The ability of the Aro settlers to call in the assistance of the Abam mercenaries gave them a great advantage, but not an invincible one, in these conflicts. On the south-west one Isu village, Umu Obom, managed to stand firm and extract recognition as landlords from the Aro, while other Isu towns were devastated. The Nkalu clan to the west, which had absorbed the remnants of these devastated Isu towns, also managed to halt Ndizuogu advances, but with great losses. To the north-east the Isuochi and Nneato towns formed an alliance to stop the Aro incursions, an example of Igbo ability to rise above the limits of traditional political units in time of necessity. Repeated Aro incursions led to warfare with every town

[44] Igwegbe, *Original History*; the date is given in the title.

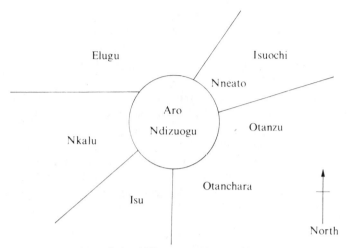

MAP 6. Aro Ndizuogu and its Neighbours.

of the Elugu to the north, whose unity was shattered as they were
driven to the hilltops while the Aro claimed the valleys. (Elugu means
'on top of the hill'.) Using Ada (Abam) mercenaries the Aro
captured and settled the towns of Ndienyi, Ujalli, and Ndikelionwu
in the Elugu territory. The Otanchara to the south-east were also
unable to resist the Aro and suffered considerable disintegration as
a result. In Otanchara smaller Aro outposts were founded on land
taken or purchased from the original owners and these became local
slave-trading centres. The Otanzu, whose territory is interspersed
with that of the Otanchara, were not raided for slaves, possibly
because they were allied with the Aro in the raids on the latter, possibly (according to another tradition) because they were descended
from an Aro trader.[45] Fed by new immigrants from Arochukwu and

[45] H. J. S. Clark, 'Intelligence Report on the Enugu Group, Awka Division, Onit-
sha Province', 1934, pp. 1–4, NAI, CSO 26/3/29827; V. Fox-Strangways, 'Intelligence
Report on the Isu Ochi, Nne Ato and Umu Chieze Clans, Okigwi Division, Owerri
Province and Awgu Division, Onitsha Province', 1932, pp. 5–6, 12, NAI, CSO 26/
3/28583; F. A. Goodliffe, 'Intelligence Report on the Otanchara Clan, Okigwi
Division, Owerri Province', 1933, pp. 10–11, 46, NAI, CSO 26/3/28860; F. A.
Goodliffe, 'Intelligence Report on the Otanzu Clan, Okigwi Division, Owerri Province', 1933, pp. 7–10, NAI, CSO 26/3/28935; I. R. P. Helsop, 'Intelligence Report
of the Nkalu Clan, Orlu District, Okigwi Division, Owerri Province', 1935, pp. 11–
12, NAI, CSO 26/4/30878; Jones, 'Intelligence Report, Isu', p. 10; C. J. Mayne, 'Intelligence Report of the Ndizuogu Village Area, Orlu District, Okigwi Division, Owerri
Province', 1935, p. 4, NAI, CSO 26/4/30836; see also Forde and Jones, *Ibo and Ibibio*,
pp. 35, 56.

by the children of local wives, Aro Ndizuogu grew until it eventually became twice the size of the mother town.[46]

The Aro were also successful in promoting themselves as agents of their Oracle in this area. According to a somewhat exaggerated account of the Ihiala district, 'It is very clear that the dominance of the Aro became so complete and the inhabitants' belief in their god Chukwu so unshakeable that no important decision in any of the towns' affairs was taken without consulting them. When any of the important administrative posts in Ihiala were to be filled, the selection was always verified by consulting Chukwu ...'[47] As was shown in the previous section, the Oracle's influence was also strong near Aboh in the mid-nineteenth century. There is some circumstantial evidence that the Ndizuogu Aro gave oracular consultations in their own settlement rather than sending the pilgrims on to Arochukwu. One member of the 1841 Niger Expedition was a Sierra Leone recaptive turned missionary named Simon Jonas. Since he was an Igbo by birth he acted as interpreter for the explorers and supplied them with this information about the Igbo east of the Niger:

The principal place of worship is called Anno; and is much larger than Aboh. The houses are high. The general trade is in slaves from the interior. The town is situated on the banks of the River Immo, which, above, flows through a rocky country ... Canoes can communicate with the River Immo, by means of connecting creeks from Aboh, by way of n'Doki ... Above Anno Simon Jonas called it Abain-him, 'the meeting of the waters'. His account was confirmed by another native.[48]

Were it not for the remarkable accuracy of the rest of his geography, one would expect that Jonas and his collaborator had placed Arochukwu on the wrong river. Instead, they seem to mean, not Arochukwu, but Aro Ndizuogu, which is on the Imo River and reachable from Aboh via Ndoki. *Aba anyim* could well apply to the conjuncture of the twin fonts of the Imo north of the town.[49]

Quite independently of Jonas's account another Sierra Leonean

[46] Udo, *Geographical Regions*, p. 66.

[47] W. R. T. Milne, 'Intelligence Report on the Achalla Group, Onitsha Division, Onitsha Province', 1933, p. 6, NAI, CSO 26/3/29001.

[48] Allen and Thomson, *Narrative*, I, 270.

[49] Unaware of the existence of Aro Ndizuogu the usually accurate Baikie (*Narrative*, p. 310) tried to harmonize Jonas' account with location of Arochukwu by placing *aba anyim* north-east (instead of north) of Ndoki and by dropping any mention of the Imo River.

missionary on the Niger in the 1850s suggested the existence of a major oracle at Ndizuogu. John Christopher Taylor collected the following geographical details at Onitsha: the Isuama were two days away; 'Aron, the consulting place of all the Ibo trade concerning Tshuku', a good three days away; and 'Bendo [Bende], the capital of Ibo', six days away.[50] Here also the most likely inference is that the oracle was at Aro Ndizuogu, almost precisely half way between Onitsha and Bende.

Evidently taking full advantage of the prestige the oracle brought them, the Ndizuogu Aro were able to compete successfully with the Nri priests in removing ritual abominations. The Nri were not without defences and were able to promote very successfully their *ozo* title system in this area during the same period. Eventually the Aro and Nri reached some sort of *modus vivendi*, since, according to Talbot, the territory was divided into a section for each and there was a 'considerable amount of business' between them, the Aro selling 'medicines' to the Nri and buying slaves in return.[51] Some time during this period a Nri 'medicine' dealer named Akpa-Nwa-Eze-Nri and an Awka trader set up an oracle named Agbala at Enugu-Ukwu (between Nri and Awka), which became very popular as a consultation place among residents of this part of the Igbo territory. This may have been designed to compete with the oracle of the Aro, but according to Talbot it was sold to the Nri by an Aro and Basden declares Agbala was a 'daughter' of the Arochukwu Oracle.[52]

[50] Crowther and Taylor, *Gospel on the Banks*, p. 252. That Ndizuogu was known as 'Aro' at that time is confirmed by a third independent source. An Igbo named Aneke, who was kidnapped in about 1820 from his home town of Nachi in southern Agbaja (Udi Division) 'was brought in succession to Aro, Bendo, and Obane'. Koelle, *Polyglotta*, p. 8. It is not hard to identify Bende and Ibani on this route; from Nachi one would pass via Aro Ndizuogu, not via Arochukwu.

The identification of Aro with Anno and Aron is based on common consonant shifts in Igbo dialects. The n/l shift is illustrated by the word for the earth goddess, which is *Ani* in the western Igbo area and *Ali* (*Ale*, *Ala*) in the eastern. The hilltop dwellers north of Ndizuogu are the *Elugu*, while *Enugu* to the north-east is the capital of Nigeria's Anambra State. The equally common l/r shift can be seen in the name for a certain kind of deity (*alosi*/*arosi*). The final 'n' is often found in nineteenth-century references to the Aro, representing a slight nasalization of the final vowel. In the interests of simplicity Koelle's stress and diacritical marks have been omitted throughout this study, but his actual transcription included an indication of nasalization.

[51] Talbot, *Peoples*, III, 596.

[52] Ibid. A very full account of this oracle is in Basen, *Niger Ibos*, pp. 77–87. The same source (p. 91) also tells of an oracle named Igwe-ka-Ala (Sky on Earth) at Umunchu, twelve miles north of Owerri.

In the same manner as they reached a *modus vivendi* with the Nri the Aro also appear to have reached agreements with the leading trading communities in this area, especially with the Awka.[53] The terms of the agreements are not known, but they evidently enabled the Aro to monopolize a major share of the slave trade in this area. According to a local history of Ndizuogu its inhabitants were accustomed to buying slaves, especially children, from impoverished local parents as well as from kidnappers.[54] Here, as elsewhere in the hinterland, village authorities became accustomed to selling criminals to the Aro.[55] The wars between the Aro and their neighbours also must have produced large numbers of slaves. Koelle's mention of the Isu (Isuama) and Elugu indicated that they were prominent among the Igbo recaptives in Sierra Leone.[56]

In general, it would seem that the Aro as traders were kept out of the riverain area and did not gain a foothold on the Niger.[57] Yet through trading agreements they were able to share in it from a distance. As representatives of their oracle(s), their presence extended to the river at least near Aboh, while through an arrangement with the Nri priests they divided the territory further north between them.

The northern area

The further north one went in the hinterland the less prominent was the physical presence of the Aro, who there, as at the coast and in the west, depended greatly on alliances with other trading groups. In the most northerly part of the Igbo territory the Aro routes and markets intersected with those of the Igala traders, who competed with the Aro and their allies for influence in the trade.

From Bende two principal routes ran north: one in a direct line to the northern fair at Uburu and the other north-west to near Okigwe, where it branched, one part connecting with Ndizuogu and Awka and the other part going north to Awgu. Just north of Awgu the Aro trade route passed through the Mgbowo village group, whose inhabitants differed from their neighbours in the strength of

[53] Webster and Boahen, *History of West Africa*, p. 180.

[54] Igwegbe, *Original History*, pp. 75–8.

[55] Milne, 'Intelligence Report, Achalla', p. 6; W. R. T. Milne, 'Intelligence Report on the Agbaja Group, Onitsha Division, Onitsha Province', 1933, p. 16, NAI, CSO 26/3/29212; Fox-Strangways, 'Intelligence Report, Isu Ochi, etc.', p. 38; Goodliffe, 'Intelligence Report, Otanzu', p. 38; Goodliffe, 'Intelligence Report, Otanchara', p. 35.

[56] Koelle, Polyglotta, p. 8.

[57] Ottenberg, 'Ibo Oracles', p. 307; Jones, 'Intelligence Report, Isu', p. 10.

their propensity for trading and their disdain for farm work. The Mgbowo became 'an important link in the Aro line of communications with Ujalli and Ndikelionwu', serving the Aro as porters and as agents for the Arochukwu Oracle. While they permitted a small Aro settlement in their town, they steadfastly deny that they were ever 'subject to or controlled by' the Aro.[58] The Aro were also allied with the Ntegbe-Nese north of Mgbowo, who were important agents in the slave trade, especially in slaves from Agbaja.[59]

These two branches came together again near the Nike village group, the most important northern agents of the Aro. The Nike fought wars with several of their neighbours, especially the Agbaja, selling some of the captives of these wars to the Aro and settling the remainder on the newly conquered lands as frontier outposts. The Aro in return supplied Abam mercenaries to the Nike and, at least on one occasion, to the Nike's enemy the Opi as well.[60]

To the east the fair at Uburu attracted a great amount of trade and continued to be an active centre for the salt trade which had initially brought it fame. Its sessions were co-ordinated with those at Bende to permit trade and traders to move smoothly from one to the other. It was also connected to Afikpo to the south-east and to the important market at Nkalagu to the north. From Nkalagu secondary routes passed north and east, while the main route continued north-west via Nike to Idah, the Igala capital on the Niger. There was some Aro trade with the North-East Igbo, but this does not appear to have become important until the latter part of the nineteenth century.[61]

Many of the slaves from this northern region were produced in the wars between the Igbo and the Igala, as well as from judicial

[58] R. de S. Stapleton, 'Intelligence Report on the Mbowo Clan, Awgu Division, Onitsha Province', 1935, pp. 1–4, NAI, CSO 26/4/30717; M. MacGregor, 'Assessment Report Awgu Division, Onitsha Province', 1927, pp. 6–7, NAI, CSO 26/3/20681.

[59] S. P. L. Beaumont, 'Intelligence Report on the Ntegbe-Nese Clan, Udi Division, Onitsha Province', 1933, pp. 11, 35–6, NAI, CSO 26/3/29601; P. P. Grey, 'Intelligence Report on the Villages of Abudu, Ama-Owelli, Isu, Obaku, Obeagu and Ugbo of the Awgu Division, Onitsha Province', 1934, pp. 2–3, 6, NAI, CSO 26/3/29803.

[60] Horton, 'Ohu System', pp. 311–13.

[61] Cf. G. B. G. Chapman, 'Intelligence Report/Assessment Report on the Ikwo Clan of the Abakaliki Division of Ogoja Province', 1930, pp. 9, 12, 48, NAI, CSO 26/3/26804; G. I. Jones, 'Assessment Report on the Ngbo and Ezengbo Clans, Abakaliki Division, Ogoja Province', 1930, p. 131, NAI, CSO 26/3/27002; J. G. C. Allen, 'Intelligence Report on the Izi Clan, Abakaliki Division, Ogoja Province', 1932, pp. 172–3, NAI, CSO 26/4/30192.

decisions and kidnapping. Contemporary records indicate that slaves from the northern area might pass either into Aro hands or into the Igala network to the north. An Igbo from the Nkalagu area, known as Eshikanyi at home and Jacob Egypt in Sierra Leone, was kidnapped and sold to the Igala about 1839 and taken to the coast for sale. An Agbaja Igbo named Aneke (*alias* Thomas O'Connor), was kidnapped twenty years earlier and sold into the Aro system passing through the Bende market and the port of Bonny.[62] Oral sources indicate that even in the most northerly part of the area the majority of the slaves passed eventually into Aro rather than Igala hands.[63]

3. CONCLUSIONS

Examined on a regional basis, Aro trading operations show a great range of organizing techniques. It was not a single coherent system but an elaborate and flexible assemblage of operations geared to local conditions. Their political power might be weak or strong, their settlements large or small, many or few, their trading structures manned at all levels by the Aro or based on alliances with non-Aro agents.

By every indication the power of the Oracle of Arochukwu was considerable throughout most of the hinterland. It was not simply a pawn used by the Aro to promote their trade, for the Oracle was powerful even in places where the Aro had little or no direct trade, such as Aboh or New Calabar. To enhance its powers the Aro had encouraged the identification of the oracular deity with *Chukwu*, the Supreme Being of the Igbo. This was at least partially successful and may help to explain why the Oracle was respected as a court of last resort among the Igbo. Perhaps because the Ibibio High God *Abassi* was never assimilated to it, the Oracle remained more feared than sought after in that area.[64] Certainly Ibibio proverbs do not express any enthusiasm about the idea of a visit to the shrine.

The enhancement of the dignity of the Oracle was not only a means of exacting heavy fines (including slaves) from petitioners, but a means of enhancing the status of the Aro as well. To harm a 'Child

---

[62] Koelle, *Polygotta*, p. 8.

[63] Afigbo, 'Trade and Trade Routes', pp. 2–3.

[64] The Ibibio call the Oracle *Ibritam Inokun*. The origin of the name is obscure, although some would derive it from *Ibit-Itam*, the drum of Itam, an Ibibio clan south of Arochukwu; see Ilogu, 'Inside Arochukwu', p. 107. The origin of the common English name for the Oracle, the Long Juju, is equally obscure.

of Chukwu' or 'God-man' was to risk supernatural sanctions which were not taken lightly in the hinterland. Moreover, contacts made in promoting the Oracle could be useful to the Aro for trading and vice versa.

However, it is quite impossible that the Oracle ever served as a conduit for any large percentage of the slaves sold at the coast. If Dike's estimate that half or more of the total number of slaves reaching the coast passed through the Oracle were true, an average of several hundred a day sustained over several decades would have had to have been 'eaten' by Chukwu. There is no indication anywhere in the written or oral sources of anything like such a volume passing through the Oracle.

The military factor was also important in Aro history, but its role was not a decisive one. The foundation legends of Aro settlements among the Igbo collected by Umo and those from among the Ibibio collected by the present writer rarely mention the use of force in the establishment of an Aro settlement. On the contrary, especially in the eastern area the Aro were often invited to end the Abam incursions. It is quite possible, of course, to see the Aro as *agents provocateurs* in this, but the evidence indicates that the Abam needed little encouragement from the Aro to engage in raids on their neighbours. While the Aro often employed the Abam and acted as agents to hire them out to others, there is no indication that the Aro were ever in control of the Abam.[65]

The Aro expansion resembled the proverbial camel with his nose in the tent and the greatest violence is associated with those Aro settlements that grew to a large size, especially Ndizuogu, Ndienyi, and the Ibibio Inokun. Most Aro settlements were small and have a peaceful history. War was hardly in the interests of traders since it led inevitably to a stoppage of trade. As the Eze Aro explained the Aro success, 'Since the Aro were *not* warlike they could penetrate to any part of the country and establish trade.'[66]

Yet the Aro lived in a tumultuous era in a society where sporadic feuds and petty conflicts were a fact of life. The Aro traders travelled

---

[65] Uku, 'Note on the "Abam"', p. 76, found those he interviewed 'generally agreed ... that the warriors were motivated not by financial considerations but by the compelling need to bring home the head of a victim', and unanimously agreed 'that the warriors were never mercenaries of the Aro'. He does note (p. 79), however, that the Aro gave chiefs a 'consultation fee' prior to guiding the warriors to an area with which they had a grouse.

[66] Interview with Chief Oji, Arochukwu.

in armed troupes and there is no question that their military might was respected and feared. Nevertheless, there is no indication that their possession of fire-arms was a decisive factor in their success, since the Aro made no effort to monopolize these weapons. Moreover, despite their close relationship with the Aro, the Abam resisted adopting fire-arms until well into the twentieth century. Apparently like their contemporaries in European cavalry units, they felt that fire-arms went against the whole *esprit* of the battle. For the Abam the proof of manhood was the head of an enemy taken in hand to hand combat. Spent cartridges or an empty powder horn were poor substitutes. Thus by all accounts their military reputation was built on the use of the fine swords and cutlasses made by the kindred Abiriba, not on guns.[67]

In comparison with the Yoruba and Dahomean states warfare east of the Niger was a very underdeveloped art. The small size and decentralization of the polities produced a correspondingly small scale of warfare. The Aro used arms to defend themselves and their allies and in some places for limited territorial gains, but their trading operations were not dependent on conquest nor their routes on armies. Their trading network could not have thrived without military measures, but it was not built or sustained by aggression.

Trade and politics have long been considered as partners in this region, but they are an abrasive team. Given the strongly independent tradition of the political units of the hinterland—a tradition shared by the Aro—attempts to interfere with local politics met with strong opposition. Only the largest Aro colonies, such as Ndizuogu and Inokun tried to dominate local affairs. Most Aro settlements were small and without territorial ambitions. Given their wealth and control of the arms trade they might have set out to create a territorial empire, but there is no indication that state-building was ever their goal among either the Igbo or the Ibibio.[68]

In their internal political organization the Aro differed more by degree than by kind from other communities of south-eastern Nigeria. In fact when G. I. Jones prepared his 1958 report on political organization in this region he chose to use the Arochukwu

[67] Basden, *Niger Ibos*, p. 385. Leonard, 'Journey to Bende', p. 206. H. D. Carleton, 'Orders for O. C. Columns, Aro Field Force', in C.O. 520/10/381: Moore to C.O., 24 Nov. 1901.

[68] J. C. Anene, *Southern Nigeria in Transition 1885–1906* (Cambridge: Univ. Press, 1966), p. 17; Ottenberg, 'Ibo Oracles', p. 301; Jeffreys, 'Assessment Report, Ikot Ekpene', p. 5.

organization as the example of a *typical* system. Essentially Aro-chukwu was governed by a council of representatives of its component parts (originally nine clans, later nineteen villages), which deliberated and decided all important matters in an open and free exchange. No segment or group of segments could dominate the others, for no village could be bound by a decision to which it did not consent in a general meeting. Although Arochukwu possessed a titled head, the Eze Aro, his powers were largely presidial like those of other town heads in the hinterland. Likewise each village was governed by a council representing its component families and was structured segmentally.[69]

Arochukwu also resembled other communities in the hinterland in having sent out individuals and small groups at various times to settle in new places. To the general reasons of land hunger and internal disputes that were operative elsewhere the Aro added the very important reason of forming trading outposts. The major difference between Arochukwu and other hinterland communities was in the relations which existed between the emigrants and their original homeland. Whereas other emigrants' ties gradually weakened as they formed new relationships abroad, the Aro managed to maintain relatively close ties and a common sense of identity between those at home (the *Aro Uno*) and those settled abroad (the *Aro Uzo*). Annual reunions were held at Arochukwu by representatives of the diaspora and travelling Aro naturally made it a point of staying at their cousins' far-flung settlements. Over time the dispersed Aro became several times as numerous as those remaining in Arochukwu.[70]

But annual meetings and common market-places were hardly enough to keep an organization together in the absence of any management structure. A segmentary government can take effective action only when there is near total agreement and what evidence there is suggests that this was not very often among the Aro. Internal disputes seem to have been frequent and bitter and the larger colonies operated in a totally independent manner. It may be that the oracle that apparently existed at Ndizuogu in the nineteenth century was an authorized franchise of Arochukwu's, but it is more likely that it represented an independent centre of Aro power. Certainly by the time British explorers made contact with the Aro in

[69] *Jones Report*, p. 5.
[70] Ukwu, 'Development of Trade', pp. 651–5.

the 1890s there were many bitter internal disputes. When Casement visited the Ibibio Inokun in 1894, he found it split into two Aro factions and learned that the Arochukwu villages of Ibom and Obinkita were at war with one another. The Aro traders of Ibibio Inokun had been unable to attend the Bende fair for four years owing to a dispute in which several of their leading men had been killed.[71] When Leonard visited Bende in 1896 he found a similar imbroglio among the Aro:

The fact was the Aro people were split up into factions on the question of trade—factions that were not merely jealous of but inimical to each other— and here at Bende, the central market and common meeting ground presumably of all factions, they were not nationally united, although they struggled hard to make it appear so ... there was no bond of unity, no patriotism was displayed, every faction played its own game, which consisted of each one trying to play off against the others.[72]

Leonard may have been inclined to exaggerate the depth of hostility in the normally fractious politics of the hinterland and it may be that the Aro were less united after several years of British pressures than they had been earlier. Still it is striking that Leonard's description went exactly contrary to the common British belief in his day that the Aro were superbly organized and at the root of all resistance to European authority. At the very least his description indicated that agreement was not achieved easily among the Aro.

The Aro did not create anything like a state. Rather than departing from the traditional segmental organization of the hinterland peoples, they depended upon it as the basis of their trading organization, distributing themselves across the hinterland in territories that mirrored the village and lineage patterns of Arochukwu.[73] Rather than departing from the political traditions of the hinterland by creating any formal structures of authority to direct this far-flung

[71] Casement, 'Report from Itu', pp. 5, 11.

[72] Leonard, 'Journey to Bende', p. 205.

[73] Shankland, 'Intelligence Report, Aro', Appendix IV, gives the following as the spheres of influence of the Aro villages (in italic): *Utuhugwu*: Akunakuna; *Oror*: Akunakuna; *Uguakuma*: Ekoi; *Amasu*: Calabar via Umon, Eki, and Uwet; *Ujari*: Enyong; *Ibom*: Enyong, Ada (Afikpo), Obubra; *Amukwa*: Uzuakoli; *Amankwu*: Enugu; *Abagwu*: Item and Ahozara (Bende); *Amanagwu*: Itu; *Obinkita*: Ibibio Country; *Amuvi*: Ahozara and Enugu; *Uguator*: Abakaliki; *Amoba*: Afikpo; *Isinkpu*: Bonny, Okrika, Ngwa, and Degema; *Atani*: Bonny, Okrika, Ngwa, and Degema; *Amangwu*: Ahozara. Forde and Jones, *Ibo and Ibibio*, p. 32, say that the Ndienyi colony was composed of settlers from *Ujalli*, *Ibom*, *Obinkita*, and *Atani*.

enterprise, the Aro continued to rely on the town-meeting mode of government by consensus, with all the imperfections inherent in it.

There is every indication that the basis of the Aro expansion and operations was economic. Moreover, the techniques of trading employed by the Aro were essentially those used by other hinterland traders, as were described in the previous chapter. The Aro created no new currencies and few new markets, relying instead on those already in existence. They were not alone in forming trading alliances and dealing in slaves and goods of local and European origin. They were not the oldest trading people in this area nor the only ones to combine trading in spiritual and material goods. Their achievement was in the skill and single-mindedness with which they pursued these ends, which gave them a virtual monopoly over long-distance trade in much of the region. While their ability to travel unmolested was due in part to the fear of divine retribution or military retaliation, local traditions strongly suggest that, like other traders, the Aro were made welcome primarily for the goods which they brought.

The Aro differed from other traders in the scale on which they operated, a scale which enabled them to transcend and combine into a single marketing grid the already existing regional networks of trade and through alliances with the other leading trading peoples to bring them into this economic structure. These alliances were based upon equality, not upon Aro domination, and the marketing grid in which all participated was controlled by none of them. Yet the Aro were the centre of this structure and ran the principal fairs that fed it. To them must go the major credit for its creation.

The Aro also differed from other trading groups in their ability to live in widely scattered settlements throughout the hinterland without losing their sense of common identity. Not just many, but most Aro came to reside outside Arochukwu and visited that town only on infrequent occasions. Like other emigrants the Aro settler soon entered by marriage into the kinship structures of his host community. His children were 'sons of the soil' and grew up fully conversant with the local dialect and culture. Yet unlike other emigrants the *Aro Uzo* did not gradually lose their former ties and become fully assimilated into the new community. Instead they firmly maintained their original culture and kinship ties. They were kinsmen of other Aro living and trading in the same area and, because the Aro trading territories were organized on the pattern of the village and lineage structures of Arochukwu, an Aro man's nearest Aro neighbours were also among his closest kinsfolk. The *Aro Uzo* had the unique system of two encapsulated residential kinship groups.

Generally the most important Aro trader in an area was regarded as the informal leader by his Aro relatives. He would call general meetings to co-ordinate trading policy and overcome any obstacles. Naturally if any Aro trader required assistance he could call upon his Aro kinsmen in the area for assistance. It was widely understood in the hinterland that to attack one Aro was to attack them all. Matters of common interest could also be discussed at regional meetings of the *Aro Uzo*, leaving the most important matters for resolution at the annual gatherings at Arochukwu. As has been shown, agreement was not an easy matter, but necessity forced solutions to the gravest problems. After Leonard's visit to Bende in 1896, for example, the Aro put aside their internal disputes long enough to agree to move the fair to neighbouring Uzuakoli to punish the Bende people for being too co-operative with Leonard.[74]

This ability to achieve voluntary agreement in time of crisis was the key to Aro organization. In part this is a characteristic of all segmentary systems, but the ability of the Aro to agree despite their dispersed settlement was due more to their great strength of common identity. Despite their fractiousness the Aro were unique among the hinterland peoples in creating not a state, but a nation, a sense of enduring communality which consistently exceeded the strength of ties to kinship groups and local settlements. This spirit was well described in a 1933 Intelligence Report on the Aro: 'The Aro were clan-conscious rather than town-conscious, and today the average man will declare with pride that he is an Aro before he gives the name of his town, recalling the spirit of St. Paul triumphantly declaring "Civis Romanus sum," followed by the information, "I come from Tarsus, no mean city." '[75]

The reasons for the development of this remarkable national spirit are difficult to assess in the absence of adequate historical records. To a degree it was a natural by-product of trading life. Constantly on the move in his trade, a man becomes less ready to give full allegiance to a narrow provincialism. This tendency can be noted among other itinerant hinterland peoples as well, such as the Awka, Nri, and Isu. This does not seem adequate to explain how the Aro, who were willing to settle far from 'home', to marry local wives and raise

---

[74] Fox, *Uzuakoli*, p. 2.
[75] Shankland, 'Intelligence Report, Aro', p. 18.

their children in a 'foreign' culture, managed to preserve this national identity. The explanation would appear to be largely in the Aro's insistence on incorporation into a host community only on the basis of a superior social standing. Thus, as was shown above, the Aro in Afikpo became an élite class. A local historian who did a study of most of the Aro settlements among the Igbo repeatedly mentions the emphasis the Aro put on preserving the distinctiveness and thus superiority of their dress, speech, and other customs.[76] Among the Ibibio and the Ngwa Igbo Aro settlers seem to have placed less emphasis on cultural distinctiveness, but no less on superior status. Frequently this took the form of a claim to be the rulers of the area, a claim which was seldom literally true. The claim to superiority was based on many things: the Aro's position as traders over farmers, their special relationship to Chukwu, their military resources, their special relationship with Europeans, the alleged superiority of their culture. Whether employed consciously or unconsciously, however, this claim acted as a bulwark against the loss of Aro national consciousness. Leonard, who was accustomed to the idea of his own superiority over all Africans, was taken aback by the boldness of the first Aro he met, who not only refused to remove his hat in the presence of the white man, but also proclaimed his superiority in the trading pidgin of the day: 'Me be "God boy"— me be "God boy." You be white man; me be "God boy." '[77]

The Aro were one of several trading peoples in south-eastern Nigeria. Their success and their limitations can be understood only in the context of their relations with other trading peoples. Throughout the parts of the hinterlands in which they operated the Aro did not exist in isolation; they were dependent on a tremendous number of 'local agents' and allies who did much of the most basic trading, leaving the Aro to concentrate on the integration, supply, and wholesale aspects of the trade. At the same time the Aro were surrounded on all sides by trading peoples similar to themselves, who operated within their own trading spheres and effectively blocked Aro expansion. To the south were the coastal entrepôts of Old Calabar, Bonny, New Calabar, and Nembe-Brass; to the west the trading communities of the Niger, the Awka and Isu on land and the Aboh, Ossomari, Onitsha, and others on the river; to the north were the Igala and to the east the Agwa'aguna, Umon, and Efik. With all of these the

---

[76] Umo, *Aro Settlements, passim.*
[77] Leonard, 'Journey to Bende', p. 191.

Aro established some sort of mutually beneficial relationship, yet all effectively blocked Aro economic expansion. There can be no clearer indication of the Aro's lack of substantial state structures and military force than their inability to break through to the coast to trade directly with European ships.

CHAPTER VI

The Slave Trade and Economic Development

THE slave trade is generally studied with a focus on the European slave traders or on the Africans who were sold into it. However, one's understanding of the economic importance of this trade to Africa is significantly altered if one looks instead at the African traders in slaves. The change does not result from assigning any lessened responsibility to the European slavers or giving any less compassion to the African victims in this nefarious trade. Rather the change comes from understanding the economic motives of the African slave traders which drew them into this trade.

For the economy of the hinterland the slave trade was a solution to a very old and difficult problem, the problem of growth. Earlier chapters have shown that the basic economy of the hinterland was subsistence production with some local redistribution of subsistence items and some regional trade in food crops, fish, and salt. While the amount of this trade was greater than in many parts of the continent, it was not great enough to remove the over-all economy from a subsistence level. To be sure one of the remarkable features of the economy was its early involvement in longer distance exchanges in certain rare and luxurious trade items, such as brass, ivory, beads, and cloth. This small but important trade in luxuries was in existence in Igbo-Ukwu days, and was more elaborately developed by the time of the first Portuguese. Although this luxury trade is historically important as evidence of the trading skill and capacity of this region, its volume also was too restricted in size and distribution to have had any great effect on the over-all economy. The problem which the region faced was expanding its trade through new efforts, new markets, or improved technology. The arrival of the Europeans did not provide a new technology, but it did open the world market to the products of south-eastern Nigeria. Of the products desired on the European market at that time the hinterland could not supply spices, gold, gums, or waxes, and so the new trade was principally in ivory and slaves during the first two centuries of trade.

At first the ivory trade expanded more rapidly. The early Portuguese purchased some and by the seventeenth century the Rio del Rey area alone was exporting up to 40,000 pounds of ivory a year and it was said to be plentiful at Old and New Calabar as well.[1] By the end of that century, however, ivory was becoming scarcer and more expensive, not because the growing slave trade had somehow driven it from the market, but more likely because two centuries of extensive hunting had diminished the number of elephants, as had the growing human population which itself was consuming a larger share of the tusks.[2] The ivory trade continued but it had lost its potential for solving the problem of growth in the hinterland.

From the point of view of the hinterland traders slaves proved a better solution to the problem of finding a viable export. Although their numbers could not be expanded indefinitely, the course of the slave trade in this region demonstrated that this trade could be sustained at a rather high volume. Moreover, because this volume was more than replenished by the naturally expanding population and because the manner in which they were obtained did not lead to a large additional loss of life, the overseas slave trade did no serious over-all damage to the hinterland economy.

The problem of economic growth in the export sector was only one aspect of the economic problems of the hinterland; the other half was economic development. Economic development is not distinct from economic growth but rather is a special kind of growth which sets off a more general expansion of the economy, stimulating diversification and specialization of labour outside the subsistence sphere and implies an ability to deal with the world market from a position of strength not dependence. The overseas slave trade, whatever its other effects, promoted economic growth; whether it led to significant economic development or simply enriched a small

[1] At the beginning of the sixteenth century ivory was plentiful on the Benin River and in 'Opuu', i.e. Igbo, and available in lesser amounts from the eastern delta and Cameroon coast, according to Pereira, *Esmeraldo*, pp. 134, 136, 140, 148. For the seventeenth century see Dapper, *Description*, p. 315, and Donnan, *Documents*, I, 193, for Royal African Company information in 1672.

[2] In 1699 James Barbot reported that New Calabar had priced itself out of the ivory market, a statement that G. I. Jones, *Trading States*, p. 89, has taken to mean that the ivory trade ceased then, but other sources make clear that the halt was only temporary; see Starke to Westmore in Donnan, *Documents*, IV, 73–4 and John Barbot, 'Description', p. 381. The ivory trade at Benin, a royal monopoly, did not decline in the eighteenth century, but neither was it ever able to expand beyond earlier volumes; see Ryder, *Benin*, pp. 206, 209, and *passim*.

class of traders without altering the over-all economy, has been an open question.

In a penetrating reappraisal of the effects of the slave trade, A. G. Hopkins argues that, for West Africa as a whole, the slave trade and the contemporary trans-Saharan trade did not in fact induce general economic development.[3] He attributes this failure to four key factors. Two factors concern the nature of the export trade. In the first place, 'the export trade was confined to staples which required little diversification of existing methods of production and no significant additional commercialization of factors in West Africa'. In addition, 'the size of the export proceeds was too small to stimulate either a wide range or a large number of new enterprises'. Hopkins's other two arguments concern the nature of the imports into West Africa. While he argues they were not the shoddy goods that are sometimes pictured, they did consist 'of consumer goods which needed hardly any further processing, and so provided few opportunities for productive investment in the domestic economy'. Secondly, while the volume and range of goods imported into West Africa in this period probably led to some enlargement of internal markets, the relatively high cost of the imports and the fact that the new wealth brought by the trade went into the hands of a relatively small group of traders, 'prevented the emergence of a mass market based upon cheap manufactures'.

The present study does not disagree significantly with Hopkins's general conclusions, but it does suggest that south-eastern Nigeria, though it did not advance to a new stage of economic development, did experience a greater degree of growth and development as a result of the slave trade than did many other parts of West Africa. For this reason its economy was able to grow more quickly when the opportunity emerged in the nineteenth century. This eighteenth-century development was in three areas. First, the slave trade promoted the growth of an integrated network of fairs, markets, and trade routes which reached into nearly every part of the hinterland, and of trading currencies adequate to carry on this trade. Second, while the slave trade was controlled by a proportionately small number of professional traders, it stimulated an already vigorous internal trade, notably in foodstuffs and handicrafts, which carried the effects of the foreign trade and imports far beyond the professional middlemen. Finally, a higher proportion of the goods

[3] Hopkins, *Economic History*, pp. 119–23.

imported into south-eastern Nigeria, notably the iron bars, did require significant additional processing and thus had a multiplier effect on the internal economy. The chief reason why imports into this region differed from those elsewhere in West Africa may have been that the higher degree of development in local industries such as blacksmithing and cloth-making enabled goods produced in south-eastern Nigeria in the eighteenth century to compete successfully with foreign ones.

1. THE MARKETING INFRASTRUCTURE

The markets and marketing system of south-eastern Nigeria have impressed all those who have studied this area. According to Polly Hill, one of the best students of rural West African economies: 'Certainly the rural periodic markets of the main acephalous societies of Eastern Nigeria, Ibibio as well as Ibo, are in terms of their number, among the most impressive in West Africa.'[4] Just as impressive as the quantity of markets has been the strong affinity of the people for the market-place. In the words of another anthropologist, whose statement about one Igbo group may be applied more widely:

If agriculture is the basic occupation of these Ibo people, trading is a close second. One might almost say that whereas they farm of necessity they trade not only of necessity but also for pleasure. Their markets are one of the main features of their lives. They provide a meeting point for the discussion of common business and the dissemination of news; they are a social event where the spice of gossip, the recreation of dancing and the zest of a bargain relieve the almost continual toil of hoeing, planting, weeding and harvesting throughout the year. Trading is the breath of life, particularly to the women...[5]

How did markets come to assume so prominent a role in this region? The high importance which they presently have presupposes a long period of development. One scholar has suggested that Igbo village markets may have developed from the custom of the rest day, i.e. a day or days out of the four-day week on which people stayed at home from the farms to do chores and craftwork, rest, visit, hold festivals, and engage in petty trade, and that a market might even be older than the village that owned it since a 'community moving

---

[4] Polly Hill, 'Notes on Traditional Market Authority and Market periodicity in West Africa', *JAH*, VII (1966), 300.
[5] M. M. Green, *Igbo Village Affairs*, 2nd edn. (London: Frank Cass, 1964), p. 37. For a description of a somewhat different marketing spirit see Paul and Laura Bohannan, *Tiv Economy* (Evanston: Northwestern Univ. Press, 1968), pp. 220–1.

into a new territory "carried" along its old market with its associated shrines and rituals'.[6] Others have related the proliferation of markets to the high ratio of population to land in this region, ratios which are among the highest in rural Africa.[7] Whatever their earliest history, these markets were important as social and economic centres, forums where one might exchange small agricultural surpluses along with greetings, news, and gossip.

No market stood alone. Each was part of a carefully worked out plan by which neighbouring markets met in rotation on set days, commonly in a four or eight-day cycle with the larger markets meeting once every four-day week, while the smaller ones met every two market weeks. Not only was this market 'ring' designed to prevent the overlapping of local markets but sometimes it kept the main market of one group from falling on the same day as their neighbour's main market as well, so that inter-group trade might be encouraged. Among the Igbo the market rings mirrored the village-group structure, the main market generally being 'located in and controlled by the senior village', while the smaller markets met in the outlying villages.[8] While the origins of this system cannot be traced in detail, it appears that from an early date the hinterland was covered with a 'tangle of individual marketing rings', through which goods could work their way slowly to places far distant from their points of origin.[9]

For much if not most of south-eastern Nigeria before the eighteenth century the primary economic function of the market-place was to redistribute within its own district the local agricultural surplus and a few local craft items such as pottery. The main function of such markets may, in fact, have been more social than economic, for as the Ibibio saying has it, 'The people who fill the markets are

[6] Ukwu I. Ukwu, 'Markets in Iboland', Ph.D. Thesis, Univ. of Cambridge, 1965, p. 33, and 'Development of Trade', p. 649.

[7] B. W. Hodder, 'Distribution of Markets in Yorubaland', *Scottish Geographical Magazine*, LXXXI (1965), 50, suggests that a critical density of about 50 persons per square mile is necessary for 'a regular pattern of periodic markets' among the Yoruba. Such a theory would account for the absence of markets among the Ekoi, who were described as 'keen traders' by Talbot, *In the Shadow*, pp. 266–7. Calabar Division as a whole had a density of 51 persons per square mile in 1921, but the density of the Ekoi areas was nearer 30 persons per square mile. In contrast, most of the hinterland west of the Cross River had densities of over 300 persons per square mile. See Talbot, *Peoples*, IV, 9–10.

[8] Ukwu, 'Development of Trade', p. 649.

[9] Ibid.

those who go empty handed.'[10] Nevertheless, in some areas, as has already been pointed out, regional trading networks did develop around certain special items, such as food, salt, cloth, beads, and metal products. The trade between the coast and the immediate hinterland, noted earliest by Pereira, is the best documented, but there were also regional networks further inland in cloth, acori beads, and the ironware of the Awka, Abiriba, and other smiths. Another example is the market at Uburu which became the centre for a regional trade in salt from a nearby salt lake. The Uburu salt was purchased by the northern Igbo and southern Igala, and the market later became one of the two great fairs of the hinterland.[11]

The periodicity of the markets, as well as the regional trade between the hinterland and the delta, was recorded by James Barbot during his visit to the Rio Real in 1699: 'In [the Igbo] territory there are two markets every week, for slaves and provisions, which the [New] Calabar Blacks keep very regularly, to supply themselves both in provisions and slaves, palm oil, palm wine, etc.; there being great plenty of the last.'[12] Although Barbot did not record the fact, the Kalabari very likely brought dried fish and locally made salt to exchange with the Igbo for slaves and food. By the time in question they would have brought European merchandise as well.

The expansion of the slave trade in the eighteenth century produced several changes in this marketing system. The interzonal markets, which had served as exchange points between the delta fishermen and the inland farmers, were expanded and their connections further inland strengthened to accommodate the trade in slaves. As was shown above, fairs at Bende and Uburu also emerged in mid-century and imposed a longer cycle and more massive volume on the old four-day cycle of markets, handling (if contemporary accounts are accurate) a major portion of the slave trade of this period. Another change took place along the major rivers, such as the Niger and Cross, where the growing trade gave new importance to markets held on islands or on sand-bars. These markets possessed both political and geographic advantages. They tended to be politically neutral, located equidistant from riverain trading

[10] W. E. Aston-Smith, 'Intelligence Report on the Ukana Group of the Ikot Ekpene Division, Calabar Province', 1931, p. 69, NAI, CSO 26/3/27604.

[11] The date of the origin of this salt trade is unknown. One author says that Uburu was a salt trading centre 'in the days of the Long Juju and before then...'; Nzekwu, 'Uburu', p. 91. Cf. Uchendu, Igbo, p. 35.

[12] Barbot, 'Abstract of a Voyage', p. 461.

communities. They were accessible from the water and from communities on both banks, while their location made them hard to disrupt by surprise and offered several avenues of escape when necessary. Such provisions were necessary as the Lander brothers discovered in 1830 at the important Igala Bank market on the Niger when they found themselves and the market under attack.[13]

The safety of a market became a prime consideration when dealing in a trade as dangerous and valuable as that in slaves, so that a secure and neutral location was an attractive asset. Inland markets located at the frontier between ethnic divisions also became important since they allowed traders from unrelated and even hostile communities to attend with a measure of safety. For quick escape, however, each group customarily sat in the part of the market nearest the road to their homes. In this land of small political units important markets became islands of political neutrality as well, and the preservation of order and justice in them became an exercise in international law.[14] Although in theory every market belonged to a village or village-group, when in session it belonged to those who attended it. The Bende fair, for example, was transferred from one site to another simply by the decision of the main Aro traders to attend elsewhere.[15]

In terms of legal jurisdiction too the larger markets had to become a law unto themselves, since those attending came from far beyond the borders of the largest political unit of any traditional jurisdiction. To deal with the legal complexities a variety of secular and religious mechanisms were used. Particularly among the Igbo there was recourse to a higher law and a greater judge by putting each market-place under the jurisdiction of a specially created market deity whose supernatural powers would punish those who violated the market-place.[16] Large markets also had their own courts whose judges sat in a special shed in the market to hear disputes. All those entering the market placed themselves under the jurisdiction of these judges. Ideas of jurisprudence left the enforcement of judicial decisions to the aggrieved person supported by his kinsmen and the public at large, making any special police unnecessary. Penalties were generally clearly understood. A thief, for example, might find himself forced to run the gauntlet naked through the market-place. Serious

[13] Lander and Lander, *Niger Journal*, pp. 232–43.

[14] Bohannan and Bohannan, *Tiv Economy*, p. 190, describe a comparable situation among the Tiv.

[15] See above, Chapter IV, note 47.

[16] Njaka, 'Igbo Political Institutions', p. 285.

or repeated theft was almost universally punished by death or sale into slavery.[17] Groups whose people got a bad reputation for unruliness might be barred from the market until they promised to exercise better restraint on their members. Despite these measures, peace was sometimes elusive. An Anang elder maintained that in his village group, 'There were no markets in those days that were held from beginning to end without fighting.'[18] The Anang have a bad reputation for disputes, but they were not alone in having unruly markets. Yet a market which acquired a reputation for violence soon lost the crowds that made it prosper, so there was strong pressure among the market traders to preserve order at all costs.

As was explained above, slaves were not normally sold in local village markets (this taking place instead in places of greater calm and privacy), but as the slaves came nearer the coast they were sold in the larger markets and fairs. In reaching the coast slaves and goods destined for export would pass through a succession of land or riverain markets, and, as was noted by both Dapper and Barbot, through several sets of traders as well.[19] In the distribution of the foreign goods received in return for these exports, however, the entire marketing system was involved. These goods first passed through the linear network of major markets and fairs and then were taken to smaller and more isolated depots, gradually distributing themselves throughout the tangle of market rings which covered most of the hinterland. The volume of trade encouraged the co-ordination of market systems on a larger and larger scale. For instance, the central markets of Itu, Enyong, Ukwa, and Umon, spread along some twelve miles of the Cross River, began to meet in a single four-day cycle.[20]

This highly developed system of market and fairs was served by an intricate web of land and water routes and by well-worn trails leading to more northern slave markets. The earliest evidence for this region suggests that transport by water was well developed before the arrival of the first Portuguese mariners. Igbo-Ukwu and Benin were served by the riverain traders on the Niger and trading canoes could have been used for the trade from the delta to the Gold Coast along the coast or through inter-coastal waterways. Pereira

[17] These conclusions are based upon the judicial sections of the intelligence reports.
[18] Interview with Chief Lawrence Udo Akpan, Ikot Obio Akpa, Afaha Obong, 18 Nov. 1972.
[19] Dapper, *Description*, pp. 315–16; Barbot, 'Description', p. 381.
[20] Interview, Mr. Udowong, Ukwa.

and later witnesses were astonished at the size of the canoes in regular use in the Bight of Biafra. There are, of course, few eye-witness accounts of the overland routes before the first European explorations in the nineteenth century, but the density of the population and the intensity of the trade presuppose the existence of footpaths connecting, at least in a meandering fashion, the villages and markets of the hinterland, Equiano tells of walking for several days along such paths in the mid-eighteenth century on his way to a riverain town.[21] As the slave trade grew, a more direct network of roads must have come into existence. Most of Koelle's informants travelled overland on their way to the coast. Much of the network of trade roads created in the period was later incorporated into the early colonial road system.[22] In the late nineteenth century the first European explorers to venture overland were impressed by the unexpected quality of the roads on which they travelled. Major A. G. Leonard, who went from Opobo to Bende in 1896, commented that parts of the routes in the Ngwa area were 'more like an avenue in England, shaded by splendid trees, than a wild roadway in Africa'.[23] Such avenues were not unique to the Ngwa, for further east the Ibibio were reported by the British Consuls to 'take a pride in making broad smooth roads from village to village. These they keep clean of weeds and planted on either side with neat hedges and fine shady trees.'[24] Consul Johnston also noted the existence of important roads from Okrika to Bende, from Bende east to the Cross River and north to the Benue, and from the middle Cross River to the Benue. Other roads, he noted, ran from rivers in the vicinity of Old Calabar to the upper Cross River, the most important of which was the one through Ododop to the Cameroon Grasslands that was described in §3 of Chapter IV. West of the Cross River Roger Casement travelled on roads which gave more evidence of heavy traffic than careful design, since his route contained stretches worn ten to twelve feet deep by erosion and barely wide enough for a porter to pass through.[25]

[21] Equiano, 'Early Travels', pp. 85–8.

[22] Ekejiuba, 'Aro Trade System', p. 15; C. U. G. Tristram, 'Intelligence Report on the Umuemenyi-Akoli Clan, Bende Division, Owerri Province', 1933, p. 6, NAI, CSO 26/3/28988.

[23] Leonard, 'Journey to Bende', p. 196. See description of other roadways Leonard encountered on pp. 191 and 201.

[24] H. H. Johnston, 'Report on the British Protectorate of the Oil Rivers', enclosed in Johnston to Salisbury, 1 Dec. 1888, F. O. 84/1882.

[25] Casement, 'Report from Itu', p. 2.

In a region of many rivers and streams bridges were a necessary part of any network of roads. Streams were often forded by means of conveniently fallen logs, but Leonard crossed the Aba River near Akirika Uku on 'a wonderful floating bridge, ... that extends for quite half a mile, winding in and out among the dense under-growth...'[26] During the rainy season when parts of their land flooded the Ododop constructed suspension bridges made of withes for the convenience of the traders to and from Old Calabar. While such engineering feats were out of the ordinary, they were not unique. Casement found several bridges during his 1894 exploration of the Ibibio country. The Kwa Ibo River could be crossed by a bamboo bridge near Ukana Ikot Ibe.[27]

Both in the market-place and on the road it was a clear principle of life in the hinterland that the trader was responsible for making his own security arrangements. There simply did not exist a public force charged with and capable of safeguarding travellers. This is in very clear contrast to the situation in the more centralized societies of West Africa where, from an early date, traders and other travellers had been charged tolls on roads and in markets for which in return they could expect the protection of the public authorities. For example, in 1941 each canoe visiting 'Gori' market on the Niger north of Idah had to pay 50 cowries per crew member and 50 more per bag of salt. The market authorities in turn paid an annual tribute of 360,000 cowries to the Fulani and a horse to the Igala king.[28]

Tolls of this nature did not generally exist in the hinterland for the simple reason that political units lacked both the authority and the means to collect them. Polly Hill has pointed out that the traditional absence of such tolls is, in fact, one of the significant features of economic life in this area.[29] Nevertheless, several recent studies of this area have argued that tolls were a general feature of pre-colonial economic life. These studies cite very few examples to back up their claims and those additional instances which have come to the attention of the present writer, with the exceptions noted below, are primarily from the colonial era and are too scattered to be the

[26] Leonard, 'Journey to Bende', p. 194.
[27] Goldie, *Dictionary*, p. 353; Casement, 'Report from Itu', p. 3, and 'Account of a Journey ... from Oron to Eket', 4 July 1894, F. O. 881/6546; interview with Chief Udoka Eshiet, Ukana Ikot Ibe, Ukana, 23 Dec. 1972.
[28] Allen and Thomson, *Narrative*, II, 84–5.
[29] Hill, 'Traditional Market Authority', pp. 309–11.

basis of such a generalization.[30] The case most cited by these studies concerns the 1896 journey of Major A. G. Leonard from Opobo to Bende. En route Leonard noticed three meeting houses (one in ruins) of a men's secret society called Okonko, and speculated that they must function as toll stations. Leonard's conclusion is suspect in view of the fact that he was looking for reasons 'to open up the trade routes', promote 'civilisation', and expand British trade and thus would have seized on any supposed impediment to free trade to justify British intervention. Leonard did not in fact pay any tolls on his journey but instead engaged in three activities which would have been familiar to any local trader: he travelled armed and in a group, gave gifts to prominent men, and swore oaths of mutual friendship. The only thing he failed to do, excusable on so short a journey, was to marry the daughters of prominent men along the way.[31]

Although tolls to permit passage were not a general feature of economic life in this region there was one clear and undisputed exception to the rule. Persons who had made an improvement in a road or waterway were allowed to collect a toll for their efforts. For example, the Ododop bridge builders mentioned above charged 'a heavy toll on all travellers who avail themselves of the accommodation'.[32] Similarly on the Enyong Creek the workmen who cleared away a fallen tree blocking the stream were allowed to collect a toll from every canoe passing by that day.[33] It was perhaps natural that powerful and greedy individuals might seek to enrich themselves by extorting unauthorized tolls from passing traders on some less substantial pretexts. An instance of this which caused trouble on repeated occasions was the effort of the inhabitants of Itu, whose position at the juncture of the Enyong Creek with the Cross River gave them a command of traffic moving between Old Calabar and

[30] Ahanotu, 'Economics and Politics', p. 41; Ofonagoro, 'Opening Up of Southern Nigeria', pp. 100–5; Ekejiuba, 'Aro Trade System', pp. 25–6. Fox, *Uzuakoli*, p. 14, speaking of the early twentieth century, says that traders coming to Bende had to pay tolls for protection, but his description of them makes them appear to be more like gift-exchanges. The Enyong town of Akani Obio levied tolls on passing canoes in the 1870s, according to Georgina A. Gollock's biography of Chief Onoyom Iya Nya in her *Lives of Eminent Africans* (London: Longmans, Green, 1928), p. 42. In this century tolls were levied on travellers through the Ikwerre Igbo area according to Forde and Jones, *Ibo and Ibibio*, p. 133.

[31] Leonard, 'Journey to Bende', pp. 190 ff.

[32] Goldie, *Dictionary*, p. 353.

[33] Interview with the Revd. J. E. Inyang, speaking for the Village Council of Ikpe Ikot Nkon, Ikpe, 26 Jan. 1973.

Umon, to extract tolls from the Efik. In 1836 it was noted: 'The Itu people are well known for their thievish propensities, and wish to levy a tax on all canoes passing their town; and the reason they assign is, that the Calabarians disturb the fish of the river before their town, and that they ought to be made to pay for it.'[34] To enforce their demands the Itu people attacked Efik canoes and held prisoners for ransom, which ultimately led to an attack on the town by the Efik assisted by Capt. John Beecroft. Things were quiet for a time but there were additional crises over several decades in mid-century.[35] The point of this dispute and others like it was the clear rejection by the traders of any toll imposed to restrict free passage except in the relatively rare cases of improvements to the route.

2. TRADING CURRENCIES

The existence of markets and routes is one way of judging the sophistication of an economy; another way is its mode of exchange. Simple barter indicates a relatively primitive level of development with goods being exchanged on an irregular or *ad hoc* basis. The use of a currency to facilitate exchanges indicates a more developed economy. A currency may operate simply as a standard of value or as a general purpose money able to measure, purchase, and store wealth. For example, the elders of one Cross River town recall a time when their ancestors conducted exchanges using short sticks of wood tied in bundles 'as a means of measuring the value of items being traded'.[36] Although this *okuk eto* (stick money) had no market value itself and its possession was not a sign of wealth, it could be used to measure the value of other goods to facilitate exchanges. These elders rightly judged such a currency to have been less useful than either their present money or the copper rods and wires which had served Cross River communities in pre-colonial days.

As the use of currencies is a way of measuring economic development, the antiquity of the trading currencies used in this region has

[34] Oldfield, 'Account of an Ascent', p. 195. The Umon people further up the Cross River may have attempted to collect tolls about the same time, leading to serious disputes with their neighbours, according to Ekejiuba, 'Aro Trade System', p. 25, who gives no source for this statement. Contemporaries attributed the dispute to other actors.

[35] King, 'Details of Explorations', p. 266. Waddell, 'Journal', VIII, 74. Hugh Goldie, 'Journal, 27 Jan. 1858', *United Presbyterian Church Missionary Record*, XIII (1 Sept. 1858), 161.

[36] Interview with Chief Offiong Etim Offiong and the Village Council of Ikot Offiong, Mbiabo, 6 Jan. 1973.

become a subject of some controversy. One curious fact is the late date at which the cowrie currencies of West Africa were adopted here. Although cowries were in use in Benin from about 1300,[37] none were found in the Igbo-Ukwu excavations and none were imported to this region by early European traders. Johnson has shown that only in the eighteenth century did cowries find acceptance in those parts of the hinterland along the Niger and bordering on the Igala.[38] Cowries were used as decorations throughout the hinterland, so this resistance may have been due to the entrenchment of other forms of money. According to Pereira, at the beginning of the sixteenth century the Portuguese paid for all their purchases on the Guinea Coast from Lagos to Mount Cameroon with copper and brass wristlets or *manilhas*, in contrast with the variety of items sold for gold on the Gold Coast.[39] This peculiar fact, plus the discovery of several copper wristlets at Igbo-Ukwu, has led the present writer to suggest that these wristlets, or manillas as they came to be called, may have been a currency in this region before the arrival of the Portuguese.[40] It has also been argued that the copper bar and wire currency of the Cross River region was pre-Portuguese in origin.[41]

Given the present state of the evidence, it is not possible to pass

[37] Five cowries were found in the early group of fillings in a disposal pit on the site of the Oba of Benin's old Palace. Charcoal from the centre of the early group of fillings has been radio-carbon dated to A.D. 1305 ± 105. See Connah, 'Archeology', p. 27.

[38] Marion Johnson, 'The Cowrie Currencies of West Africa', *JAH*, XI (1970), 32–7. A full description of the currencies of the hinterland is in G. I. Jones, 'Native and Trade Currencies in Southern Nigeria during the Eighteenth and Nineteenth Centuries', *Africa*, XXVIII (1958), 43–53. See also M. D. W. Jeffreys, 'The Cowrie Shell: a Study of its History and Use in Nigeria', *Nigeria*, No. 15 (1938), 221–6, 256.

[39] Pereira, *Esmeraldo*, pp. 134–48.

[40] David Northrup, 'The Growth of Trade among the Igbo before 1800', *JAH*, XIII (1972), 229n; cf. Shaw, *Igbo-Ukwu*, II, plates 313–18, 321–3. M. D. W. Jeffreys has also argued on the basis of other evidence that the use of manillas was pre-European in origin in West Africa, but he would derive them from ancient Egypt: 'Some Negro Currencies in Nigeria', *South African Museums' Association Bulletin*, V.16 (1954), 410–11. Another writer has accepted the relation between the Portuguese and Igbo-Ukwu wristlets, but has turned the argument on its head, maintaining that the existence of manillas at Igbo-Ukwu proves that those sites cannot be earlier than the arrival of the Portuguese; see Lawal, 'Dating Problems', pp. 6–7.

It must be granted that the manilla shape is a common one and probably cannot be traced to a single source. Irish Bronze Age wristlets are illustrated in A. H. Quiggins, *A Survey of Primitive Money*, rev. edn. (London: Methuen, 1963), p. 89, and gold ones from Kent dated to 1050–850 B.C. may be seen on display in the British Museum and in C. H. Read, *A Guide to the Antiquities of the Bronze Age*, 2nd edn (London: British Museum, 1920), p. 51.

[41] Latham, 'Currency', pp. 599–600.

final judgement on these contentions. It is possible, however, to separate the argument into two parts and defuse one of them. On the one hand there is the debatable evidence for the origins of the manilla, copper bar, and wire currencies; on the other hand is the question of whether sophisticated currencies came into use only through introduction by European traders. Specialists in this area will no doubt continue to debate the origins of these brass and copper currencies, but a judgement on the second question does not depend on the outcome of this debate. For there were in existence in this region iron currencies which owe nothing to the European presence since they were not used or duplicated by them. In fact this iron money was probably pushed out of the market by the vast amounts of trading currencies and iron supplied by the European traders.

Iron money may have been the oldest form of currency in use in south-eastern Nigeria since it was already well established when it was first reported by Europeans in the seventeenth century. Dapper reported its existence in the vicinity of the Rio Real: 'In the Province of Moco, a kind of iron money is made, each piece of which is as big as the palm of one's hand and has a tail a span in length.[42] Three pieces of iron money of the exact size and shape Dapper described are in the British Museum Ethnography Collection, having been 'dug up in the Midden at the Long Juju, Aro Chuku' by M. D. W. Jeffreys in 1929.[43]. Currency of this type was still used in remote parts of the Ogoja area well into this century.[44]

A second type of iron currency, perhaps of greater antiquity, was of a much smaller size, measuring only half an inch or so in length and resembling in shape a miniature arrow-head, or a hook, or a

[42] Dapper, *Description*, p. 315. The Moco, as was indicated above, are to be identified with the Anang Ibibio. Barbot, 'Description', p. 380, expands upon Dapper's definition slightly: 'The money of *Moko* is of iron, in the shape and figure of a thornback, flat, and as broad as the palm of the hand, having a tail of the same metal of the length of the hand.'

[43] Museum of Mankind, 'Register of Antiquities, Ethnographical', vol. VIII (1932): (12-6) No. 5, and 'Register of Antiquities: Ethnographical, Large Collections', vol. 17 (Africa 3): 1954 AF 23 (No. 682a & b). Jeffreys, 'Some Negro Currencies', pp. 406, 412–13, explains how he came into possession of these iron tokens. He also describes cutting through a mound containing amulets and money discarded by consultants along an ancient path to the Arochukwu Oracle. There he discovered an iron manilla lying deeper than the common trading ones of the eighteenth and nineteenth centuries, but not so deep and thinner manillas of pure copper (such as had been traded by the sixteenth-century Portuguese). At the bottom he found small iron octahedrons $1\frac{1}{2}$ inches long. Cowries were found throughout.

[44] Jones, 'Native and Trade Currencies', p. 48.

squashed tack. Equiano recalled such a currency in use among his
Igbo group in the mid-eighteenth century: '... we have some small
pieces of coin, if I may call them such. They are made something
like an anchor; but I do not remember either their value or denomi-
nation.'[45] There were some in use in a limited fashion among the
Igbo in this century, the leading men of Awka never being without
a small supply.[46]

Given the available evidence, it is not possible to indicate how
widely these currencies were in use or exactly how they were used,
but indirect evidence would suggest that they were a general currency. Iron currencies are common enough in this part of Africa.
Baikie reported quite similar iron money among several peoples
along the Benue, which he judged had been in use before the introduction of cowries to that area.[47] The importation of iron bars both
as a trading currency and as an abundant supply of iron must have
greatly diminished value of these older and much smaller iron currencies. The growing popularity of cowries, manillas, and copper
bars and wires would have driven them from the market-place. Thus,
although iron tokens were general-purpose money both for the
Moko and for Equiano's people in the seventeenth and eighteenth
century, they survived in later centuries only for some special and
perhaps largely ceremonial purposes. Both north of the Benue and
among the Awka Igbo the iron money in more recent times was used
to purchase domestic slaves. Awka men used the small tokens in
sacrifices and in purification ceremonies, after which the iron pieces
were 'cast away into the bush'. Clients of the Arochukwu Oracle
were expected to bring five of the larger tokens as offerings. In other
Igbo areas the payment of iron money could effect the quasi-per-
manent transfer of land, which under ordinary circumstances would

[45] Equiano, 'Early Travels', p. 75.

[46] Basden, *Niger Ibos*, pp. 330–40; Meek, *Law and Authority*, pp. 103–4. The Igbo
called this small iron currency *umumu*. The word (and thus probably the coins themselves) appear to be of Ibibio origin. Goldie's *Dictionary*, pp. 318–19, 389, lists the
word *umumuquakabang*, meaning 'a sort of tenterhook used by coopers', which is
composed of the words *unumi* (a seizure; securing, holding), *uquak* (iron), and *abang*
(barrel), i.e. an iron hook for holding barrels together. Barrel-making became an
occupation in Old Calabar only with the growth of the palm-oil trade in the nineteenth
century. Before that the word *umumuquak* (iron hook) may have referred to the small
iron tokens of that shape used as coins, from which the Igbo took the word *umumu*.
It must be said on the other side, however, that Goldie lists no such word in his dictionary and that there is no record of the use of this currency among the Ibibio.

[47] Baikie, *Narrative*, p. 416. For a general treatment see Lars Sundström, *The Trade
of Guinea* (Upsala: Akademisk Avhandling, 1965), pp. 200–16.

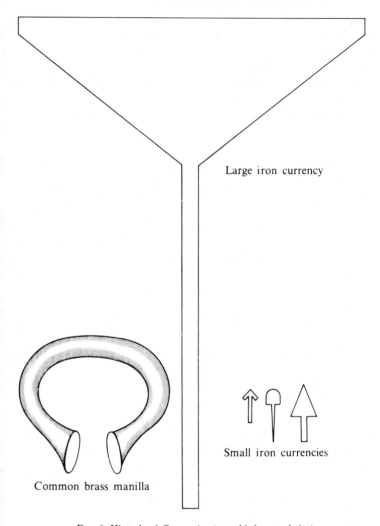

Large iron currency

Common brass manilla

Small iron currencies

FIG. 6. Hinterland Currencies (two-thirds actual size).

have been impossible. Since the total value of the thirty small tokens involved in the transaction was little more than a halfpenny, it was clearly the ratification of the transfer rather than an additional payment which was involved.[48] Among the Ekoi small iron tokens

[48] Ibid., pp. 114–15; Basden, *Niger Ibos*, pp. 339–40; Ekejiuba, 'Aro System of Trade', p. 14; Meek, *Law and Authority*, p. 104.

called *akpa* are still given as part of a bride's 'dowry' and, in case
the marriage does not last, only these need be returned to the groom
to dissolve the bond.[49] From these examples it may be concluded
that iron currency has been used in recent times for quite special
purposes: to establish rightful claim to something (land, wife, slave)
or to rid oneself of a spiritual debt (sacrifice, purification). These
purposes may be understood as 'survivals' of earlier, more general
functions and are thus additional indications of the antiquity of this
form of money.[50]

The growth of trade with Europe introduced new trading currencies both at the coast and in the hinterland. By the end of the
seventeenth century the standard measure of value on the Rio Real
was the iron bar and on the Cross River it was the copper rod (which
had earlier been the standard of value on the Rio Real). James Barbot relates how after arriving at the Rio Real in 1699 the value of
each item in his cargo was re-computed in iron bars since that was
the 'standard coin' there. A ship arriving from London the next year
had its cargo invoiced solely in that currency.[51]

In addition to functioning as a standard for measuring value at
the coast, copper rods also became a general purpose money all
along the Cross River, and northwards among the Tiv as well.[52]
Because their value was so high, one iron bar being equal to four
copper rods, iron bars did not become general-purpose money,
although at the coast 'avaricious men' in Bonny were said to hoard
them.[53] Instead, brass manillas became a general-purpose currency
in the south-central part of the hinterland and cowries eventually
became important along the Niger and in the north.[54]

[49] Personal communication from Mr. E. U. Eko, manager, Standard Bank, Ikot
Ekpene, South East State, Nigeria, a native of Ejagham Ekoi.

[50] For a discussion of cultural survivals being used in the reconstruction of African
history see Jan Vansina, 'The Use of Ethnographic Data as Sources for History',
in *Emerging Themes in African History* (London: Heinemann Educational Books,
1968), pp. 108–9.

[51] Barbot, 'Description', pp. 459–60. 'Invoice of Merchandise Loaded on board
the *Affrica* Galley bound for Gold Coast and New Calabar, 23 Oct. 1700', in Donnan,
Documents, IV, 77–9.

[52] Bohannan and Bohannan, *Tiv Economy*, p. 237, argue that among the Tiv the
rods were 'a general-purpose currency *only within the prestige sphere*'. That qualification would be removed for earlier periods of economic history by Latham, 'Currency',
p. 601.

[53] Adams, *Remarks*, p. 263.

[54] Jones, 'Native and Trade Currencies', p. 48. Cf. O. O. Amogu, 'The Introduction
into and Withdrawal of Manillas from the "Oil Rivers" as Seen in Ndoki District',
Nigeria, No. 38 (1952), 134–9.

As the trade expanded the demand for these currencies grew proportionately. Since, with the partial exception of cowries which also entered this region from the north, the principal currencies were supplied by European traders, this demand is apparent in the European records. Iron bars and copper rods had uses other than as currencies, but it is still worth noting that the records of two seventeenth-century ships bound for New Calabar show that two-thirds of their cargoes consisted of iron bars, copper rods, and manillas.[55] With the growth of the palm-oil trade in the early nineteenth century the demand for specie in the hinterland became intense. King Obi Osai of Aboh indicated to Niger explorers in 1832 and again in 1841 that the trade item he desired most was cowries.[56] On the Cross River shortages of specie often held up trade. A trading guide published in 1819 advised merchants to bring an ample supply of copper rods to Old Calabar as the Ibibio Proper, one of the Efik's principal trading partners, would accept only those in exchange for their palm-oil.[57] Likewise, a report on the trade in that river a decade later warned that if ships failed to bring an ample supply of specie they might have to wait up to six months to obtain a cargo of slaves instead of ten days to a fortnight.[58]

The peoples of the hinterland adapted the imported bars, rods, and manillas to the needs of their own marketing systems. With the exception of cowries, which were equally useful for small or large transactions, the hinterland markets used the coastal currency as the upper tier of a two tier currency system. The rods and manillas were useful for the upper tier but had too high a value to be used for small purchases or bargains argued down to fractions of a unit. A lower tier was devised to fill this need. The simplest system was along the Cross River where copper rods were split lengthwise and made into wires about 18″ long and bent in two like a hairpin. Called *sitim* by the Ibibio, they were in great demand for the hinterland markets.[59] Elsewhere small salt-cakes, steel wire, large and small cowries

[55] Hutchinson, 'Slaver's Diary', p. 60. 'Invoice of *Affrica* Galley', in Donnan, *Documents*, IV, 77–9.

[56] Laird and Oldfield, *Narrative*, I, 271; Allen and Thomson, *Narrative*, I, 219.

[57] Lt. Edward Bold, *The Merchants' and Mariners' African Guide* (London: Longman, 1819), p. 78.

[58] Badgley, 'Report on Old Calabar River'.

[59] Waddell, 'Journal', I, 26. In the nineteenth century, when brass rods had come to replace the copper ones on the Cross River, the Efik called the rods *afia okuk* (white coppers) and the wires *obubit okuk* (black coppers). The latter were said to

functioned as a lower tier.[60] Needless to say, the number of different currencies led to considerable overlapping and intermingling of currency zones, but this does not appear to have caused any particular confusion or to have impeded trade. Like complexities of political life, those of economic life were considered normal. Traders in the hinterland had less trouble with currency changes than Americans on a European holiday.

3. THE IMPACT OF THE IMPORTS

The Africans who participated in the slave trade did so in order to obtain goods which they could not get in sufficient quantities through any other means. It is often argued that these goods received in return for slaves compounded the destructiveness of that trade in several ways: that the goods brought by the slave ships were, on the whole, frivolous and worthless trifles (such as cast-off clothing, beads, mirrors, and other glittering objects), items destructive of African society (such as strong drink and fire-arms), and manufactures (such as hardware and cloth) which undermined traditional African industries and thus kept Africa in a state of underdevelopment.[61] It is therefore worth examining the types of goods which came into south-eastern Nigeria to determine if they conformed to this pattern.

During the early centuries of the overseas trade coastal Africans had exhibited an almost insatiable demand for metals in the form of iron bars, copper rods, and copper or brass wristlets (manillas). In Pereira's early sixteenth-century account the coastal Ijo of the Rio Real traded with the Portuguese exclusively in manillas, preferring pure copper ones to those of brass. In the next century the trade reported there by Dapper was much the same: the Dutch paid for their purchases with grey copper manillas and small polished copper rods.[62] By the end of the century, with the slave trade beginning to boom, unfabricated metals were still the most desired trade commodity, and iron was gaining a larger share of the trade. For

be made by the Igbo (perhaps by the Abiriba smiths). See Goldie, *Dictionary*, pp. 6, 255.

[60] Allen, 'Intelligence Report, Isi', p. 175; Baikie, *Narrative*, pp. 78–90; Adams, *Remarks*, p. 116.

[61] A typical summary of this line of argument is in Basil Davidson, *A History of West Africa to the Nineteenth Century* (Garden City: Doubleday & Company, Inc., 1966), pp. 293–5.

[62] Pereira, *Esmeraldo*, p. 146; Dapper, *Description*, pp. 315–16.

example, most of the cargo of a Royal African Company ship trading in New Calabar in 1677 consisted of 1,420 iron bars, 6,500 copper rods, and 10,000 manillas.[63] The *Affrica* galley, which called at the same port in 1700, had nearly 60 per cent of its cargo in iron bars, with additional amounts of copper bars and manillas; its captain had been advised by the ship's owner that 'Iron Barrs is the Staplest Comodity there.'[64]

While the imports of the eighteenth century are less well documented than one would like, unfabricated metals appear to have remained a substantial part of the trade but with finished goods becoming more important. These included Indian textiles, beads of various origins, and British hardware such as pewter basins and tankards, knives, and bells. Although fire-arms had been traded on the Guinea coast by the early Portuguese,[65] guns and powder evidently did not become an important item of trade in the Bight of Biafra until some time in the first half of the eighteenth century. They were not mentioned by Barbot in 1699 at New Calabar, but were an important item of trade in Equiano's area a half century later.[66] In the first half of the nineteenth century, as will be shown in Chapter VIII, imported cloth, salt, hardware, arms, and ammunition all increased tremendously in this region.

The impact of these imports on south-eastern Nigeria was not so negative as traditional evaluations have suggested. There were, it is true, items in the cargoes brought to the Bight of Biafra by the slave ships which must appear frivolous in the context of West Africa's material needs in that era: gilt mirrors, fancy clocks, fine table-ware, paintings, organs, even (for Old Calabar) entire prefabricated wooden and cast-iron houses. Such items enhanced the standing of the major coastal traders in the eyes of their European counterparts, who were otherwise inclined to adopt a condescending manner toward Africans. The favourable impression made on European traders was vindication of such display. Other apparently frivolous items of trade, such as beads and small bells, were intended for use in the costumes of men's masquerade societies. The considerable importance and utility of such societies, whose displays were a means

[63] Hutchinson, 'Slaver's Diary', p. 60.

[64] Letter of Thomas Starke to James Westmore, 22 Oct. 1700, in Donnan, *Documents*, IV, 74, 77–91.

[65] Wilks, 'Medieval Trade Route', p. 339, who says this trade was apparently banned by Pope Sixtus IV (1471–84).

[66] Barbot, 'Abstract of a Voyage'; Equiano, 'Early Travels', p. 75.

of ritualizing social standing and competition among villages, was discussed in Chapter IV. In any event such items of display were only a small portion of the goods reaching the hinterland.[67]

The charge that personally or socially harmful goods constituted a major part of those goods traded for slaves likewise needs to be examined carefully. Given the degree to which fire-arms added to internal disorders to other regions their presence in the cargoes for this coast suggests that they may have been a culprit there as well. Yet as was argued above, while guns were used for protection in travel (and surely for hunting), they do not appear to have found too important a place in warfare in the hinterland. Indeed, compared to the situation west of the Niger south-eastern Nigeria seems to have suffered few large-scale or lengthy wars. Though minor skirmishes were a fact of frequent occurrence, it is not possible to blame them on fire-arms or to suggest that such incursions were more bloody because of the presence of fire-arms. According to Equiano swords, javelins, bows, and arrows were used equally with fire-arms in these local battles,[68] a circumstance which continued through the pre-colonial era.

The scourge of the missionaries, 'demon rum', does not appear to have been imported into the hinterland in significant amounts until the nineteenth century. The ship *Arthur* did carry a small amount of brandy to New Calabar in 1677, noting that it was 'for the Negroes'.[69] The probable meaning of this cryptic remark is brought out by Bold a century and a half later when he notes that ships trading on this coast should being a quantity of rum 'for dashes', i.e. as gifts to the local merchants who were accustomed to opening and closing transactions over drinks and to receiving spirits as courtesy presents.[70] Although the liquor trade increased sharply in the nineteenth century the greatest increases came after the overseas slave trade was over.[71] The impression one gets from the seventeenth and eighteenth-century sources is that more alcoholic beverages were

---

[67] Jackson, *Journal*, pp. 74–5, 88; William F. Daniell, 'On the Natives of Old Callebar, West Coast of Africa', *Journal of the Ethnological Society of London*, I (1848), 220–2; Waddell, *Twenty-Nine Years*, pp. 243–4. Jackson was in Bonny in 1826; Daniell in Old Calabar in 1841. See also Simmons, 'Ethnographic Sketch', p. 8.

[68] Equiano, 'Early Travels', p. 77.

[69] Hutchinson, 'Slaver's Diary', p. 60.

[70] Bold, *African Guide*, p. 80.

[71] For a study of the liquor trade see E. A. Ayandele, *The Missionary Impact on Modern Nigeria 1842–1914* (London: Longmans, 1966), Chapter 10, 'The Triumph of Gin'.

sold by Africans to European seamen and with more harmful results than the reverse.

The argument that European-supplied imports promoted the underdevelopment of Africa is in substance the reverse of the previous two points, since it stresses that these imports, instead of being worthless or destructive, were of such a high quality and low price that African-made goods could not compete with them, and that as a result the mining-smelting-smithing, spinning-weaving-dying, and other African industries or complexes were gradually swamped by the imports. There is some truth in this argument, but when, why, and to what degree this occurred can be understood best in the context of the specific cases of metals and cloth examined below.

As was indicated in Chapter I, metal-working has a long history in this region and was already well developed by the time of the Igbo-Ukwu culture. Both iron and copper alloy products were excavated at Igbo-Ukwu, and there is evidence elsewhere of extensive lead mining to provide sinkers for the nets of coastal fishermen.[72] The iron was mined locally, but copper can have reached this area only from rather distant sources, most probably to the north. Thus the copper and brass imported from European traders replaced and gradually increased the supplies that had once been imported from elsewhere.

The copper and brass were put to several uses. Smiths turned much of it into body ornaments. The metal that had evidently been associated with royalty at Igbo-Ukwu was being worn in finger-thick neck torques by the otherwise naked coastal fishermen at the beginning of the sixteenth century. In the seventeenth century the people of the Rio Real divided the polished copper rods brought by the Dutch into three pieces which they twisted into bracelets and collars.[73] In the next century, Equiano indicates, the 'women of distinction' in his area wore 'golden' (i.e. brass) ornaments in profusion on their arms and legs.[74] By the nineteenth century this custom was widely observed, women of wealthy families wearing several pounds of brass coils on each leg and often on their arms as well. Bells and other objects often of elaborate design were also cast in brass or bronze by local craftsmen.[75] Finally, as was shown above, brass and

---

[72] Pre-colonial lead mining in the hinterland is discussed by Mr. N. Francis of the Nigerian Base Metals Corporation in Allen, 'Intelligence Report, Izi', p. 13.

[73] Pereira, *Esmeraldo*, p. 126; Dapper, *Description*, pp. 315–16.

[74] Equiano, 'Early Travels', p. 73.

[75] Waddell, *Twenty-Nine Years*, pp. 256, 371, for Old Calabar. Brass coils on the arms and legs of girls near the Efik settlement of Ikot Offiong were seen by the Revd.

copper bars and manillas were also used extensively as trading currencies.

The iron imports were put to greater and more utilitarian uses. One product was the elaborately decorated double-edged swords frequently mentioned in connection with this region. Pereira says they were 'of the same type as the white Moors of Barbary carry'; Barbot illustrates a fine example of one; Equiano mentions them as being used in battle in this area; and an 1841 Niger explorer saw them being made at Idah 'of admirable metal, nicely engraved and a few inlaid with portions of deeper coloured or more highly oxydized iron'.[76] Local smiths also made high quality knives, axes, hoes, spear heads, arrow tips, gongs, and, in the late nineteenth century, even fire-arms.[77] There is no doubt that over a period of time the imported iron reduced the amount of local iron-mining and smelting, although such activities continued in some areas into the twentieth century. By the nineteenth century mining had ceased in the Kwa Mountains north of Old Calabar and Idah smiths were using only imported iron.[78] At the same time as local iron-mining and smelting declined, blacksmithing expanded making use of the imported iron to produce tools, weapons, and other iron objects in growing quantities. It was only after the 1830s and 1840s, when the slave trade was substantially over, that British hardware and cutlery began to be imported in quantities great enough to offer competition to the hinterland smiths, but before the century was out the inroads of the Birmingham foundries had become substantial.[79]

Hugh Goldie, *Calabar and Its Mission* (Edinburgh: Oliphant Anderson and Ferrier, 1890), p. 21. Louisa Anderson says King Eyo Honesty II's wives and daughters could scarcely move because of the weight of such ornaments in a letter to Young Friends, 16 Apr. 1849, NLS MS. 2981. For the Niger area see Stone, 'Intelligence Report, Umueri', p. 3. Hartle, 'Bronze Objects', pp. 25–8, describes objects from a site later dated to A.D. 1495 ± 95. Taylor reported that Awka smiths made embellished brass keys of dexterous composition in Crowther and Taylor, *Gospel on the Banks*, p. 299. See also, F. I. Ekejiuba, 'Preliminary Notes on Brasswork of Eastern Nigeria', *African Notes*, IV (1967), 11–15.

[76] Pereira, *Esmeraldo*, p. 146; Barbot, 'Description', plate 26; Equiano, 'Early Travels', p. 77; Allen and Thomson, *Narrative*, I, 323.

[77] Thomas, *Anthropological Report*, I, 129; Basden, *Niger Ibos*, pp. 318–21; Talbot, *Peoples*, III, 927.

[78] Waddell, *Twenty-Nine Years*, p. 326; Allen and Thomson, *Narrative*, I, 323. The Old Calabar smiths used an English bellows, while those at Idah used one made locally.

[79] 'Report from the Select Committee', 1842, appendix No. 36. Jones, *Trading States*, p. 89.

Although the Indian and British cottons sold in the Bight of Biafra during the era of the slave-trade were in the form of yard goods, one cannot develop a line of argument parallel to the relation of hinterland smiths to iron bars. Cotton yard goods did not give rise to a great tailoring industry for the simple reason that the peoples of the hinterland were accustomed to wearing the cloth in untailored lengths as 'wrappers'. Yet despite the quantities of cloth imported there is little indication that the local spinning-weaving-dying complex suffered from the competition. Instead the production of cotton cloth in the hinterland appears to have expanded in this period.

Archaeological evidence from Benin and Igbo-Ukwu, plus the testimony of early traders and explorers, make it clear that for many centuries Africans of this region produced two kinds of cloth for their own use and for export to neighbouring regions: a cotton (or cotton-like) cloth and a cloth made from other fibres such as raffia or the bark of certain trees.[80] The quality of both types could vary with the skill of the workmen and the use for which the cloth was intended. Equiano reports that women in his area made long pieces of cotton cloth which, after being dyed blue, were the usual clothing of both sexes, while much of the cotton cloth the Ibibio bought from the Igbo was of a thick, towel-like weave, and members of the Old Calabar Ekpe Society bought a finely woven cloth from the Igbo with alternating blue and white triangles and mystical *nsibidi* writing in the designs.[81] Likewise the standard raffia cloth of the Ibibio was suitable for clothing while other raffia cloth was intended only for salt-bags or fish-nets, and the Niger Igbo made a 'chief's cloth' from the silky fibres of green palm leaves and another linen-like cloth from the downy underbark of a certain tree.[82]

An Igbo folk-tale, also common elsewhere in West Africa, says that the first hunter to make an animal net learned to do so by watching a spider spin a web and that, after some prodding by his wife, he went on to weaving a kind of grass cloth.[83] It may well be, as this tale implies, that non-cotton cloth was common in south-eastern

[80] See Chapter I.

[81] Equiano, 'Early Travels', pp. 72–3; interview with Chief Akpan, Afaha Obong; interview with the Revd. Inyang, Ikpe; Duke, 'Diary', p. 51; Simmons, 'Ethnographic Sketch', p. 76. For *nsibidi* see R. F. G. Adams, 'Obɛri Ɔkaine: a New African Language and Script', *Africa*, XVII (1947), 24–34.

[82] Interview with the Revd. Inyang, Ikpe; interview with Mr. Udowong, Ukwa. Basden, *Niger Ibos*, p. 327.

[83] Recorded by Mary Kingsley, *Travels in West Africa*, 2nd edn. (London: Macmillan, 1904), pp. 529–32.

Nigeria before the introduction of cotton-spinning and weaving. In any event the use and manufacture of cotton cloth appears to have originated in the area bordering the Edo along the Niger and among the Igala to the north and spread gradually to the east and south. The earliest recorded Igbo case is that of Equiano's people west of the Niger, which was cited above. There was an extensive cotton cloth industry of uncertain antiquity, north-west of Enugu in the Nsukka area, while east of Enugu in the Nkalagu and Ngbo areas much cotton was grown and woven into cloth which continued to clothe most of the population there well into the twentieth century.[84] Along the lower Imo river the village of Akwete, which had been a raffia weaving centre, switched to the manufacture of cotton cloth some time ago.[85] Most of these cloth-weaving centres came to supply not only their own needs, but provided exports to distant places carried by the Aro and other traders.

Despite the tremendous imports of Indian and European cloth during both the eighteenth and nineteenth centuries, both cotton and non-cotton cloths continued to enjoy a large local market and were traded over considerable distances. In some instances this tenacity was due to a strong African preference for certain designs and weaves. For example, Baikie saw an Igbo cloth with elaborate perforations woven in for sale at several markets along the lower Benue river in 1854, and Waddell reported that indigo cloth from the Niger had a ready market in Old Calabar in the same era.[86] In part, too, the failure to adopt imported cloth was due to its higher cost. In 1894 Casement observed that the wives of Aro traders resident among the Ibibio 'often dressed in a piece of good cloth', while the less prosperous Ibibio women in the next settlement 'wore only a strip of bark cloth'.[87] Yet this reason does not explain the popularity which local textiles continued to enjoy in communities clearly able to afford imported cloth. For example, at the end of the eighteenth century the women of Old Calabar still dressed primarily in raffia cloth and even in 1866 the Okrika, a major trading people on

[84] Boston, 'Ethnographic Field Work', p. 5; Afigbo, 'Trade and Trade Routes', pp. 4–5; Jones, 'Assessment Report, Ngbo and Ezengbo', p. 150; W. P. Livingstone, *Dr. Hitchcock of Uburu* (Edinburgh: United Free Church of Scotland, 1920), p. 58, quoting Dr. Hitchcock in 1914.

[85] Udo, *Geographical Regions*, pp. 74–5. Raffia weaving has continued among the neighbouring Anang Ibibio. The largest Anang town, Ikot Ekpene, has recently begun promoting itself as 'Raffia City'.

[86] Baikie, *Narrative*, pp. 287–8; Waddell, *Twenty-Nine Years*, p. 327.

[87] Casement, 'Report from Itu', p. 11.

a main route from Bende to Bonny, were clothed primarily in raffia cloth.[88] In Onitsha imported cloth, while greatly desired, was still so rare in the late 1850s that 'very little difference is made between the quality of cotton cloths', nearly all cloth being made locally even twenty years later.[89] The conclusion is inescapable that, despite the apparent abundance of the imports, foreign cloth remained rare enough in the hinterland not to be able to compete with traditional local products; both in price, and, still more important, in quality and design local textiles were preferred.

Any evaluation of the impact of imported goods on south-eastern Nigeria must make due allowance for the great gaps in evidence, particularly the paucity of eye-witness accounts, except at the coast. Nevertheless, it does not appear that these goods were generally harmful in themselves or in their impact on local industries during the era of the overseas slave trade. In the case of unfabricated metals, which, though gradually declining from nearly 100 per cent of the cargoes in the early sixteenth century to 13 per cent in the early nineteenth, remained very substantial in volume, Europe was actually a supplier of raw materials for the expansion of hinterland smithing.

4. INTERNAL TRADE

The commerce of the slave trade era may be divided into three parts: the export trade in slaves, the trade in imported goods in exchange for the slaves, and the trade internal to Africa which coexisted with these two. It is this last and oldest part of the hinterland's trade that is now to be considered. Over many centuries before the eighteenth century a complex system of local and regional trade had developed within south-eastern Nigeria and other trade between it and other parts of the continent. The expansion of the slave trade had not displaced this internal trade, but had added to it and merged with it to form new and more complex patterns of commerce which lay the

---

[88] Henry Schroeder, *Three Years Adventures of a Minor, in England, Africa, the West Indies, South-Carolina, and Georgia*, by William Butterworth (pseud.) (Leeds: Thomas Inchbold, 1831), p. 44. Livingstone to Clarendon, 2 Aug. 1866, *Parl. Papers* 1867, lxxiii (3816-I), p. 29.

[89] Crowther and Taylor, *Gospel on the Banks*, pp. 30, 34, 436; Adolphe Burdo, *The Niger and Benueh: Travels in Central Africa* (London: Richard Bentley, 1880), p. 128. Crowther says that Onitsha people used no dyes, but Burdo describes in detail the use of indigo dye. Unless one of them is mistaken—and Burdo is not entirely reliable—this means that the local cotton cloth industry in this period was able not merely to hold its own, but to *expand* in competition with imported cloth.

foundation for significant additional growth and development in the next century.

The continuing importance of the internal trade in the eighteenth century should not be underestimated for the surviving records indicate that it was substantial. For example, the itinerant traders who visited the local markets in Equiano's area brought 'fire-arms, gunpowder, hats, beads and dried fish'. The first three items were imports, and the beads may have been as well, but the fish had surely been caught and dried along the coast since Norwegian dried cod (stock fish) was not imported in quantity until the late nineteenth century.[90] The absence of metals from the list is not surprising since they would have been sold directly to the local smiths rather than in the market-place. Equiano indicated that brass body ornaments and iron swords were common in his area; both were probably crafted locally from imported metal. The absence of imported cloth from the list is to be explained differently, since he indicated that his people made their own cotton cloth, against which, evidently, Indian textiles could not compete successfully. In exchange for the goods the traders brought, Equiano's people sold 'odoriferous woods', 'salt of wood ashes', and some slaves, of which the first two were surely part of the internal trade.[91]

A trade in quite similar goods was observed by Niger explorers in the early 1830s between Aboh and the markets further up the river. The Aboh traders took upriver: 'powder, yams, beads, cloth, iron bars, and knives'. Although these goods were said to have come to Aboh, through three or four intermediaries, from the European ships, the yams were clearly a local product. In return the Aboh traders received 'slaves, rice, goats, fowls, calabashes, mats, country beads, horses of a small breed', ivory, and kola nuts.[92] In this case most of the slaves and ivory would have been intended for export, but some of the ivory and food and all of the horses, beads, and kola would have been for internal consumption.

It is clear from these examples that there did not exist, except at the coast, any simple exchange of slaves for imported goods. The slave trade was intertwined with the internal trade. As the trade in slaves expanded so did the market for all sorts of other goods. Only a portion of these material wants was met by imported goods; the

---

[90] Jones, *Trading States*, p. 89.
[91] Equiano, 'Early Travels', pp. 72–7.
[92] Laird and Oldfield, *Narrative*, II, 180–1.

rest was met from expanded internal production. As was shown in the previous section, a great deal of eighteenth-century consumer demand was met by locally produced salt, cloth, hardware, and a great variety of other goods.

The operations of the Aro traders may also serve to illustrate the conjunction of internal and overseas trade. Although the Aro are best known as slave traders, they might more correctly be called specialty traders, since they dealt in every conceivable article of high value and scarcity. One of the items which the Aro specialized in was hardware, much of which was made from imported metals by the hinterland smiths with whom the Aro had special agreements. So important did metal goods become in the trade of the Aro that one of the principal things which the explorer Baikie knew of them was that they were 'skilled artisans and manufacture swords, spears, and metallic ornaments, specimens of all of which I have seen and can therefore testify to their being very neatly finished'.[93] Baikie would not have been the first mistakenly to credit the merchant with the talent of the manufacturer. The Aro also became major traders in the kinds of specially woven cloths needed for certain festivals and masquerades, driving prices up to such heights that it is claimed some people were tempted to sell away their children to get the coveted cloths.[94] At least in some areas the Aro (and other traders as well) turned a handsome profit selling the rights and secret lore necessary to set up certain of the secret societies. The most important men's society in the Cross River area, Ekpe, had been sold by the Ekoi to the Efik at Old Calabar, who sold it to the Enyong, who sold it to others including the Aro, who in turn sold it to many other communities.[95] Of course, the Aro were also active in marketing their Oracle and the charms and shrines that were associated with it.

The internal trade of the eighteenth century was not confined to these exchanges in specialty goods, which were destined for a

[93] Baikie, Narrative, pp. 310–11.

[94] Igwegbe, Original History, p. 78. For the Aro as cloth merchants see Talbot, Peoples, I, 183; interview with Chief Akpan, Afaha Obong; interview with Messrs. Mefo and Ibe, Idemile; interview with the Revd. Inyang, Ikpe.

[95] Talbot, Peoples, III, 779–80. Interview with Chief Obong, Afaha Obong; interview with Chief John Umoh Eka, Nkwot Ikot Umo, Ikono, 21 Nov. 1972; interview with Chief Ibah, Enyong. The Aro also marketed another secret society called Okwa on the middle Cross River according to L. E. H. Fellows, 'Intelligence Report on Ikom, Nkum, and Obokum Mbaba Villages, Ikom Division, Ogoja Province', 1934, NAI, CSO 26/3/29966.

relatively élite portion of the population. There was another sort of internal trade in basic goods produced by the ordinary farmers, especially in the southern portion of the hinterland. There had long been a trade in provisions (yams, palm-oil, palm wine, small livestock) from the inland farmers to the coastal fishermen and traders. As the coastal states in the eighteenth century came to devote an increasing proportion of their energies to the slave trade, they came to depend almost exclusively for provisions upon their inland neighbours, setting off a major industry producing and distributing these goods. Since inland trading communities also specialized in trade, they too came to depend more upon their neighbours for provisions. This internal food trade cannot be separated from the export trade in provisions for the slave ships; both will be dealt with more fully in the next chapter which considers the development of commercial agriculture in the hinterland.

The centuries of the Atlantic trade saw great changes in the economy of south-eastern Nigeria. The nature of these changes and their causes have often been obscured by over-simple analyses which ignore or minimize the significance of events not directly involving Europeans. A theory popular in the nineteenth century and still current relates changes in African economies primarily to the movement from the overseas slave trade to the 'legitimate' trade of the abolitionists. The slave trade, some argue, produced massive destruction of African lives and institutions and grossly perverted African economies to a cruel trade in human lives, while the goods received for these slaves were of an essentially harmful nature and of low quality, being accepted by Africans too ignorant of economic realities to know or care about the difference.

Economic realities in this region were directly contrary to the main thrusts of this theory. While it is true that the slave trade was cruel and produced a climate of fear and suspicion, its social and economic effects which can be measured were surprisingly benign. Certainly in the cases of population growth and the expansion of economic institutions the slave trade was not the calamity it has often been said to have been. The entrepreneurial spirit of the hinterland peoples organized the trade in slaves on the basis of their already well-developed marketing networks. Moreover, slaves were traded for, and along with, a great variety of other goods, both local and imported. Instead of a destructive effect, the era of the slave trade saw a great expansion of this marketing network into a comprehensive grid of markets and fairs and a vast expansion of the over-all volume of trade in the hinterland of which slaves were only a part.

It must also be stressed that the peoples of the hinterland chose the goods they received in return for the slave exports with great care. While social display and pageantry encouraged the importation of many items which appear frivolous on ships' invoices, when seen in their social context these goods assume a more reasonable role. Such exotic and decorative goods were, however, but a small part of the total imports. Most imports contained a large portion of useful consumer goods, such as clothing, which supplemented locally produced supplies without unduly capturing the markets of local craftsmen. Finally, an important share of the imported goods consisted of goods which encouraged the development of the African economy. Abundant imports of metals supported and expanded the hinterland smithing industry, putting metal tools into the hands of an increasing number of people. Metals and imported cowries were also at the basis of hinterland currency systems. Only after the withdrawal of the British from the slave trade in 1807 and especially after the end of the overseas slave trade do the nature and quality of the imports change, as the effects of the industrial revolution begin to be felt.

The eighteenth-century trade also promoted development in south-eastern Nigeria by adding to the buying power of a large number of individuals. It is true that the profits of the overseas trade were not distributed evenly in the hinterland, benefiting the professional traders more than the non-traders and the coastal traders more than inland ones, but the fact that organized warfare and large scale raids played no significant role in the enslavement of individuals for export meant that the enslavement of individuals was governed primarily by economic motivation. The material rewards to individual kidnappers or pawners may have been small in proportion to the ultimate selling price of a slave in the Americas, but they were sufficient to create and extend a vast trade in a relatively brief period of time. Thus the profits of the trade were distributed more widely in this region than in parts of Africa where force and central control were more important in the slave trade. The developing trade in provisions added substantial numbers of small consumers to the market for imported local cloth or beads, hoes or knives made from imported iron bars, for gunpowder, for hunting, etc. Thus both the methods of the slave trade and the highly developed internal trade distributed the benefits of economic growth beyond a small élite.

It is the conclusion of this chapter that the slave trade not only offered an effective, though cruelly exploitative, solution to the problem of economic growth in south-eastern Nigeria by providing a market for slaves, the one export that the region was able to furnish in quantity at this stage of its economic development, but that the slave trade also led to sufficient economic development of the region to enable it to move to an even more profitable, yet unexploitative, trade in the early nineteenth century. This new trade in palm-oil did not wait for the slave trade to come to an end but expanded along with that older trade during the first four decades of the century. This fact is itself the clearest illustration of the development which the slave trade had promoted.

CHAPTER VII

The Growth of Agricultural Exports

THE previous chapter suggested that selling slaves had solved the problem of a profitable and sustainable export trade in the Bight of Biafra. Slaves were not, however, a satisfactory solution either in social and humanitarian or in economic terms. Many of the more thoughtful African slave traders in south-eastern Nigeria as elsewhere were aware of the cruelty and disruptiveness of the trade in slaves, but were unwilling to discontinue a trade which was of so much economic importance.[1] From a strictly economic point of view the trade in slaves, while not the disaster it is sometimes said to have been, was very limited in its developmental aspects. It is quite true that the *over-all* trade of the eighteenth century had promoted the expansion of the infrastructure, stimulated some African industries, and increased internal trade, but the trade in *slaves* had slowed rather than encouraged this process. The procurement of slaves, like that of ivory, was not labour-intensive, nor did it demand of any great labour specialization or technical advances, and thus had little direct developmental effect on the over-all economy.

More important in its developmental aspects was the trade in provisions. During the eighteenth century hinterland farmers had fed not only the trading communities but the slaves and crews in the overseas trade as well. This trade was of great economic importance because it was labour-intensive and because it encouraged regional labour specialization, trends that the nineteenth-century palm-oil trade would accelerate, furthering the process of economic development in the hinterland.

1. THE PROVISIONING TRADE

Although the provisioning trade had greatly expanded during the eighteenth century, its origins were much earlier. As was shown above, agricultural imports had long been important to the coastal

[1] For example, King Obi Osai of Aboh told Niger explorers 'that he was very willing to do away with the slave trade, if a better traffic would be substituted'. Allen and Thomson, *Narrative*, I, 218.

communities whose soils were too saline and/or swampy to grow all of their own food. This interzonal trade had expanded along with the overseas trade because of the growing population of these coastal entrepôts and the tendency of these communities to neglect fishing, farming, and eventually salt-making, in preference for trading.

Provisioning the trading ships added substantially to this trade. Along with slaves the early Portuguese traders had regularly bought yams and livestock in substantial amounts on the Rio Real.[2] As the slave trade grew in the late seventeenth and eighteenth centuries so did the demand for provisions. Ships often remained in port for months at a time while collecting a complement of slaves, and the crews and accumulating slaves all had to be fed from local resources during this stay. When the ships sailed, they took on additional supplies. By the mid-seventeenth century 'It was a standing convention of the trade that the sellers should deliver with each slave sufficient food (maize or yams and palm oil) to maintain him during the voyage to the West Indies ...'[3] How long such a convention lasted and how well it was observed are unclear. As early as 1677 the growing demands of the slave trade had led to the separation of the provisions trade from the trade in men. Because of the expanding slave trade it had become impossible for hinterland farmers to supply all of the food required, especially out of the harvest season,[4] so that a portion of the food needs had to be met from other sources. Slave ships began to secure some of their supplies before their arrival at Gulf of Guinea ports. In the latter part of the seventeenth century Royal African Company ships regularly brought along dried 'biskett', dried peas, horse beans from London, other beans from La Rochelle, lard from Holland, and maize purchased on the Gold Coast.[5] Additional supplies were purchased outside of southern Nigeria before attempting the two-month trans-Atlantic voyage. Because the currents and winds in the Gulf of Guinea made it necessary to sail east and south along the coast before one could pick up the easterly winds south of the equator, slave ships would stop at the islands of São Tomé, Principe, or Annobon, or at Cape Lopez to take on water, wood, and provisions.[6] These patterns continued throughout

[2] Pereira, *Esmeraldo*, p. 146.

[3] Hutchinson, 'Slaver's Diary', p. 141.

[4] Ibid., 142.

[5] Ibid., 141; Barbot, 'Description', p. 547; Barbot, 'Abstract of a Voyage', p. 456.

[6] Barbot, 'Description', pp. 383, 395, 403–6, 541–2. Accounts of provisioning in this manner by ships leaving Whydah in 1693 and 1725–7 may be found in Thomas

the period of the slave trade, the only change being that from the 1770s or earlier yams were also purchased at the island of Fernando Po to which ships often sent their tenders while awaiting a cargo on the Cross River, Rio del Rey, or Cameroon estuary.[7]

Despite these supplies from elsewhere slave ships continued to rely on the coastal ports for food to last them during the several months they remained in port, during the two to three-week voyage to São Tomé or one of the other provision stations, and for part of their supplies during the trans-Atlantic voyage. In 1699, for example, James Barbot bought 50,000 yams at Bonny which had been brought down from the hinterland, as well as livestock, palm wine, firewood, and water which he paid for in goods equal to the value of at least thirty-two male slaves. By the time his ship-load of 583 slaves reached São Tomé the yams were gone.[8] The ship *Dragon*, which took on 212 slaves at Old Calabar in 1698, had paid 360 copper bars for provisions, more than the cost of eight slaves.[9] These late seventeenth-century records suggest that the cost of provisions in the Bight of Biafra was equal to about 5 per cent of the value of the cargo of slaves. Comparable records for the eighteenth century are lacking but observers indicate that there continued to be a brisk trade in provisions to the slave ships.[10]

Astley, ed., *A New General Collection of Voyages and Travels* (London: Thomas Astley, 1745–7), II, 413–14, 462–3, 480. During voyages from Benin and Warri in the 1770s and 1780s provisions were obtained from Principe by J. B. Landolphe, *Mémoires du Captaine Landolphe*, ed. J. S. Quesné (Paris: Arthus Bertrand et Pillet ainé, 1823), I, 54, 177 and II, 9.

[7] Falconbridge, *Account of the Slave Trade*, p. 10, says ships call at São Tomé or Principe for supplies. The yam trade at Fernando Po was described by Captain John Ashley Hall in the *Abridgements of the Minutes of Evidence, taken before a Committee of the Whole House, to whom it was referred to consider of the Slave Trade* (London: 1790), II, 211, and by Capt. William Fitzwilliam Owen, *Narrative of Voyages to Explore the Shores of Africa, Arabia, and Madagascar* (London: Richard Bentley, 1833), II, 342–3. Waddell, 'Journal', VII, 64, estimated that Fernando Po sold a million pounds of yams a year to ships and to the mainland.

[8] Barbot, 'Abstract of a Voyage', pp. 460, 465.

[9] Ibid., 465, quoting 'Journal' of John Grazelhier.

[10] Antera Duke's diary of life in Old Calabar in the 1780s makes reference to frequent sales of yams by the thousands to slave ships; Duke, 'Diary', pp. 80, 91, 92. Nearer the turn of the century other observers remarked on the large quantities of yams, plantain, and palm-oil supplied to slave ships; see Schroeder, *Three Years Adventures*, p. 98 and Nicholls to African Assn. in Hallett, *Records*, p. 207. In 1828–9 an Old Calabar chief had even contracted to supply the small colony of British subjects on Fernando Po with livestock, grain, fruit, and other provisions; Badgley, 'Report on the Old Calabar River'.

Yams were one of the chief items purchased. As the staple food of southern Nigerians, they were desired by the slave captains for at least part of the middle passage on the theory that a familiar diet would promote good health among their slaves. Although records are inadequate to calculate the volume of the trade in provisions as a whole, a rough calculation of the yam trade can be made for the eighteenth century. At the beginning of the century an experienced trader estimated that 100,000 yams were required to feed 500 slaves during the middle passage,[11] apparently in the case when yams were to be the main element in the diet. As was mentioned above this was not the normal case. In 1699 James Barbot had bought only 50,000 for his 583 slaves and 22 years earlier Captain Hingston had put his needs at 30,000 for a cargo of 347 slaves; in 1778 Captain Landolphe had bought 35,000 large yams at Warri for a cargo of 410 slaves.[12] If these figures are representative, then an average of 85–6 yams per slave would have been a typical cargo. This would mean a trade from the Bight of Biafra ranging from just under 400,000 yams per annum at the beginning of the eighteenth century to 1,200,000 at that century's end. The actual trade from the hinterland to the coast would have been several times this amount since slaves and crew also had to be fed during the many months spent in port assembling a cargo and the coastal inhabitants themselves consumed vast amounts. Moreover, yams were but one of the items supplied from the hinterland. The livestock trade must also have been substantial, although sufficient figures are not available to estimate its volume. Nevertheless, it is clear that throughout the main period of the slave trade there was a substantial trade in agricultural produce from this coast.

Bonny and New Calabar were physically unable to expand their production to meet this demand or even to feed themselves. Old Calabar possessed vast uncultivated fertile territories to its north and east, but these were not developed as plantations until the nineteenth century.[13] Therefore, the entire increase in food shipments to the coastal ports in the seventeenth and eighteenth centuries was produced by the individual farmers of that part of the hinterland most readily accessible to these ports. In the egalitarian hinterland land-

[11] Barbot, 'Abstract of a Voyage', p. 465.

[12] Ibid., 460; Hutchinson, 'Slaver's Diary', V, 32; *Mémoires du Capt. Landolphe*, I, 174. Yams came in two basic sizes: a smaller or slave's yam and a larger king's yam. See Barbot, 'Abstract of a Voyage', p. 460 and Starke to Westmore in Donnan, *Documents*, IV, 80.

[13] Latham, *Old Calabar*, p. 48, describes the settlement of Akpabuyo.

holdings were uniformly modest in size and the surplus production of many thousands of households, gradually assembled through the complex network of local and area markets and regional fairs for shipment to the coast, was thus required to sustain this trade.[14] As the trade expanded the provisions would have come from a wider area and from greater distances. At the beginning of the eighteenth century Bonny was accustomed to sending large canoes upstream, evidently to Okrika, for yams; later in the century they reportedly bought yams from Okrika and from Andoni to the east.[15] These places were not themselves major producers, but were the markets to which yams came from further away, Andoni having excellent connections by water to the Ibibio of the lower Imo River and Okrika drawing on the neighbouring Ogoni country[16] and lying on a main route from the Bende fair. In the nineteenth century Baikie reported that most of the yams at Bonny came from that fair.[17] Old Calabar was likewise drawing supplies of yams from outside its own territories. Antera Duke's diary for 1785 makes references to canoes returning from 'Boostam', i.e. Umon on the Cross River, with thousands of yams. Twenty years later a visitor in Old Calabar reported that 'Howatt', i.e. Uwet on the Calabar River, 'trades with Old Calabar people for nothing but yams...'[18] Thus the same ports which handled the trade in slaves were also the focus of a distinct trade in provisions drawing upon the production of several thousand households.

[14] According to the estimates of a yam-growing area of Western Nigeria in 1928–30, a typical household with a farm of one acre could produce 9,000 lb. of yams a year of which 2,000 lb. (c. 650 yams) could be sold as surplus. See C. Daryll Forde and Richenda Scott, *The Native Economies of Nigeria*, ed. Margery Perham (London: Faber and Faber, 1946), p. 82. Estimates of yam production in south-eastern Nigeria are more difficult to come by since much of the region has concentrated on higher-yielding cassava-production in the twentieth century, but in a 1935 study of a yam-growing region on the left bank of the Cross River (Umor of Yakö) a typical household produced a comparable harvest to that in Western Nigeria (ibid., 58). Nearer the coast, however, yields may have been smaller. An Anang farmer can expect a yield of 6,000 lb. of yams per acre, and production in Ngwa in the 1920s was put at only 3,000 lb. per acre. See Udo, *Geographical Regions*, p. 7, for Otoro in Anang and A. Leeming, 'Assessment Report on Aba Native Court Area, Aba Division', 1927, p. 14, NAI, CSO 26/3/20610.
[15] Barbot, 'Abstract of a Voyage', p. 460; Penny in 'Report of Committee of Council', 1789.
[16] Alagoa, *History*, p. 148.
[17] Baikie, *Narrative*, p. 336.
[18] Duke, 'Diary', pp. 80, 90–1; Nicholls to African Assn. in Hallett, *Records*, p. 204.

2. PALM-OIL PRODUCTION

Long before the export trade in slaves and provisions had begun to taper off, a new product of the hinterland farms, palm-oil, began to pass in volume through the coastal ports. The palm-oil trade grew rapidly in the early decades of the nineteenth century and for a time slave ships and palm-oil ships competed for the attentions of the coastal merchants. About 1840, when the external trade in slaves was finally brought to an end, the expanding oil trade enabled the coastal entrepôts to continue prospering. Unlike other parts of West Africa which suffered some degree of economic dislocation when they could no longer buy their imports with slaves, the ports of the Bight of Biafra hardly seemed to miss an economic heartbeat.

In order to understand the economic importance of the palm-oil trade three aspects of it need to be considered: the production of the oil, its transport to the coast, and the changes which took place both north and south of the oil-palm belt as a result of this trade. The first two will be considered in the remainder of this chapter, the last in the following chapter.

The palm-oil was produced by thousands of hinterland households in the same areas which had previously supplied provisions for the coastal communities and for the slave-ships. Palm-oil had formed a part of the provisions trade and thus the export of palm-oil may be traced back to the early sixteenth-century Portuguese who purchased palm-oil from the Niger Delta for resale at Elmina on the Gold Coast.[19] Near the end of that century England imported some oil, but the real growth dates from the 1770s. By the mid-1780s Liverpool was importing an average of 40 tons a year, which was mostly from this coast.[20]

The trade in palm-oil increased gradually during the last years of

---

[19] Pereira, *Esmeraldo*, p. 138. An analogous development in English agricultural sales had taken place in the sixteenth century. The growth of the English army had stimulated regional grain production; when military demands fell in peace-time the farmers turned to exporting across the channel. See Alan Everitt, 'The Marketing of Agricultural Produce', in *The Agrarian History of England and Wales*, IV: Joan Thirsk, ed. *1500–1640* (London and New York: Cambridge University Press, 1967), pp. 521–2, 524.

[20] Hartley, *Oil Palm*, p. 10, for the sixteenth-century trade. For the eighteenth century see Falconbridge, *Account of the Slave Trade*, p. 52, where exports from Bonny are mentioned. Antera Duke refers to sales of two- to four-ton lots at Old Calabar in his 'Diary', *passim*. Figures for imports of palm-oil into Liverpool from 1772 are in Latham, *Old Calabar*, p. 56.

TABLE 4 *Palm-Oil Trade (in tons), 1815–64*

	Exports from Old Calabar	Exports from Bonny	Imports into U.K. from Western Coast of Africa[a]
1815	1,200	?	2,064
1821	2,000	?	5,124
1828	2,000	?	6,327
1833	4–5,000	?	13,350
1847	5,217	7,773	?
1848	4,634	8,450	?
1849	2,782	8,227	20,950
1850	4,260	6,730	19,324
1851	2,838	12,421	25,520
1855	4,090	16,124[b]	32,490
1864	4,500	16–17,000[b]	27,241

[a] Excluding British Possessions.
[b] Including New Calabar.
Sources: For all Old Calabar figures: Latham, *Old Calabar*, appendix 1. For Bonny 1847–51: Latham, *Old Calabar*, p. 67. For Bonny 1855, 1864: Thomas J. Hutchinson, 'General Report on the Bight of Biafra', 20 June 1856, F.O. 2/16/69A (covering the period 1 July 1854–1 July 1855) and Burton to Russell, 15 Apr. 1864, F.O. 84/1221. For imports into U.K.: *Parl. Papers* 1845 xlvi (187), 'Palm Oil: Quantity Imported into United Kingdom (1790–1844'; *Annual Statement of the Trade and Navigation of the United Kingdom with Foreign Countries and British Possessions in the Year 1853* (London: H.M. Stationery Office, 1855), p. 234; *Annual Statement . . . 1856*, p. 305; and *Annual Statement . . . 1865*, p. 322.

the eighteenth century and the first decade of the nineteenth, averaging over 150 tons a year in the 1790s and more than three times that in the next decade. The greatest increases came after the withdrawal of British ships from the slave trade in 1807 and the conclusion of the Napoleonic wars. In 1819 the exports of the Bight of Biafra to Liverpool reached 3,000 tons, in 1829 some 8,000 tons, in 1839 it was 13,600 tons.[21] In the mid-1850s the British consul for the Bight of Biafra calculated its oil trade in excess of 25,000 tons a year, while a decade later the consular report put the trade at 40–42,000 tons per annum.[22]

This remarkable growth of trade was dependent on two complementary circumstances: the great demand for oil of this type in

[21] Robert Jamieson, *Commerce with Africa*, rev. edn. (London: Effingham Wilson, 1859), p. 20. Jamieson bases his figures on 'custom house and other documents'.

[22] Thomas J. Hutchinson, 'General Report on the Bight of Biafra', 20 June 1856, F.O. 2/16. Richard Burton, 'General Report on Consulate (extract)', Burton to Russell, 15 Apr. 1864, *Parl. Papers* 1865 (3503–1) lvi.

Britain and the capability of south-eastern Nigeria to respond effectively to this demand.

The first set of circumstances was clearly understood by historians of British trade, but the African aspect has been both neglected and misrepresented. In his *Economic Revolution in British West Africa* Allan McPhee attributed the growing British demand for palm-oil to three factors: the increased demand for fats and oils of all sorts due to England's growing population; the increasing consumption *per capita* of fats and oils due to the 'new vogues' for washing with soap and lighting with candles, both of which were made largely of palm-oil in this period; and finally the tremendous amounts of lubricants for the new metal machinery of the factories and railroads.[23] By 1862 competition from the new supplies of mineral oil and gas would put an end to the boom period of the palm-oil trade, although this would be offset partly by the trade in palm kernels (for a light, edible oil) beginning about 1870.[24] These later vicissitudes, however, fall outside the scope of this study.

McPhee judged that the reason for the rise in African exports of palm-oil was 'more simple'. Despite the 'economic backwardness' of the West African hinterland, which he felt was due to the 'savagry' of its inhabitants and the 'primitive' processes of production, marketing, and transport in use, only a relatively small amount of labour was necessary to prepare the oil and get it to the waiting British ships.[25] In reality the production, marketing, and transport of such volumes of oil were hardly simple or easy matters, nor, although technology of the hinterland was comparatively unsophisticated, could so vast a trade have been sustained by a region as backward as McPhee suggested. Instead, the palm-oil exports of south-eastern Nigeria were possible only because of the centuries of economic development which had already taken place in conjunction with internal and external trade, plus the ability to adapt quickly in changing economic conditions.

Although oil-palm trees are found, at least in small numbers, throughout the region as far north as the Benue Valley, they grow in greatest profusion in a belt just behind the coastal swamps extending inland some 125 miles from the coast. The growth of this oil-

[23] Allan McPhee, *The Economic Revolution in British West Africa* (London: George Routledge, 1926), pp. 30–1.

[24] Jones, *Trading States*, pp. 73, 90.

[25] McPhee, *Economic Revolution*, pp. 10, 32.

palm belt has resulted from the penetration of cultivators into the primary rain forest of this region many centuries ago. As the upper canopy of the rain forest was cleared away, a secondary growth of oil-palms took its place. While it was not traditional for the hinterland cultivators to plant oil-palms, they did take care to protect adult trees, as well as seedlings, which had taken root naturally. By this process, which has been termed 'semi-cultivation', the oil-palm has attained a natural density in south-eastern Nigeria which is unsurpassed in any other part of the continent. These trees are commonly found on land under active cultivation, but are thickest in the patches of semi-wild 'palm-bush' which has not been cultivated for several decades.[26]

The density of the oil-palm also varies considerably from one part of the oil-palm belt to another. Thus, while averaging perhaps forty to fifty trees per acre of palm bush throughout the region, the area between Ikot Ekpene, Abak, and Opobo may be double that, while the Orlu area has only half the average density. High densities also exist along the Ikpe Creek and near (but not along) the Niger south of Onitsha. The hinterland behind Old Calabar generally did not have a high concentration of oil-palms because it was too thinly settled.[27]

This proliferation of oil-palms is a clear sign that their value was recognized early by the hinterland cultivators. Further indication of the early utilization of this tree can be deduced from linguistic evidence. The words for oil-palm (as well as those for the indigenous yam and kolanut species) in the languages of the Niger Delta developed their distinct forms in the very distant times before these languages themselves separated from their common source. One may reasonably conclude from this that these plants were known to and used by the speakers of the 'protolanguage' of the Niger Delta.[28]

In ancient times as today the principal use of the palm-oil would have been as food, since it is both tasty and nourishing. Because

[26] Hartley, *Oil Palm*, pp. 1–9. Udo, *Geographical Regions*, pp. 66–7.

[27] A. F. B. Bridges, 'Report on Oil Palm Survey in Ibo, Ibibio and Cross River Area', 1938, Appendix VII, p. 1, Rhodes House Library, Oxford, MSS. Afr. s. 679. Martin, *Oil Palm*, pp. 9–10. F. S. Purchas, 'Assessment Reports, Onitsha Division, Onitsha Province', 1927, p. 3, NAI, CSO 26/3/20676. See Latham, *Old Calabar*, p. 86, for the Akpabuyo area of the Old Calabar hinterland.

[28] Williamson, 'Food Plant Names', pp. 158–9. The languages being considered are Izi-Ukwani Igbo, Edo, Itsekiri-Igala, Abua-Ogbia, Ogoni, and Efik-Ibibio.

the trees were abundant and required little tending, in most areas of the hinterland their use and ownership was communal to the local resident group.[29] In the nineteenth century as palm-oil assumed a commercial value, a number of changes took place in the ownership and exploitation of oil-palms, a topic which will be considered later. Before that change can be considered it is necessary to examine how the oil was produced and marketed in the nineteenth century.

The manufacture of palm-oil was anything but the simple process McPhee imagined. The clusters of palm-nuts grow at the top of the oil-palm, so that the first step was to climb the tree, cut down the clusters and lug them home. Next the individual nuts had to be separated from the core and cooked until soft. The remainder of the process, as it was performed near Creek Town, Old Calabar, in 1851, was witnessed by Hope Waddell:

> There were three troughs of wood inclined, about six feet long each and two broad. In one of them a man was tramping the nuts while another kept throwing a little water over them. The man and nuts were at the upper end, the water and its oily accompanyment which flowed from them gathered in and filled the lower end. The oily matter is skimmed off the water and afterwards boiled leaving much refuse. Very little could be made in a day by such a slow and imperfect and wasteful process. The oil contained in the external pulp is easily enough procured in this way. But it is small compared to the quantity of nuts required to furnish it...[30]

Waddell witnessed the making of soft or edible oil, which was two or three times as arduous a process as that required to produce the less refined semi-hard oil for the export trade. Nevertheless, the amount of time and effort involved was very considerable. Twentieth-century studies of palm-oil production by traditional methods in this area suggest that 300 pounds of palm-fruit (25–30 clusters) are required to produce a 36-pound tin of semi-hard oil. The labour involved equals three to five person/days per tin, half or more of the work being done by women.[31] Assuming an average of four days' labour per tin and 62 tins per ton, the person/days devoted to the production of palm-oil for export from south-eastern Nigeria would have risen from 750,000 in 1819 to 10,000,000 in 1863–4. While the production methods were necessarily somewhat crude, the exertion and dedication were very considerable.

[29] Bridges, 'Oil Palm Survey', Appendix IX, pp. 9, 16.
[30] Waddell, 'Journal', VIII, 55.
[31] Bridges, 'Oil Palm Survey', Appendix VII, p. 1; Forde and Scott, *Native Economies*, p. 52.

The growth of the palm-oil trade in the early nineteenth century greatly enhanced the economic value of the common oil-palms, leading to important changes in their management. Before the expansion of the palm-oil trade oral sources indicate that oil-palms, like other valued forest plants or like the village stream or spring, had been considered a communal resource, subject only to such regulations as were deemed necessary to maintaining public order. Because supplies far exceeded demand, the oil-palms were endowed with only minor economic value. With the growth of the oil trade, however, the economic value of oil-palms was sharply enhanced, which in turn occasioned changes in their management. In most parts of the southern hinterland a community's trees were reallocated among its smaller component units, each unit receiving control of the trees on and adjacent to its farmland. From communal control the oil-palms passed to lineage or familial control. The process stopped far short of individual tenure, but in the twentieth century there has been a persistent movement in that direction. This solution to the enhanced economic status of the oil-palm was in clear accord with the overall tendency of hinterland societies to seek a balanced distribution of wealth and power among their component parts as well as to avoid centralizing political or economic power. As one might expect, this change in oil-palm management began, as did the trade itself, among the Ibibio and spread with the trade among the Igbo.[32]

In other parts of the hinterland, however, the communal management of oil-palms was retained, but their use was more closely regulated. In general, the retention of a form of communal management was characteristic of places which were also deeply involved in commerce and may represent an earlier stage of accommodation than the change to familial management. The Mboli and Ndoki Igbo, adjacent to the delta, several southern Ibibio groups, and the Ikpe Ibibio on the Enyong Creek have all retained an essentially communal system of management in the twentieth century, although they have used different institutions to regulate oil-palm use.[33] In

---

[32] Bridges, 'Oil Palm Survey', Appendix IX.
[33] C. J. Mayne, 'Intelligence Report on the Mbolli Clan, Ahoada Division, Owerri Province', n.d., NAE, CSE 1/85/3861; Ennals, 'Intelligence Report, Ndoki', p. 32; D. A. F. Shute, 'Intelligence Report on the Oniong and Nung Ndem Clans of Eket Division, Calabar Province', 1932, p. 25, NAI, CSO 26/3/27935; D. Bayley, 'Intelligence Report on the Ibesikpo Clan of the Uyo District, Calabar Province', 1934, pp. 11–12, NAI, CSO 26/3/29699; Johnson, 'Intelligence Report, Ukanafun', p. 26; interview with the Revd. Inyang, Ikpe.

some cases, the component villages or age-sets of a community were allotted set times for their members to cut palm fruit, a sign of an unusual degree of concentration of power in the village council which may be linked to trading organization. In a number of southern Ibibio communities, on the other hand, the right to cut palm fruit was wholly or partially restricted to members of certain men's secret societies, which had also usurped many traditional powers of the village councils.[34] No matter which system was adopted, however, the over-all result was to distribute the benefits of the trade to the producers in an egalitarian manner. Even the secret societies had open membership, and were generally representative of the community at large. Under these conditions it was impossible for the profits of the trade to accrue to a small class of cash croppers. The palm-oil trade of south-eastern Nigeria was thus firmly based upon the efforts of individual family groups, unlike the situation in neighbouring Dahomey in the 1850s and 1860s where royal plantations were set up.[35]

South-eastern Nigeria also differed from nineteenth-century Dahomey in making no efforts to increase the number of oil-palms. While Kings Gezo and Gelele promoted the planting of oil-palms on plantations, no such effort was needed by the Ibibio and Igbo who already had the densest concentration of oil-palms in the world. It would also appear that the small size of family land holdings prevented even the possibility of tree-farming on an economic scale, as indeed it does generally to this day.

Examined from the production end, it is clear that the trade in palm-oil rested upon a different segment of society than the trade in slaves: individual farming families. It was this group of producers who were most important in the economic revolution taking place in south-eastern Nigeria and who sustained in existence the hinterland and coastal traders (and the European shippers as well) who claimed the greater share of the profits.

3. PALM-OIL MIDDLEMEN

The palm-oil trade was structured very differently in its initial stages from the slave trade. The large volumes of palm-oil came from a

[34] Shute, 'Intelligence Report, Oniong', p. 25; Bayley, 'Intelligence Report, Ibesikpo', p. 26; interview with Chief Ibok, Nung Asang.
[35] For Dahomey see Coquery-Vidrovitch, 'Traite des esclaves'. Only in the hinterland of Old Calabar was any attempt made to establish plantations at this time, but these were more for food production than for palm-oil.

limited portion of the southern hinterland and were collected through the local market networks. In contrast, slaves were obtained a few at a time from a much wider area of the hinterland and avoided using the local markets. Thus in its initial stages the palm-oil was handled largely by local traders, while at the comparable level the slave trade was already largely monopolized by the professional hinterland traders like Aro. However, as palm-oil moved into the final stages of its transport to the coast it was handled in much the same ways as slaves. The southern fair at Bende became an oil centre and, until the founding of Opobo in 1869, palm-oil was shipped from the same coastal ports that were important in the slave trade.

During the early and middle years of the nineteenth century, when the new trade in palm-oil was rising and the slave trade had come under increasing attack and finally suppression, both exports passed through these ports without serious disruption.[36] Nevertheless, this was a period of great political and social change for these states. Their increasingly tumultuous history, which has attracted the attention of several historians,[37] was not due to the changes in exports but to the increasing pressures within and among these states and between them and the European merchants and officials at the coast. The great increase in the volume of trade promoted the expansion of the canoe houses, which had been founded in the late eighteenth and early nineteenth centuries, into larger amalgams which Jones has named 'canoe house groups'. In Bonny in the 1830s and somewhat later in New Calabar internal crises developed when merchant-king rulers who had managed to combine royal birth with mercantile acumen were followed by others lacking this combination. In the ensuing struggles the economic interests of the canoe house groups clashed with royal authority based on descent and led to European intervention. This struggle reached its greatest intensity in Bonny, where the non-royal head of the Anna Pepple House, Jaja (a man of slave origins), led his people out of Bonny to found the new

---

[36] 'It is indeed one of the curious facts of West African history that the one region where a peaceful changeover to legitimate commerce took place was the region where in the past the slave-trade had been most active', according to Roland Oliver and Anthony Atmore, *Africa since 1800*, 2nd edn. (London: Cambridge University Press, 1972), p. 38. The point of this chapter is to explain why that fact was not at all curious.

[37] The analysis that follows of the political and social history of the coastal states in the nineteenth century is based upon the following studies: Dike, *Trade and Politics*, Chapters III–VII; Jones, *Trading States*, Parts III and IV; Latham, *Old Calabar*, Chapters 6 and 7.

trading port of Opobo in 1869. The site was chosen to cut Bonny off from the richest oil markets up the Imo River and resulted in Opobo becoming the premier oil port. In Old Calabar intense internal rivalry among the wards and towns for control of the key political offices resulted in witchcraft accusations and pogroms which claimed the lives of hundreds of slaves and freeborn citizens.

In addition to these internal conflicts this period was also one of increased competition among the coastal entrepôts for access to the leading oil markets. Old Calabar's early lead in the trade was captured by the eastern delta states of Bonny and New Calabar, who battled with each other for exclusive trading rights at the inland oil markets. In addition, the nineteenth century also witnessed an intensification of the conflict between the coastal states and the European merchants. The latter were able to increase their leverage through manipulation of the credit system at Bonny and Old Calabar and through the involvement of the British government. Early British anti-slave-trade patrols and blockades had been followed by increased interference in local politics, treaties with the trading states, the appointment of a consul (1849), the use of exemplary and often illegal force, and finally the declaration of a Protectorate over the Niger Coast in 1884. Nevertheless, in the period up to the declaration of the protectorate it was still, in Jones's words, 'the European traders [who] had ... to conform to the African trading organization'.[38]

The political and social changes taking part in the coastal states have largely obscured the relative continuity in economic structures and activities which marked this critical period of external trade. Through their inland trading partners the coastal middlemen encouraged the expansion of the new palm-oil trade.

The first part of the hinterland to become involved in the palm-oil trade in a big way lay along the Cross River. During the last decade of the eighteenth century and the early years of the nineteenth, palm-oil became important enough to be recorded as a separate item of trade in British statistics.[39] At this period palm-oil was probably still part of the general trade in provisions and surely came from the Ibibio Proper, who are mentioned in a 1698 account as supply-

[38] Jones, *Trading States*, p. 82.
[39] 'Account of the Quantity of Palm Oil annually imported into the United Kingdom from the Western Coast of Africa, since the Year 1789, to the 31st day of December 1844', *Parl. Papers* 1845, xlvi (187).

ing general provisions to slaving ships.[40] Few details of the turn of the century palm-oil transactions have been preserved, but Bold's 1819 guide for English traders in 'legitimate' commodities placed Old Calabar's main oil markets among the Ibibio Proper with other important oil markets further upriver among the Mbiabo and Enyong, and an additional market among the Efut south-east of Old Calabar.[41] Efik sources also preserve important details of this period. The Efik of Old Calabar, it was indicated in Chapter II, had probably moved down the Cross River to their present location some time in the seventeenth century, after having settled for a time among the Uruan clan of the Ibibio Proper. Other Efik clans, the Enyong and Mbiabo, continued to inhabit parts of the river north of Old Calabar and were important trading partners for their Old Calabar cousins in the slave and food trades. About the time that the palm-oil trade began to expand there were important initiatives by various Efik groups to form or strengthen settlements and alliances with Ibibio Proper groups in the same area. In this the traders of Creek Town, Old Calabar, were more successful than their Duke Town rivals.[42] In forging or renewing these trading links the Efik of Old Calabar did not depart in any dramatic way from the techniques of the slave trade and the provisioning trade.

For the coastal states of the Rio Real the transition to palm-oil was effected in much the same manner as on the Cross River, although the transition began later. Bold's *Guide* reported that Bonny and New Calabar, which were then exporting 'a considerable quantity of palm-oil, ... might become a formidable market for that article with a little encouragement, particularly on the New Calabar side'.[43] Bold's expectations of increased palm-oil trade were fulfilled

[40] Barbot, 'Abstract of a Voyage', p. 465. Barbot bought supplies from the 'kings' of 'Agbisherea', evidently Ibibio Proper chiefs.

[41] Bold, *African Guide*, p. 78. Naturally these places were listed only by approximate versions of their actual names or nicknames: 'Ecricock', 'Aniung', 'Egbosherry', and 'Little Cameroons'. 'Aniung' is clearly Enyong. The nicknames 'Ecricock' (the Mbiabo clan of the Efik, most likely Ikot Offiong town) and 'Egbosherry' (Ibibio Proper) were explained in Chapter I. 'Little Cameroons' must not be confused with the big Cameroon Estuary on the other side of Mount Cameroon from Old Calabar, for Antera Duke recorded in his 'Diary' (p. 43) that he was able to walk from Qua Town, Old Calabar, to Cameroons in six hours one morning in 1786. As Goldie's *Dictionary* (p. 357) makes clear, it is the Efut country south-east of Old Calabar which is meant, for it was called Cameroons and the Efik bought palm-oil there which had been brought from places further inland.

[42] See below, Chapter VIII, §1.

[43] Bold, *African Guide*, p. 72.

in the 1820s, but it was Bonny not New Calabar which became the premier port. As a visitor to the Rio Real in 1826, Capt. William F. Owen, noted in his journal: 'eleven years back one vessel could with difficulty procure a cargo of palm-oil in the river Bonny, while at present from eight to ten are annually laden with it'.[44]

It appears that the oil was drawn from the same hinterland markets that were supplying slaves as well at this early period. Areas which had long supplied the delta communities with foodstuffs would also have begun to send their oil to the coast, but direct references to the oil sources of the Rio Real ports exist only from the mid-nineteenth century when the trade was already well established. At that time Bonny traded along the lower Imo River drawing upon the oil-rich Ibibio and Ngwa Igbo areas to the east and north of the river. Her chief Ibibio trading stations were Egwanga, Essene, Urua Awak, Ekeffe, and Uruata. Those among the Ndoki Igbo, who served the Ngwa, were Ohambele, Akwete, and Obunku.[45] New Calabar also became active in the palm-oil trade, relying for supplies on many places which had been their markets earlier. In the later part of the nineteenth century New Calabar's main oil markets were along the Engenni-Orashi, Sombreiro, and New Calabar Rivers, but in mid-century there are indications that New Calabar tapped markets along the Imo River as well. The explorer Baikie learned in 1854 that New Calabar had much trade with Ozuzu, a part of the Ikwerre Igbo, where there was 'plenty of palm oil . . . and abundance of cocos and yams'.[46] In 1859 the British consul reported that Bonny chiefs were willing to reopen the Ibibio and Ohambele markets on the Imo

[44] Owen, *Narrative*, II, 343.

[45] The British Consul in the Bight of Biafra from 1855 identified Bonny's chief oil markets as 'Iguangu' (= Egwanga), 'Sebrotonme' (?), 'Oriante' (= ? Urua Nta), 'Kufe' (= Keffe, Ekeffe), 'Orata' (= Uruata), 'Egbanaje' (= Egbanifeh). All of these, he said, were in 'Qua' (= Ibibio). See T. J. Hutchinson, *Impressions of Western Africa* (London: Longman, 1858), p. 104. Goldie, *Dictionary*, p. 360, named Nungasang, Essene's clan name, as a district of the Ibibio Proper with which Bonny traded. Waddell, *Twenty-Nine Years*, p. 418, learned from eye-witnesses that 'Ahombly' (= Ohambele) was the principal oil market in Ndoki. In his General Report of 15 Apr. 1864, Consul Richard Burton said that 'Akwitta' (= Akwete) on a tributary of the Imo River 'supplies a quantity of oil' to Bonny. He also mentioned oil markets at other places along the Imo: 'Ohombola' (= Ohambele), and 'Ommoba' (= Umuoba). See *Parl. Papers* 1865, lvi (3503-I), p. 43. A 1931 Intelligence Report states that there were six main oil markets before the founding of Opobo in 1869–70: Essene, Azumini, Ohambele, Uruata, Akwete (which had sub-markets as Asa, Ohundu, and Mkporo), and Obunku. See H. Webber, 'Intelligence Report on Bonny District, Owerri Province', 1931, p. 83, NAI, CSO 26/3/27226.

[46] Baikie, *Narrative*, p. 309.

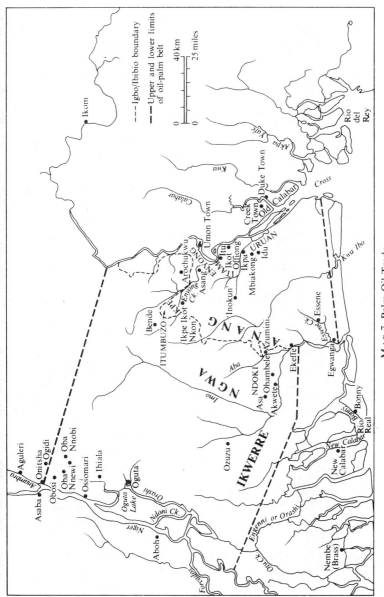

MAP 7. Palm-Oil Trade.

River to New Calabar in return for the settlement of a dispute which was blocking Bonny's access to Nembe-Brass. Details of this and other disputes which led to the later nineteenth-century system of exclusive markets have been examined by Jones.[47]

Along the third major artery into the palm-oil belt, the Niger River, there was also no sharp break between the slave-trade and the early palm-oil trade. The basic pattern of markets along the river, which had been set before 1500, changed only slightly; access to the major oil-producing areas—mostly east of the river—followed routes which had been developed earlier, but with considerable expansion and the emergence of some new riverside markets. As in the delta the trade in palm-oil here developed later than along the Cross River, although there had been a small trade in palm-oil for centuries, including exports to the early Portuguese mariners.[48]

Aboh, a merchant town at the neck of the delta, had long been the chief nexus of trade on the lower Niger and by 1830 the Landers could report that palm-oil had become as important as slaves in its trade.[49] During the following decade palm-oil rapidly increased in importance and volume as the slave-trade was brought to an end. The dimensions of the trade and its connection with the trade in provisions is clear from this early 1830s description by the explorer Macgregor Laird:

At daybreak I was much pleased to see a fleet of canoes of all sizes leaving the town for the purpose of collecting palm-oil, yams, and other provisions, for it gave an assurance of the regular and industrious habits of the people. There could not have been less than from one hundred to one hundred and fifty; and in the evening they came dropping in with their cargoes of yams, bananas, and palm-oil in large gourds. It was the most gratifying proof of regular and honest industry that I had yet seen in Africa.[50]

By 1841 Aboh had become 'the largest town in the Delta of the Niger' with a population of 7,000–8,000 and was said to dominate the Niger from the Forcados River north to near Onitsha.[51] Aboh had, of course, played a leading role in the trade along the lower Niger for several centuries, but much of the credit for its outstanding success in the first half of the nineteenth century appears to have been due

[47] *Trading States*, pp. 145–50.
[48] See Chapter I, §3.
[49] Lander and Lander, *Journal*, p. 253.
[50] Laird and Oldfield, *Narrative*, I, 98.
[51] Allen and Thomson, *Narrative*, I, 239, 233.

to its king, Obi Osai, whose superior intelligence and organizational skill impressed a whole generation of Niger explorers.[52]

From Aboh the oil went to the delta ports by canoe, the routes taken determined by the seasons of the year and the politics of the moment. The most direct route went from Aboh via the Ndoni Creek to the Orashi River and south along the Otu Creek and the Brass River to Brass. Some oil was shipped overseas directly from Brass, but because the bar across the mouth of the Brass River was difficult for large ships to cross safely most of the oil was trans-shipped to Bonny. During the rainy season it was possible to take a more direct route to Bonny along the Orashi and Engenni Rivers.[53] The relations among the delta peoples also influenced the choice of this route. Obi Osai told the 1841 Niger Expedition, 'I have some misunderstanding with the people between Aboh and Bonny; but I can [communicate] through the Brass people.'[54]

The growth of the palm-oil trade demonstrates the capacity for rapid change and over-all economic growth which had developed during the earlier decades of overseas trade. The demand for palm-oil and the fortuitous concentration of oil-palms in this region were beyond the control of African traders and producers, but the rapidity and magnitude of their response to new opportunity was possible because of their highly developed commercial skills and institutions. The earlier trade in provisions both for export and to supply the trading communities had drawn upon the same area of the hinterland and, by accustoming the farming households of this region to

[52] Laird and Oldfield, *Narrative*, I, 101, where Laird described him as 'the most intelligent black man I have met, and far superior to those on the coast'. John Beecroft was well received by Obi Osai in September 1835; see 'Substance of a Letter', pp. 424–5. Allen and Thomson, who met the king in 1841 when he was in his fifties, found his 'features ... pleasing and his countenance expressive of kindness; with an air of dignity and self possession like one used to command'; and also remarked on his force of character, superior judgement, and mild and equitable administration of justice; see *Narrative*, I, 207, 234. Only the Landers were sparing in their praise of Obi, an understandable occurrence since, though he had rescued them from an attack on the Igala Bank market, he then held them for ransom. 'In most African towns and villages', the captive explorers lamented in Aboh in 1830, 'we have been regarded as demi-gods, treated in consequence with universal kindness, civility, and veneration; but here alas! what a contrast—we are classed with the most degraded and despicable of mankind, and are become slaves in a land of ignorance and barbarism, whose savage natives have treated us with brutality and contempt.' See Lander and Lander, *Journal*, p. 257.

[53] Laird and Oldfield, *Narrative*, I, 102–3, 341. Lander and Lander, *Journal*, p. 253. Cf. Jones, *Trading States*, pp. 145–50.

[54] Allen and Thomson, *Narrative*, I, 226.

regular surplus production and by creating a system for marketing and conveying this produce to the coastal states, had prepared the way for a greatly expanded overseas trade in one of those provisions. The earlier trade had also developed the skills and institutions of the coastal middlemen and their inland commercial partners which were used for assembling and exporting palm-oil. Despite intense internal and external pressures these sophisticated traders were able to develop a major trade in palm-oil while simultaneously expanding their trade in slaves. Thus when circumstances beyond their control ended the latter trade, they suffered far less economic dislocation than did trading states elsewhere along the western coast of Africa.

Although there was a strong continuity in the economic institutions and activities of this period, the rise of the palm-oil trade represented a major turning point in the economic history of south-eastern Nigeria. The nature and significance of this departure is examined in the next chapter.

CHAPTER VIII

Agricultural Exports and Economic Development

DURING the first six decades of the nineteenth century the exports of the Bight of Biafra had altered, at intervals of about twenty years, from a trade predominantly in slaves, to a greatly expanded trade in which both slaves and palm-oil were dominant, to a trade primarily in palm-oil.[1] The significance of these changes in the economy of this region and of the changeover elsewhere in West Africa from slaves to 'legitimate' items of trade is a matter both complex and controversial. The two most recent historical studies of this question have in fact drawn diametrically opposite conclusions from the evidence. Commencing with a survey of the most common economic activities in West Africa, J. E. Flint decided that:

European economic contact with West Africa, at least before 1880, was essentially peripheral to the West African economy ... Seen from the viewpoint of African traditional society at the time the triumph of legitimate commerce was less than revolutionary. In general, African societies provided the European traders with new commodities without undertaking any major changes in their own internal economic structures. The palm oil trade is the major illustration of this phenomenon ...[2]

A. G. Hopkins reached conclusions directly contrary what he called the 'traditional view, which stresses continuities with the past', arguing instead that 'the structure of legitimate commerce marked an important break with the past and signified a new phase of growth of the market, a phase which can be seen as the start of the modern economic history of West Africa'.[3] He too finds a major illustration of his argument in the palm-oil trade.

---

[1] After 1870 the main exports consisted of palm-oil and palm-kernels.
[2] J. E. Flint, 'Economic Change in West Africa in the Nineteenth Century', in Ajayi and Crowder, *History*, II, 390, 397. Although these quotations are taken from widely separated parts of Flint's chapter, it is felt that their juxtapositioning here does not distort his meaning.
[3] Hopkins, *Economic History*, p. 124.

Not only do these two historians disagree strongly in their over-all conclusions about this period, but they also reach opposite assessments on the component parts of the larger argument. Flint stresses the continuity of economic life and traditional technology, arguing that the palm-oil trade 'was accomplished by traditional methods and traditional means of transport, extended in scale and size'; Hopkins agrees that methods and technology changed little, but argues that the great expansion of scale in this sector of the economy, in contrast to the slave trade, 'enabled small-scale farmers and traders to play an important part in the overseas exchange economy for the first time' and led to 'a marked increase in the com-mercialization of labour and land ...'[4] While Flint points out the inutility of nineteenth-century exports to West Africa, 'which were by their nature quickly consumed and contributed almost nothing to the quality of the economy or to its development', Hopkins stresses that these 'mainly cheap, mass-produced goods ... offered large numbers of inconspicuous Africans opportunities of material improvement' and in developing a mass market opened the way for the latter establishment of modern industries within West Africa to satisfy it.[5]

While such divergence of interpretation is symptomatic of the need for more research on this topic, it will be apparent that the arguments which have been advanced so far in this study share Hop-kins's more optimistic line of interpretation. European economic contact was not peripheral to the economy of this region in the early and middle years of the nineteenth century and the palm-oil trade did indeed mark the beginning of a major step forward in economic development. The discussion of the economic activities of the palm-oil producers in the previous chapter is in full accord with Hopkins's conclusions as is the section of this chapter on the hinterland palm-oil traders. The discussion later in this chapter of the effect of nine-teenth-century imports on south-eastern Nigeria is also closer to Hopkins's argument but pays greater attention to the role of imports in undermining local production. One important aspect of economic change which neither author emphasizes in his over-all survey of West Africa is the growth of internal trade as a result of the legiti-mate trade. In south-eastern Nigeria the diminished internal trade in

---

[4] Flint, 'Economic Change', p. 398; Hopkins, *Economic History*, pp. 125–6.
[5] Ibid.

some items was more than offset by the greatly increased markets in food and labour, as well as in manufactures such as canoes. This important point will also be elaborated in this chapter.

1. HINTERLAND PALM-OIL TRADERS

From the markets to which it had been brought by the producers the palm-oil passed through a series of intermediaries before reaching the coast. The routes and techniques for transporting palm-oil differed of necessity from those used for slaves. For one thing nearly all the oil sold came from the oil-rich southern portion of the hinterland, while slaves had been drawn from all parts of the hinterland and beyond. Moreover, the palm-oil trade made greater use of creeks and rivers than did the slave trade. As was shown above, most slaves were marched overland as far as the nearest way station to one of the coastal ports, slaves destined for Bonny, for example, customarily passing through a series of hinterland markets before reaching the Imo River where they were transferred to Bonny canoes. One reason for favouring overland routes where possible was to enable the slaves to transport themselves. Equally important was the fact that the major slave traders of the hinterland, such as the Aro, and Ekoi, were landlubbers, who had neither the skill nor the inclination to use waterways. Only on the Niger where riverain skills were common, did slaves travel any distance by canoe, and even there such people as the Onitsha or Asaba Igbo remained unproficient in aquatic transport, concentrating their trading skills on their own dry hinterlands.

The great bulk of the palm-oil, however, could not be transported overland except in relatively small amounts and over relatively short distances. While a slave trader might have been able to escort a dozen or more slaves and guard them at the same time, a single person could carry only one headload of oil and required armed escorts in addition. The solution to the transport of palm-oil was to make increasing use of the creeks, streams, and smaller rivers of the hinterland.

Transport of palm-oil by canoe led to the growth of strategically placed waterside markets along the streams and rivers of the palm-oil belt. Some of these had played a role in the slave trade and/or the provisioning trade, but the nineteenth century produced a great increase in their numbers and importance. In addition, the necessity of moving great quantities of oil to and from these markets at regular intervals promoted the growth of local traders and porters. Thus along with the initiatives of the coastal middlemen in the growth of the palm-oil trade attention must also be given the efforts of these market organizers and traders.

Along the Cross River the oil trade gave a major boost to several communities of traders intermediate between Old Calabar and the producers. Because of their geographical location and skill in using inland waterways as routes for the palm-oil, these communities were able to achieve a position in the oil trade comparable in scope though not in scale to that of the Aro in the slave trade. This achievement has been obscured by the fact that none of them ever attained the fame or ubiquity of the Aro, but their combined achievement was enough to deserve more attention than it has hitherto received. Two communities, the Ikpa and the Enyong, that were notably successful in the early Cross River oil trade, may thus illustrate the role and techniques of the intermediate palm-oil traders along the Cross River.

Ikpa was favoured in the oil trade by nature and by history. It lay in an area the density of whose population was already proverbial in the nineteenth century,[6] and as a result of human intervention the area was also known for the density of its oil-palm forest. Only eight miles up a navigable creek, Ikpa was accessible to the largest canoes used in the oil trade, and as a part of the Uruan clan, was linked by tradition with the Efik traders, whose sojourn in Uruan had lasted for several generations.[7] It is possible that Ikpa had traded with Old Calabar for slaves and provisions before the palm-oil trade became important. In any event its trade was worth a fight for Eyo Honesty I, the leading Creek Town trader, became a national hero of Old Calabar by defeating the 'pirates' of Mbiakong at the mouth of the Ikpa Creek, who had sought to restrict the movement of Efik traders on the Cross River.[8] After their defeat Mbiakong and other nearby peoples began to sell their oil to Creek Town traders at Ikpa market and sometime in the 1830s a second market was opened in Ikpa for the Duke Town

[6] Goldie, *Dictionary*, pp. 358–9, cites the proverbs: *Mbiakong nte mfang ikot* (Mbiakong is like the leaves of the bush), and *Idu nte ntan esien* (Idu is just like sand).

[7] See Chapter II, §2.

[8] Eyo Honesty I, *alias* Willy Honesty, was born Eyo Nsa and died in 1820. He is to be distinguished from his more famous son, Eyo Honesty II, who became King of Creek Town in the late 1830s. See Latham, *Old Calabar*, pp. 26–8. For Eyo I's victory see *Hart Report*, p. 129.

traders.[9] By mid-century Ikpa had become Old Calabar's premier oil market.[10]

Palm-oil was brought to Ikpa from its own palm forests, from other Uruan communities, and from the oil-rich Itam clan further inland which also supplied the Efik oil market at Ikot Offiong and Itu.[11] Oral sources indicate that palm-oil also came down the Ikpa Creek and its tributaries from Ibibio communities near the Aro trading settlement of Inokun, where 'little beaches', i.e. creekside markets, had been established.[12] As the oil trade grew Creek Town traders intermarried with the leading Ikpa families and settled in Ikpa to buy oil as it came in. Later in the century foreign companies also established depots at Ikpa Beach.[13]

Further up the Cross River were the Enyong people who controlled the oil-trade along a creek named after them. The Enyong were a branch of the Efik who had remained on this portion of the Cross River when the main branch had descended the river to found Old Calabar. Although primarily fishermen, the Enyong had engaged in the slave trade as intermediaries between Arochukwu and Old Calabar.[14] The growth of the oil trade gave the Enyong an opportunity to use their traditional expertise in canoes to reach the oil-producing communities further up the Enyong Creek. The earliest report of the Cross River oil trade, Bold's 1819 *Guide*, mentioned the Enyong by name as one of the River's principal oil markets.[15] Oral sources indicate that the Enyong derived a large part of their oil from the Ikpe and Itumbuzo clans many hours journey up the creek.[16] The Enyong had agreements with communities all along the creek and its tributaries to keep the waterway free of fallen

[9] Interviews with Chief James Udo Akang of Mbiakong, Chief Jacob Eyo Akpan, Obong Isong of Mbiakong, and other elders of the town, 25 Nov. 1972. Latham, *Old Calabar*, p. 88, cites the records of Black Davis, a Duke Town trader, for 3 Sept. 1839, to document Duke Town's activities at Ikpa.

[10] Goldie, *Dictionary*, p. 359, names Ikpa as the 'largest oil market of the Calabar people', and Waddell, *Twenty-Nine Years*, p. 243, shows it as the 'great oil market' on his map of the Cross River region.

[11] Hugh Goldie, 'Journal', 6 Nov. 1848, in *Missionary Record*, IV (Sept. 1849), 132.

[12] Interview with Chief Ikpo, Ibiono.

[13] Interview with Chief Philip Bassey Ikpe, regent for the Obong Isong of Ikpa, Chief Asuquo Okon, 5 Dec. 1972. The warehouses and residences built for foreign traders may still be seen at Ikpa Beach.

[14] See Chapter V, §2.

[15] See Chapter VII, note 41.

[16] Interview with Chief Ibah, Enyong, and interview with the Revd. Inyang,

trees and other obstacles to navigation, for which set fees were paid by the Enyong oil traders.[17] All along the creek marketing beaches were established as collection points for the oil from nearby communities, giving scope to local traders to organize the trade to the beaches. According to one Ikpe source: 'At the mouth of every tributary creek there would be huts and people would being their oil there. And the bulk trader would buy whatever oil and kernels were there. And if it filled his canoe he would go back and return on the [next] market day.'[18] The most important of these markets was Ikpe Ikot Nkon, which was also an important stop on an Aro trade route. Through the market passed much of the oil from the communally held oil-palms of Ikpe.[19] The oil from the Enyong Creek was sold to Old Calabar traders at the Asang market a few miles upstream from the Cross River or at Itu at the mouth of the creek.

Additional supplies reached Old Calabar from the middle Cross River, passing through the Umon middlemen, whose commanding position on an island in the river ensured them control of the traffic between the lower and middle river. The oil passing through Umon hands came chiefly from the Agwa'aguna people on the left bank of the river.

It is not possible to describe the operations of the intermediate traders in the central portion of the hinterland in as great detail as on the Cross River, but there too some interesting changes are discernible. While the palm-oil trade on the Cross River remained tied to the traditional four-day market cycle,[20] Waddell observed in 1846 that the trade at Bonny was carried on differently. The network of fairs which had developed during the slave trade continued to dominate the trade. Once a month 'a whole fleet' of canoes went up the Imo River loaded with European trade goods and after the fair was over they returned with 'a thousand puncheons of oil at a time', which was sold to the waiting European ships.[21] Eight years later Baikie learned that the Bende fair 'had declined but little' as a result

---

Ikpe. The canoe time from a point about ten miles up the Enyong Creek to Ikpe Ikot Nkot was estimated at 19 hours by Major H. D. Carleton, 'Orders for O.C. Columns, Aro Field Force', in Moore to C.O., 24 Nov. 1901, C.O. 520/10/381.

[17] See Chapter VI, §1.

[18] Interview with Revd. Inyang, Ikpe.

[19] Ibid.

[20] For the operation of this market ring see Chapter VI, §1.

[21] Waddell, *Twenty-Nine Years*, p. 270.

of the termination of the overseas slave trade and had become an important depot for palm-oil.[22]

Some of the oil sold at Bende appears to have come from the Agwa'aguna people east of the Cross River, who in 1841–2 became embroiled in a violent dispute with Umon when they attempted to by-pass the latter traders and sell directly to Efik traders. This dispute dragged on for several decades, robbing Old Calabar of a fifth of its former oil exports.[23] No longer able to ship their oil to Old Calabar, the Agwa'aguna sought out another route to the coast. By 1842, Beecroft learned, they had found it: the oil was sold to the Igbo on the west bank, who, in turn, sold it to New Calabar and Bonny.[24] It is highly likely that the Agwa'aguna oil was passing through the Bende fair, since the most direct route from Agwa'aguna would have been by canoe to Ikun Beach[25] and then overland 20–25 miles to Bende. From the fair the oil would have gone as far or farther by headload before reaching the Imo River and then by canoe to the delta.[26] The rapidity with which this oil found an alternative route to the coast illustrates both the high degree of commercial development in the hinterland and the role which overland transport was able to play even in the bulky oil trade. It also suggests the role

[22] Baikie, *Narrative*, pp. 309–10.

[23] Beecroft reported that Umon was shipping palm-oil to Old Calabar during his 1841 ascent of the river (see 'On Benin', p. 190), but that a quarrel over a piece of land had ruptured the trade by the time of his ascent of the river a year later (see King, 'Details of Explorations', p. 272). Waddell described expeditions of Old Calabar chiefs in 1846 and 1848 to settle the dispute with Umon, attributing the dispute to the earlier slaughter of Agwa'aguna traders and retainers at Umon town 'on pretense of an old quarrel', which is essentially the reason for the stoppage cited by European traders in 1856. See Waddell, *Twenty-Nine Years*, pp. 285–8, 365–6, 470, and Supercargoes to Hutchinson, 30 June 1856, enclosure No. 1 in Hutchinson to Clarendon, 20 Feb. 1857, *Parl. Papers* 1857, xlvi (0.2). Goldie seems to strike at the root cause in attributing the stoppage and the resultant incidents to the attempt of the Agwa'aguna 'to drive a direct trade with Calabar' in palm-oil which would have by-passed the Umon market and robbed them of their profits; see Goldie, *Dictionary*, p. 361. The annual loss to Old Calabar was put at 1600–1800 puncheons by the Old Calabar kings in 1851; see Beecroft to Palmerston, 9 Oct. 1851, and enclosures, F.O. 84/858. Peace between Umon and Agwa'aguna was finally restored in January 1888 through the mediation of Acting Consul Harry H. Johnston; see Johnston to Salisbury, 9 Feb. 1888, F.O. 84/1881.

[24] King, 'Details of Explorations', p. 272.

[25] Ikun was said to be an Agwa'aguna town by Hugh Goldie, 'Notes of a Voyage Up the Calabar or Cross River in November 1884', *Scottish Geographical Magazine*, I (1885), 276. It is in fact an Ibibio town, but probably had a colony of Agwa'aguna traders.

[26] See maps 4 and 7 for probable routes.

played by the Aro in the oil trade, a point which will be taken up shortly.

The main terminus of the trade route south from Bende was Ohambele on the Imo River. When the first Europeans advanced into that portion of the hinterland in 1850, they observed about 200 canoes there loading with oil.[27] The majority of the palm-oil shipped from Ohambele probably came from places less distant than Bende. According to Ohambele traditions, traders from the Ika and Anang Ibibio as well as the Ngwa Igbo brought oil directly to Ohambele until the rise of Azumini on an intervening creek in the 1860s drew away much of that trade.[28] The importance of the Ngwa trade was also attested to in an 1873 letter from the Bonny chiefs in which that region was said to supply two-thirds of the palm-oil sent to Akwete and Obunku.[29] It is not likely that all trade in palm-oil was dominated by the cycle of fairs. Places like Ohambele which were closely tied to Bende clearly did operate in that fashion, but oral sources indicate that smaller markets, such as Essene and Ekeffe farther downstream, drew their oil only from their own territories and would have used the traditional four-day market cycle.[30]

Along the Niger, as was shown earlier, Aboh had become a major intermediary between the delta and the hinterland for palm-oil by the 1930s. Little oil was produced by Aboh itself, most supplies being brought from riverside markets to the north. By mid-century, Samuel Crowther reported, Onitsha was Aboh's 'chief oil market'.[31] Onitsha in fact lies near the northern limit of the oil-palm belt, but had the singular advantage of occupying high ground on the river's edge. While the banks of the river to the south were low and swampy for a depth of several miles, Onitsha had excellent overland connections from the river to the east and south-east. For this reason it had become a trading centre in early times, connected to the nearby Igala Bank market described in Chapter I. With the rise of the palm-

[27] Waddell, *Twenty-Nine Years*, p. 418.

[28] Interview with the elders of Ohambele, Ndoki, 15 Jan. 1973. The rise of Azumini is associated with the career of Jaja of Opobo. The trade of Azumini with the Anang and Ika became so intense that a 1926 report recommended that these three groups might all be administered together. See H. H. Marshall, 'Obong Village Group of the Anang Sub-Tribe, Abak District, Calabar Province', 1933, p. 12, NAE, CSE 1/ 85/4905A.

[29] King and Chiefs of Grand Bonny to Bonny Court of Equity, 30 May 1873, enclosure in Livingstone to Granville, F.O. 84/1377.

[30] Interview with elders of Ekeffe, Inen, Southern Anang, 11 Jan. 1973.

[31] Crowther and Taylor, *Gospel on the Banks*, p. 17.

oil trade Onitsha became a natural focus for the oil-rich Ihiala,
Nnewi, and southern Idemile areas to its south-east. Some oil would
also have reached Onitsha from Ogidi in northern Idemile and from
the Aguleri area on the lower Anambra River.[32] The organization
of the early trade to Onitsha is remembered this way at Oba in southern Idemile:

The market at Onitsha was not the present one, but one called Otu Moye.
There was another market at Obosi waterside called Otu Obosi ... We sold
the Onitsha people palm kernels, palm oil, and coconuts, all of which came
from Oba and places south-east of us ... It was not easy to go to Onitsha
in those times; there were dangers along the way and life was not secure ...
The men went to Onitsha in groups for safety, though some strong women
would accompany them. We went first to Obosi whose people would accompany us to Onitsha ... There were no roads in those days and the paths did
not go very straight to Onitsha. We had to cross one stream on the way by
means of a hanging bridge made of ropes. The trade went from hand to hand:
Oba to Obosi to Onitsha, that is, you had to have a relative in Obosi to handle
your trade to Onitsha.[33]

The attendance of Oba, Obosi and several other village-groups in
this area at Onitsha market was recorded by Crowther in 1854.[34]
Asaba, across the river from Onitsha, did not share so much in the
oil trade since little palm-oil was produced on that side of the river.

Midway between Onitsha and Aboh, on the eastern side of the
Niger, was another important palm-oil collection centre, Ossomari.
Located in the swampy margin of the river, Ossomari had few oil-
palms itself, but it was connected by creeks to the Orashi River,
to Oguta Lake, and by other streams and paths to the oil-rich Isuama
Igbo hinterland. Crowther noted that Ossomari was trading between
Aboh and this thickly populated hinterland in 1854 and oral sources
place Ossomari's main feeder markets at Okija, Ihiala, and Oguta.[35]
Ossomari was also able to by-pass Aboh by shipping oil down the
Orashi River to New Calabar and Bonny, a procedure which may
have led to the conflicts with Aboh remembered in Ossomari traditions. Intermarriage, however, was common between the two towns
on the Niger and they eventually reached an agreement dividing

[32] Oil-palms are 'plentiful' in Ihiala, Nnewi, Nnobi (south Idemile) and 'fair' in
Ogidi, Onitsha, and Aguleri, according to Purchas, 'Assessment Report, Onitsha',
p. 3.
[33] Interview with Messrs. Mefo and Ibe, Idemile.
[34] See map 3.
[35] Crowther, *Journal*, p. 23; Henderson, *King in Every Man*, p. 69.

the trade between them.[36] In the second half of the century traders from Brass and New Calabar established direct contact and settlements along the south shore of Oguta lake, which made Oguta one of the most important palm-oil markets in this region and probably cut both Aboh and Ossomari off from a portion of the trade.[37]

Even without these later developments, commerce along the Niger retained its historic complexities, palm-oil being one commodity in the over-all trade. This complexity and the roles of areas north of the oil-palm belt, are suggested in this mid-century résumé by Crowther: 'Abo [Aboh] people bring salt and other goods from the lower parts of the river, as far as Igara [Igala], which are also taken to the Confluence by the people of Idda [Idah], and are sold for cowries or ivory, and the cowries are brought to Onitsha market, to purchase palm oil.'[38]

In tracing the growth of the palm-oil trade in the first six decades of the nineteenth century it is important to avoid losing sight of the role of the small producers and local traders. While the direct evidence of their activities is inversely proportional to their actual importance, it is obvious from the volume of the trade that a multitude of small traders were at the base of the trade at the local level: men and women carrying calabashes of oil on their heads from the village markets to the creekside beaches, local wholesalers organizing and supervising the trade, specialists marketing the imported goods received for the oil. It is also necessary to appreciate the importance of the waterside trading centres which served the new trade. The rise of these groups in the nineteenth century was largely outside the trading structures of the coastal middlemen and the hinterland traders who had dominated the slave trade. Before concluding this section, therefore, it is useful to examine the 'crisis' which the rise of the palm-oil trade produced in the older hinterland trading communities.

For the Aro the suppression of the overseas slave trade and the simultaneous rise of the palm-oil trade was a blow to their trading hegemony in the central hinterland. Nevertheless their decline was only gradual and relative until they faced a more direct attack by

[36] Kaine, *Ossomari*, p. 31; B. G. Stone, 'Intelligence Report on the Riverain Villages of the Onitsha Division, Southern Section, of the Onitsha Province', 1932, p. 9, NAI, CSO 26/3/28740; Henderson, *King in Every Man*, pp. 69–70.

[37] Udo, *Geographical* Regions, p. 50.

[38] Crowther and Taylor, *Gospel on the Banks*, p. 30.

British forces in the early twentieth century.[39] There are several reasons for this. First the slave trade ended slowly. The overseas slave trade did not begin to decline until the 1830s by which time the Aro settlements were well established. The large demand for domestic slaves throughout the century, while very much smaller than the former export trade, continued to provide a measure of traditional employment to the Aro. Moreover, while they had specialized in the slave trade, the Aro had also traded a vast array of other items, so that the end of the overseas slave trade did not bring an end to their trading prominence. They continued to trade in items of high value from local and overseas sources, and to act as agents for their oracle at Arochukwu, which was often consulted by coastal traders to settle political disputes in their states.[40] Finally, the Aro were not entirely shut out of the new palm-oil trade. While they never adapted themselves to water navigation, they did become quite active in the new trade in some places as by using their trading contacts, organizational skill, and capital. They were notably active along the Cross River where it is hard to avoid seeing their hand in the capture of the Agwa'aguna oil for Bende and Bonny. Similarly in the oil-rich Anang and Ngwa areas oral sources report that the Aro were often local wholesalers in the oil trade.[41] Later in the century the Aro also came to play an important role in the oil trade to the west at Oguta as well. In evaluating the ways in which the Aro adjusted to this crisis in their trading hegemony, it is important to recall that they were not organized as a single trading company but as diverse and scattered communities that were free in the nineteenth century, as they had been in the eighteenth, to exploit the local situation in whatever ways they found best. As Chapter V has shown, that was not accomplished without conflict among Aro factions, but it did enable them to come through a major trading crisis with a relatively less important but none the less substantial role in the hinterland's trade.

[39] See A. E. Afigbo, 'The Nineteenth Century Crisis of the Aro Slaving Oligarchy of South-Eastern Nigeria', *Nigeria*, Nos. 110–12 (1974), pp. 66–73.

[40] See above Chapter V, §2.

[41] Interviews with Chief Ebu, Okun; Chief Akpan, Afaha Obong; Chief Udonyah, Okono. Interview with Mr. Asuquo Okori, an Aro trader of Ndi Chioka, Arochukwu, resident at Ikpe Ikot Aqua, Ikono, Abak Division, 14 Dec. 1972. Interview with Chief Jonah Udo, an Aro trader resident in Ikot Obio Ama, Ikono, Abak Division, 14 Dec. 1972. Interview with Chief Charles Esu, Ikwen, Otoro, Ikot Ekpene Division, 18 Feb. 1973. These local traditions were confirmed by interviews at Arochukwu with Chief Oji and Chief Asiegbu.

Of the major trading peoples of the hinterland it is the Aro whose activities in the nineteenth century are best known. However, it would appear that the other professional trading communities were also able to continue as major dealers in internal manufactures and foreign imports. Certainly the growth of title societies in the western part of the hinterland gives every indication of their continued commercial prosperity.[42]

2. NINETEENTH-CENTURY IMPORTS

During the first half of the nineteenth century major changes took place in the trade goods reaching West Africa from overseas. Newbury's careful research has demonstrated that the magnitude of the trade between Western Europe and West Africa increased by a factor of about six or seven between 1820 and 1850.[43] A high proportion of this increase took place in the Bight of Biafra where the slave trade and the palm-oil trade were both increasing, the former until the 1830s and the latter until the 1860s when palm-oil prices fell, owing to competition from newly available mineral oil. At the same time as the export trade was increasing imports were also growing in magnitude, and great changes were taking place in the proportions of the various goods that were imported. Many of these imports in the early nineteenth century were goods that the hinterland had once largely furnished for itself: salt, hardware, cloth, and clothing. Later in the century Jamaican rum, American tobacco, and Norwegian dried cod also came to be imported in much greater amounts.

Some indication of the actual volumes of goods traded can be gathered from Newbury's studies of British exports to 'Western Africa' in the nineteenth century. Although the figures cover the entire coast from the Senegal River to the Cape of Good Hope, a substantial proportion of that trade was with the Bight of Biafra. Over-all trade with this part of Africa increased very sharply during this period, but for some items the advancement was quite spectacular. Cotton cloth led the list, increasing by a factor of 50 in the first half of the century, with exports of iron bars in second place, growing by a factor of 18. Both of these items experienced the major portion of their growth after 1825. Salt, tobacco, and rum handled by British

---

[42] See above Chapter IV, §4.
[43] Newbury, 'Prices and Profitability', p. 92.

TABLE 5

'An Abstract of a Cargo Suitable to Purchase 100 tons of Palm Oil at [Old] Calabar, at £14 per ton.'

	pounds sterling	copper rods[a]
100 tons of Salt	100	6,200
50 barrels of Gunpowder	150	15,000
200 Soldiers' Muskets	185	8,000
200 Photaes[b]	180	6,000
300 Romals, assorted[b]	162	7,200
130 Allijars[b]	50	2,400
100 Sastracundies[b]	60	2,400
20 pcs. Langee handkerchiefs[b]	25	800
20 pcs. Pullicat[b]	25	800
100 pcs. Chintz, English	90	2,400
6 puncheons of Brandy	66	4,480
Beads, iron bars, copper rods, hardware, earthenware, hats, caps, etc.	247	10,620
Totals	1,340[c]	66,300

Source: Adams, *Remarks*, pp. 250–5.

[a] The actual value of a copper rod was about 6*d*. Therefore, by Adams' figures the gunpowder trade was very profitable, while most of the cloth trade was not.

[b] Indian textiles.

[c] Adams lists a total of £1,400, which is in accord with what the table is supposed to show, but his figures do not add up to that number.

merchants increased more slowly (by factors of 3 or 4) and more steadily in the first half of the century.[44]

The changes taking place in the Bight of Biafra in the earlier part of the century may be seen in the sample cargoes suggested for Old Calabar by two English guides for palm-oil traders, which are presented in tables 5 and 6 and analysed in table 7. At that time iron bars and copper rods still held a sizeable, though reduced, share of the cargoes, the rods being needed as currency to facilitate the expansion of the palm-oil trade,[45] but goods for the consumer market

[44] C. W. Newbury, 'Credit in Early Nineteenth Century West African Trade', *JAH*, XIII (1972), 82–3, and Newbury, 'Prices and Profitability', pp. 91–4. For other recent evaluations of the effects of imports see Flint, 'Economic Change', pp. 387–91, for all of West Africa, and Latham, *Old Calabar*, pp. 73–9, for the imports through that port. Both agree that European imports had little adverse effect on the African cloth industry through the middle of the century.

[45] See above Chapter VI, §2.

TABLE 6
Cargoes Suitable for the Purchase of Palm-Oil at Old Calabar

(A) For 10 crews[a] of palm-oil @ 12 copper rods each		(B) For 500 crews of palm-oil @ 16 copper rods each	
10 crews of salt	40	1,000 crews of salt	4,000
4 kegs of powder	8	1 barrel of powder	300
		10 guns	400
4 iron bars	16	220 iron bars	880
		200 copper rods	200
1 pc. Romal	24	50 pcs. Romal	1,200
4 yds Pocket	12	130 yds. Pocket	390
2 striped caps	8	24 striped caps	96
1 wedge of soap	8	15 wedges of soap	120
		7 bandana handkerchief	56
		24 looking glasses and	
small articles	4	small articles	358
total	120	total	8,000

Source: Edward Bold, *The Merchants' and Mariners' African Guide* (London: Longman, 1819), p. 81.

[a] A unit of measure equal to 10–12 gallons.

including cloth and clothing, fire-arms and ammunition and mineral salt had greatly increased in importance. As the figures quoted above indicate, these goods all increased their share of the trade much more in the next quarter century.

The changes in the kinds of goods being traded in the first half of the nineteenth century of course reflect the impact of the British industrial revolution on the world market, with British cotton

TABLE 7
Trade Items for Old Calabar as Percentages of Total Cargo

	Table 5 total £s	Table 5 total rods	Table 6A rods	Table 6B rods
salt	7%	9%	33%	50%
cloth/clothing	44	33	37	22
iron/copper	a	a	13	14
guns/powder	25	35	7	9
soap	—	—	7	2
brandy	5	7	—	—
other	18	16	3	4

[a] Included in 'other'.

goods largely replacing Indian ones and the salt of British mines undercutting local African production. Yet the external factor did not solely determine the nature of the trade; African preferences still played a major role in shaping the exports to each sector of the African coast, as Bold's and Adams's guides amply illustrate. These African preferences were not simply a matter of taste or caprice, but also depended on the trading conditions at each African port which in turn were shaped by its competitive position on the coast and its inland trading relations. On the Rio Real early in the century competition between Bonny and New Calabar kept prices lower than at Old Calabar. Whereas at the latter port Bold said it was necessary to have a good selection of fine Indian cloth, he noted that on the Rio Real 'common Manchester cloths suffice'.[46] Adams indicated that at Bonny, where the palm-oil trade was not so well developed, salt was less in demand than at Old Calabar and the goods he suggested for purchasing 100 tons of palm-oil at Bonny consisted in very large part of gunpowder and muskets.[47]

In the middle part of the century Niger explorers concerned with expanding 'legitimate' trade between West Africa and Britain regularly inquired about African preferences. In 1834 King Obi of Aboh replied with a clear list of his priorities: 1. cowries, 2. red cloth, 3. red beads (mock coral), 4. soldiers' jackets, 5. Romals and Bandana handkerchiefs, 6. rum, 7. muskets and powder.[48] At Onitsha in the late 1850s Crowther was told that American leaf-tobacco was the best trade item, with substantial demand for iron bars and salt as well.[49]

In calculating the effects of these changes in imports, it is important to keep in mind that the nature of the imports into this region was determined by this relation between African preferences and the competitive position of goods on the world market. It has already been argued that because of the quality and design of their works the hinterland smiths were able to hold on to most of their former trade until mid-century and the cloth-makers still longer.[50] On a

---

[46] Bold, *African Guide*, pp. 79, 72.

[47] Adams, *Remarks*, pp. 263, 252.

[48] Laird and Oldfield, *Narrative*, I, 271. Seven years later, asked the same question, King Obi gave a very similar reply: 1. cowries, 2. cloth, 3. muskets and powder, 4. handkerchiefs, 5. coral beads, 6. hats, 7. salt. The higher priority given to fire-arms is the only notable change; Allen and Thomson, *Narrative*, I, 219–20.

[49] Crowther and Taylor, *Gospel on the Banks*, p. 436.

[50] See above Chapter VI, §4.

great many other items the hinterland remained wholly or substantially self-sufficient well into the nineteenth century. Dried fish from the coast, for example, remained a staple of the inter-zonal trade between the saline littoral and the agricultural interior for centuries until replaced by Norwegian stockfish late in the century.[51] Locally grown tobacco likewise eventually lost its hold on the local market to the superior American leaf, but not until about the middle third of the century.[52] In salt, too, south-eastern Nigeria remained self-sufficient until about 1800, but then its demand for imported salt became as dramatic as its previous holdout had been. For this reason the case is worth examining in more detail.

The salt needs of the populations of the hinterland had been met from early times from both vegetable and mineral sources. The mineral salt was generally preferred, although because sources were unevenly distributed, many communities had to rely on less satisfactory substitutes. Mineral salt came from various salt springs and a few salt lakes, like Uburu, but most was prepared along the coast by evaporating sea water.[53] As was shown in Chapter I, the trading of coastal salt was one of the underpinnings of early hinterland trade, a situation which evidently extended to vegetable salts as well, since one of the main items Equiano's people sold to itinerant traders was salt they made from wood ashes.[54]

Even though the Portuguese had discovered a virtual island of salt off the coast of Senegal, in the fifteenth century,[55] they made

[51] Jones, *Trading States*, p. 89.

[52] James Penny testified that no market for imported tobacco existed at Bonny and New Calabar because of local supplies from the interior. See 'Report of the Committee of Council concerning the present State of the Trade to Africa and particularly the Trade in Slaves', *Parl. Papers* 1789, lxxxiv (646ᵃ), part I. Crowther noted the great popularity of American leaf tobacco in Onitsha in the late 1850s. See Crowther and Taylor, *Gospel on the Banks*, p. 436. Imported tobacco is often mentioned by oral sources as having been an early trade item.

[53] See Chapter I, note 23.

[54] Equiano, 'Early Travels', p. 75. Goldie, *Dictionary*, p. 357, tells of an Ekoi town called Emafi whose saline springs supported a salt trade. This may be the same place referred to by Talbot, *Peoples*, III, 920, who also describes (p. 919) the making of salt by the Ijo from the leaves and roots of the mangrove tree. A Niger explorer heard of a town called Ojogo some 130 miles north of the Niger-Benue Confluence where salt was dug from pits in the dry season; see Hutchinson, *Narrative*, p. 254. For the salt lake at Uburu, see (Nzekwu), 'Uburu', for the making of vegetable salt among the Nsukka Igbo see Afigbo, 'Trade and Trade Routes', p. 7.

[55] John W. Blake, *European Beginnings in West Africa, 1454–1578* (London: Longmans, 1937), p. 90.

no effort to market salt along the Bight of Biafra and local supplies there evidently remained adequate for local needs until the late eighteenth century. Then the situation reversed. Adams reported that the demand for salt at Cameroon and Old Calabar was 'extensive' and that one could expect the demand for it at Bonny to surpass the then current fifty tons per ship as the oil trade grew.[56] In 1819 Bold advised ships calling at Old Calabar, that so far as salt was concerned, 'you cannot bring too much'.[57] The reasons for the sudden increase in imports of European salt were related to increases in the over-all volume of trade and the population of the hinterland, but particularly to the low prices and vast quantities at which European merchants could supply it. Salt had long commanded high prices in the hinterland and even in 1854 a 20–30-lb. bag sold for £1 sterling just north of Idah, the price of a ton in Old Calabar a half-century earlier.[58] Bold noted that the near monopoly which the Liverpool merchants enjoyed in the palm-oil trade in the Bights of Benin and Biafra in his day was due to 'their facility for procuring fine salt, and at an infinitely cheaper rate than any other port'.[59]

The impact of this new salt trade on the traditional producers was swift and sure. A town on the western side of the mouth of the Cross River, called Tom Salt's Point, which was supporting itself by making salt in 1805, was prohibited from continuing that industry by the chiefs of Old Calabar later in the century lest their salt 'interfere in the market with the salt imported by European traders'.[60] Elsewhere along the coast the story was similar. Although the Landers saw salt still being made near Brass in 1830, 'salt making virtually ceased in the delta' in the course of the nineteenth century.[61] Salt continued to be sent northward from the coast in raffia bags or blue clay cups,[62] but it may have been largely imported salt in traditional packages.

---

[56] Adams, *Remarks*, p. 263.

[57] Bold, *African Guide*, p. 79.

[58] Hutchinson, *Narrative*, p. 254. See Tables 5–7.

[59] Bold, *African Guide*, p. iv. A visitor to Old Calabar in 1828 likewise noted, 'The principal cargo of the Liverpool vessels who trade for palm oil, is salt, of which the natives are very fond.' See *Holman's Voyage*, p. 17.

[60] Henry Nicholls to African Assn., 15 Feb. 1805, in Hallett, *Records*, p. 197. Goldie, *Dictionary*, pp. 355–6.

[61] Lander and Lander, *Niger Journal*, p. 268; Jones, *Trading States*, p. 89.

[62] Blue cups were observed being made north of Bonny by Waddell, *Twenty-Nine Years*, p. 411. The trade in salt in grass bags (called *trona*) was reported by several

Any evaluation of the impact of imported goods on this region must make due allowance for the great lacunae in evidence, particularly the paucity of eye-witness accounts in the hinterland. The greatly expanded trade in slaves and palm-oil during the first six decades of the nineteenth century produced greater changes in the hinterland economy than had the previous six decades of the slave-trade. While the imports of the eighteenth century had promoted rather than undermined traditional internal trade, the nineteenth century saw increasing dependence upon imported goods. The rapid inroads of foreign salt marked the earliest and most dramatic destruction of African production, but as the century wore on, the cheap and plentiful goods of the industrial revolution gained a larger and larger share of the hinterland market.

3. THE NEW HINTERLAND ECONOMY

The significance of this dependence on foreign goods is difficult to gauge from the limited historical sources. One might view these developments as evidence of the enormous competitive advantage of industrial capitalism, which had reduced the hinterland to the role of supplier of unfree labour and then raw materials while destroying its internal economy. There is evidence, however, that a more complex interpretation should be placed upon the declining self-sufficiency of the hinterland: that it was part of a process of labour specialization resulting from the economic growth taking place in the hinterland. First of all, the case of salt aside, there is no indication that the increased imports of cotton goods and hardware actually did lead to a decline in local production of these items. As was argued in Chapter VI, it appears instead that local weavers and smiths were able to hold their own during this period. The imports signalled not declining production but rising consumption due to the prosperity brought by the palm-oil trade.

This argument gains support from the fact that there was a similar expansion of trade (in items other than palm-oil) *within* the hinterland during the same period. This trade was in three key items: (1) large canoes for transporting the palm-oil to the

---

Niger explorers, even north of Idah: Allen and Thomson, *Narrative*, I, 198; Hutchinson, *Narrative*, p. 254; Crowther, *Journal*, p. 41.

coastal ports, (2) food to replace that lost by the concentration of labour in the production and transport of palm-oil, and (3) labour in the form of seasonal migrant labour and domestic slaves destined for the major trading communities, especially the coastal ports, and also for newly opened food producing areas. The economy of south-eastern Nigeria was becoming more specialized and more integrated as it solved the economic problems posed by the increased trade. Transport bottlenecks were broken by the development of canoe factories in places where the largest trees had not been cut previously. The labour required to man these canoes and meet other labour needs was supplied by the employment of free and unfree persons from elsewhere. The food, clothing, and tools of these trading communities were likewise drawn from more distant parts of the hinterland and from overseas. The specialization of labour in the production and transport of palm-oil thus had an impact outside the oil-palm belt as well as within it. After the overseas trade came to an end the growth of an internal trade in food, canoes, and domestic slaves enabled areas outside the oil-palm belt to continue to participate in the trading networks which had developed in the course of the overseas slave trade. Thus the growth of the palm-oil trade resulted in a strengthening of ties not only between the producers and the oil-consuming nations but also between the northern and southern parts of the hinterland.

The trade in canoes may be taken up first. As was described earlier in this chapter, the palm-oil travelled from the producers to small trading beaches in calabashes. From these beaches it was taken, still in calabashes or in specially made wooden barrels,[63] to major depots such as Ikpa, Ohambele, or Aboh, where the oil was readied for shipment to the coast. At this point the oil was generally transferred to one of the units of measure employed at the coast: the smaller 'crew' of 11 or 12 gallons and the 'puncheon' of 220 to 240 gallons. The standardization of these units was not achieved very rapidly and the tendency was for the units to become larger as the century wore on.[64]

The oil reached the largest inland depots in specially made canoes

[63] Interview with Chief Eshiet, Ukana.
[64] Sizes also varied from port to port: Bold's 1819 *African Guide*, pp. 80, 85, listed the standard crew at Old Calabar at 9·5 gallons, while just down the coast at the Cameroon Estuary it was 12 gallons.

of sizes appropriate to the creeks and rivers on which they had to travel. The expansion of the palm-oil trade created a demand for canoes beyond what had ever been needed for the slave and food trades, so that the manufacture of canoes, especially of the largest sort,[65] became a major industry in many places. When the Landers were rescued from Aboh in 1830 by King Boy Amin of Brass, they travelled in such a vessel: a fifty-foot giant drawing $4\frac{1}{2}$ feet of water, propelled by 40 paddlers, carrying passengers and a heavy load of goods, and with cannons fore and aft.[66] Such giants were not unusual and seventy-foot, 150-man monsters were not unknown. In time of war the king of Aboh was able to assemble from his chiefs a fleet of about 300 canoes, 'many armed with muskets and cannons in the bows'.[67] In the 1850s Brass was said to have no fewer than 100 large canoes, some capable of carrying six 220-gallon puncheons of oil at a time.[68] Although no estimates are available of the resources of the canoe houses of Bonny, in 1847 King Eyo Honesty of Creek Town, Old Calabar, was said by his son to possess 400 canoes and the next year he led a fleet of 60 large war-canoes on an expedition to Umon.[69]

Guiding the large canoes through the narrow delta creeks was no easy task. Even with the current it took four days for a canoe to reach Brass from Aboh and the return trip against the current took seven or eight days of hard paddling.[70] Yet these routes were plied assiduously by the coastal trading houses; one Niger explorer notes, 'The distance which they get over in these large canoes is astonishing: they think nothing of paddling for 24 hours without ceasing, except to have refreshment for a very little while.'[71] Likewise in the delta and on the Cross River the exertion of the 'pullah-boys' was legendary.

The canoe industry which grew up to fill these needs was important on its own and soon had extended to places distant from the coastal

[65] At the beginning of the sixteenth century Pereira (*Esmeraldo*, p. 146) stated that the canoes used for slaves and provisions on the Rio Real were the largest in all Guinea, each made of the trunk of a single tree and holding up to 80 men. For a general exposition see Robert Smith, 'The Canoe in West African History', *JAH*, XI (1970), 515–33.

[66] Lander and Lander, *Journal*, pp. 259–60.

[67] Allen and Thomson, *Narrative*, I, 236.

[68] Crowther and Taylor, *Gospel on the Banks*, p. 12.

[69] Waddell, *Twenty-Nine Years*, pp. 320, 372.

[70] Laird and Oldfield, *Narrative*, II, 321.

[71] Ibid., I, 175.

ports. Bonny is reported to have obtained its canoes from the Brass section of the delta and from Aboh,[72] but Old Calabar relied on much further-flung suppliers. Some were located far up tributaries of the Cameroon Estuary to the east,[73] but most came from the middle section of the Cross River. There the giant trees needed to make the one-piece vessels still stood in the forest, though the dimensions of this trade in the nineteenth century must have greatly depleted the supplies and forced the industry to move further upstream. These 'Atam' canoes, as they were known to the inhabitants of the lower river, were sold at Umon even after the oil trade had dried up, and at Itu and Ikot Offiong. Though these giants are no longer made, they are still remembered by the descendants of the nineteenth-century palm-oil traders. 'It is unfortunate that canoes of that size are not available now;' lamented an old Enyong chief, 'they were big enough to carry seven barrels of oil.'[74] On a voyage up the Cross River in 1884 Goldie examined one of the canoe factories near Okurike: '... we saw a number of canoes in the process of manufacture, this being a principal industry in the upper parts of the river. They are so far roughly prepared, and the purchaser finishes them to suit his taste or purpose. They are made of large hard-wood trees, capable of conveying the palm-oil puncheons, carried to market by the Calabar traders.[75] Since in normal service in the palm-oil trade a canoe would develop major cracks after about five years, and even with repairs could be made to last only another ten to fifteen years, there was a steady business in replacing canoes even after the trade itself levelled off.[76]

The second area of growing internal trade was in foodstuffs, a trade item of great antiquity in this region. The earliest discernible stage had been the trade between the delta fishermen and the farmers just inland from them. The growth of the overseas trade in the seventeenth and eighteenth centuries had led to a great expansion of this

[72] Evidence of John Arden Clegg, supercargo in Bonny from 1825, to the Select Committee on the British Possessions on the West Coast of Africa, *Parl. Papers* 1842, xi (551), p. 98. See also Alagoa, 'Trade and States', p. 324.

[73] Goldie, *Dictionary*, p. 357, says Old Calabar got canoes from 'Ekumbe', evidently the people of the town of Kumba on the Moungo River in West Cameroon.

[74] Interview with Chief Ibah, Enyong.

[75] Goldie, 'Notes of a Voyage', p. 276.

[76] Harris, 'Trade at Ikom', p. 129. She also learned of the existence of a canoe industry near Ikom, which must have begun operations soon after the inauguration of the overseas palm-oil trade and lasted until 15 or 20 years ago. The shells were 70–80 feet long, made from trees from the 'Boki' country north of Ikom.

trade, not just to feed the growing delta population in the coastal ports, but also for the slaves before and during their voyages to the Americas. During the nineteenth century the population of the delta ports continued to increase, while still producing very little of their own food. Moreover, although the need to provision slave cargoes ended with the overseas slave trade, a new demand for foodstuffs developed throughout the southern hinterland. The palm-oil trade greatly increased the number of people involved in the production and marketing of palm-oil. All this labour was withdrawn from the agricultural sector. In addition, some trading communities, such as Arochukwu and Ndoki, almost ceased to farm at all,[77] and others must have reduced their attention to agriculture. In most cases food could be purchased from neighbouring peoples less involved in commerce, but the increasing demands for food within the oil-palm belt strained the capacity of this region to supply the needs of the growing coastal towns. Thus a third stage of the food trade was reached drawing on supplies grown in the northern hinterland to meet the needs of the coast and southern hinterland.

Old Calabar had depended upon the Ibibio farmers west of the Cross River for much of its food supply and in the 1780s was receiving shipments of yams from the middle Cross River via the Umon Market.[78] These supply routes were secure enough in 1828-9 for Duke Ephraim to contract to supply the British settlement of 1,300 on the island of Fernando Po with beef, fruit, and grain.[79] Livestock was also an important part of the food trade down the river: an 1836 explorer reported that the Ibibio supplied trading towns on the Cross River with dwarf cattle, sheep, and goats and also noticed 50–60 head of 'fine cattle' grazing in the market-place at Ikot Offiong. These must have been raised further north, outside the sleeping-sickness zone, since only the tsetse-resistant dwarf cattle could have survived for long near Ikot Offiong.[80] The cattle must have been resting before shipment to Old Calabar, a fact confirmed by another

[77] Shankland, 'Intelligence Report, Aro', p. 2; Ennals, 'Intelligence Report, Ndoki', p. 32. Ennals writes, 'In the farming season men from the Nguru area of Owerri division, the Osus in Okigwi division and Ibibios were hired to cut palm nuts and to clear the bush and even to farm the land.'

[78] Duke, 'Diary', p. 39, mentions a 'Boostam' (i.e. Umon) canoe returning to Old Calabar with slaves and yams.

[79] Badgley, 'Report on the Old Calabar River', and Owen to Under Secretary of State, 6 Mar. 1829, C.O. 82/2.

[80] Oldfield, 'Account of an Ascent', pp. 196–7.

explorer in 1841 who noted that large numbers of livestock reached Calabar via the Umon market.[81]

By mid-century a serious and probably chronic shortage of yams had arisen in the Ibibio area. Yams, which had been selling to Old Calabar at five for a copper wire, jumped to five coppers each. In 1848 and again in 1850 prophets warned of dire consequences if there were not a return to traditional prices.[82] It is unclear whether these warnings were inspired by vested interests in Old Calabar or if they had any lasting effect, but about this time Old Calabar must have begun to tap the yam production further up the Cross River, especially in the area above Afikpo where the Igbo were moving into the underpopulated but fertile savanna lands. These North-East Igbo became famous for the size of their farms and of their yams. Along the Okpoku tributary of the Cross River these Igbo yam farmers set up markets which supplied 'enormous quantities' of yams to both the Efik of Old Calabar and to the Ibibio Proper.[83] It is not easy to document the movement of the North-East Igbo into this area or the beginning of their trade in yams down the river. Calculations made in 1930 from unusually deep genealogies put the founding ancestor of one clan three centuries earlier and Harris has taken Beecroft's sighting of conical roofs in 1842 as presumptive evidence that the North-East Igbo reached the Cross River by that time.[84] That the Aro also became involved in this trade is evident from the report of Aro traders resident at the Eke Mohan market on the Okpoku River early in this century.[85]

Bonny's yam supply had come from the Okrika area at the edge of the delta during the slave trade, but by the middle of the nineteenth century most of their yams were being funnelled through the Bende fair, perhaps also originating in the middle Cross River area.[86]

On the Niger River, too, the leading towns of Aboh and Idah became dependent on external supplies of foodstuffs and the production of surplus crops became a profitable trade for neighbouring

[81] Beecroft, 'On Benin', p. 190.

[82] Hugh Goldie's 'Journal' for 23 Oct. 1848 and 20 Nov. 1850 in *Missionary Record*, IV (Sept. 1849), 130, and VI (Sept. 1851), 131.

[83] Allen, 'Intelligence Report, Izi', pp. 170–1.

[84] Chapman, 'Intelligence Report, Ikwo', p. 7; Rosemary L. Harris, *The Political Organization of the Mbembe, Nigeria* (London: H.M. Stationery Office, 1965), p. 83.

[85] Livingstone, *Dr. Hitchcock*, p. 57. See also G. I. Jones, 'Ecology and Social Structure among the North Eastern Ibo', *Africa*, XXXI (1961), 117–34.

[86] Baikie, *Narrative*, p. 336.

peoples.[87] In their cases the food was drawn partly from their own fertile hinterlands, but the food trade from the middle to the lower Niger also grew sharply in this period. Crowther noted that the Basa people around the confluence were supplying large amounts of food crops to the important riverain market of Gbegbe, near Idah.[88]

The third trade ancillary to the palm-oil was in domestic slaves. Even after the end of the overseas trade, there remained a strong internal demand for slaves for both labour and prestige. There is no clear evidence of where these slaves were obtained, but it is likely that the oil-palm belt produced a smaller percentage than it had before the beginning of the palm-oil trade. The prosperity brought by this trade should have reduced the number of persons sold on account of economic hardship, though captives, criminals, and social misfits would have continued to be sold. As a result an increasing proportion of the domestic slaves must have been drawn from areas of the hinterland not involved in the oil trade. In mid-century, for example, King Eyo Honesty II explained that his very numerous domestic slaves 'came from different countries . . . in which they had no other trade.'[89]

Domestic slavery was not a new institution in south-eastern Nigeria, if one is to judge by the mention of slaves in the foundation accounts of many hinterland communities. At first domestic slaves were used primarily as ways of displaying wealth and increasing the numbers of a family unit. During the nineteenth century the numbers of these slaves increased sharply and their functions became more economically specialized, especially in the northern hinterland and among the trading communities of the coast and the main arteries of transport. In the major oil-producing areas there does not appear to have been any unusual influx of slaves to assist in the harvesting and preparation of the oil, except in areas which were also heavily involved in the transport of the oil. The already dense population of the oil-palm belt appears to have handled the increased labour demands by increased effort and by devoting less time to food production. This was economically the simplest solution since drastic increases in the population would have complicated the food shortages still further. What slaves were purchased from traders were

[87] Crowther and Taylor, *Gospel on the Banks*, p. 438.

[88] Ibid. For the location and movement of the Basa see Daryll Forde, Paula Brown, and Robert G. Armstrong, *Peoples of the Niger–Benue Confluence* (London: International African Institute, 1955), pp. 19–20 and map.

[89] Waddell, *Twenty-Nine Years*, p. 429.

incorporated into the existing family units and did not long constitute a distinct labour group or social class.[90]

At the coast and among the leading trading communities of the hinterland there was a dramatic increase in domestic slavery in this period, in part in response to the demands for manpower of the palm-oil trade. Old Calabar, Bonny, and New Calabar came to be populated primarily by persons of unfree status and the trading communities of Aboh, Asaba, Onitsha, Ossomari, Ndoki, and the many Aro settlements had large numbers of slaves in their service.[91] The magnitude of change in the coastal ports may be gauged by the fact that contemporary estimates of their populations showed a growth rate of 20 per cent a decade.[92] In the trading communities domestic slaves were employed in a variety of jobs connected with commerce: paddling canoes, marketing, portage of palm-oil, raising food crops to feed those employed in the trade. The situation

[90] Goldie, *Dictionary*, p. 358, wrote of the Ibibio: 'Singular to say, there is no slavery existing amongst them, any stranger bought as a slave being adopted into the family purchasing him; ...' That this was true for the children of bought slaves was confirmed by oral testimony throughout the area.

[91] Domestic slavery in the coastal communities is discussed in Dike, *Trade and Politics*, pp. 34–7, and in Jones, *Trading States*, chapter iv and x. A large portion of the population of Ndoki trading communities near the lower Imo River were slaves; in Akwete freeborn were a minority. See Ennals, 'Intelligence Report, Ndoki', pp. 2–3, 14.

On the Niger the leading trading community of Aboh had a large number of domestic slaves, who were said by Allen and Thomson to be well treated, *Narrative*, I, 251–2. Laird met a woman near Aboh who owned over 200 slaves, whom she employed in raising yams, making palm-oil, and trading on the river; see Laird and Oldfield, *Narrative*, I, 99–100. At Ossomari leading traders were said to have owned 100 slaves each; see Kaine, *Ossomari*, p. 41. Slaves were also common at Onitsha, where the men farmed and the women traded; see Talbot, *Peoples*, III, 701.

At Afikpo on the Cross River, where there were many Aro settlers, 'Household slaves, *ohu*, and the matrilineal cult slaves, *osu*, existed in substantial numbers', according to Ottenberg, *Leadership and Authority*, p. 26.

[92] The population of the main towns of Old Calabar (Duke Town, Creek Town, and Henshaw Town) had been estimated at 3,800 in 1805 by Nicholls in Hallett, *Records*, p. 206. Forty years later Waddell put their total at 9,500–10,600; see Waddell, 'Journal', I, 23–5. In another forty years the population was pegged at 15,000; see H. H. Johnston, 'Report on the British Protectorate of the Oil Rivers (Niger Delta)', Johnston to Salisbury, 1 Dec. 1888, F.O. 84/1882. The same source put the population of Aboh in the 1880s at 8,000, while a half-century earlier it had been said to have had only 4,800–6,000 inhabitants. See Laird and Oldfield, *Narrative*, I, 102. When Capt. Crow visited Bonny in the late eighteenth century he had calculated its population at 3,000, but in 1864 Richard Burton said their were 5,000 permanent inhabitants and another 4,000 'floating', i.e. continuously on the move between the port and the up-country markets. See Crow, *Memoirs*, p. 197 and Burton to Russell, 15 Apr. 1865, *Parl. Papers* 1865, lvi (3503–1), p. 43.

described by Waddell at Old Calabar was generally true of other trading communities:

Most of the slaves are employed in farming and trading. The former cultivate a portion of land, allotted by their masters for their own use, and generally supply the town markets with the produce. Their labour is much less continuous and severe than that of West Indian slaves. If called into towns to work, they receive a small allowance. Those employed in canoes are fed, and are in crews of six to ten to each canoe, under a captain or supercargo. He has a commission on his trade and may trade on his own account a little, but not in palm oil, or so as to neglect his master's interests. The canoe people traffic in provisions, buying with English goods up country, and selling to the townspeople, ships, and mission houses.[93]

While the slaves at the coast were not incorporated into existing family structures, both they and the free population were part of the trading houses which had much of the same effect in minimizing the social stigma borne by an economically prosperous slave. Though many abuses of the weak by the strong could and did take place, slavery itself was no bar to success in coastal society. As the British Consul reported later in the century: 'It is a curious fact and an evidence of the mild character of the slavery in the Niger Delta, that nearly all the leading men in the Oil Rivers at the present time are ex-slaves,—such as Yellow Duke of Old Calabar, Ja-Ja of Opobo, Waribu and Oko Jumbo of Bonny, and William Kia of Brass.'[94]

The case in the northern part of the hinterland provided a vivid contrast: there the large numbers of slaves—some living in separate slave villages—held a low status from which there was no means of escape. Among the Northern Igbo generally domestic slaves of this type seem to have become common in the nineteenth century. The best known example, the system of separate villages of slaves among the Nike Igbo traders, was not typical of the area. Horton, who has studied this system, is of the opinion that it came into existence, at least indirectly, as a result of the trade in food.[95] A larger and clearer case of the use of domestic slave labour in the food trade is among the North-Eastern Igbo yam farmers. As was shown above, the major theme of their history in the nineteenth century was the

[93] Waddell, *Twenty-Nine Years*, pp. 319–20.

[94] Johnston, 'Report', 1888. This statement is repeated in 'Report by Major Macdonald of his Visit as Her Majesty's Commissioner to the Niger and Oil Rivers', 13 Jan. 1890, F.O. 403/131 (5913).

[95] Horton, 'Ohu System', pp. 311–36.

conquest of vast tracts of land to be used in the growing of yams for sale to the south. These farmers evidently used the wealth accruing to them from the sale of yams to purchase slaves from Aro and other traders on the middle Cross River.[96] The slaves had dwellings within the compounds of the masters, but were unable to raise the social status of themselves or of their descendants. The slaves were used to conquer[97] and occupy the lands on the frontier. Slaves were provided with personal farm plots, but their labour was also used on their owners' farms.

The growth of the palm-oil trade demonstrates clearly the flexibility and continuity of trading patterns in south-eastern Nigeria. The palm-oil trade differed from the slave trade in being based upon the efforts of small producers and employing new routes of transport, yet it did not mark so sharp a break with the past as is sometimes claimed. The new trade operated through the traditional local markets and made use of the routes and techniques which had come into being much earlier for the provisioning trade to the coast. Even some of the old slave routes and markets eventually converted to palm-oil after the overseas trade came to an end. The greatest change inaugurated by the palm-oil trade was the creation of a new class of small consumers at the same time as the Industrial Revolution was flooding African markets with inexpensive manufactures. However, only a portion of the expansion went into external trade; the growth of internal trade, especially in canoes, food, and domestic slaves, was of equal or greater importance since it had a multiplier effect on the economic growth of the hinterland.

[96] For this and many of the details that follow see Allen, 'Intelligence Report, Izi', Appendix I; Chapman, 'Intelligence Report, Ikwo', pp. 63–5; G. B. G. Chapman, 'Intelligence Report on the Ezza Clan, Abakaliki Division, Ogoja Province', 1932, pp. 66–7, NAI, CSO 26/3/28179; and Jones, 'Ecology and Social Structure', *passim*.

[97] The only amelioration of status a slave could obtain among the North-Eastern Igbo was by taking a human head in battle and presenting it to his master. For this he was granted exemption from being killed or sold away. See Allen, 'Intelligence Report, Izi', pp. 23–4.

Conclusion

THE region adjoining the Bight of Biafra was one of the chief sources of slaves during the peak decades of the Atlantic slave trade and it was even more prominent in the palm-oil trade of the nineteenth century. Because of the commercial importance of this region, the political and economic relations between the African coastal states and the Europeans who traded there have been the subject of several scholarly works. This study has sought to build upon these earlier works by considering the commercial importance of this region in a larger context: extending the time span to include the period before the arrival of the first Europeans, expanding the geographical focus to include the hinterland as well as the coast, and examining the development of internal commerce along with the growth of overseas trade. These new approaches have led to a revised understanding of the main divisions and directions of hinterland commerce.

Generally speaking the economic history of this region may be divided into three periods, which correspond to the three stages of development of long-distance West African trade suggested by Claude Meillassoux.[1] The earliest period which can be defined, the time of the Igbo-Ukwu finds, may correspond to Meillassoux's stage of 'immediate exchange', although there is too little information to be sure. At this stage the primary motive of long-distance trade would have been to obtain particular objects without reference to the profitability of the exchange. Located at the tail end of intercontinental trade routes extending to Europe and Asia, south-eastern Nigeria sought to acquire, in whatever way possible, rare metals, beads, and other items for use in ceremonial regalia. Whatever profits were made by hinterland persons engaged in this trade were probably largely incidental to the purposes of these exchanges, though the profit motive may have been stronger in the local trade in cloth and ironware.

By the fifteenth century parts of the region had attained a more advanced stage of economic activity. The acquisition of goods for 'profit motive', i.e. for their exchange value rather than their specific

---

[1] *Development of Indigenous Trade*, pp. 68–9. Meillassoux does not suggest that these stages correspond to the historical periods that are proposed here.

utility, had become a feature of long-distance trade along the lower Niger River and along the coast as far west as the region of modern Ghana. By this era some of the internal trade of this region may also be classified at the 'market profit' stage on the basis of the existence of currencies in iron and (possibly) copper and the likely existence of at least semi-professional trading communities. Mining, salt-making, some farming, and various craft industries were also tied into this trade which made use of the developing market system. However, this region was still a relative backwater in Africa, and the volume and value of its exchanges were low.

The arrival of the Portuguese and other Europeans produced no abrupt changes in the economy of the region, but did provide opportunities for expanding the volume of trade and acquiring new or cheaper goods. Rather than inaugurating a new phase in this region's economy the Portuguese and their goods were absorbed into the pre-existing African economy. It is unlikely that either the form or the content of trade with the early Portuguese along this coast represented a departure from established trading patterns. This new overseas outlet grew only slowly in the sixteenth and seventeenth centuries. The potential for growth was delayed as European interests focused on trade with Asia and the Americas. The size of the trade was also limited by the type and quantity of goods which Africans could supply. South-eastern Nigeria possessed no gold and the trade in ivory was limited by the size of the elephant population. Nevertheless, by the seventeenth century the expanding overseas trade had encouraged the establishment or movement of trading communities both at the coast and in the hinterland and the consolidation of the commercial and social ties between them. However, one must avoid assigning too great a role in these developments to the stimulus of European trade in this period since, as was pointed out in Chapter II, other internal factors also influenced the movements and relations of hinterland peoples.

The growth of the trade in slaves in the eighteenth century was a temporary and imperfect solution to the problem of finding an item of trade which was strongly desired by Europeans and which could be supplied in regular quantities by Africans. While this trade should still be included within the 'market profit' stage of economic activity, the slave trade did not extend the profit motive much more widely in this region and produced important changes in the commercial infrastructure. It has been stressed that these changes were not due to the fact that the trade was in slaves, which as an item of trade had no direct developmental impact, but to the great expansion in the over-all volume of trade both internal and overseas of which slaves were the central item but not the economically most important one. This era saw major changes in the political and economic structures of the coastal trading communities and the expansion of hinterland trading communities, especially of the Aro. Local markets were drawn into a more general grid of large feeder markets and fairs, which were connected to each other and to the coastal entrepôts by regular trade routes. General-purpose currencies, some using tokens supplied from overseas, became more common, and complex, profit-motivated negotiations accompanied each transfer of goods.

The impact of the slave trade on Africa has been the subject of much heated debate, frequently with far too little attention to the details of its operation within Africa. For this reason this study has sought to uncover those aspects of the slave trade which are capable of being quantified or otherwise measured. In general, although the export was human beings, the slave trade in south-eastern Nigeria was conducted in much the same way as commerce in any other item of high value. Only at the point of initial enslavement were non-commercial procedures at work and this was true of only a portion of the cases of enslavement. Some slaves were obtained by raids and many more through kidnapping or judicial processes, all of which lay outside commercial transactions. Many others, however, were sold by relatives as a result of debt or other economic conditions. Once in the hands of slave traders the slaves were sold and resold by relays of slavers until they reached the plantations of the Americas. Despite the great number of slaves shipped from this coast, the fact that the trade was distributed over many decades and drew evenly on all parts of the region meant that no area of any size suffered depopulation. On the contrary, south-eastern Nigeria became one of the most densely settled regions in Africa.

In return for the slaves exported, Europeans sold a wide variety of articles. Some few were the 'worthless trifles' so often cited, but many were greatly desired consumer goods which were traded widely in the hinterland. Iron bars actually stimulated hinterland industry by freeing smiths from dependence on inefficient local iron-smelting, thus greatly increasing the availability of locally made tools and weapons.

In some portions of the hinterland in the eighteenth century and more generally in the first half of the nineteenth century the growth of trade in agricultural products may be considered to have inaugurated a new stage in economic development in which 'manufacturing profit' became a feature of commerce. According to Meillassoux's definition, in this stage of development 'goods acquired are used in the production of goods for export, the latter being used in the acquisition of the former'. This stage is associated with industrial production, but it also includes 'the importing of food to feed producers of goods for export'. During the eighteenth century the professional trading communities of the coast and hinterland came to rely for food upon the production of neighbouring farmers. In the nineteenth century, while the coastal peoples continued their role as middlemen in the overseas trade, the farmers of the southern hinterland dramatically increased the labour they devoted to producing palm-oil. Their growing specialization in production for export led to shortages of food which were met by increased production in the northern portion of the region partially through the use of slave labour. At the same time the transport requirements of the oil trade stimulated canoe production, also primarily in the northern hinterland. In large part the food imports and canoes were paid for with goods received from abroad in exchange for the palm-oil.

This agricultural trade relying on the efforts of thousands of hinterland households had a different economic base from that of the slave trade. It was labour-intensive, encouraged labour specialization, and resulted in a closer integration of the hinterland economy through a greater volume of internal trade. Moreover, these changes in labour utilization also altered consumption patterns. 'As a general proposition', Hopkins has pointed out, 'the more equal the distribution of incomes, the smaller the demand for luxury items and the greater the demand for cheap mass-produced goods.'[2] The palm-oil which lubricated British machinery also created customers for the cheap salt, cottons, and hardware produced by mechanized industry.

It is important to understand the relation between the palm-oil trade and the trade in slaves. Contrary to opinions common since the early nineteenth century, the rise of the palm-oil trade, at least in south-eastern Nigeria, was not dependent upon the decline of the overseas slave trade. In fact the trade in both items expanded during

[2] Hopkins, *Economic History*, p. 127.

the first three decades of the nineteenth century. Instead, the rapidity of the rise in palm-oil exports from this coast, while associated with many changes in productive and distributive methods, was possible only because of the economic changes which had occurred in the previous century as a consequence of the slave trade. The eighteenth century had enlarged professional trading communities, expanded markets, trade routes, and currencies, and added monthly fairs— all of which were readily employed in the palm-oil trade. More directly the growth of the provisioning trade as an adjunct of the trade in slaves prepared the way for an agricultural trade which was free of the slave trade. The region had found a way to obtain foreign goods through employing at home the labour which it once was forced to export to the Americas.

This economic transformation raises the question of whether the natural growth of the palm-oil trade might not have rendered the export of slave labour uneconomic and thus brought that nefarious trade to an end without the need for European patrols, blockades, and seizures, with their imperialist consequences. That answer cannot be known for certain, but the circumstances of the slave trade suggest that competition from the palm-oil trade would not have done so, at least not with any dispatch. For one thing the population of south-eastern Nigeria appears to have been large enough to mean that no labour shortage was created by the volume of the slave trade in the nineteenth century. Moreover, so long as the overseas demand for slave labour continued, it was more profitable for African traders to sell slaves than to employ them. Only after the export of slaves had been stopped by force were slaves employed in large numbers in agricultural production.

This suggests that in the first half of the nineteenth century, as earlier, the economic development of the region was linked to changes in the world economy. European demand for palm-oil and opposition to the overseas slave trade set the limits of trade just as the arrival of the first European ships in the fifteenth century had opened the way for economic growth in this region. Yet one must guard against reducing the African role to conditioned responses to European initiatives. This study has sought to demonstrate how the previous level of development and the scale of the efforts of the inhabitants of this region enabled it to capture a share of the available overseas market disproportionate to its size.

It is true that the necessary concomitant to economic growth was increased dependence upon the vicissitudes and inequalities of a Europe-centred world economy. The ultimate value or harm in this relationship must be left for other scholars to judge, influenced as they must be by its twentieth-century consequences. This study ends in the 1860s with the peoples of this region politically independent and palm-oil prices at record highs. It has seemed wise to end here to avoid being unduly influenced in tracing pre-colonial economic development by the economic, political, and social changes of the decades that followed.

Another important feature of this region has been the absence of large-scale political units or even of major efforts to create such units, despite a high degree of economic activity. Though the economy altered significantly, the political systems remained remarkably constant in most of the inland parts of the region, aside from efforts at curbing the potentially disruptive power of trading wealth. Robin Horton has suggested that segmentary lineage systems of the 'pure type', which are characteristic of 'a good deal' of the central portion of south-eastern Nigeria, are strongly resistant to the development of large-scale states. He gives three reasons for this:

First, the individual in such systems thinks of the locus of his political allegiance as varying with context, whereas the state requires from him an allegiance which endures through all possible contexts. Again, the stress on equivalence and opposition as the dominant mode of relationship between coordinate segments militates against any one segment emerging as a 'royal lineage' charged with providing rulers recognized as such by all the others. Finally, the stress on equivalence and opposition of segments and their representatives acts as a block against the role specialization and division of labour necessary in the development of a consequential state organization. Between the 'pure type' segmentary lineage system and the state, then, there seems a great gulf fixed.[3]

So strong does the lineage idiom become, Horton argues, that it persists despite considerable variances between it and the changing reality in which it operates.[4]

One may question how accurately Horton's mode fits the historical dynamics of this particular region, especially those portions not of the 'pure type', but one risks being drawn away from the historical realities of the region and into counter-historical speculations over why states did not emerge here. Since Horton agrees that such

[3] Horton, 'Stateless Societies', pp. 111–12, 117.
[4] Ibid., 83–9.

lineage organization would not persist under all historical conditions, his argument may be reduced to the statement that the political organization of south-eastern Nigeria was able to cope with the conditions of the pre-colonial period without major structural change. The history of this region thus demonstrates the fallacy in the assumption that some form of large-scale state structure (empire, tribal-state, nation-state) must be associated with vigorous economic activity. Such was not the case in medieval Europe, where the most active commercial centres were the city-states of northern Italy, southern Germany, and the Netherlands. It is the rise of the modern nation-state and the international capitalist economy in early modern Europe that requires explanation, not their absence in other times and places.[5]

In south-eastern Nigeria the long process of commercial development which this study has examined occurred with little regard for large state structures or for national or ethnographic frontiers, belying the common belief that African history must be written in terms of kings and tribes. It was economics not ethnicity, trade not rulers which governed the main lines of this region's pre-colonial past.

[5] Immanuel Wallerstein, *The Modern World-System: Capitalist Agriculture and the Origins of the European World-Economy in the Sixteenth Century* (New York and London: Academic Press, 1974).

Appendix A

Origins of Slaves Shipped from Ports in the Bight of Biafra, 1821–2

Ship	Port	Year	Number Emancipated				
			Igbo	Ibibio	Hausa	Other	Total
ʌnna Maria	By	1821	308	57	8	28	401
)ona Eugenia	By	1821	41	37	—	—	78
ʹonstantia	OC	1821	92	59		3	154
ʹonceição	OC	1821	9	45	—	—	54
ʟa Caridad	By	1821	116	16	—	4	136
ʟa Nueva Virgen	By	1821	65	31	—	9	105
)efensora da Patria	OC	1822	60	16	1	3	80
Subtotal	By		530	141	8	41	720
Per Cent	By		74	20	1	6	100
Subtotal	OC		161	120	1	6	288
Per Cent	OC		56	42	*	2	100
Grand Total			691	261	9	47	1,008
Per Cent			68	26	*	5	100

ʙy = Bonny, OC = Old Calabar, * = less than 1 per cent.
ʂource: F.O. 84/9 Sierra Leone (General): Woods to Bandinel, 5 July 1821, and F.O. 84/15
ʂierra Leone (General): Woods to Bandinel, 5 Jan. 1822 [1823].

Appendix B

'The Following Countries Are Called Ibo in Sierra Leone . . .' According to Koelle, *Polyglotta*, p. 8

Koelle's Spelling[1]	Modern Spelling	State of Nigeria	Forde & Jones, *Ibo & Ibibio*[2]
Mbɔfia or Mbɔhia[3]Ohafia		Imo	IV.B.2
Elugu[4]	Elugu	Anambra	I.A.4–9, I.B.
Uŋgua	Ngwa	Imo	II.C.9
Ɔzozu	Ozuzu	Rivers	II.B.8
Okua or Ndɔki	Ukwa or Ndoki	Imo	II.C.11
Ishelu[5]	Ishielu	Anambra	I.B.31
Ohuasora[6]	Awhawzara	Imo	I.B.18, 20, 21, 37–40, V. 6–13
Abadsha[7]	Agbaja	Anambra	I.B.15
Bɔm[8]	Kalabari	Rivers	
Mudiɔka[9]	Umudi Awka	Anambra	I.A. 10–27
Isoama[10]	Isuama	Imo	II.A.1–10
Oru	Oru	Imo	II.A.11
Mbɔli[11]	Mboli or Eleme	Rivers	II.B.16
Upani or Obani[12]	Bonny	Rivers	
Amɔni[13]	Umon?	Cross River	

[1] Koelle's spelling has been modified here and his indications of stress and nasalization have been omitted.

[2] Classification of Igbo-speaking peoples only: I = Northern, II = Southern, III = Western, IV = Eastern, V = North-Eastern, etc.

[3] Koelle places Mbɔfia west of *Ikun*, east of *Benda*, north of *Otutu*, and south of *Ebiriba*. Ohafia is west of Ikun (a market town in Ibibio Ukwa), east of Bende, north of Ututu, and south of Abiriba.

[4] Niger explorers in the mid-nineteenth century reported that Elugu was a name for the Igbo people east and north of Onitsha. See Baikie, *Narrative*, p. 443, for a list of Elugu towns.

[5] Koelle puts *Ishelu* east of *Igala* and his informant was sold to the *Igala*. Ishielu was on a slave route to Idah, the capital of the Igala kingdom. He also gives the spellings *Ishiele* and *Ishiel*.

[6] Awhawzara was considered an Igbo sub-tribe by Talbot, *Peoples*, IV, 41.

[7] Koelle's informants placed *Abadsha* east of *Ebenebe* (a town between Enugu and Onitsha), three days south-west of *Igala*, one day from *Aki* (very likely Achi, north-west of Awgu). The informant was born in *Naki* (probably Nachi in southern Agbaja).

[8] New Calabar was called *Bom* by the Ozuzu, according to Baikie, *Narrative*, p. 309. Hugh Goldie (*Dictionary*, p. 358) identified *Ibumanyi* as 'an Ibo tribe in the delta of the Niger, or between [Old] Calabar and the Niger'. Although the Kalabari were Ijo in origin, they had purchased large numbers of domestic slaves from the Igbo hinterland. Captain Crow (*Memoirs*, p. 198) reported that when he visited the delta in 1790, the 'king of New Calabar [Amakiri II] and Pepple, King of Bonny, were both of Eboe [Igbo] descent, of which also are the mass of the natives.'

[9] 'People who came from this area [Nri-Awka to Nnewi] were in the past collectively known as *Umudi Awka*,' according to Forde and Jones, *Ibo and Ibibio*, p. 32.

[10] Koelle's informant placed *Isoama* west of *Oru* and *Ŋkalo*, which are Oru and Nkalu (II.A.11 and I.A.26). Nkalu is more north than west of Isuama. Baikie, *Narrative*, p. 443, gives a list of Isuama towns.

[11] The proper name for this group is Eleme, Mbolli being a name given them by Igbo strangers, according to Mayne, 'Intelligence Report, Mbolli', p. 2. Forde and Jones call it Obia.

[12] Elsewhere Koelle makes it clear that Bonny was only near, not in, Igbo country. He says that what the English called Bonny was also called *Obane*, *Bane* and *Bone*.

[13] Koelle's informant said that the river which flowed near Ohafia 'comes from the Amɔni country, where a different language is spoken'. Umon is down-river from Ohafia and is not Igbo-speaking, although many residents do speak Igbo as a second language.

Appendix C

Known Ships and Slaves from the Bight of Biafra, 1659–1702

Ship	Owner	Port	Year	Total	Men	Boys	Women	Girls
St. Jan	WIC[a]	By[b]	1659	195	81	6	105	3
Arthur	RAC	NC	1678	348	187	10	141	10
Dragon	?	OC	1698	212	102	43	53	14
Bridgewalter	RAC	NC	1702	221	101	20	88	12
Canterbury	RAC	OC	1702	94	29	18	37	10
Total				1,070	500	97	424	49

[a]WIC = Dutch West India Company, RAC = English Royal African Company.
[b]By = Bonny, NC = New Calabar, OC = Old Calabar.
Source: Donnan, *Documents*, I, 141–4, 226–34, 419–20; II, 34–5, 37.

Slaves from the Bight of Biafra Captured by the British Navy and Liberated in Sierra Leone, 1821–39

Ship	Registry	Port	Captured		Emancipated and Registered				
			Year	Total	Total	Men	Boys	Women	Girls
Anna Maria	S[a]	By[b]	1821	491	401	191	73	81	56
Dona Eugenia	P	By	1821	83	78	32	5	27	14
Constantia	P	OC	1821	244	154	51	33	33	37
Conceição	P	OC	1821	56	54	22	11	5	16
La Caridad	S	By	1821	149	136	60	25	15	36
La Nueva Virgen	S	By	1821	130	105	55	11	14	25
Esperança Felis	P	OC[c]	1822	187	85	36	8	28	13
Vecua	S	By	1822	325	217	114	42	38	23
Ycanam	S	By	1822	380	12	6	2	1	3
Defensora da Patria	P	OC	1822	100	80	20	20	25	15
San José Xalaça	P	OC	1822	20	17	13	0	4	0
Josefa	S	By	1822	216	183	158	25	0	0
Commerciante	P	Cm	1822	179	167	68	17	59	23
Intrepida	S	By	1825	290	235	106	25	39	65

[a] S = Spanish, P = Portuguese, D = Dutch, B = Brazilian.

[b] By = Bonny, OC = Old Calabar, Cm = Cameroon estuary, Bs = Brass (Nun River), NC = New Calabar, G = Gabon.

[c] Although this vessel was captured at Lagos, the overwhelming majority of those emancipated were identified as Igbo, Ibibio, and coastal Cameroonians, suggesting that the vessel had loaded its slaves in the Bight of Biafra, probably at Old Calabar.

Appendix D—continued

Ship	Registry	Port	Captured		Emancipated and Registered				
			Year	Total	Total	Men	Boys	Women	Girls
Ana	S	CM–OC	1825	202[d]	130	50	40	22	18
Charles	D	OC	1825	265	243	128	37	23	55
La Fortunée	D	By	1826	245	120	52	17	28	23
Invincival	B	Cm	1826	440	250	83	56	57	54
Lynx	D	Bs	1827	265	251	110	29	45	67
Fama	S	OC	1827	100	95	47	24	7	17
Silverinha	B	OC	1827	266	209	52	45	40	72
Emelia	S	By	1827	282	175	127	46	2	72
Creola	B	OC	1827	308	288	94	47	70	0
La Fanny	D	OC	1828	279	252	146	30	41	77
Voadora	B	Cm	1828	64[e]	61	2	21	0	38
Josephina	B	Cm	1828	79	74	26	22	9	17
Clementina	B	Cm	1828	271	156	44	44	41	27
Henriette	D	OC	1828	367[f]	292	128	36	89	39
Minerva da Conceição	B	G	1828	105	82	16	21	29	16
Arcenia	B	Cm	1828	448	269	93	75	46	55
Campeadora	S	By	1828	229[g]	212	71	78	27	36
El Juan	S	By	1828	407	378	137	91	78	72
La Coquette	D	OC	1828	220	185	74	26	49	36
Jules	D	OC	1829	220	207	111	23	24	49
La Jeune Eugénie	D	OC	1829	50	46	14	8	16	8
Mensageira	B	By	1829	226[h]	117	10	49	6	52
Hirondelle	D	OC	1829	78[i]	55	49	0	5	1
Panchita	S	OC	1829	291	259	112	39	73	35

Ship			Year						
Ceres	B	Cm	1829	279	128	30	41	10	47
Emilia	B	By	1829	157	148	42	30	26	50
Cristina	S	Bs	1829	348	216	80	32	61	43
Octavio	S	By	1829	366	335	158	61	61	55
Altimara	S	Bs	1830	249	185	68	30	42	45
Santiago	S	By	1830	165	153	77	16	27	33
Marinerito	S	OC	1831	496	376	220	78	49	29
Regulo	S	By	1831	207	164	127	28	6	3
Frasquita	S	By	1832	290	228	131	62	19	16
Prueva	S	By	1832	308	274	215	43	9	7
Carolina	S	Bs	1832	426	369	190	87	49	43
Desengano	S	By	1833	220	209	128	66	12	3
Veloz Mariana	S	NC	1833	290	265	151	58	28	28
Indio	S	By	1833	117	108	52	24	9	23
Josefa	S	By	1833	280	191	100	38	23	30
Caridad	S	By	1833	120	107	26	32	5	44
Virtude	S	OC	1833	350	314	135	78	49	52
El Primo	S	By	1833	342	335	139	82	53	61
Vengador	S	By	1834	405	376	192	59	50	75
La Pantica	S	OC	1834	317	269	132	71	30	36
Indagadora	S	NC	1834	375	367	221	45	57	44
Clemente	S	By	1834	415	401	236	97	22	46

[d] Captured with 103 slaves from Bimbia (Cameroon Estuary) and four from Old Calabar, to which the captors added 50 from the Spanish slaver *Teresa*, taken at Old Calabar, and 45 more from the Spanish slaver *Isabella*, also taken at Old Calabar. The *Teresa* was lost in a tornado en route to Sierra Leone with only six of the remaining 198 slaves aboard being rescued. The *Isabella* also disappeared en route to Sierra Leone, either as the result of a storm or of pirates, along with 228 slaves, the crew, and the British prize crew.

[e] Not including 170 captives landed on Fernando Po.
[f] Not including 59 captives landed on Fernando Po.
[g] Not including 152 captives landed on Fernando Po.
[h] Not including 127 captives landed on Fernando Po.
[i] Not including 34 captives landed on Fernando Po.

Appendix D—continued

Ship	Registry	Captured			Emancipated and Registered				
		Port	Year	Total	Total	Men	Boys	Women	Girls
Sutil	S	OC	1834	307	210	47	86	15	62
Formidable	S	OC	1834	728	378	130	107	60	81
Minerva	S	OC	1835	650	444	141	184	41	78
Iberia	S	By	1835	313	305	143	43	44	75
El Manuel	S	By	1835	387	375	212	52	45	66
Bienvenida	S	G	1835	430	362	132	118	39	73
Numero Dos	S	By	1835	154	141	67	13	24	37
Volador	S	By	1835	487	418	207	53	84	74
Semiramis	S	By	1835	477	421	221	100	40	60
Argos	S	By	1835	429	359	189	60	53	57
Conde de los Andes	S	Bs	1835	282	267	99	70	53	45
Norma	S	By	1835	234	218	60	51	45	62
Isabella Segunda	S	By	1835	374	342	142	58	64	78
Ligeira	S	Bs	1835	198	192	48	57	34	53
Segunda Iberia	S	Bs	1835	260	233	69	70	44	50
Vandolero	S	NC	1836	377	342	142	58	64	78
Seis Hermanos	S	NC	1836	187	169	68	13	57	31
Felicia	S	By	1836	401	352	179	53	65	55
Vigilante	P	By	1836	270	231[/]	80	45	43	63
Mindello	P	Cm[k]	1836	268	254	45	114	22	73
Joven Carolina	P	OC	1836	421	377	145	96	46	90
Atalaya	S	By	1836	118	87	41	4	12	30
Felix	P	By	1836	557	463	239	50	83	91
Esperança	P	By	1836	471	404	193	43	77	91

Esperança	P	By	1836	438	386	191	59	65	71
Victoria	P	NC	1836	380	310	158	59	33	60
Olimpia	P	Cm	1836	282	238	45	94	16	83
Serea	P	OC	1836	22	21	6	5	5	5
Gata	P	By	1836	111	99	27	28	13	31
Temerario	P	By	1837	349	229	106	24	40	59
Esperança	P	By	1837	108	89	85	4	0	0
Paquete de C. Verde	P	By	1837	576	434	190	59	77	108
Dolores	S	OC	1837	314	282	84	86	22	90
Cobra de Africa	P	Cm	1837	162	95	19	22	27	27
Primoroza	P	By	1837	182	136	85	18	8	25
Vibora de C. Verde	P	Cm	1837	269	217	102	50	33	32
Felicidade	P	By	1837	335	274	220	41	4	9
Ligeira	P	Bs	1837	313	279	113	79	53	34
Felicidades	P	OC	1838	559	404	176	96	57	75
Dous Irmãos	P	By	1838	306	234	136	31	30	37
Prova	P	OC	1838	225	193	87	36	28	42
Paquete Felis	P	By	1838	195	187	102	38	32	15
Prova	P	Bs	1838	328	293	149	73	25	46
Magdalena	P	Bs	1838	320	293	167	38	32	56
Ontario	P	Bs	1838	219	199	123	41	9	26
Passos	S	OC	1839	87	81	33	17	17	14
Pomba da Africa	P	OC	1839	157	115	36	19	24	36
Sedo ou Tarde	P	OC	1839	23	21	9	2	7	3
Totals				30,380	24,502	11,171	5,024	3,713	4,594

_J_ Landed at Fort Nassau on the Gold Coast.

_k_ Seized with 140 slaves from Bimbia (Cameroon estuary), 100 from Cape Lopez, 25 from Gabon, and 3 from Ambiz.

Sources: F.O. 84/4–270 and F.O. 315/31–6.

Sources

I. PERSONAL INTERVIEWS

Aba Division: Mr. J. Whemekwa Wamuo, Aba Township, 12 Feb. 1973.

Abak Division: Chief Lawrence Udo Akpan, Ikot Obio Ikpa, 18 Nov. 1972; Chief Udo Udo Obong, Ikot Ibit Ekpe, 18 Nov. 1972; Chief Jonah Udo, Ikot Obio Ama, Ikono Clan, 14 Dec. 1972; Chief Udo Udo Akpan Ntuk, Ikot Obio Ama, Ikono Clan, 14 Dec. 1972; Mr. Asuquo Okori, Ikpe Ikot Aqua, 14 Dec. 1972; Chief Dick Ubom Udom and Chief Benson Akarundut, Ikot Ibritam, 11 Jan. 1973; Chief D. K. Eshiet, Ntak Obio Akpa, Ikot Okoro, 11 Jan. 1973; elders of Ekeffe (Chief Benson Udo Idiong, Chief Frank Akpan Ekerete, Chief Thompson Eke, Chief Silas Josiah Ibanga, Chief Etim Udom), Keffe Waterside, Inen, 11 Jan. 1973.

Arochukwu Division: His Highness Chief Kanu Oji, Paramount Chief of Arochukwu, and advisors, 12 Dec. 1972; Mr. Fidelis Emmanuel Sunday Okoro, Ndi Okoro, Obinkita, Arochukwu, 13 Feb. 1973; Mr. Kanu Merem and Mr. Kanu Nwankwo, Ndi Akweke, Obinkita, Arochukwu, 13 Feb. 1973; Chief Robert N. Asiegbu, Ndi Chioka, Obinkita, Arochukwu, 13 Feb. 1973.

Calabar Division: Chief Ekpenyong Ibah, Ikot Nya Asaya, Enyong, 19 Dec. 1972; Chief Offiong Etim Offiong and Village Council, Ikot Offiong, Mbiabo, 6 Jan. 1973; Mr. Odiong Udowang, spokesman for Village Council, Ukwa Eburutu, 14 Feb. 1973.

Eket Division: Chief James Isangetighi and Mr. Edet Jonah Ubong, Etebi, 23 Jan. 1973.

Idemmile Division: Mr. Anyaebosim Mefo and Mr. Maurice Ibe, Okozu, Oba, 30 Dec. 1972.

Ikot Ekpene Division: Chief Akpan Akpan Ebu, Okuku of Oku Clan, Ikot Ama, Central Anang, 9 Nov. 1972; Mr. John Inokun, Ikot Ebak, Afagha Clan, 8 Dec. 1972; Chief Udoka Eshiet, Ikot Ibe, Ukana, 23 Dec. 1972; Chief Charles Esu, Ikwen, Otoro, 18 Feb. 1973.

Itu Division: Chief Ekwere Udonyah, Ibiaku Ikot Edet, Ikono, 20 Nov. 1972; Chief John Umoh Eka, Nkwot Ikot Umo, Ikono, 21 Nov. 1972; Chief Ekpenyong Akpan, Ekoi Atan Ubom, Ikpe, 20 Dec. 1972; Chief Akpan Udo Essien, Obong Ikpa Isong of Ikpe, Ebam Ukot, 20 Dec. 1972; elders of Uku Iboku, 6 Jan. 1973; the Revd. J. E. Inyang, spokesman for Village Council, Ikpe Ikot Nkon, 26 Jan. 1973.

Opobo Division: Chief the Honourable Ntuen Ibek, M.B.E., Essene, Ikpa Nung Asang, 20 Dec. 1972.

Oron Division: Chief Peter Eyo Etim, Oron Township, 24 Jan. 1972; Chief Thomas Edet Eta and elders, Esuk Oron, 24 Jan. 1972; Chief Solomon Isangedighi, Chief Luke Edeke, Chief Augustus Isangedighi, and Chief T. U. Okon, Udesi (Urua Eye), 28 Jan. 1973.

Ukwa Division: Elders of Ohambele (Messrs. Jeremiah Inglis Ekeke, Johnson Isaac Wabara, Dickson Wagomo Ekeke, Samuel A. Ngubo, Amos Nwankwonta, Nwachuku Nwagbara Idi, William Balibo), Ohambele, Ikweke, Ndoki, 14 Jan. 1973.

Uyo Division: Chief James Udo Akang, Mbiakong, Uruan, 25 Nov. 1972; Chief Jacob Eyo Akpan, Obong Isong, Mbiakong, Uruan, 25 Nov. 1972; Chief Thompson Ekpo, Ikot Udo, Ibiaku, Ibiono, 28 Nov. 1972; Chief James Russell, Ikot Akpan Odung, Itak, 28 Nov. 1972; Mr. Patrick Etim Ita, Ifiayong Usuk, Uruan, 4 Dec. 1972; Chief Philip Bassey Ikpe, Regent for the Obong Isong and spokesman for the elders, Ikpa, Uruan, 5 Dec. 1972.

II. PUBLIC RECORDS

1. Great Britain. Public Record Office, London

F.O. 2: GENERAL CORRESPONDENCE. AFRICA

Correspondence with the Consuls in the Bight of Biafra for the years 1850–72 is found in files 4–5, 7–16, 19, 25, 29, 35, 40, 42, 45–8. Correspondence with Dr. William B. Baikie concerning his Niger explorations in the years 1853–60 is in files 18, 23, 27, 31–2, 34. The following reports by Roger Casement of his explorations in 1894 are in files 63–4: 'Report of an Attempted Journey from Itu ... to the Opobo River', 10 Apr. 1894; 'Account of a Journey ... from Essene on the Opobo to Ikorasan ... on the Qua Ibo River', 2 May 1894; 'Account of a Journey ... from Okoyong to Okurike', 6 June 1894; 'Account of a Journey ... from Oron to Eket', 4 July 1894.

F.O. 84: SLAVE TRADE

Correspondence with the British Slave Trade Commissioners in Sierra Leone concerning important aspects of the slave trade in the Bight of Biafra for the years 1819–45 is in files 3–4, 9–10, 15–16, 21–2, 28, 38, 48–50, 63–7, 76–9, 87–90, 101–5, 116–18, 127, 134–5, 147–9, 166–9, 188–94, 212–14, 231–8, 268–72, 301–3, 308A–11, 344–6, 391–3, 499–500, 505–7, 557. The more important correspondence with the British Consuls in the Bight of Biafra (and with the later Commissioners of the Oil Rivers Protectorate) for the years 1849–91 is in files 775, 816, 858, 886, 920, 975, 1001, 1030, 1061, 1087, 1117, 1147, 1176, 1203, 1221, 1249, 1265, 1277, 1290, 1308, 1326, 1343, 1356, 1377, 1881–2, 1940–1, 2110–11.

F.O. 315: SLAVE TRADE. SIERRA LEONE.

The 'Registers of Slaves Emancipated' in the years 1819–48, containing the name, age, sex, physical characteristics, and (sometimes) the ethnic identification of each slave, are in files 31–6.

F.O. 403: CONFIDENTIAL PRINT. AFRICA.

General matters relating to the decision to establish an Oil Rivers Protectorate and its early administration, covering the years 1842–92, are in files 4, 12, 18–20, 31–4, 71–4, 132–5, 171.

Of more than ordinary interest are:

file 16 (4092): Proceedings of H.M.S. *Pioneer* on the River Niger. Correspondence. 1879.

file 76 (5753): Report on the British Protectorate of the Oil Rivers (Niger Delta) by H. H. Johnson. 1888.

file 131 (5913): Report by Major Macdonald of his Visit as Her Majesty's Commissioner to the Niger and Oil Rivers. 1890.

F.O. 881: CONFIDENTIAL PRINTS.

Of interest are prints numbered:

89. Memo. Fernando Po and Annabon 1778–1839. Bandinel. 1839.

671. Report. Baikie's Expedition up Kwara and Niger. 1855.

824. Report. Slave Trade. West Coast of Africa. 1859.

2193. Treaties, etc. Old Calabar. 1841–72.

2197. Draft. Order in Council. Old Calabar, etc. 1871.

5753. Report on the British Protectorate of the Oil Rivers (Niger Delta) by H. H. Johnson. 1888.

6546. Report. Journey from Oron by Roger Casement. 1894.

C.O. 82: FERNANDO PO.

Files numbered 1–10 are primarily concerned with the proposal to establish a Slave Trade Commission on the Spanish island of Fernando Po. The negotiations are excellently summarized in F.O. 881/89. There is some information on trade in these files as well.

2. Great Britain. Parliamentary Papers

1789 lxxxiii (635–45). Minutes of the Evidence taken Before a Committee of the House of Commons ... to consider the Circumstances of the Slave Trade.

1789 lxxxiv (646a). Report of the Committee of Council ... concerning the present State of the Trade to Africa, and Particularly the Trade in Slaves ...

1790 lxxxvii (698); 1790 lxxxviii (699); 1790–91 xcii (745–47). Minutes of Evidence taken before a Committee of the House of Commons ... appointed to take the Examination of Witnesses respecting the African Slave Trade.

1798–99 cvi (965–6). Minutes of Evidence taken on the Third Reading of the Bill to prohibit the Trading for Slaves on the Coast of Africa, within certain Limits.

1822 xxii (103). Papers relating to the Slave Trade.

1842 xi–xii (551). Report from the Select Committee appointed to inquire into the State of the British Possessions on the West Coast of Africa.

1847–8 xxii (272, 366, 536, 622). Reports. Minutes of Evidence taken before the Select Committee on the Slave Trade.

1849 xix (308, 410). Reports. Minutes of Evidence taken before the Select Committee on the Slave Trade.

865 x (412). Report from the Select Committee on the State of British Settlements on the Western Coast of Africa.

Correspondence with the British Consuls for the Bight of Biafra may be found in these volumes:

854–5 lvi (0.4)	1864 lxvi (3339–I)
1856 lxii (0.2)	1865 lvi (3503–I)
1857 xliv (2282)	1866 lxxv (3635–I)
1857–8 lxi (2443–I)	1867 lxxiii (3816–I)
1859 xxxiv (2569–I)	1867–8 lxiv (4000–I)
1860 lxx (2749)	1868–9 lvi (4131–I)
1861 lxiv (2823–I)	1870 lxi (140)
1862 lxi (2959)	1871 lxii (339)

1863 xxi (3160), including dispatches from Dr. Baikie.

3. *Great Britain. Museum of Mankind* (*British Museum—Ethnography*), *London*

Registers of Antiquities, Ethnographical
Registers of Antiquities, Ethnographical, Large Collections

4. *Nigeria. National Archive, Ibadan*

CALPROF 1–5 contains some records of British activities in the Bight of Biafra and in the Bight of Benin before 1891, including pre-Consular and Consular papers, Court of Equity records, and manumission papers.

ALLEN, J. G. C., 'Intelligence Report on the Izi Clan, Abakaliki Division, Ogoja Province', 1932, CSO 26/4/30192.

ASTON-SMITH, W. E., 'Intelligence Report on the Ukana Group of the Ikot Ekpene Division, Calabar Province', 1931, CSO 26/3/27604.

—— 'Intelligence Report on Otoro or Northern Anang Group, Ikot Ekpene Division, Calabar Province', 1933, CSO 26/3/28780.

BAYLEY, D., 'Intelligence Report on the Ibesikpo Clan of the Uyo District, Calabar Province', 1934, CSO 26/3/29699.

BEAUMONT, S. P. L., 'Intelligence Report on the Ntegbe-Nese Clan, Udi Division, Onitsha Province', 1933, CSO 26/3/29601.

CHADWICK, E. R., 'Intelligence Report on Olokoro Clan, Bende Division, Owerri Province, 1935, CSO 26/4/30829.

CHAPMAN, G. B. G., 'Intelligence Report/Assessment Report on the Ikwo Clan in the Abakaliki Division, Ogoja Province', 1930, CSO 26/3/26804.

—— 'Intelligence Report on Ezza Clan, Abakaliki Division, Ogoja Province', 1932, CSO 26/3/28179.

CHUBB, L. T., 'Intelligence Report on the Ibere Clan, Bende Division, Owerri Province', 1933, CSO 26/3/28869.

CLARK, H. J. S., 'Intelligence Report on the Enugu Group, Awka Division, Onitsha Province', 1934, CSO 26/3/29827.

CURWEN, R. J. N., 'Intelligence Report on the Ediene and Itak Clans of the Ikot Ekpene Division, Calabar Province', 1931, CSO 26/3/27615.

DEWHURST, J. V., 'Intelligence Report on the Ututu Clan, Arochuku District, Calabar Province', 1932, CSO 26/3/28779.

ENNALS, C. T. C., 'Intelligence Report on the Ndoki Clan, Aba Division, Owerri Province', 1933, CSO 26/3/29281.

FELLOWS, L. E. H., 'Intelligence Report on Ikom, Nkum, Obokum Mbaba Villages, Ikom Division, Ogoja Province', 1934, CSO 26/3/29966.

FOX-STRANGWAYS, V., 'Intelligence Report on the Isu Ochi, Nne Ato and Umu Chieze Clans, Okigwi Division, Owerri Province and Awgu Division, Onitsha Province', 1932, CSO 26/3/28583.

GOODLIFFE, F. A., 'Intelligence Report on the Otanchara Clan, Okigwi Division, Owerri Province', 1933, CSO 26/3/28860.

—— 'Intelligence Report on the Otanzu Clan, Okigwi Division, Owerri Province', 1933, CSO 26/3/28935.

GORGES, E. H. F., 'Intelligence Report on the Ubium Clan of the Eket Division, Calabar Province', 1935, CSO 26/4/31351.

GREY, P. P., 'Intelligence Report on the Villages of Abudu, Ama-Owelli, Isu, Obaku, Obeagu and Ugbo of the Awgu Division, Onitsha Province', 1934, CSO 26/3/29803.

HARDING, H. J. M., 'Mbiabo Clan Intelligence Report', 1932, CSO 26/3/28862.

—— 'Intelligence Report on the Ibiono Clan (Idioros and Strangers upon Ibiono Clan), Itu District, Enyong Division, Calabar Province', 1933, CSO 26/3/28881.

HAWKESWORTH, E. G., 'A Report on the Okun and Afaha Clans of the Ikot Ekpene Division, Calabar Province', CSO 26/3/26506.

HELSOP, I. R. P., 'Intelligence Report on the Nkalu Clan, Orlu District, Okigwi Division', 1935, CSO 26/4/30878.

JACKSON, JOHN, 'Assessment Report upon the Asa Native Court Area of the Aba Division', 1927, CSO 26/3/20610.

JAMES, H. P., 'An Assessment Report on the Abak District of the Ikot Ekpene Division, Calabar Province', 1927, CSO 26/3/20678.

JEFFREYS, M. D. W., 'Assessment Report—Ikot Ekpene District, Calabar Province', 1927, CSO 26/3/20687.

JOHNSON, S. E., 'Afaha Obong Village Group of the Afaha Clan of the Anang Sub Tribe', 1932, CSO 26/3/28242.

—— 'Intelligence Report on the Ukanafun Clan in the Abak District of the Calabar Province', 1933, CSO 26/3/29627.

JONES, G. I., 'Assessment Report on the Ngbo and Ezengbo Clan, Abakaliki Division', 1930, CSO 26/3/27002.

LEEMING, A., 'Intelligence Report on Aba Native Court Area, Aba Division, Owerri Province', 1927, CSO 26/3/20610.

—— 'Intelligence Report on the Isu Clan, Okigwi Division, Owerri Province', 1935, CSO 26/4/31354.

MacGREGOR, M., 'Assessment Report Awgu Division, Onitsha Province', 1927, CSO 26/3/20681.

MACKENZIE, J. G., 'Intelligence Report on the Emohua Clan, Ahoada Division, Owerri Province', 1933, CSO 26/3/28871.

MAYNE, C. J., 'Intelligence Report on the Ndizuogu Village Area, Orlu District, Okigwi Division, Owerri Province', 1935, CSO 26/4/30836.

MEEK, C. K., 'Intelligence Report on the Isu Group of the Owerri Division', 1932, CSO 26/3/28057.

MILNE, W. R. T., 'Intelligence Report on the Achalla Group, Onitsha Division, Onitsha Province', 1933, CSO 26/3/29001.

—— 'Intelligence Report on the Agbaja Group, Onitsha Division, Onitsha Province', 1933, CSO 26/3/29212.

MOULT, V. H., 'Intelligence Report on Oguta Native Court Area, Owerri Division', 1934, CSO 26/3/29835.

NEWINGTON, W. F. H., 'Intelligence Report on the Ekpeya Clan, Ahoada Division, Owerri Province', 1931, CSO 26/3/28956.

PLEASS, C. J., 'Intelligence Report on the Ubakala Clan, Bende Division, Owerri Province', 1934, CSO 26/3/29828.

PORTER, J. C., 'Intelligence Report on the Okrika Clan, Degema Division, Owerri Province', 1933, CSO 26/3/29004.

SEALY-KING, L., 'Intelligence Report on the Okoyong Clan of the Calabar Province', 1932, CSO 26/3/27674.

SHANKLAND, T. M., 'Intelligence Report on the Aro Clan, Calabar Province', 1933, CSO 26/3/29017.

SHUTE, D. A. F., 'Intelligence Report on the Oniong and Nung Ndem Clans of Eket Division, Calabar Province', 1932, CSO 26/3/27935.

STAPLEDON, R. de S., 'Intelligence Report on the Mbowo Clan, Awgu Division, Onitsha Province', 1935, CSO 26/4/30717.

STONE, B. G., 'Intelligence Report on Umueri Villages of Awka and Onitsha Divisions, Onitsha Province', 1932, CSO 26/3/28323.

—— 'Intelligence Report on the Riverain Villages of the Onitsha Division, Southern Section, of the Onitsha Province', 1932, CSO 26/3/28740.

—— 'Intelligence Report on the Anam Villages, Onitsha Division, Onitsha Province', 1934, CSO 26/3/29576.

TRISTRAM, C. U. G., 'Intelligence Report on the Umuemenyi-Akoli Clan, Bende Division, Owerri Province', 1933, CSO 26/3/28988.

WEBBER, H., 'Intelligence Report on Bonny District, Owerri Province', 1931, CSO 26/3/27226.

WILLIAMS, G. A., 'Intelligence Report on Okpo Mbu Tolu Clan, Ahoada Division, Owerri Province', 1932, CSO 26/3/28074.

5. Nigeria. National Archive, Enugu

ALLEN, J. G. C., 'Supplementary Intelligence Report No. 1 on the Ngwa Clan, Aba Division', 1933, CSE 1/85/3708.

—— 'Supplementary Intelligence Report No. 2 on the Ngwa Clan, Aba Division', 1933, CSE 1/85/3709.

ALLEN, J. G. C., 'Supplementary Intelligence Report No. 3 on the Ngwa
Clan, Aba Division', 1934, CSE 1/85/3710.

DICKINSON, E. N., 'Intelligence Report on Ezennihitte Clan in Owerri Province', 1932, CSE 1/85/4817.

FLOYER, R. K., 'Intelligence Report on the Uwet Sub-Tribe', 1931, CAL-
PROF 53/1/547.

JEFFREYS, Melvin David Waldegrave, 'Notes on the Ibibio: Thesis for a
Diploma in Anthropology', 1931, CSE 1/85/3831.

MARSHALL, H. H., 'Intelligence Report on the Obong Village Group of the
Anang Sub-Tribe, Abak District, Calabar Province', CSE 1/85/4905A.

—— 'A Report on the Umuma Area, Aba Division, Owerri Province', 1934,
CSE 1/85/5426A.

MAYNE, C. J., 'Intelligence Report on the Mbolli Clan, Ahoada Division,
Owerri Province', n.d., CSE 1/85/3861.

SAVORY, R. T., 'Intelligence Report on the Ikwerri Clan, Ahoada Division,
Owerri Province', 1939, CALPROF 53/1/577.

III. PRIVATE PAPERS AND THESES

AHANOTU, Austin Metumara, 'The Economics and Politics of Religion: A
Study of the Development of the Igbo Spirit of Enterprise 1800–1955', Ph.D.
dissertation, University of California, Los Angeles, 1971.

ANDERSON, William, 'Journal', United Presbyterian Church papers, NLS
MS. 8944 (1851–2), MS. 2982 (1853).

—— 'Notes on O[ld] C[alabar], 1846–85', United Presbyterian Church papers
NLS, MS. 2983.

BRIDGES, A. F. B., 'Report on Palm Oil Survey in Ibo, Ibibio and Cross
River Area', 1938, Rhodes House Library, Oxford, MSS. Afr. s. 679.

NJAKA, Elechukwu, N., 'The Igbo Political Institutions and Transition',
Ph.D. dissertation, University of California, Los Angeles, 1971.

NWABARA, Samuel Nwankwo, 'Ibo Land: A Study in British Penetration
and the Problem of Administration, 1860–1930', Ph.D. dissertation, Northwestern University, 1965.

OFONAGORO, Walter Ibekwe, 'The Opening Up of Southern Nigeria to
British Trade, and its Consequences: Economic and Social History, 1881–
1916', Ph.D. dissertation, Columbia Univ., 1972.

TURNER, Capt. (presumed author), 'Voyage. Ship Magistrate towards Old
Calabar commencing Tuesday 15th Dec. 1840', National Maritime Museum,
London, MS. LOG/M/23.

—— 'Voyage in the Celma to Old Calabar, 1847', National Maritime
Museum, London, MS. LOG/M/23.

UKWU, Ukwu Iguwo. 'Markets in Iboland', Ph.D. dissertation, University
of Cambridge, 1965.

WADDELL, Hope Masterton. 'Journal of the Old Calabar Mission', United
Presbyterian Church papers, vol. 1 (1846), MS. 7739: vol. 7 (1849–50), MS
7740; vol. 8 (1850–1), MS. 7741; vol. 9 (1851–3), MS. 8953; vol. 10 (1853–

5), MS. 7742; vol. 11 (1855–6), MS. 7743. (Extracts from some of the missing volumes were printed in the *United Presbyterian Church Missionary Record*, e.g. XI (1856), 198–9; XII (1857), 43, 89, 109, 146; XIII (1858), 87–9, 176–82.)

IV. PUBLISHED WORKS CITED

ADAMS, Capt. John, *Remarks on the Country Extending from Cape Palmas to the River Congo*, London: G. & W. B. Whittaker, 1823; reprinted by Frank Cass, 1966.

ADAMS, R. F. G., 'Oberi Okaime: a New African Language and Script', *Africa*, XVII (1947), 24–34.

AFIGBO, Adiele Eberechukwu. 'Efik Origins and Migrations Reconsidered', *Nigeria*, No. 87 (1965), 267–80.

—— 'The Eclipse of the Aro Slaving Oligarchy of South-Eastern Nigeria, 1901–27', *JHSN*, VI (1971), 3–24.

—— 'The Aro of Southern Nigeria: A Socio-Historical Analysis of Legends of their Origin', *African Notes*, VI.2 (1971), 31–46, and VII.1 (1972), 91–106.

—— 'Mono-causality and the African Historiography: the Case of Efik Society and International Commerce', *Transactions of the Historical Society of Ghana*, XIV (1973), 117–27.

—— 'Trade and Trade Routes in Nineteenth Century Nsukka', *JHSN*, VII.1 (1973), 77–90.

—— 'The Nineteenth Century Crisis of the Aro Slaving Oligarchy of South-Eastern Nigeria', *Nigeria*, No. 110–12 (1974), 66–73.

AJAYI, J. F. A., and CROWDER, Michael, eds., *History of West Africa*, 2 vols., London: Longmans, 1971, 1974.

AKINJOGBIN, I. A., *Dahomey and its Neighbours, 1708–1818*, Cambridge: Univ. Press, 1966.

ALAGOA, Ebiegberi Joe, *The Small Brave City-State: a History of Nembe-Brass in the Niger Delta*, Ibadan: Ibadan Univ. Press, 1964.

—— 'Oral Tradition among the Ijo of the Niger Delta', *JAH*, VII (1966), 405–19.

—— 'Long-distance Trade and States in the Niger Delta', *JAH*, XI (1970), 319–29.

—— 'The Development of Institutions in the States of the Eastern Niger Delta', *JAH*, XII (1971), 269–78.

—— 'The Niger Delta States and their Neighbours 1600–1800', In Ajayi and Crowder, *History of West Africa*, I.

—— *A History of the Niger Delta*, Ibadan Univ. Press, 1972.

ALLEN, William and THOMSON, T. R. H., *A Narrative of the Expedition . . . to the River Niger in 1841*, 2 vols., London: Richard Bentley, 1848.

ALUTU, John O., *A Groundwork of Nnewi History*, Enugu: the author, 1963.

AMOGU, O. O., 'The Introduction into, and Withdrawal of Manillas from the "Oil Rivers" as Seen in Ndoki District', *Nigeria*, No. 38 (1952), 134–9.

ANENE, Joseph C., 'The Protectorate Government of Southern Nigeria and the Aros 1900–1902', *JHSN*, I.2 (1956), 20–6.

—— 'Benin, Niger Delta, Ibo and Ibibio Peoples in the Nineteenth Century', in J. F. Ade Ajayi and Ian Espie, *A Thousand Years of West African History*, Ibadan Univ. Press, 1965.

—— *Southern Nigeria in Transition 1885–1906: Theory and Practice in a Colonial Protectorate*, Cambridge: Univ. Press, 1966.

ANSTEY, Roger, *The Atlantic Slave Trade and British Abolition, 1760–1810*, London: Macmillan, 1975.

ARDENER, Edwin, *Coastal Bantu of the Cameroons, Ethnographic Survey of Africa, Western Africa*, Part XI, London: International African Inst., 1956.

—— 'Documentary and Linguistic Evidence for the Rise of the Trading Polities between Rio del Rey and Cameroons, 1500–1650', in *History and Social Anthropology*, ed. I. M. Lewis, A. S. A. Monograph #7. London: Tavistock Publications, 1968.

ARNOLD, Margaret, 'A Port of Trade: Whydah on the Guinea Coast', in *Trade and Markets in the Early Empires*, ed. K. Polanyi, *et al.*, Glencoe: Free Press, 1957.

ASTLEY, Thomas, ed., *A New Collection of Voyages and Travels*, 4 vols., London: Printed for Thomas Astley, 1745–7; reprinted by Frank Cass, 1972.

AYANDELE, E. A., *The Missionary Impact on Modern Nigeria 1842-1914: a Political and Social Analysis*, London: Longmans, 1966.

AYE, Efiong U., *Old Calabar through the Centuries*, Calabar: Hope Waddell Press, 1967.

BAIKIE, William Balfour, *Narrative of an Exploring Voyage up the Rivers Kwora and Binue in 1854*, London: John Murray, 1856.

BARBOT, James, 'An Abstract of a Voyage to *New Calabar* River, or *Rio Real*, in the Year 1699', in Churchill and Churchill, *Collection of Voyages*, V.

BARBOT, John, 'A Description of the Coasts of North and South Guinea . . .', in Churchill and Churchill, *Collection of Voyages*, V.

BASDEN, George Thomas, *Among the Ibos of Nigeria*, Philadelphia: J. B. Lippincott, 1921.

—— *Niger Ibos*. London: Seeley Service, 1938.

BEECROFT, John, 'Substance of a Letter received from J. Becroft [*sic*], Esq., relative to his recent Ascent of the Quorra, dated Fernando Po, 28th February, 1836', *JRGS*, VI (1836), 424–6.

—— 'On Benin and the Upper Course of the River Quorra or the Niger', *JRGS*, XI (1841), 184–90.

BLAKE, John W., *European Beginnings in West Africa, 1454–1578*, London: Longmans, 1937.

—— *Europeans in West Africa 1450–1560*, London: Hakluyt Society, 1942.

BOHANNAN, Paul and Laura, *Tiv Economy*. Evanston: Northwestern Univ. Press, 1968.

—— and DALTON, George, eds., *Markets in Africa*. Evanston: Northwestern Univ. Press, 1962.

BOLD, Lt. Edward, *The Merchants' and Mariners' African Guide*, London: Longman, Hurst, Rees, Orme and Brown, 1819.

BOSMAN, Willem, *A New and Accurate Description of the Coast of Guinea*, 2nd edn. London: J. Knapton, 1721.

BOSTON, J. S. 'Notes on Contact between the Igala and the Ibo', *JHSN*, II.1 (1960), 52–8.

—— 'Ethnographic Field Work', *Annual Report of the Antiquities Service for the Year 1956–57*. Lagos: Federal Government Printer, 1961.

—— *The Igala Kingdom*. Ibadan: Oxford Univ. Press, 1968.

BOWEN, R. L., 'Obi Oputa of Aboh', *Nigeria*, No. 22 (1944), 64–5.

BURDO, Adolphe, *The Niger and Benueh: Travels in Central Africa*, trans. Mrs. George Sturge, London: Richard Bentley, 1880.

BURTON, Richard Francis, *Wanderings in West Africa*, 2 vols., London: Tinsley Brothers, 1863; reprinted by Johnson Reprint Corp., New York: 1970.

BUTTERWORTH, William, see Schroeder, Henry.

CARDI, Count C. N. de, 'A Short Description of the Natives of the Niger Coast Protectorate, with Some Account of Their Customs, Religion, Trade, etc.', in Mary Kingsley, *West African Studies*.

CHILVER, E. M., 'Nineteenth Century Trade in the Bamenda Grassfields, Southern Cameroons', *Afrika and Übersee*, XLV (1962), 233–58.

—— and KABERRY, P. M., 'Sources of the Nineteenth-Century Slave Trade Two Comments: I. The Cameroons Highlands', *JAH*, VI (1965), 117–19.

CHUBB, L. T., *Ibo Land Tenure*, 2nd edn., Ibadan University Press, 1961.

CHURCHILL, Awnsham and John, compilers, *Collection of Voyages and Travels*, vol. V, London: Printed by arrangement from Messrs. Churchill, for H. Lintot and John Osborn, 1746.

CLARK, David J., 'Three "Kwa" Languages of Eastern Nigeria', *Journal of West African Languages*, VIII (1971), 27–36.

CLARKSON, Thomas, *The History of the Abolition of the African Slave Trade*, 2 vols., London: Longman, Hurst, Rees, and Orme, 1808.

CONNAH, Graham, 'Archaeology in Benin', *JAH*, XIII (1972), 25–38.

—— *The Archaeology of Benin*, Oxford: Clarendon Press, 1975.

COOKEY, S. J. S., 'An Igbo Slave Story of the Late Nineteenth Century and its Implications', *Ikenga*, I.2 (July 1972), 1–9.

COQUERY-VIDROVITCH, Cathérine, 'De la traité des esclaves à l'exportation de l'huile de palme et des palmistes au Dahomey: xixe siècle', in Meillassoux, *Development of Indigenous Trade*.

COURSEY, D. G., *Yams: an Account of the Nature, Origins, Cultivation and Utilization of the Useful Members of the Dioscoreaceae*, London: Longmans, Green, 1967.

CROW, Captain Hugh, *Memoirs of the Late Capt. Hugh Crow of Liverpool*, London: Longmans, Rees, Orme, Brown, and Green, 1830.

CROWTHER, the Revd. Samuel Adjai, *Journal of an Expedition up the Niger and Tshadda Rivers ... in 1854*, London: Church Missionary House, 1855.

CROWTHER, the Revd. Samuel Adjai, and TAYLOR, John Christopher, *The Gospel on the Banks of the Niger: Journals and Notices of the Native Missionaries on the Niger Expedition of 1857–1859*, London: Dawsons, 1859.

CURTIN, Philip D., *The Atlantic Slave Trade: A Census*, Madison: Univ. of Wisconsin Press, 1969.

—— 'Measuring the Atlantic Slave Trade', in *Race and Slavery in the Western Hemisphere*. Edited by Stanley L. Engerman and Eugene D. Genovese. Princeton Univ. Press, 1975.

—— and VANSINA, Jan, 'Sources of the Nineteenth Century Atlantic Slave Trade', *JAH*, V (1964), 185–208.

DAAKU, Kwame Y., *Trade and Politics on the Gold Coast, 1600–1720*, London: Oxford, 1970.

—— 'Trade and Trading Patterns of the Akan in the Seventeenth and Eighteenth Centuries', in Meillassoux, *Development of Indigenous Trade*.

DALBY, David, 'Provisional Identification of Languages in the *Polyglotta Africana*', *Sierra Leone Language Review*, No. 3 (1964), 83–90.

DANIELL, William F., 'On the Natives of Old Callebar, West Coast of Africa', *Journal of the Ethnological Society of London*, I (1848), 210–24.

DAPPER, Olfert, *Description de l'Afrique*, Amsterdam: Chez Wolfgang, Waesberge, Boom and van Someren, 1686.

DAVIDSON, Basil, with Buah, F. K., and the advice of Ajayi, J. F. Ade, *A History of West Africa to the Nineteenth Century*, Garden City: Doubleday and Company, 1966.

DAVIES, K. G., *The Royal African Company*, New York: Atheneum, 1970.

DIKE, Kenneth Onwuka. *Trade and Politics in the Niger Delta 1830–1885*, Oxford: Clarendon Press, 1956.

DONNAN, Elizabeth, ed., *Documents Illustrative of the History of the Slave Trade*, 4 vols., Washington: Carnegie Institute of Washington, 1930–35; reprinted New York: Octagon Books, 1965.

DUKE, Antera, 'The Diary of Antera Duke', ed. Simmons, Donald C., in Forde, *Efik Traders*.

EKEGHE, Ogbonna O., *A Short History of Abiriba*, Aba: International Press, 1956.

EKEJIUBA, Felicia Ifeoma, 'Omu Okwei, the Merchant Queen of Ossomari; a Biographical Sketch', *JHSN*, III.4 (1967), 633–46.

—— 'Preliminary Notes on Brasswork of Eastern Nigeria', *African Notes*, IV (1967), 11–15.

—— 'The Aro Trade System in the Nineteenth Century', *Ikenga*, I.1 (1972), 11–26.

—— 'The Aro System of Trade in the Nineteenth Century', *Ikenga*, I.2 (1972), 10–21.

—— 'Igba Ndu: An Igbo Mechanism of Social Control and Adjustment', *African Notes*, VII.2 (1972), 9–24.

EKUNDARE, R. Olufemi, *An Economic History of Nigeria, 1860–1960*, London: Methuen, 1973.

ELTIS, David, 'The Export of Slaves from Africa 1821–1843', *Journal of Economic History*, XXXVII (1977), 409–33.

EQUIANO, Olaudah, *Equiano's Travels. His Autobiography. The Interesting Narrative of the Life of Olaudah Equiano or Gustavus Vassa the African*, abr. and ed. Paul Edwards, New York: Frederick A. Praeger, 1967.

—— 'The Early Travels of Olaudah Equiano', ed. G. I. Jones, in *Africa Remembered: Narratives by West Africans from the Era of the Slave Trade*, ed. Philip D. Curtin. Madison: Univ. of Wisconsin Press, 1967.

EVERITT, Alan, 'The Marketing of Agricultural Produce', in *The Agrarian History of England and Wales*, volume iv: *1500–1640*, ed. Joan Thirsk. London: Cambridge Univ. Press, 1967.

FAGE, John D., 'Some Remarks on Beads and Trade in Lower Guinea in the 16th and 17th Centuries', *JAH*, III (1962), 343–7.

—— *A History of West Africa*, Cambridge: Univ. Press, 1969.

—— 'Slavery and the Slave Trade in the Context of West African History', *JAH*, X (1969), 393–404.

—— 'The Effect of the Export Slave Trade on African Populations', in *The Population Factor in African Studies*, ed. R. P. Moss and R. J. A. R. Rathbone, Univ. of London Press, 1975.

FALCONBRIDGE, Alexander, *An Account of the Slave Trade on the Coast of Africa*, London: J. Phillips, 1788.

FLINT, John E., 'Economic Change in West Africa in the Nineteenth Century', in Ajayi and Crowder, *History of West Africa*, II.

FORDE, Cyril Daryll, ed., *Efik Traders of Old Calabar*, London: Oxford Univ. Press, 1956.

—— BROWN, Paula, and ARMSTRONG, Robert G., *Peoples of the Niger–Benue Confluence*, Ethnographic Survey of Africa, Western Africa, Part X, ed. Daryll Forde, London: International African Institute, 1955.

—— and JONES, G. I., *The Ibo and Ibibio-Speaking Peoples of South-Eastern Nigeria*, Ethnographic Survey of Africa, Western Africa, Part III, ed. Daryll Forde, London: International African Institute, 1950.

—— and KABERRY, Phyllis M., eds. *West African Kingdoms in the Nineteenth Century*, London: Oxford Univ. Press, 1967.

—— and SCOTT, Richenda. *The Native Economies of Nigeria*. Edited by Margery Perham. London: Faber & Faber, 1946.

FORTES, Meyer, and EVANS-PRITCHARD, E. E., eds., *African Political Systems*, London: Oxford Univ. Press, 1940.

FOX, A. J., *Uzuakoli: a Short History*, London: Oxford Univ. Press, 1964.

GOLDIE, Hugh, 'Journal', *Missionary Record*, IV (Sept. 1849), 130–2, VI (Sept. 1851), 131.

—— *Dictionary of the Efik Language*, Glasgow: Dunn & Wright, 1862; reprinted Ridgewood, N.J.: Gregg Press, 1964.

—— 'Notes of a Voyage Up the Calabar or Cross River in November 1884, with a Map by the Revd. R. M. Beedie', *Scottish Geographical Magazine*, I (1885), 273–83.

GOLDIE, Hugh, *Calabar and Its Mission*, Edinburgh: Oliphant Anderson & Ferrier, 1890.

GOLLOCK, Georgina A., 'Chief Onoyom Iya Nya' in *Lives of Eminent Africans*, London: Longmans, Green, 1928.

GRAY, Richard and BIRMINGHAM, David, eds., *Pre-Colonial African Trade: Essays on Trade in Central and Eastern Africa before 1900*, London: Oxford Univ. Press, 1970.

GREAT BRITAIN, House of Commons, *Abridgment of the Minutes of Evidence, taken before a Committee of the Whole House, to whom it was referred to consider of the Slave Trade*, 4 vols., London: H.M.S.O., 1789–1791.

GREEN, Margaret Mackesen, *Igbo Village Affairs*, 2nd edn., London: Frank Cass, 1964.

GREENBERG, Joseph H., *The Languages of Africa*, 2nd edn., Bloomington: Indiana Univ. Press, 1966.

GREEVES, M., 'Identification of Fibres and Weaves in Cloth Fragments from Feature 21 in Cutting II on the Clerks' Quarters Site', in Connah, *Archaeology in Benin*.

GROVES, the Revd. W., 'The Story of Udo Akpabio of the Anang Tribe, Southern Nigeria', in *Ten Africans*, ed. Margery Perham, London: Faber and Faber, 1936.

HAIR, P. E. H., 'The Enslavement of Koelle's Informants', *JAH*, VI (1965), 193–203.

——— 'Ethnolinguistic Continuity on the Guinea Coast', *JAH*, VIII (1967), 247–68.

HALLETT, Robin, ed., *Records of the African Association, 1788–1831*, London: Thomas Nelson, 1964.

HARRIS, J. S., 'Some Aspects of Slavery in Southeastern Nigeria', *Journal of Negro History*, XXVII (1942), 37–54.

HARRIS, Rosemary L., *The Political Organization of the Mbembe, Nigeria*, London: H.M.S.O., 1965.

——— 'The History of Trade at Ikom, Eastern Nigeria', *Africa*, XLII (1972), 122–39.

HART, A. Kalada, *Report of the Enquiry into the Dispute over the Obongship of Calabar*, Official Document No. 17 of 1964, Enugu: Government Printer, 1964.

HARTLE, Donald, 'Bronze Objects from the Ikeka Garden Site, Ezira', *West African Archaeological Newsletter*, No. 4 (Mar. 1966), 25–8.

——— 'Radiocarbon Dates', *West African Archaeological Newsletter*, No. 9 (May 1968), 73.

HARTLEY, C. W. S., *The Oil Palm (Elaeis Guineensis)*, London: Longmans, 1967.

HAVINDEN, M. A., 'The History of Crop Cultivation in West Africa: a Bibliographical Guide', *Economic History Review*, 2nd Ser., XXIII (1970), 532–55.

HENDERSON, Richard Neal, *The King in Every Man; Evolutionary Trends in Onitsha Ibo Society and Culture*, New Haven: Yale Univ. Press, 1972.

HILL, Polly, 'Notes on Traditional Market Authority and Market Periodicity in West Africa', *JAH*, VII (1966), 295–311.

HODDER, B. W., 'Distribution of Markets in Yorubaland', *Scottish Geographical Magazine*, LXXXI (1965), 45–55.

HOLMAN, James, *Holman's Voyage to Old Calabar*, ed. Donald Simmons, Calabar: American Association for African Research, 1959.

HOPKINS, Anthony G., *An Economic History of West Africa*, New York: Columbia Univ. Press, 1973.

HORTON, James Africanus, *West African Countries and Peoples*, Edinburgh: At the Univ. Press, 1969.

HORTON, Robin, 'From Fishing Village to City-state: A Social History of New Calabar', in *Man in Africa*, ed. Mary Douglas and Phyllis M. Kaberry, London: Tavistock Publications, 1969.

—— 'Stateless States in the History of West Africa', in Ajayi and Crowder, *History of West Africa*.

HORTON, W. R. G., 'The Ohu System of Slavery in a Northern Ibo Village-Group', *Africa*, XXIV (1954), 311–36.

HUTCHINSON, Thomas Joseph, *Narrative of the Niger, Tshadda and Binue Exploration*, London: Longmans, 1855.

—— *Impressions of Western Africa*, London: Longman, Brown, Green, Longmans, & Robert, 1858; reprinted London: Frank Cass, 1970.

HUTCHINSON, William F., 'A Seventeenth Century Slaver's Diary', *Elder Dempster Magazine*, IV (1925), 60–2, 141–3; V (1926), 32–4.

IGWEGBE, Richard Ohizo, *The Original History of Arondizuogu from 1635–1960*, Aba: International Press, 1962.

ILOGU, E., 'Inside Arochukwu', *Nigeria*, No. 53 (1957), 100–18.

ISICHEI, Elizabeth, 'Historical Change in an Ibo Polity' Asaba to 1885', *JAH*, X (1969), 421–38.

—— *The Ibo People and the Europeans: the Genesis of a Relationship—to 1906*, London: Faber and Faber, 1973.

—— *A History of the Igbo People*, New York: St. Martin's Press, 1976.

JACKSON, Richard Mather, *Journal of a Voyage to the Bonny River on the West Coast of Africa in the Ship Kingston from Liverpool*, Letchworth: Garden City Press, 1934.

JAMIESON, Robert, *Commerce with Africa*, revised edn., London: Effingham Wilson, 1859.

JEFFREYS, Mervin David Waldegrave, 'The Cowrie Shell: a Study of its History and Use in Nigeria', *Nigeria*, No. 15 (1938), 221–6, 256.

—— 'Some Negro Currencies in Nigeria', *South African Museums' Association Bulletin*, V.16 (1954), 405–16.

—— 'Umundri Tradition of Origin', *African Studies*, XV (1956), 119–31.

—— 'Efik Origin', *Nigeria*, No. 91 (1966), 297–9.

JOHNSON, Marion, 'The Cowrie Currencies of West Africa, Part I', *JAH*, XI (1970), pp. 17–49.

JONES, Gwilym Iwan, 'Who are the Aro?' *Nigerian Field*, III (1939), 100–3

—— 'Political Organization of Old Calabar', in Forde, *Efik Traders*,

—— *Report of the Position, Status and Influence of Chiefs and Natural Rulers in the Eastern Region of Nigeria*, Enugu: Government Printer, 1958.

—— 'Native and Trade Currencies in Southern Nigeria during the 18th and 19th Centuries', *Africa*, XXVIII (1958), 43–53.

—— 'Ecology and Social Structure among the North-Eastern Ibo', *Africa*, XXXI (1961), 117–34.

—— *The Trading States of the Oil Rivers*, London: Oxford Univ. Press for the International African Institute, 1963.

—— 'Introduction to the Second Edition', in Waddell, *Twenty-Nine Years*, 2nd edn.

JONES, William Orville, *Manioc in Africa*, Stanford: Stanford Univ. Press, 1959.

KAINE, Esama, *Ossomari, a Historical Sketch*, Onitsha: the author, 1963.

KANU-UMOH, R., *Slave Markets in East Nigeria*, Umuahia-Ibeku: Language Academy, n.d.

KING, J. B., 'Details of Explorations of the Old Calabar River, in 1841 and 1842 by Captain Becroft . . . and Mr. J. B. King', *JRGS*, XIV (1844), 260–83.

KINGSLEY, Mary, *Travels in West Africa*, London: Macmillan, 1897.

—— *West African Studies*, London: Macmillan, 1899.

KLEMP, Egon, ed., *Africa on Maps Dating from the Twelfth to the Eighteenth Century*, Leipzig: Edition Leipzig, 1968.

KOELLE, Sigismund Wilhelm, *Polyglotta Africana*, London: Church Missionary House, 1854; reprinted with a new introduction by P. E. H. Hair, Graz, Austria: Akademische Druck-U. Verlagsanstalt, 1963.

LAIRD, Macgregor and OLDFIELD, R. A. K., *Narrative of an Expedition into the Interior of Africa . . . in 1832, 1833, and 1834*, 2 vols., London: Richard Bentley, 1837.

LANDER, Richard and John, *Journal of an Expedition to Explore the Course and Termination of the Niger*, London: J. Murray, 1832.

—— *The Niger Journal*, ed. and abr. Robin Hallett, New York: Frederick A. Praeger, 1965.

LANDOLPHE, J. F., *Mémoires de Capitaine Landolphe, continant l'histoire de ses voyages pendant trente-six ans, aux côtes d'Afrique et aux deux Amériques*, editée par J. S. Quesné, 2 vols., Paris: Arthus Bertrand et Pillet ainé, 1823.

LATHAM, A. J. H., 'Currency, Credit and Capitalism on the Cross River in the Pre-colonial Era', *JAH*, XII (1971), 599–605.

—— *Old Calabar 1600–1891: The Impact of the International Economy upon a Traditional Society*, Oxford: Clarendon Press, 1973.

LAWAL, Babatunde, 'Dating Problems at Igbo-Ukwu', *JAH*, XIV (1973), 1–8.

LEONARD, Arthur Glyn, 'Notes of a Journey to Bende', *Journal of the Manchester Geographical Society*, XIV (1898), 190–207.

LIEBER, J. W., *Efik and Ibibio Villages*, Occasional Publication No. 13, Ibadan: Institute of Education, Univ. of Ibadan, 1971.

LIVINGSTONE, William Pringle, *Dr. Hitchcock of Uburu*, Edinburgh: Foreign Mission Committee of the United Free Church of Scotland, 1920.

MCCULLOCH, Merran, LITTLEWOOD, Margaret, and DUGAST, I., *Peoples of the Central Cameroons, Ethnographic Survey of Africa: Western Africa*, IX, London: International African Institute, 1954.

MCPHEE, Allan, *The Economic Revolution in British West Africa*, London: George Routledge, 1926.

MARTIN, Anne, *The Oil Palm Economy of the Ibibio Farmer*, Ibadan: Ibadan Univ. Press, 1956.

MARWICK, William, *William and Louisa Anderson: A Record of Their Life and Work in Jamaica and Old Calabar*, Edinburgh: Andrew Elliott, 1897.

MAUNY, Raymond, 'Que faut-il appeler "pierre" d'agris?' *Notes Africaines*, IV.42 (1949), 33–6.

—— 'Akori Beads', *JHSN*, I (1958), 210–14.

MEEK, Charles Kingsley, *Report on the Social and Political Organization in the Owerri Division*, Lagos: Government Printer, 1934.

—— *Law and Authority in a Nigerian Tribe*, London: Oxford Univ. Press, 1937.

MEILLASSOUX, Claude, ed., *The Development of Indigenous Trade and Markets in West Africa*, London: Oxford Univ. Press for the International African Institute, 1971.

MIDDLETON, John, and TAIT, David, eds., *Tribes Without Rulers*, London: Routledge and Kegan Paul, 1958.

MORGAN, W. B., 'The Forest and Agriculture in West Africa', *JAH*, III (1962), 235–9.

MORTON-WILLIAMS, Peter, 'The Oyo Yoruba and the Atlantic Trade', *JHSN*, III (1964), 25–45.

MOTA, A. Teixeira da, *Topónimos de Origem Portuguesa na Costa Ocidental de Africa Desde o Cabo Bojador ao Cabo de Santa Caterina*, Bissau: Centro de Estudos da Guiné Portuguesa, 1950.

MURDOCK, George Peter, *Africa: Its People and Their Cultural History*, New York: McGraw-Hill, 1959.

NAIR, Kannan Kutty, *Politics and Society in South Eastern Nigeria 1841–1906: A Study of Power, Diplomacy and Commerce in Old Calabar*, London: Frank Cass, 1972.

NEWBURY, Colin W., 'Trade and Authority in West Africa from 1850 to 1880', in *Colonialism, in Africa 1870–1960*, I: *The History and Politics of Colonialism 1870–1914*, eds. L. H. Gann and Peter Duignan, Cambridge: Univ. Press, 1969.

—— 'Prices and Profitability in Early Nineteenth Century West African Trade', in Meillassoux, *Development of Indigenous Trade*.

—— 'Credit in Early Nineteenth Century West African Trade', *JAH*, XIII (1972), 81–95.

NORTHRUP, David, 'The Growth of Trade among the Igbo before 1800', *JAH*, XIII (1972), 217–36.

—— 'New Light from Old Sources: Pre-Colonial References to the Anang Ibibio', *Ikenga*, II.1 (1973), 1–5.

—— 'The Compatibility of the Slave and Palm Oil Trades in the Bight of Biafra', *JAH*, XVII (1976), 353–64.

—— 'African Mortality in the Suppression of the Slave Trade: The Case of the Bight of Biafra', *Journal of Interdisciplinary History*, IX (1978), 47–64.

NZEKWU, J. O., 'Onitsha', *Nigeria*, No. 50 (1956), 200–23.

NZEKWU, Onuora, 'Uburu and the Salt Lake', *Nigeria*, No. 56 (1958), 84–96.

—— 'Gloria Ibo', *Nigeria*, No. 64 (1960), 72–88.

NZIMIRO, Ikenna, *Studies in Ibo Political Systems*, London: Frank Cass, 1972.

OBI, Samuel Nwanko Chinwuba, *The Ibo Law of Property*, London: Butterworths, 1963.

OLDENDORPS, Christian Georg Andreas, *Geschichte der Evangelischen Brüder auf den Carabischen Inseln*, Barby: Christian Friedrich Laux, 1777.

OLDFIELD, R. K., 'A Brief Account of an Ascent of the Old Calabar River in 1836', *JRGS*, VII (1837), 195–8.

OTTENBERG, Simon, 'Ibo Oracles and Intergroup Relations', *Southwestern Journal of Anthropology*, XIV (1958), 295–317.

—— *Leadership and Authority in an African Society: The Afikpo Village-Group*, American Ethnological Society Monograph 52, Seattle and London: Univ. of Washington Press, 1971.

—— and OTTENBERG, Phoebe, 'Afikpo Markets: 1900–1960', in *Markets in Africa*, ed. Paul J. Bohannan and George Dalton. Evanston: Northwestern Univ. Press, 1961.

OWEN, Capt. William Fitzwilliam, *Narrative of Voyages to Explore the Shores of Africa, Arabia, and Madagascar*, 2 vols., London: Richard Bentley, 1833.

PARTRIDGE, Charles, *Cross River Natives*, London: Hutchinson, 1905.

PEREIRA, Duarte Pacheco, *Esmeraldo de Situ Orbis, Côte Occidentale d'Afrique du Sud Marocain au Gabon*, ed. and trans. Raymond Mauny, Bissau: Centro de Estudos da Guiné Portuguesa, No. 19, 1956.

POLANYI, Karl, *Dahomey and the Slave Trade*, Seattle: Univ. of Washington Press, 1966.

QUIGGIN, Alison Hingston, *A Survey of Primitive Money*, rev. edn., London: Methuen, 1963.

READ, C. H., *A Guide to the Antiquities of the Bronze Age in the Department of British and Medieval Antiquities*, 2nd edn., London: British Museum, 1920.

REYNOLDS, Edward, *Trade and Economic Change on the Gold Coast*, London: Longmans, 1974.

RODNEY, Walter, 'African Slavery and Other Forms of Social Oppression on the Upper Guinea Coast in the Context of the Atlantic Slave-Trade', *JAH*, VII (1966), 432–3.

R UEL, Malcolm, *Leopards and Leaders: Constitutional Politics among a Cross River People*, London: Tavistock Publications, 1969.

R YDER, A. F. C., 'Dutch Trade on the Nigerian Coast during the Seventeenth Century, *JHSN*, III.2 (1965), 195–210.

R YDER, Alan F. C., *Benin and the Europeans, 1485–1897*, London: Longmans, 1969.

S ANDOVAL, Alonso de, S. J., *De Instauranda Aethiopum Salute*, Bogota: Empressa Nacional de Publicaciones, 1956 (a reissue of *Naturaleza . . . de Totos Etiopes*, Sevilla: Francisco de Lira, 1627).

S CHÖN, James Frederick, and C ROWTHER, Samuel, *Journals of the . . . Expedition up the Niger in 1841 . . .* 2nd edn., London: Frank Cass & Co. Ltd., 1970; (originally published London: Church Missionary Society, 1842).

[S CHROEDER, Henry], *Three Years Adventures of a Minor, in England, Africa, the West Indies, South-Carolina, and Georgia*, by William Butterworth (pseudonym), Leeds: Thomas Inchbold, 1831.

S HAW, Thurstan, *Igbo-Ukwu*, 2 vols., London: Faber and Faber, 1970.

—— 'Those Igbo-Ukwu Radiocarbon Dates: Facts, Fictions and Probabilities', *JAH*, XVI (1975), 503–7.

S IMMONS, Donald C., 'An Ethnographic Sketch of the Efik People', in Forde, *Efik Traders*.

S MITH, Robert, 'The Canoe in West African History', *JAH*, XI (1970), 515–33.

S NELGRAVE, Capt. William, *A New Account of Some Parts of Guinea and the Slave-Trade*, London: James, John, and Paul Knapton, 1730.

S PENCER, Julius, 'The History of Asaba and Its Kings', *Niger and Yoruba Notes*, VIII (1901), 20–1.

S TEVENSON, Robert Findlay, *Population and Political Systems in Tropical Africa*, New York: Columbia Univ. Press, 1968.

S UNDSTRÖM, Lars, *The Trade of Guinea*, Upsala: Akademisk Avhandling, 1965.

T ALBOT, Percy Amaury, *In the Shadow of the Bush*, London: William Heinemann, 1912.

—— *Life in Southern Nigeria: The Magic, Beliefs and Customs of the Ibibio Tribe*, London: Macmillan, 1923.

—— *The Peoples of Southern Nigeria: A Sketch of Their History, Ethnology and Languages*, 4 vols., London: Oxford Univ. Press, 1926.

T HOMAS, Northcote Whitridge, *Anthropological Report on the Ibo-Speaking Peoples of Nigeria*, 4 vols., London: Harrison and Sons, 1913–14.

U CHENDU, Victor Chikezie, *The Igbo of Southeast Nigeria*, New York: Holt, Rinehart and Winston, 1965.

U DO, Edet, A., 'The Ibo Origin of Efik by A. E. Afigbo: A Review', *Calabar Historical Journal*, I.1 (1976), 154–72.

U DO, Reuben K., *Geographical Regions of Nigeria*, Berkeley: Univ. of California Press, 1970.

UKA, N., 'A Note on the "Abam" Warriors of Igbo Land', *Ikenga*, I.2 (1972), 76–82.

UKWU, Ukwu Iguwo, 'The Development of Trade and Marketing in Iboland', *JHSN*, III (1967), 647–62.

UMO, R. Kanu, *History of Aro Settlements*, Lagos: Mbonu Ojike, n.d.

VANSINA, Jan, 'The Use of Ethnographic Data as Sources for History', in *Emerging Themes in African History*, ed. T. O. Ranger. London: Heinemann Educational Books, 1968.

VASSA, Gustavus (see Equiano, Olaudah).

VOEGELIN, C. F. and F. M., 'Languages of the World: African Fascicle One', *Anthropological Linguistics*, VI.5 (May 1964).

WADDELL, Hope Masterton, *Twenty-Nine Years in the West Indies and Central Africa; A Review of Missionary Work and Adventure 1829–1858*, London: T. Nelson and Sons, 1863: reprinted as 2nd edn. with introduction by G. I. Jones, London: Frank Cass, 1970.

[WATTS, John]. *A true Relation of the inhuman and unparallel'd Actions, and barbarous Murders of Negroes or Moors, committed on three English-men in Old Calabar in Guinny*. London: Thomas Passinger, 1672.

WEBSTER, J. B., and BOAHEN, A. A., *History of West Africa: The Revolutionary Years—1815 to Independence*. New York: Praeger Publishers, 1970.

WELSH, Master James, 'A Voyage to Benin beyond the Country of Guinea (1588)', in Hakluyts' *Voyages*, VII.

WILKS, Ivor, 'A Medieval Trade-Route from the Niger to the Gulf of Guinea', *JAH*, III (1962), 337–41.

—— *Asante in the Nineteenth Century*, Cambridge Univ. Press, 1975.

WILLIAMSON, Kay, 'Some Plant Names in the Niger Delta', *International Journal of American Linguistics*, XXXVI (1970), 156–67.

WINSTON, F. D. D., 'Nigerian Cross River Languages in the Polyglotta Africana', *Sierra Leone Language Review*, III (1964), 74–82 and IV (1965), 122–8.

Index

Aba, 97, map 4
Aba Ala, map 5
Aba River, 155
Abaja, map 3
Abak, 125, 185, map 5
Abalama, 47, 51
Abam (Igbo), 63; raids by 68, 119, 121; agents of Aro, 116–17, 125, 131–2, 136, 139; settlers at Ohambele, 129; mercenaries, 136; map 2
Abiriba, 116; smiths 41–2, 103, 121, 139, 151; mercenaries 69n; trade with Aro, 104
Aboh, 24–6, 28, 98, 130, 216–17; traders of, 25, 64, 68, 101, 103, 131, 144, 163, 172; foundation of, 45–7; market, 64; Aro influence at, 130, 133, 137; palm-oil trade of, 194–5, 204–6, 215; food trade to, 219; domestic slaves at, 220; maps 2, 3, 7
Achan Ika, map 5
acori, see beads
Ada (Igbo), 116, 119–20
Adams, John, sea captain and writer, on African trade goods preferences, 211, 213
Adamugu, 25
Adua, map 4
Afaha Obong, map 5
Afigbo, A. E., writer, on effects of European trade, 16n; on Aro, 118
Afikpo (Igbo), 75, 120–1, 129, 131, 136, 144, 219; domestic slaves of, 221n; map 4
Agbaja (Igbo), 62–3, 82–3; enslavement of, 104, 136–7
agriculture, 11–12, 225; trade in products of, 21, 217–20; *see also* food
Aguka, 45; *see also* Nri
Aguleri, 45; palm-oil of, 205; maps 2, 5, 7
Aguleri River, 68
Agwa'aguna, 35, 41–2, 82, 101, 144; palm-oil of, 202–3, 207; map 2

Ajalli, map 4
Aka Eze, map 4
Akan, 14, 89
Akanu, map 5
Akirika Uku, 155; map 5
Akpa, 35–6, 38
Akpa Yafe River, 11; maps 2, 4, 7
Akri, 47; *see also* Aboh
Akunakuna, 38, 73; *see also* Agwa'aguna
Akwete, 125, 170, 192; palm-oil trade of, 204; domestic slaves in, 221n; maps 4, 7
Akwukwu, map 3
Alagoa, E. J., writer, on Aro, 94n
alcohol, imports of, 166–7, 208, 211
Allen, J. G. C., writer, on Ngwa, 33
Amakiri, king of New Calabar, 88
Amanagwu, 122
Amasu, trade of, 122
Amuro, map 5
Anambra River, 205; map 7
Anang (Ibibio), 15, 30n, 63, 129, 153; enslavement of, 51n, 63; trade of, 119; *and* Aro, 124, 128, 207; 'king' of, 125; palm-oil trade of, 204, 207; maps 2, 7
Anderson, William, missionary, on warfare, 69n
Andoni (Ibibio), 15, 30n, 51n; salt making of, 21; yam trade of, 181
Andoni River, 39
Aneke (*alias* Thomas O'Connor), 137
Anene, J. C., writer, on Aro, 118
Angola, 51
Anstey, Roger, writer, on population, 81
Antera Duke, 58, 67, 191n; on yam trade, 181
Anyang, 102
Aro (Igbo), 4, 34, 64, 82, 94n, 199–200, 226; earliest mention of, 36; settlements and colonies, 48, 104, 113, 120–45, 207, 221; trade and traders, 48, 62, 85, 88, 104, 113–45, 170, 173, 189; *and* religion, 71, 104, 114–16, 121; *and* slave trade, 75, 114–45, 137, 173, 223;

Aro (Igbo)—*contd.*
    alliances, 97, 99, 104; language, 63;
    theories of success of, 114–19, 137–45;
    areas of activity, 119–37; cultural
    identity, 127–8, 142–4; *and* palm-oil
    trade, 204, 206–8; *and* food trade, 219,
    223
Aro Expedition, 118
Arochukwu, 10, 37, 41, 63, 75, 101, 113,
    120, 125, 159; traders of, 4, 85, 114;
    foundation of, 34–5, 37–8, 42, 48, 103,
    116, 119, 122; trade with Old Calabar,
    60; *and* slave trade, 86; immigrants
    from, 114, 132; villages of, 122, 124,
    141n; Ibibio proverb about, 126;
    farming in, 218; maps 2, 4, 5, 7; *see
    also* Amanagwu, Amasu, Atani, Ibom,
    Obinkita, Ujari
Asa, map 7
Asaba, 24–5, 27, 47, 131; foundation of,
    46; palm-oil trade of, 205; domestic
    slaves at, 221; maps 2, 3, 7
Asang, 122, 202; maps 4, 5, 7
Ashanti, 1, 3, 89
Ashimini, 51
assagai, 23, 40–1
associations: secret societies, 108–110,
    156, 173, 188; title societies, 108, 110–
    12; masquerade societies, 165; *see also*
    Ekpe, Okonko, Ozo
Atam, canoes of, 217; map 4; *see also*
    Nde Ekoi
Atani, 124n
Atan-Onoyon, map 5
Awgu, 135; map 4
Awka (Igbo), 104, 143–4, 160; smiths 18,
    102, 151; traders 102–3, 131, 133;
    agreements with Aro, 104, 134; maps
    2, 4
Aye, Efiong U., writer, on Ekpe society,
    109
Azara, map 4
Azumini, palm-oil trade of, 204; maps 4,
    5, 7

Baikie, William Balfour, writer, 27; on
    Oracle of Chukwu, 115; on trade
    routes, 115, 122; on Aro, 133n, 173;
    on iron currencies, 160; on Igbo cloth,
    170; on yam trade, 181; on palm-oil
    trade, 192, 202
Bamenda, 64, 102; *see also* Cameroon
    Grasslands

Bantu languages, 14, 39; North-west, 60,
    62, 79
Banyang, 108
Barbot, James, writer, 87; on Rio Real,
    106, 147n, 151, 153, 162, 165; on pro-
    visions trade, 179–80
Barbot, John, writer, 23, 41, 168; on Rio
    Real, 52–3; on Old Calabar, 53
Basa, 220
Basden, George Thomas, writer, on
    Agbala oracle, 134
Bauchi, 64
beads, at Ugbo-Ukwu, 19, 24, 28; *acori*,
    19, 40–1, 151; from Forcados River,
    23, 26; from Mount Cameroon, 23,
    40; from Rio del Rey, 40–1; trade in,
    94, 146, 165, 172, 224
Beecroft, John, British Consul, 157, 219;
    on palm-oil trade, 203
Bende, 34, 65, 68, 82, 121, 124n, 125,
    129–30, 134–5, 141, 143, 207; fair,
    105–7, 117, 119–20, 137, 141, 151–2,
    181, 189, 202–4, 219; roads to and
    from, 154, 171, 181; maps 2, 4, 5, 7
Benin, Bight of, 1
Benin City, 46, 87, 158; trade of, 25–7;
    textiles at, 169; map 1
Benin Kingdom and Empire, 27; iron
    knives from, 18n; textiles from, 19,
    169; trade of, 26, 86, 153; influences
    along Niger River, 44–7, 89, 92
Benin River, trade on, 21, 23, 26, 147n;
    map 1
Benue River, 6, 14, 25, 100–1, 170; roads
    to, 154; map 1
Benue Valley, 5n, 160, 184; slaves from,
    179
Biafra, Bight of, 2, 10n, 39, 42, 86, 197;
    slave trade from, 50–65, 68, 77–80, 81,
    85, 102, 107; coastal states of, 86–9,
    117; provisions trade from, 179–80;
    palm-oil trade from, 182–3; imports
    of, 208–14; map 1
Biakpan, map 4
Birmingham, England, foundries of, 168
Birmingham, David, writer, on slave
    trade and state systems, 5n
blood pacts, 97–8
Bocqua market, 64; *see also* Ikiri market
Boki, 102; map 4
Bold, Edward, writer, on palm-oil mar-
    kets, 191, 201; on African trade good
    preferences, 211, 213

Bonny, 21, 46, 51, 57, 60, 64, 86, 144; trade and traders of, 24–5, 28, 49, 52, 64, 88, 129, 162, 179, 181; foundation of, 43–4, 47; slave trade from, 77; slave trade to, 101–2, 106, 137, 199; political development of, 88–9, 189–90; *and* Aro, 124n; palm-oil trade of, 191–2, 195, 202–5, 207; competition with New Calabar, 211; salt imports, 213; canoes of, 216; food trade to, 219; domestic slaves in, 221–2; maps 2, 4, 7

Bonny River, 11; map 7

Boy Amai-kunno, king of Brass, 98, 216

brass, trade in, 146, 167; ornaments, 167n, 168n, 172

Brass, 24–5, 28, 57, 60, 64, 98, 144, 194, 216–17; slave trade to, 101; palm-oil trade to, 195, 206; salt making at, 213; domestic slavery at, 222; maps 2, 7; *see also* Nembe

Brass River, 195

Brazil, slave trade to, 52; traders of, 55

bridges, 155–6

British: trade and traders, 54, 156, 175, 183–4, 208–9; explorers, 140; imperialism, 141, 156, 207; beliefs about Aro, 116, 141; consuls, 154, 183, 190, 192, 222; exports, 208–9

bronze objects at Igbo-Ukwu, 18, 20, 23; *cire perdue* process of casting, 17n, 20

Calabar River, 11, 37, 39, 104, 122, 181; maps 2, 4, 7

Cameroon, slaves from 79; ivory from coast of, 147n; salt trade to, 213

Cameroon Grasslands, 64, 68; slaves from, 79; slave route from, 102, 154; map 4

Cameroon Mountains, 5n, 64

Cameroon River, 50, 64, 179, 217; map 1

canoe houses, 89, 100, 113, 189, 216

canoes, 11–12, 22, 24–5, 27, 66, 86, 153–5, 157, 181, 195; armed, 103, 216; in palm-oil trade, 199–203, 215–17, 221–2, 227

Cape Lopez, 178

Cape of Good Hope, 208

Caravalies, 51, 59; *see also* Elem Kalabari, Kalabari, New Calabar, Old Calabar

Casement, Roger, writer, on Aro, 124n, 125, 129, 141; on roads and bridges, 154–5; on women's clothing, 170

Chukwu, Oracle of, 35, 114–16, 121, 127–8, 130, 133–4, 136–8, 160, 173, 207; Ibibio proverb about, 126, 128

Clarkson, Thomas, writer, on slave raids along Cross River, 66

cloth; *see* textiles

commercial organization: of small-scale societies, 4–6, 90–113, 224, 229–30; interpersonal relations, 94–5, 97–100, 108–113; credit system, 190; periods of, 224–29; *see also* blood pacts, gift-exchange, marriage alliances, oaths, troupes

Congo, Kingdom of, 50–1

copper: objects at Igbo-Ukwu, 18, 23, 28, 167; trade in, 40, 158, 163–5, 167; currencies, 157–60, 162–3, 219; imports of, 209

cowries, 25, 155, 158, 160, 162–3, 175, 206, 211

Creek Town (Old Calabar), 37–8, 42, 67, 99, 186, 216; traders, 191, 200–1; maps 2, 4, 7

crime, enslavement as punishment for, 153

Cross River, 11, 14, 31, 34–5, 37–9, 41, 47, 50, 53, 63, 67–8, 114; trade and traders on, 31, 38, 40, 43, 87, 119, 122, 151, 156, 158, 179, 200–3; means of enslavement on, 66–7, 73–4, 102; marriage alliances along, 99; Aro settlements on, 120; markets on, 153; roads to, 154, currencies along, 162–3; palm-oil trade along, 190–1, 200–3, 207; canoe trade on, 217; food trade on, 218; maps 1, 2, 4, 7

Crowther, Samuel Adjai, writer, on Opuu, 27; on Aro, 130; on palm-oil trade, 204–6; on African trade good preferences, 211, 212n; on food trade, 220

Cuba, slave trade to, 56, 115

currencies, 148, 157–64, 175, 226, fig. 6; functions of, 157, 162; stick money, 157; *see also* copper, cowries, iron, manillas

Curtin, Philip D., writer, 7; on volume of slave trade, 54–6; on provenance of slaves, 60; on organization of slave trade in south-eastern Nigeria, 86

Dahomey, Kingdom of, 1, 89, 139, 188
Dapper, Olfert, writer, 40, 52, 66, 153; on currencies, 159, 164
Delta, Niger, *see* Niger Delta
Dick Ebro, 66
Dike, K. Onwuka, writer, on population movements, 13n; on effects of European trade, 16; on Aro, 115–16, 118, 137
Duke, Antera; *see* Antera Duke
Duke Ephraim (Efiom Edem), 72, 88, 218
Duke Town (Old Calabar), 37–8, 42, 58, 66–7, 88; traders, 191, 200–1; maps 2, 4, 7
Dutch, 39, 164, 167; traders, 23, 42, 52–3, 55

Eastern Igbo, 15
economic growth and development, 224–5; defined, 147; *and* slave trade, 147–9, 157, 164–7, 171–2, 174–7, 225–6; *and* legitimate trade, 197, 214, 223, 227–9
Edo, 14, 170; influence along Niger, 44–6
Effiat, map 2
Efik (Ibibio), 14–15, 34, 36–9, 43, 74, 91, 173, 201; language, 63; traders, 87, 101, 144, 157, 163, 200; alliances, 191; map 2
Efut, 39–41; palm-oil market, 191; map 2
Egbo, *see* Ekpe
Egwanga, 192; map 7
Eha Amufu, map 4
Eke Mohan market, 219
Ekeffe, 192; palm oil trade, 204; maps 4, 5, 7
Ekejiuba, Felicia I., writer, on Aro, 94n, 117
Eket (Ibibio), 15
Ekoi, 14n, 38, 92, 161, 173; traders, 40, 101, 199; *see also* Nde Ekoi, Obang Ekoi
Ekoi (Ibibio), 63, 119; map 2
Ekpe, secret society, 108–110; at Old Calabar, 88, 108–10, 169, 173; origins of 108–9; spread of, 110, 173
Ekpemiong, 125
Ekundukundu, map 4
Ekwere Azu, map 5

Elem Kalabari, 43–4, 87; *see also* New Calabar
Elmina, 23, 182
Elugu (Igbo), 63, 132, 135; map 6
Engenni River, 46, 130; palm-oil trade on, 192, 195; maps 2, 7
English traders, 42, 52–3, 191; *see also* British
Enugu, 18, 170
Enugu-Ukwu, 134
Enyong (Ibibio), 15, 38, 48, 122, 173, 217; trade agreements with Aro, 104, 201; market, 153, 191; palm-oil trade of, 200–2; maps 2, 7
Enyong Creek, 34, 35n, 37, 119, 122, 201; tolls on, 156; map 7
Equiano, Olaudah, writer, 58–9; on procurement of slaves, 68, 70; on warfare, 69n, 90, 166, 168; on kidnapping, 76; on political organization, 90, 91n; on traders, 94, 103, 172; on iron currency, 160; on trade in fire-arms, 165, 172; on metal ornaments, 167; on weaving and dying, 169–70; on vegetable salt, 212
Eri, 45; *see also* Nri, Umueri
Eshikanyi (*alias* Jacob Egypt), 137
Essene, 125, 192; Aro settlement at, 126; palm-oil trade of, 204; maps 4, 5, 7
Esuk Ododop, map 4
Ewe, 14
Eyo Honesty I, 200
Eyo Honesty II, on slave trading, 67, 83–4, 220; on famine, 74; marriages of, 99; canoes of, 216
Eze Aro; *see* Kanu Oji
Eze Nri, 45
Ezi-Owelli, map 3

Fage, J. D., writer, 7, on population, 80–2
fairs, 105–7, 112, 148, 202, 228; and Aro, 106–7; *see also* Bende, Uburu
Falconbridge, Alexander, writer, on procurement of slaves, 69, 76–7, 106
farming, *see* agriculture
Fernando Po, 39; purchase of yams at, 179; sale of food to, 218; map 1
fire-arms, 103; introduction of, 36; trade in, 94–5, 164–6, 210–11; *and* Aro power, 116, 139; African manufacture of, 168
fish, trade in, 21, 94, 146, 151, 172, 211; imports of, 211

fishing and fishermen, 11, 16, 21, 86; trade of, 86, 174, 217

Flint, J. E., writer, on legitimate commerce, 197–8

Fon, 1, 3

food, trade in, 52–3, 75, 146, 148, 151, 172, 174, 177–81, 191, 217–20, 222, 227–8; shortages of, 74–5, 219, 227; see also agriculture, fish, livestock, palm-oil, yams

Forcados River, 19n, 21, 23, 26, 46, 194; maps 1, 7

Fox, A. J., writer, on Aro, 117

French traders, 52, 54–5

Fulani, raids by, 64, 79, 102; tribute paid to, 155

Gaboe, 26, 28; see also Aboh

Gbegbe market, 220

Ghana, ancient, 37

Ghana, modern, 1, 14, 225

gift-exchange, 97, 156

Gold Coast, 1, 20, 41, 158, 178; trade to, 22–3, 39, 182

Goldie, Hugh, writer, on enslavement by Ibibio, 72; on slave route to Old Calabar, 102; on Oracle of Chukwu, 128; on canoe manufacturing, 217

Gray, Richard, writer, on commerce and political organization, 5n

Great Duke Ephraim, see Duke Ephraim

Green, M. M., writer, on Igbo markets, 149

Guinea, Gulf of, 1, 3, 6, 19, 50, 89, 158, 165, 178

hardware, 164–5, 173, 208

Harris, J. S., writer, on enslavement in Bende area, 65, 68

Harris, Rosemary L., writer, 219

Hausa, 45; enslavement of, 56, 60, 62, 64

Hill, Polly, writer, on markets, 149; on tolls, 155

Hingston, Captain, 77, 180

Hopkins, A. G., writer, 7; on effects of slave trade, 148; on legitimate trade, 197–8; on consumption patterns, 227

Horton, James Africanus, writer, on Igbo political organization, 90

Horton, Robin, writer, on stateless societies, 5n, 229

hunting, 20–1

Ibakachi, map 5

Ibani, 43–4; see also Bonny

Ibeme, 33

Ibeno (Ibibio), 15

Ibere, 34; map 2

Ibesit, map 5

Ibiakpa, map 5

Ibibio, 2, 4, 10, 13–15, 33–5, 37, 44, 48, 119, and passim; enslavement of, 51, 59, 62–3, 65; language, 14, 15n, 30, 33, 40, 63; beliefs, 70–1, 137; political and social organization, 91–3; and Aro, 122, 123–29, 144; trade roads, 154; currencies, 163; trade of, 169, 192, 218; oil-palm management, 187–8; map 1; see also Anang, Andoni, Efik, Ekoi, Enyong, Ibeno, Ibibio Proper, Ibiono, Ika, Ikono, Ikpe, Itam, Ito, Itumbuzo, Nkwot, Ukwa, Uruan

Ibibio Proper, 15, 36, 125; enslavement of, 63; currency demands of, 163; palm-oil trade of, 190–1; food trade to, 219; map 2

Ibiniukpabi, 35; see also Chukwu, Oracle of

Ibiono (Ibibio), and Aro, 124

Ibo, 3, 4; see also Igbo

Ibom, 37, 124n; trade of, 122; war with Obinkita, 141

Ibritam, 35; see also Chukwu, Oracle of

Ibung Okpo Eto, map 5

Idah, 24–5, 45–6, 213, 220; traders from Bonny at, 64n; market of, 100, 155; trade routes to, 136; swords of, 168; traders of, 206; food trade to, 219; map 4

Idemile, 205

Idu, 200n, map 7

Ifoko, 87

Ifuho, map 5

Igala, 14, 27, 44–8, 158; enslavement of, 64, 101; trade and traders, 64, 135, 144, 151, 206; marriage alliances, 99; textiles, 170; map 1

Igala Bank market, 24–5, 64, 152, 204

Igala Kingdom, 24, 45, 136; traders of, 25; emigrants from, on lower Niger, 45–6, 89; markets, 64, 100; tribute paid to, 155; see also, Idah

Igbira, 25, 27; of Panda, 64

Igbo, 2, 14, 30, 33–5, 43–4, and passim; language, 14, 30, 43–4; divisions of, 15; contacts with Ibibio, 33–5, 48, 92,

Igbo—*contd.*
169; contacts with Igala, 45–8, 92, 99; contacts with Ijo, 92; on Niger 43–7; enslavement of, 51, 59, 62–5, 101; beliefs, 70–1, 137, 152; political and social organization, 91–5; trade of, 151; map 1; *see also* Abam, Ada, Afikpo, Agbaja, Aro, Awka, Eastern Igbo, Elugu, Ika, Ikwerre, Ishielu, Isu, Isuama, Isuochi, Mboli, Ndoki, Ngwa, Nkwerre, North-Eastern Igbo, Northern Igbo, Ohafia, Otanchara, Otanzu, Owerri, Southern Igbo

Igbo-Ukwu, 23–4, 102, 169; remains found at, 17–20, 158; dating of, 17–18; economy of, 20–1, 146, 153, 224; culture of, 45; map 2

Igwegbe, Richard O., writer, on Aro, 117

Ihiala, 133; palm-oil of, 205; map 7

Ihuba, map 4

Ijo, 14, 30, 51, 164; language, 30, 43–4; contacts with Igbo, 43–4, 48; states, 108; map 1

Ika (Ibibio), 204

Ika (Igbo), 59, 94n

Ikiri market, 25, 64n

Ikom, 101–2, 217; map 7

Ikono (Ibibio), 63

Ikot Akpan Nsek, map 5

Ikot Ama, map 5

Ikot Ekpene, 185

Ikot Ibritam, 127; map 5

Ikot Ikpene, map 5

Ikot Itunko, 37; *see also* Creek Town

Ikot Nta, map 5

Ikot Ntuk, map 5

Ikot Obio Ama, map 5

Ikot Offiong, 99, 157, 191n; palm-oil market, 201; canoe trade, 217; food trade, 218; maps 4, 7

Ikot Okoro, map 4, 5

Ikot Udo, map 5

Ikot Ukana, map 5

Ikot Umo Essien, map 5

Ikot Usukpong, map 5

Ikpa, palm-oil trade of, 200–1, 215; market, 201; map 7

Ikpa Creek, 200–1

Ikpe (Ibibio), 63, 119–20, 187; palm-oil of, 201; map 7

Ikpe Creek, 185

Ikpe Ikot Nkon, 119, 202; maps 5, 7

Ikpo, map 5

Ikun Beach, 203; map 4

Ikwerre (Igbo), 88, 130, 192; map 7

Imo River, 11, 31, 33, 39, 43, 49, 88, 92, 129, 133, 170, 181; markets on, 106, 126, 190, 192, 199, 202–4; Aro settlement on, 131; maps 2, 4, 7

imports, 208–14; effects of 148, 164–71, 175, 198, 209n, 211–14, 226; magnitude of, 208–9

Inen Nsai, map 5

Inokun: name for Aro, 126; Aro settlement, 124–5, 137, 141, 201; maps 4, 5, 7

Intelligence Reports, 70, 76, 125, 128, 143

iron: objects of, at Igbo Ukwu, 18; imports of, 18, 149, 160, 163, 165, 168, 208–9, 211, 226; mining, 18, 167–8; trade in, 104, 121, 151, 172; currencies, 159–63, 225

Ishielu (Igbo), slaves from, 63, 83n

Isichei, Elizabeth, writer, on effects of slave trade, 7n

Isiko, map 5

Isu (Igbo), 104, 112, 131, 135, 143–4; map 6

Isuama (Igbo), 62–6, 82, 104, 133, 135; palm-oil trade of, 205

Isuochi (Igbo), 131; map 6

Isuorgu, 34; map 2

Itam (Ibibio), 201; map 7

Ito (Ibibio), 63, 122

Itsekiri, 87

Itu, 122, 124–5, 156–7; market of, 153, 201–2; canoe trade of, 217; maps 4, 5, 7

Itumbuzo (Ibibio), palm-oil of, 201; maps 5, 7

ivory trade, 146–7, 225; at Igbo-Ukwu, 21; on Benin River, 21, 147n; in Niger Delta, 21, 147; at Mount Cameroon, 21, 40, 147; on Rio del Rey, 40, 147; on Rio Real, 52, 147; at Old Calabar, 53, 147; on Niger River, 172, 206

Iyankpo, 47

Izombe, map 4

Jaja, King, founder of Opobo, 189–90, 222

Jeffreys, M. D. W., writer, on iron currency, 159

Johnson, H. H., British Consul, on roads, 154

Johnson, Marion, writer, on cowries, 158

Jonas, Simon, on Aro, 133
Jones, G. I., writer, on salt making in Niger Delta, 21; on foundation of Old Calabar, 38; on Owerri Daba, 51–2; on political change, 92, 189; on Ika Igbo, 94n; on Isu Igbo, 112; on Aro, 129; on ivory trade, 147n; on trading patterns, 190.
judges, at markets, 152

Kakanda, 64, 101
Kalabari Ijo, 51, 59, 87, 130, 151; see also New Calabar
Kamalu: Aro name, 43, 129; Bonny king, 129, New Calabar king, 129
Kanu Oji, Paramount Chief of Aro-chukwu (Eze Aro), on Oracle of Chukwu, 71; on slave trade, 71, 76; on Aro success, 137
kidnapping, 70, 75–9, 121, 136
Koelle, S. W., writer, 59, 62–4, 74, 101, 104, 119, 154; on procurement of slaves, 79
Kru, 14
Kwa, 37, 39, 41; language, 14; map 2
Kwa Ibo River, 11, 58, 68, 155; maps, 2, 7
Kwa Mountains, 41; iron mining in, 168
Kwa River, 11, 39; maps 2, 4, 7

Lagos, 57, 89, 158
Laird, Macgregor, writer, on palm-oil trade, 194
Lander, Richard and John, writers, 28, 152, 216; on palm-oil trade, 194; on salt making, 213
Landolphe, J. F., writer, 180
Latham, A. J. H., writer, on Efik trade, 87
Leonard, A. G., writer, 105n, 141, 143–4; on roads and bridges, 154–5; on tolls, 156
Liberia, 14
Little Kwa River, 39
Little Popo, 89
Liverpool, England, palm-oil trade to, 182–3, 213
livestock, 20; trade in, 21, 27–8, 174, 178–80, 218–19
Long Juju, 35, 38, 71, 128, 159; see also Chukwu, Oracle of
Lundu, map 4

McPhee, Alan, writer, on palm-oil trade and production, 184, 186
Makor, map 5
Mamfe, 102; map 4
manillas, 158, 160, 162–5, 225
market, 94, 149–53, 174–5, 181, 225; Onitsha, 95; Igala, 100–1; rings, 106, 150–1, 153, 202, 204; origins of, 149; riverain, 151, 199, 201; location of, 152; law, 152–3; palm-oil, 199–207, 223; see also fairs
marriage alliances, 98–100, 201, 205; by Aro, 127
Mauny, Raymond, writer, on Opuu, 27
Mbiabet, map 5
Mbiabo, foundation of, 36; palm oil market, 191
Mbiakong, 200; proverb about, 200n; map 7
Mboko, see Ibeme
Mboko Ofokobe, 97
Mboli (Igbo), 187
Mbudikom, 102n
Meillassoux, Claude, writer, on stages of commercial development, 224–27
metal, at Igbo-Ukwu, 17–18, 167; trade in, 41, 164–5, 171, 175, 224
Mgbowo, 135–6; map 4
mining, 225; iron, 18, 167–8; lead 167n
missionaries, 8, 9, 36, 59
Moco, see Moko
Moko, 30n, 159–60; see also Anang
Mount Cameroon, 39; trade at, 21, 40, 158; map 1

Nde Ekoi, enslavement of, 101; canoes of, 217
Ndi Nze, 110, 112; see also Ozo
Ndienyi, 132; map 4
Ndikelionwu, 132, 136; map 4
Ndizuogu, 62, 68, 74, 113, 135, 137, 139; origins and growth, 131–3; oracle at, 133–4, 140; slave trade of, 135; maps 4, 6
Ndoki (Igbo), 10, 43–4, 88, 129–30, 133; foundation of, 44; trade of, 48–9, 52; oil-palm management of, 187; palm-oil markets of, 192; farming in, 218; domestic slaves of, 221; maps 2, 7
Ndoni Creek, 195; map 7
Nembe, 144, 194; maps 2, 7; see also Brass

New Calabar, 28, 46, 51, 86–8, 144, 194; foundation of, 43; trade of, 52, 57, 60, 64, 88, 147, 151, 165–6, 180; slave trade from, 77; slave trade to, 101, 106; political development of, 88, 189–90; Aro influence at, 129–30, 137; palm-oil trade of, 191–2, 203, 205–6; competition with Bonny, 211; domestic slaves in, 221; maps 2, 4, 7
New Calabar River, 11, 192; map 7
Ngbo, 170
Nguru, map 4
Ngwa (Igbo), 10, 33–5, 63, 82, 91–2, 95; and Aro, 124, 129, 144, 207; trade routes among, 154; palm-oil trade of, 192, 204, 207; maps 2, 7
Ngwa Uku, 33
Niger-Benue Confluence, 24–5, 64, 100–1, 206
Niger-Congo languages, 14
Niger Coast Protectorate, 190
Niger Delta, 11, 14, 15, 23, 31, 86, 129, and passim; states of, 24, 66; trade and traders of, 25–6, 31, 49, 98, 147n, 182; trade routes to, 100–1; slave trade of, 116; slavery in, 222; map 1
Niger Expeditions, of 1831–2, 163, 172, 211; of 1841, 133, 163, 168, 195; of 1854, 27
Niger River, 2, 5n, 6, 11, 14, 22, 27, 43, 45, 68, 170, 185, and passim; trading patterns on, 24–8, 100–1, 199, 206, 225; trading communities on, 31, 44–7, 49, 89, 91–2, 144, 199; markets on, 151–2, 155, 194; currencies on, 158; palm-oil trade on, 194–5; food on, 219–20; maps 2, 3, 4, 7; see also Aboh, Asaba, Idah, Igala Bank market, Ikiri market, Onitsha, Ossomari
Niger Valley, 4, 10, 43
Nike, 68, 136; trade of, 62–3; domestic slaves in, 222; map 4
Nkalagu, 136–7, 170; map 4
Nkalu, 131; map 6
Nkpor, map 3
Nkwerre (Igbo), smiths and traders, 102–3, 131; agreements with Aro, 104; map 3
Nkwot (Ibibio), 63; map 2
Nneato, 131; map 6
Nnewi, 69n; palm-oil of, 205; maps 3, 7
North-Eastern Igbo, 15, 136, 219, 222–3; domestic slaves of, 222–3

Northern Igbo, 15; domestic slaves of, 222
Nri, 45–6, 143; foundation of, 45–6; priests of, 45–6, 71, 111, 131, 134–5; map 2
Nsugbe, map 3
Nsukka, 170
Ntegbe-Nese, 136; map 4
Nteji, map 3
Nto Edino, map 5
Nto Ndang, map 5
Nun River, 46; map 1
Nung Akwibit, map 5
Nung Asang, see Essene
Nung Ita, map 5
Nung Okoro, 125
Nupe kingdom, 25, 27, 101; slaves from, 64
Nyamkpe, Ekpe grade, 109

oaths, 97, 156
Oba, 205; maps 3, 7
Oba Nnobi, map 7
Obang Ekoi, map 4
Obegu, 129; map 4
Obero, 34; map 2
Obi Osai, King of Aboh, 103n, 195n; on slave procurement, 67–8; marriage alliances of, 98; trade goods desired by, 163, 211; palm-oil trade of, 194–5
Obinkita, trade of, 122, 124–5; settlements among Ibibio, 124–5; structure of, 124–5; meaning of name, 124n; war with Ibom, 141
Obohia, maps 4, 5
Obokwe, map 4
Obosi, 205; maps 3, 7
Obunku, 192; palm-oil trade of, 204
Ododop, 30–40, 102; roads and bridges of, 154–6; maps 2, 4
Odoro Ikpe, 119
Ofonagoro, Walter I., writer, on marriage alliances, 99
Ogbu, map 3
Ogidi, 205; map 7
Ogoja, 159
Ogoni, 88, 181; map 2
Ogurugu, map 4
Oguta, marriage alliances of, 98; trade and traders of, 129–31; Aro settlements near, 130, 207; palm-oil trade of, 205–7; maps, 3, 4, 7
Oguta Lake, 205–6; maps 3, 7

Ohafia (Igbo), 116; slaves from, 63, 83n, 121; map 2

Ohambele, 129; palm-oil market, 204, 215; maps 4, 7

Ohanze, map 5

Oil Rivers, 1, 222

oil-palms, density of, 10, 20, 184–5, 200; care of, 12, 20, 185; oil-palm belt, 184–5, 215; linguistic evidence about, 185; management of, 187–8, 202

Oji River, 18

Okigwe, 135; map 4

Okija, 205

Oko Jumbo, 222

Okonko, secret society, 110, 156

Okop, map 5

Okoyong, 39, 41, 69n; map 2

Okpoku, 219

Okporo Enyi, map 5

Okposi, 105n; map 4

Okrika, 129; foundation of, 44; trade of, 48, 88, 130, 181, 219; political and economic development of, 89; trade route to, 154; apparel in, 170–1; maps 2, 4

Okurike, canoes from, 217

Oláudah Equiano, see Equiano, Olaudah

Old Calabar, 40–1, 57, 60, 66, 122, 144, and passim; foundation of, 34, 36–9, 42, 48–9, 201; trade of, 53–4, 87, 147, 163, 170; trade routes to, 64, 101, 122, 155–6, 181; slave trade from, 77, 179; slave trade to, 101–2, 115; enslavement at, 66; warfare in, 69n; political development of, 88, 110, 190; Ekpe society in, 108–110; agriculture in, 180; palm-oil trade of, 191, 200–3, 211; imports of, 209, 213; canoes of, 216–17; food trade of, 218–19; domestic slavery in, 221–2; maps 2, 4, 7

Old Calabar River, see Calabar River

Old Town (Old Calabar), 37–8, 42, 67; map 2

Oldendorps, C. G. A., writer, 59

Oloko, map 4

Olokoro, 34; map 4

Onitsha, 10, 25, 62, 134, 185, 194; foundation of, 46–7; market, 95, 206; trade and traders of, 98, 113, 131, 171, 211; title-holders at, 111; palm-oil trade of, 204–6; domestic slaves at, 221; maps 2, 3, 4, 7

Opi, 136

Opobo, 125, 154, 156, 185; and Aro, 124; founding of, 189–90

Opuu, 21, 26–8, 30n, 147

oracles, 134; Agbala, 134; Igwe-ka-Ala, 134n; see also Chukwu, Oracle of

Orashi River, 130; palm-oil trade on, 192, 195, 205; maps 2, 7

Orlu, 62, 185

Oron Creek, map 4

Ossomari: foundation of, 46–7; trade of, 62, 103; traders of, 68, 131, 144; palm-oil trade of, 205–6; domestic slaves at, 221; maps 2, 3, 7

Otanchara (Igbo), 132; map 6

Otanzu (Igbo), 132; map 6

Ottenberg, Simon, writer, on Aro 117; on Afikpo Igbo, 120

Otu Creek, 195; map 7

Owen, William F., writer, on palm-oil trade, 192

Owerri (Igbo), 99, 129; map 4

Owerri Daba, 51, 130

Owo, map 5

Oye-Eboe, 94

Ozo, title society, 110–12, 133

Ozuzu, 63, 192; maps 4, 7

palm kernels, trade in, 184

palm-oil, trade in, 1, 6, 23, 57, 73, 126, 163, 174, 176, 182–3, 188–96, 197–208, 214–18, 220–4, 227–8; as food crop, 20, 185; production of, 182–8, 227; transportation of, 199–200; prices of, 208, 229

Panda, 25; Aboh traders at, 64n

Parker, Isaac, on slave raids by Efik, 66–7

pawning, 73

Pennsylvania, 59

Pepple, King of Bonny, 88

Pereira, Duarte Pacheco, writer, 21–3, 26–8, 39, 50, 59, 151; on canoes, 153–4; on manillas, 158, 164; on swords, 168

Peru, 59

political organization and change, 13–15, 51, 85–9, 112, 224; of societies along Gulf of Guinea, 3–5, 85, 89, 155; of coastal states, 85–9, 189–90; of hinterland societies, 90–3, 229–30; of Aro, 139–40; see also trading states, canoe houses

population density, 10–11, 13, 74–5, 104, 118, 122, 200; of Benue Valley, 5n; effects of slave trade on, 80–3, 147, 226; *and* markets, 150n; rise of, in coastal states, 221

population movement, 13, 30–49, 82, 225; *and* founding of Ngwa, 33–4; *and* founding of Arochukwu, 34–5 *and* founding of Old Calabar, 36–9, 42; into Niger Valley and Delta, 43–9, 89; along Cross River, 119

Porto Novo, 89

Portuguese, 1, 6, 17, 20, 22, 29, 46, 86, 146, 153; early African trade of, 19n, 23, 26, 158, 164–5, 178, 182, 194, 212, 225; *and* introduction of new food crops, 12; on São Tomé, 50–1, 57; trade in slaves, 52–3, 55

pottery: at Igbo-Ukwu, 17, 20; trade in, 150

Principe, 52, 178; map 1

provisions, *see* food

Qua, *see* Kwa

Qua River, *see* Kwa River

Rio da Cruz, 11, 39; *see also* Cross River

Rio del Rey, 11, 23, 40–1; trade in, 40–2, 52, 147, 179; maps 1, 2, 4, 7

Rio Formoso, *see* Benin River

Rio Real, 11, 21, 23, 27–8, 44, 50, 52, 154, 162, 167; trade in, 87, 106, 151, 164, 178, 211; palm-oil trade in, 191–2; maps 1, 2, 4, 7

Royal African Company, 52–3, 77, 147n, 165, 178

Ruel, Malcolm, writer, on leopard societies, 108–9

Sahara, 45; trade across, 23–4, 28, 148, 224

salt: making of, 21, 27–8, 44, 151, 173, 212–13, 225; internal trade in, 105, 146, 151, 155, 212–13; as currency, 163; imports of, 165, 208, 210–13, 227

Sam Jorze da Mina, *see* Elmina

Sandoval, Alonso de, writer, on slave trade, 50–1, 59, 66

São Tomé, 50–2, 55, 57, 178–9; map 1

São Tomé blacks, 51, 59

Senegal River, 208

Shaw, Thurstan, writer, on Igbu-Ukwu, 17, 19, 23, 45

Sierra Leone, 15; Joint Commissions in, 55, 60; census, 56; recaptives, 59, 62–3, 77, 82, 101, 104, 115, 119, 133

slave ships: *St. Jan*, 52; *Dragon*, 53, 179; *Eagle Galley*, 53; *Arthur*, 77, 166; *Affrica*, 162n, 165

slave trade, 1, 6, 50–8, 85–6, 146, 199, 206–7, 224–6; on Benin River, 23; on Forcados River, 23; at Mount Cameroon, 40; in Rio del Rey, 40–1; on Cameroon River, 50; to São Tomé, 50–1; in Rio Real, 52–3, 60, 86–9; on Cross River, 53–4, 60, 86–9, 101–2; to Virginia, 54; on Niger River, 98, 100–1, 172; volume of, 54–8, 85, 107; sources of, 58–65, 79–80, 101–2; effects of, 80–4, 146–8, 162, 164–7, 171–2, 174–7, 225–6, 228; British measures against, 190

slaves and slavery: ethnic identity of, 58–65; means of enslavement, 65–84, 115–16, 121, 132, 136, 153, 175, 177, 226; domestic, 73–4, 82, 160, 220–23

smelting, 167–8, 226; at Igbo-Ukwu, 18

smiths and smithing, 149, 167–8, 171–2, 175, 211, 226; at Igbo-Ukwu, 18; at Panda, 25; at Abiriba, 41

social organization and values: individualism, 90, 93; descent groups, 90–93; interpersonal relations, 94–5, 97–100, 108–13; continuity in, 107–8, 111–12; *see also* associations, blood pacts, gift-exchange, marriage alliances, oaths

societies, *see* associations

Sokoto Caliphate, 68

Sombreiro River, 192

Southern Igbo, 15

Spain, 51

Spanish traders, 55

states, *see* political organization

Stevenson, R. F., writer, on Aro, 118

sugar, 50, 52

swords, 21, 168, 172

Talbot, P. Amaury, writer, on warfare, 68; on Aro, 115–17, 134

Taylor, John Christopher, missionary, 134

textiles, 169–71; trade in, 21, 23, 74, 104, 146, 151, 169–70; at Igbo-Ukwu, 17–19, 169; at Panda, 25; at Benin, 19, 169; imports of, 164–5, 169, 171–3,

175, 208, 210–11; Indian, 165, 169–70, 211; British, 169, 210–11, 227; weaving of, 149, 167, 169–70, 172–3, 211; dyeing of, 169; raffia, 169–71; bark cloth, 170

Tibara, 102n

Tiv, 14, 162

tobacco, imports of, 208, 211–12

tolls, 155–7

Tom Salt's Point, 213

trade routes, 100–4, 223; to Gold Coast, 22–3, 153, 225; trans-Saharan, 23–4, 28, 148, 224; on lower Niger, 24–8, 100–1, 153; to Rio del Rey, 40–1; to Old Calabar, 101–2, 122; among Ibibio, 126–7, 154–5, 202; to Bonny, 129–30, 171, 199; among Igbo, 129–30, 135–6, 154–5; growth of, 148, 153–5, 228

traders, 225–6; coastal, 86, 190, 206; hinterland, 86, 103, 148, 189, 226; intermediary, 88, 104; on Niger, 153; palm-oil, 188–9, 199–208

trading states and communities: coastal 86–9, 108; hinterland, 100–5; Aro, 117–18

Trevor-Roper, H. R., writer, on immigration, 48

troupes, trading, 103–4; Aro, 104, 113, 117, 139

Uburu, fair, 105–7, 117, 120, 135; salt trade of, 151, 212; map 4

Udo, Reuben, K., writer, on Aro, 116

Udo Akpabio, on travel, 95

Ujalli, 131, 136

Ujari, trade of, 122

Ukana Ikot Ibe, 155

Uke, map 3

Ukpom, map 5

Ukwa (Ibibio), 63; market, 153; map 2

Ukwu, Ukwu I., writer, on Aro, 117; on markets, 149–50

Umo, R. Kanu, writer, on Aro, 117

Umon, 38, 99; trade of, 101, 144, 157, 181; market, 153, 218–19; palm-oil trade of, 202–3; relations with Old Calabar, 216; canoe trade of, 217; maps 2, 4, 7

Umu Obom, 131

Umu Osoko, map 5

Umueri, 45–6

Umuoji, map 3

Urua Awak, 192

Uruan (Ibibio), 37–8, 42, 191, 200–1; maps 2, 7

Uruata, 192

Uruk Obong, map 5

Utu, map 3

Ututu, map 5

Uwet, 41, 48, 122, 124; trade agreement with Aro, 104; yam trade of, 181; maps 2, 4

Uzuakoli, 105n, 143; map 4

Virginia, slave trade to, 54

Waddell, Hope M., writer, on beads at Uwet, 41; on slave trade, 67, 78–9, 83–4; on polygyny, 99; on cloth, 170; on palm-oil production, 186; on palm-oil trade, 202; on domestic slavery, 222

war, 14, 139, 166; for slaves, 51, 65–9, 121, 124, 175; between Nnewi and Abiriba, 69n; between Old Calabar and Okoyong, 69n; by Ndizuogu, 131–2, 137; by Nike, 136; and Aro success, 116–17, 138–9

Waribu, 222

Warri, 46, 87, 180

West Africa, 55–6, 62, 72, 81, 148, 158, 182; legitimate trade in, 197; trade of, 208–9, 224

West Indies, 52, 59, 62, 178, 222

Western Igbo, 15

Whydah, 89

William Kia, 222

yams, 12, 20; trade in, 27–8, 75, 172, 174, 178–81, 192, 218–19, 223; production of, 181, 219, 223

Yellow Duke, 222

Yoruba, 1–2, 13–14, 89, 139

Zumper, 64n